MW01156456

HOUSE DIVIDED
THE BREAK-UP OF DISPENSATIONAL THEOLOGY

Other books by Greg L. Bahnsen

Theonomy in Christian Ethics, 1977
Homosexuality: A Biblical Perspective, 1978
By This Standard: The Authority of God's Law Today, 1985
No Other Standard: Theonomy and Its Critics, 1991
Theonomy, An Informed Response, 1991, with other authors
Always Ready: Directions for Defending the Faith, 1996

Other books by Kenneth L. Gentry, Jr.

The Christian Case Against Abortion, 1982
The Christian and Alcoholic Beverages, 1982
The Charismatic Gift of Prophecy: A Reformed Analysis, 1986
Before Jerusalem Fell: Dating the Book of Revelation, 1989 [1997]
The Beast of Revelation, 1989 [1994]
*The Greatness of the Great Commission: The Christian Enterprise in a
      Fallen World,* 1990
Theonomy, An Informed Response, 1991, with other authors
He Shall Have Dominion: A Postmillennial Eschatology, 1992 [1997]
Lord of the Saved: Getting to the Heart of the Lordship Debate, 1992
*God's Law in the Modern World: The Continuing Relevance of Old
      Testament Law,* 1993

HOUSE DIVIDED

THE BREAK-UP OF DISPENSATIONAL THEOLOGY
(Second Printing)

Greg L. Bahnsen

and

Kenneth L. Gentry, Jr.

Institute for Christian Economics
Tyler, Texas

©Copyright, Institute for Christian Economics, 1989 [1997]

Library of Congress Cataloging-in-Publication Data

Bahnsen, Greg L.
  House divided : the break-up of dispensational
theology / Greg L. Bahnsen and Kenneth L. Gentry, Jr.
    p.   cm.
  Includes bibliographical references and index.
  ISBN 0-930464-27-3
    1. Dispensationalism. 2. Dominion theology.
  3. Kingdom of God. 4. House, H. Wayne. Dominion
    theology. I. Gentry, Kenneth L.
  II. Title.
  BT157.B32   1997
  230'.0463--dc21   97-5054
                                                        CIP

Published by the Institute for Christian Economics
P.O. Box 8000, Tyler, TX 75711

Printed in the United States of America

For the cause of Christ
and His Glory

Ye are the salt of the earth: but if the salt have lost his savour, wherewith shall it be salted? it is thenceforth good for nothing, but to be cast out, and to be trodden under foot of men. Ye are the light of the world. A city that is set on an hill cannot be hid. Neither do men light a candle, and put it under a bushel, but on a candlestick; and it giveth light unto all that are in the house. Let your light so shine before men, that they may see your good works, and glorify your Father which is in heaven. Think not that I am come to destroy the law, or the prophets: I am not come to destroy, but to fulfill. For verily I say unto you, Till heaven and earth pass, one jot or one tittle shall in no wise pass from the law, till all be fulfilled. Whosoever therefore shall break one of these least commandments, and shall teach men so, he shall be called the least in the kingdom of heaven: but whosoever shall do and teach them, the same shall be called great in the kingdom of heaven (Matthew 5:13-19).

At the heart of the problem of legalism is pride, a pride that refuses to admit spiritual bankruptcy. That is why the doctrines of grace stir up so much animosity. Donald Grey Barnhouse, a giant of a man in free grace, wrote: "It was a tragic hour when the Reformation churches wrote the Ten Commandments into their creeds and catechisms and sought to bring Gentile believers into bondage to Jewish law, which was never intended either for the Gentile nations or for the church."[1] He was right, too.

S. Lewis Johnson (1963)[2]

---

1. He cites Barnhouse, *God's Freedom*, p. 134.
2. S. Lewis Johnson, "The Paralysis of Legalism," *Bibliotheca Sacra*, Vol. 120 (April/June, 1963), p. 109.

TABLE OF CONTENTS

CONCLUSION

APPENDIXES

PUBLISHER'S FOREWORD

by Gary North

Devout postmillenarianism has virtually disappeared.

Alva J. McClain (1956)[1]

Dispensationalists should be open to, sensitive to, and ready to enter-tain any future development of theology based on a proper theological method, giving primary consideration to the ongoing work of interpreting the Scripture. Many dispensationalists are encouraging this, and that is why development can be seen within the system.

Craig A. Blaising (1988)[2]

Dispensationalism, as a theologically defensible system, is now in the aorist tense.

Gary North (1989)

Behind my rhetoric, there is always a bedrock theme lurking. The cover of this book reveals my theme. (Gary DeMar suggested the title, while I selected the cover. The two authors provided the text.) In the early writings of Francis Schaeffer, we read of modern philosophy's two-storey universe. The bottom storey is one of reason, science, predictable cause and effect, i.e., Immanuel Kant's *phenomenal* realm. This view of the universe leads inevitably to despair, for to the extent that this realm is dominant,

---

1. Alva J. McClain, "A Premillennial Philosophy of History," *Bibliotheca Sacra* (1956), p. 113.
2. Craig A. Blaising, "Development of Dispensationalism by Contemporary Dispensationalists," *Bibliotheca Sacra* (July-September 1988), p. 255.

man is seen to be nothing more than a freedomless cog in a vast impersonal machine.

In order to escape the pessimistic implications of this lower-storey worldview, humanists have proposed an escape hatch: a correlative upper-storey universe. The upper storey is supposedly one of humanistic "freedom": faith, feeling, emotion, personality, randomness, religion, non-cognitive reality, i.e., Kant's *noumenal* realm. It also supposedly provides meaning for man, but only non-cognitive ("irrational") meaning. It is meaning which is meaningless in rational ("lower storey") terms.

There is no known point of contact or doorway between these two realms, yet modern man needs such a doorway to hold his world and his psyche together. This is why the modern world is in the midst of a monumental crisis, Schaeffer argued.

Schaeffer got the core of this idea from his professor of apologetics at Westminster Theological Seminary, Cornelius Van Til, although you would not suspect this by reading Schaeffer's footnotes. Van Til argued throughout his long career that all non-Christian philosophy from the Greeks to the present is dualistic: a war between the totally rational and the totally irrational. Creating a memorable analogy, Van Til said that the irrationalist and the rationalist are like a pair of washerwomen who support themselves by taking in each other's laundry. The intellectual problems created by each school of thought are unresolvable in terms of its own presuppositions, and so the defenders of each system seek temporary refuge in the very different but equally unresolvable problems of the rival school.

Why do they do this? Because non-Christian man prefers to believe anything except the God of the Bible, who issues His covenant law and holds all men responsible for obeying it, on pain of eternal judgment. They would prefer to dwell in an incoherent dualistic universe of their own devising rather than in God's universe, dependent on His grace.

The Two-Storey World of Orthodox Christianity

The New Testament teaches that there are two realms of existence in this world: the eternal and the temporal. Each of these realms is itself divided: life vs. death. Jesus said: "He that believeth on the Son hath everlasting life: and he that believeth not the Son shall not see life; but the wrath of God abideth on him" (John 3:36). The one who rejects Jesus Christ as Lord and savior is *already dead*. He shall not see life, either in this world or the next.

These two realms — time and eternity — are linked together by the sovereign God of the Bible, who created all things. It is Jesus Christ, as God the Creator, who binds all things together; it is Jesus Christ

> Who is the image of the invisible God, the firstborn of every creature: For by him were all things created, that are in heaven, and that are in earth, visible and invisible, whether they be thrones, or dominions, or principalities, or powers: all things were created by him, and for him: And he is before all things, and by him all things consist. And he is the head of the body, the church: who is the beginning, the firstborn from the dead; that in all things he might have the preeminence. For it pleased the Father that in him should all fulness dwell; And, having made peace through the blood of his cross, by him to reconcile all things unto himself; by him, I say, whether they be things in earth, or things in heaven (Col. 1:15-20).

Thus, the kingdom of God encompasses all the creation. It alone is the source of unity. The two realms — time and eternity — are united under God's covenant. Men participate in this unified kingdom either as covenant-keepers or as covenant-breakers. Heaven is linked to earth by God's law, which is why Jesus taught His people to pray: "Thy kingdom come. Thy will be done in earth, as it is in heaven" (Matt. 6:10). The progressive manifestation of the kingdom of God on earth — "thy kingdom come" — is seen in the progressive subduing of the world in terms of God's revealed law: "thy will be done." Thus, the link between heaven and earth is God's covenant: *faithfulness* (through Jesus Christ, empowered by the Holy Spirit) to God's covenant law. The link between hell and earth is also God's covenant: *rebellion* against God's covenant law.

This covenantal and therefore *legal* link between heaven and earth is explicitly denied by modern fundamentalism. Fundamentalism denies the continuing authority of God's law. Thus, fundamentalism faces the same dilemma that humanism faces: a radical break between the upper storey and the lower storey.

The Two-Storey World of Fundamentalism

Fundamentalism's lower storey is the world of work, economics, professional training, art, institutions, authority, and power, i.e., the "secular" realm. This realm is governed, not in terms of the Bible, but in terms of supposedly universal "neutral reason" and natural law. (So far, this is basically the thirteenth-century worldview of Thomas Aquinas and the medieval scholastic philosophers.) The Bible supposedly does not speak directly to this realm, we are assured by both the fundamentalists ("We're under grace, not law!") and the secular humanists ("This is a pluralistic nation!"). Thus, there is no theological or judicial basis for Christians to claim that they are entitled to set forth uniquely biblical principles of social order. Above all, Christians are not supposed to seek to persuade voters to elect political rulers who will enforce biblical laws or principles. This means that rulers must not be identifiably Christian in their social and political outlook. Christians are allowed to vote and exercise civil authority only insofar as they cease to be explicitly biblical in their orientation. In short, only *operational humanists* should be allowed to rule. This is political pluralism, the reigning political gospel in our age — in an era which believes that only politics is gospel.[3]

Crumbs from Humanism's Table

This view of the world — "the world under autonomous man's law" — leads Christians to an inescapable pessimism regarding the church's present and its earthly future, for this view asserts that Christians will always be under the humanists' table, eating the

---

3. Gary North, *Political Polytheism: The Myth of Pluralism* (Tyler, TX: Institute for Christian Economics, 1989).

crumbs that may occasionally fall from that table. This view of the relationship between the saved and the lost in history is the reverse of what the Bible teaches: "Then came she and worshipped him, saying, Lord, help me. But he answered and said, It is not meet to take the children's bread, and to cast it to dogs. And she said, Truth, Lord: yet the dogs eat of the crumbs which fall from their masters' table. Then Jesus answered and said unto her, O woman, great is thy faith: be it unto thee even as thou wilt. And her daughter was made whole from that very hour" (Matt. 15:25-28). Because modern fundamentalism has reversed the biblical worldview in this regard, it promotes a despair similar to that which is promoted by the humanists' view of the lower-storey world of science and technology. It destroys freedom under God.

The Upper Storey

To escape this inherent despair, fundamentalists have turned to their own version of the humanists' escape hatch: an upper-storey universe. This upper storey is the world of faith, expectation, and hope: the heavenly realm. It is a hope in heaven—a world above and beyond this world of Christian powerlessness and defeat. With respect to this world, there is a preliminary way of escape: the Christian family and the church. In other words, Christians find solace in the time that remains after the work day is over and on weekends. This world of temporary rest and recreation—a realm of exclusively individual healing—does not and cannot heal the State or society in general. God's healing is limited to individual souls, families, and churches. Why? We are never told precisely; it just is.[4]

Fundamentalists believe that the individual Christian must live in both realms during his stay on earth, but he is not sup-

---

4. A growing number of Christians now contend that God's healing can work in education, too. This has split churches all over the nation. The idea that Christians need to start their own private schools, pulling their children out of the humanistic, tax-supported, officially "neutral" public schools, is regarded as a heresy by most Christians, who continue to tithe their children to the Moloch State.

posed to take the first realm very seriously — the realm of the calling
or vocation. This is why fundamentalists have invented the phrase,
"full-time Christian service": it contrasts the world of faith where
ministers and missionaries work with the world where the rest of
us work. This distinction is very similar to the monastic outlook of
Roman Catholicism, which distinguishes between the "secular
clergy" — parish priests who work with common people in their
common affairs — and the "regular clergy," meaning the monks
who have retreated from the normal hustle and bustle of life (the
"rat race"). Yet your average fundamentalist would be shocked to
learn that he is thinking as a Roman Catholic thinks. He would
probably deny it. But he has to think this way, for he has adopted
the Roman Catholic (scholastic) doctrine of law: "natural law" for
the lower storey, and God's revelation for the upper storey.

A Culturally Impotent Gospel

Fundamentalists believe that Christians are not supposed to
devote very much time, money, and effort to transforming the
"secular" world. We are assured that it cannot be transformed, according to Bible prophecy, until Jesus comes physically seven
years after the Rapture to set up His One World State with head-
quarters in Jerusalem. Anything that Christians do today to build
a better world will be destroyed during the seven-year tribulation
period.[5] John Walvoord, former president of Dallas Theological
Seminary, insists: "Well, I personally object to the idea that premillennialism is pessimistic. We are simply realistic in believing
that man cannot change the world. Only God can."[6] "Realism"

---

5. In the early 1960's, I was told that the Stewart brothers, who financed the
creation of formerly dispensationalist Biola College (then called the Bible Institute of Los Angeles), and who also financed the publication and distribution of
the tracts that became known as *The Fundamentals*, shipped crates of Bibles to
Israel to be hidden in caves there, so that Jews could find them during the Great
Tribulation. I was told years later by an amillennial pastor that Arabs later used
pages in these Bibles for cigarette paper, which may just be a "sour grapes" amillennial apocryphal legend. The point is this: Why waste money on Bibles to be
hidden in caves? Answer: because of a specific eschatology.

6. *Christianity Today* (Feb. 6, 1987), p. 11-I.

sounds a lot better than "pessimism," but the psychological results are the same: retreat from cultural involvement. As Christians, we must be content with whatever the humanists who control the "lower realm" are willing to dish out to us, just so long as they leave us alone on Sunday.

The former president of Grace Theological Seminary, Alva J. McClain, wrote a five-and-a-half-page essay on "A Premillennial Philosophy of History" for Dallas Seminary's *Bibliotheca Sacra* in 1956. This essay should be read by every dispensationalist, not to learn what this view of history is, which the essay never says, but to learn that a major theologian of the movement did not bother to describe it. McClain rejected postmillennialism, although he did admit that "Classical postmillennialism had plenty of defects, but it did make a serious attempt to deal with human history."[7] He then dismissed — in one paragraph per error — modern liberalism, neo-orthodoxy, amillennialism (Louis Berkhof), and all those who think "there will never be such a 'Golden Age' upon earth in history. . . ."[8] This left exactly half a page for a thorough discussion of the premillennial view of history. He never said what this is. He simply concluded, "The premillennial philosophy of history makes sense. It lays a Biblical and rational basis for a truly optimistic view of human history."[9]

McClain refused even to mention the key historical issue for those living prior to the Rapture: What is the basis of *our* optimism regarding the long-term future of our earthly efforts? Clearly, dispensationalists have none. The results of our efforts, they would have to say if they had the courage to discuss such things in public, will all be swallowed up during the great tribulation after the Rapture. This is a self-consciously pessimistic view of the future of the church, and it has resulted in cultural paralysis whenever it has been widely believed by Christians; therefore, the intellectual leaders of dispensationalism refuse to discuss it forthrightly. It is just too embarrassing. They use the language of post-

---

7. McClain, "A Premillennial Philosophy of History," p. 112.
8. *Ibid.*, p. 115.
9. *Ibid.*, p. 116.

millennial optimism to disguise a thoroughgoing pessimism. They keep pointing to the glorious era of the millennium in order to defend their use of optimistic language, never bothering to point out that the seven years that precede it will destroy the results of gospel preaching during the entire Church Age. After all, every Christian will have been removed from the earth at the Rapture (an explicit denial of the historical continuity predicted in Christ's parable of the wheat and tares: Matthew 13:20, 38-40). McClain's essay is representative of what has passed for world-and-life scholarship within dispensationalism since 1830.

While McClain may have fooled those who read *Bibliotheca Sacra* regularly, the troops in the pews have not been fooled. Dave Hunt is willing to say publicly what dispensationalism means, and without any apologies. Dispensational theology obviously teaches the defeat of all the church's cultural efforts before the Rapture, since the millennium itself will be a cultural defeat for God, even with Jesus reigning here on earth in His perfect body.

> In fact, dominion — taking dominion and setting up the kingdom for Christ — is an *impossibility,* even for God. The millennial reign of Christ, far from being the kingdom, is actually the final proof of the incorrigible nature of the human heart, because Christ Himself can't do what these people say they are going to do. . . .[10]

Here we have it without any sugar-coating: there is no connection between the upper storey of God's spiritual kingdom and the lower storey of human history, not even during the millennium. The two-storey world of fundamentalism is so radically divided that even God Himself cannot bind the two together. That is an impossibility, says Hunt. In the best-selling writings of Dave

---

10. Hunt, "Dominion and the Cross," Tape 2 of *Dominion: The Word and New World Order* (1987), published by Omega Letter, Ontario, Canada. See his similar statement in his book, *Beyond Seduction*: "The millennial reign of Christ upon earth, rather than being the kingdom of God, will in fact be the final proof of the incorrigible nature of the human heart." *Beyond Seduction: A Return to Biblical Christianity* (Eugene, OR: Harvest House, 1987), p. 250.

Hunt, the legacy of Scofield has come to fruition: a cultural rose which is all thorns and no blooms. The seminary professors can protest that this is not the "real" dispensationalism, but this complaint assumes that the movement's scholars have produced a coherent alternative to pop-dispensationalism. They haven't.

Dispensationalists say that Christians *in principle* are impotent to change things in the "lower storey," and to attempt to do so would be a waste of our scarce capital, especially time. While the academic leaders of dispensationalism have been too embarrassed to admit what is obviously a consistent cultural conclusion of their view of history, the popularizers have not hesitated, especially in response to criticisms by the Reconstructionists. Writes dispensationalist newsletter publisher Peter Lalonde regarding a friend of his who wants Christians to begin to work to change the "secular world":

> It's a question, "Do you polish brass on a sinking ship?" And if they're working on setting up new institutions, instead of going out and winning the lost for Christ, then they're wasting the most valuable time on the planet earth right now, and that is the serious problem in his thinking.[11]

Because this attitude toward social change has prevailed within American Christianity since at least 1925 (the aftermath of the Scopes "Monkey Trial"),[12] those who attempt to dwell only in the "lower storey" — non-Christians — have had few reasons to take Christians very seriously. American Christians have been in self-conscious cultural retreat from historic reality and cultural responsibility for most of this century.[13] Meanwhile, as non-Christians have become steadily more consistent with their own worldview, they have begun to recognize more clearly who their ene-

---

11. "Dominion: A Dangerous New Theology," Tape 1 of *Dominion: The Word and New World Order.*
12. George Marsden, *Fundamentalism and American Culture: The Shaping of Twentieth-Century Evangelicalism, 1870-1925* (New York: Oxford University Press, 1980), Chapters 20-23.
13. Douglas W. Frank, *Less Than Conquerors: How Evangelicals Entered the Twentieth Century* (Grand Rapids, MI: Eerdmans, 1986).

mies really are: Christians who proclaim the God of the Bible, i.e., the God of final judgment. Thus, we are now seeing an escalation of the inherent, inevitable conflict between covenant-keepers and covenant-breakers in the United States.

The Great Escape

Modern premillennial fundamentalism officially believes that there is only one biblical solution to this escalating conflict: the so-called Rapture. Premillennialists do not place the Rapture at the end of history, as postmillennialists and amillennialists do; they place it in the midst of history. It serves them psychologically as the hoped-for Great Escape Hatch. This is the "hope of historical hopes" for Bible-believing fundamentalists, as Dave Hunt insists in his 1988 book, *Whatever Happened to Heaven?*

The theological world of fundamentalism is a two-storey world, and those who lived psychologically in that upper storey were content, up until about 1979, to let the humanists run things in the lower storey. But the Rapture has been delayed again and again, and those who have been running things "downstairs" are getting pushy in their monopolistic control over education, politics, the media, and just about everything else. Fundamentalists are at long last getting sick and tired of being pushed around. They want to have a greater voice in running the affairs of the lower storey. But the older version of fundamentalism teaches that this is a false hope, both morally and prophetically, while the secular humanists still argue that the Christians have no authority, no moral right, to exercise such authority. After all, we are told by both fundamentalists and secular humanists, this is a pluralistic nation. (*Pluralism* means that Christians have no legal rights except to pay taxes to institutions controlled by humanists.)

So, we find that fundamentalism is splitting apart psychologically. The "lower storey" activists are tired of listening to the escapism of the "upper storey" pietists. As the activists grow increasingly impatient with the arguments of the passivists, they begin to abandon the theology that undergirds passivism: original Scofieldism. Fundamentalism in general now has only two legitimate hopes: the imminent Great Escape of the Rapture or the long-term overturning of the older two-storey fundamentalist theology. Either Scofieldism's promise must come true, and very soon, or else it will be abandoned.

What about the former hope, i.e., the Rapture? It is fading fast. Dispensationalists have been repeatedly frustrated by the public announcement of, and subsequent delay of, the Rapture. A lot of them have now begun to lose interest in that much-abused doctrine. For at least a decade, we have not heard sermons by television evangelists about the imminent Rapture. Jimmy Swaggart, just before his downfall in 1988, openly proclaimed himself to be the last of the Rapture-preaching preachers, and so he may have been. Since 1979, the dispensationalist dam has begun to leak. The pent-up lake of frustrated Christian social concern and social relevance is now pouring through holes in the dam. When it finally breaks, as hole-ridden dams must, the world of dispensationalism will be swept away.

The Death of Dispensational Theology

If dispensational theology were still strong and healthy, it might be able to delay the looming transformation of the dispensational movement. But it is not healthy. Theologically speaking, meaning *as a coherent system*, dispensational theology is dead. Its brain wave signal has gone flat. It has now assumed room temperature. RIP. It was not killed by its theological opponents. Its defenders killed it by a thousand qualifications. They revised it into oblivion. Like a man peeling an onion, dispensational theologians kept slicing away the system's embarrassing visible layers until there was nothing left. The last remaining layer was removed by H. Wayne House and Thomas Ice in their 1988 book, *Dominion Theology: Blessing or Curse?*

As an intellectual system, dispensationalism never had much of a life. From the beginning, its theological critics had the better arguments, from George Bush in the 1840's to Oswald T. Allis's classic study, *Prophecy and the Church*, published in 1945. But the critics never had many followers. Furthermore, the critics were trained theologians, and dispensationalists have never paid much attention to trained theologians. Besides, there were not very many critics. Because dispensationalists had no self-consciously scholarly theology to defend and no institutions of somewhat higher learning until well into the twentieth century, their critics thought that they could safely ignore the dispensational movement. They always aimed their published analyses at the academic Christian community. They thought they could call a halt to the spread of dispensationalism through an appeal to the Scriptures and an appeal to the scholarly Christian community. They were wrong. Theirs was a strategic error; popular mass movements are not directly affected by such narrow intellectual challenges. Indirectly over time, yes, but not directly. Few people adopt or abandon their theological views by reading heavily footnoted and carefully argued scholarly books. Thus, the appeal of dispensational theology was not undermined by its theological opponents; instead, it collapsed of its own weight. Like a former athlete who dies of a heart attack at age 52 from obesity and lack of exercise, so did dispensational theology depart from this earthly veil of tears. Dispensational theologians got out of shape, and were totally unprepared for the killer marathon of 1988.

The Heart, Mind, and Soul of Dispensationalism

The strength of dispensationalism was never its formal theological argumentation, but rather its ethical and motivational conclusions, namely, that Christians have almost no influence in this world, will never have much influence, and most important, are not morally responsible before God for exercising lawful authority in this so-called "Church Age." The dispensational system was adopted by people who wanted to escape from the burdens of cultural responsibility. This retreatist mentality has been freely admitted by Thomas Ice's former associate, David Schnittger:

> North and other postmillennial Christian Reconstructionists label those who hold the pretribulational rapture position pietists and cultural retreatists. One reason these criticisms are so pain-

ful is because I find them to be substantially true. Many in our camp have an all-pervasive negativism regarding the course of society and the impotence of God's people to do anything about it. They will heartily affirm that **Satan is Alive and Well on Planet Earth,** and that this must indeed be **The Terminal Generation**; therefore, any attempt to influence society is ultimately hopeless. They adopt the pietistic platitude: *"You don't polish brass on a sinking ship."* Many pessimistic pretribbers cling to the humanists' version of religious freedom; namely Christian social and political impotence, self-imposed, as drowning men cling to a life preserver. [14]

To justify this otherwise embarrassing motivation — cultural withdrawal — fundamentalist Christians adopted the doctrine of the pre-tribulation Rapture, the church's hoped-for Escape Hatch on the world's sinking ship. The invention of the doctrine of the pre-tribulation Rapture in 1830 by either J. N. Darby (the traditional dispensational view) or by a young Scottish girl during a series of trances (Dave MacPherson's revisionist view) was the key element in the triumph of dispensationalism. It has therefore been the steady decline of interest in this doctrine during the 1980's that has publicly marked the demise of the dispensational system. Dave Hunt wrote *Whatever Happened to Heaven?* in 1988, but this is not what he really was asking. What his book asks rhetorically is this: *What Ever Happened to Fundamentalists' Confidence in the Doctrine of the Pre-Tribulation Rapture?* (Heaven has been close by all along; the pre-tribulation Rapture hasn't.)

The appeal of this doctrine was very great for over a century because it offered Christians a false hope: to be able to go to heaven without first going to the grave. Traditional dispensationalists want to become modern Elijahs: not as he lived his life, which was painful, risky, and highly confrontational with the religious and political authorities (1 Kings 18), but as he ended his life, when God's chariot carried him to heaven (2 Kings 2). Fundamentalists regard the critics of dispensationalism as enemies of "the

---

14. David Schnittger, *Christian Reconstruction from a Pretribulational Perspective* (Oklahoma City, OK: Southwest Radio Church. 1986), p. 7.

blessed hope," namely, the hope in life after life. They fully understand what the postmillennialist is telling them: "You are going to die!" For over a century, dispensationalism's recruits in the pews refused to listen to such criticism. They traded their God-given heritage of Christian cultural relevance — which requires generations of godly service and compound growth in every area of life — for a false hope: getting out of life alive. It was a bad bargain. It was a mess of pottage in exchange for the birthright.

The culmination and epitaph of the dispensational system can be seen on one short bookshelf: the collected paperback writings of "serial polygamist" Hal Lindsey and accountant Dave Hunt, plus a pile of unread copies of Edgar C. Whisenant's *On Borrowed Time* and *88 Reasons Why the Rapture Is in 1988* (1988), which predicted that the Rapture would take place in September of 1988, and which Mr. Whisenant claims sold over six million copies in 1988. We could also add all the 1970's titles by Salem Kirban, before he switched his interest to the topic of nutrition.

That these authors best represent dispensationalism in our day is denied (always in private conversation) by the faculty and students of Dallas Theological Seminary, but the embarrassed critics have ignored the obvious: the dispensational movement is inherently a paperback book movement, a pop-theology movement, and always has been. It does not thrive on scholarship; it thrives on sensational predictions that never come true. Anyone who doubts this need only read Dwight Wilson's book, *Armageddon Now!* (Baker Book House, 1977, which ICE will reprint soon).

1988

The year 1988 was the year of the public demise of dispensational theology: no Rapture. The church is still here despite the 40th year of "the generation of the fig tree," i.e., the nation of Israel, which is itself involved in something like a civil war rather than an invasion by the USSR. Whisenant's book appeared, confidently prophesying the Rapture for September, 1988.[15] Dave

---

15. Later, he said it would be by January of 1989. Then he updated it to September of 1989. By then, his victimized former disciples were not listening to him any more.

Hunt's *Whatever Happened to Heaven?* also appeared. Meanwhile, former Dallas Seminary president Lewis Sperry Chafer's 8-volume *Systematic Theology* (1948) — the one and only comprehensive theology in the history of the dispensational movement — went out of print, and only a shortened two-volume version has been published by his heirs at Dallas Seminary. (Keep your eye on what got cut, not simply on what remains!)

Then, in October, came the book by House and Ice, *Dominion Theology: Blessing or Curse?* It was a hardback dispensational book. It also appeared on the surface to be a scholarly book. Therefore, it sank without a trace; fundamentalist readers are not interested in scholarly books. *House Divided* buries that ill-conceived effort, and in so doing, buries the last vestiges of dispensational theology. More people will read this grave marker than will read the original book. (Have *you* read the original book, cover to cover? Only if you are Rev. Ice or Professor House, I suspect. Or one of their mothers. Maybe.)

What Is This Book All About?

I am directly responsible for the publication of *House Divided*, and I was indirectly responsible for the publication of *Dominion Theology: Blessing or Curse?*, as I shall explain. Thus, it is appropriate that I explain what I think *House Divided* is all about. It is about the public burial of an expired theological system. What is even more significant about this burial is that its official defenders are almost as active in gathering dirt to shovel on the casket as its theonomic critics are.[16]

As you read this book, keep in the back of your mind this thought: *House and Ice have quietly revised the fundamental doctrines of traditional dispensational theology.* They no longer believe that the old dispensational theology can be successfully defended, a suspicion obviously shared by Dallas Seminary Professor Craig Blaising, as

---

16. See, for example, John MacArthur, Jr., *The Gospel According to Jesus* (Grand Rapids, MI: Zondervan/Academie, 1988), which documents the antinomianism of conventional dispensationalism.

revealed by the citation with which I opened this Foreword. For example, they (House) argue that the death penalty is still valid in New Testament times because this was part of Noah's covenant (Gen. 9:5-6) — a pre-Mosaic covenant.[17] This was Calvinist theologian John Murray's argument a generation ago.[18] It is a bit odd to see dispensationalists appealing to traditional covenant theology when defending dispensationalism against theonomy. Professor House in this case has dressed John Murray's covenant theology in Lewis Sperry Chafer's clothing. It is not that the dispensational Emperor has no clothes; it is that the few presentable clothes that he has were stolen from his long-term rival's wardrobe.

It should also be noted that Charles Ryrie played a similar academic game in *Dispensationalism Today* back in 1965. He used arguments very similar to O. T. Allis's covenant theology to defend traditional dispensationalism against the discontinuity-based attacks by ultradispensationalists (e.g., E. W. Bullinger, C. R. Stam, J. C. O'Hair). I refer here to the devastating and utterly irrefutable (for a Scofield dispensationalist) argument of the ultradispensationalists that Acts 2 (Pentecost) was clearly a fulfillment of Joel 2. Peter specifically referred to the prophecy in Joel 2 in Acts 2:16-20. This means that an Old Testament prophet forecasted the events of Acts 2. This poses a horrendous problem for Scofieldism. Dispensational theology has always taught that the so-called "Church Age" — also called "the great parenthesis" — was completely unknown in the Old Testament and not predicted by any prophet. But Peter said that Pentecost was known to an Old Testament prophet, Joel. The conclusion is inescapable: *the church could not have begun at Pentecost; it must have started later.* This is exactly what the ultradispensationalists argue — a heretical idea, clearly, but absolutely consistent with the dispensational view of the church as the great parenthesis.

---

17. House and Ice, *Dominion Theology: Blessing or Curse?* (Portland, OR: Multnomah Press, 1988), p. 130.

18. John Murray, *Principles of Conduct: Aspects of Biblical Ethics* (Grand Rapids, MI: Eerdmans, 1957), p. 118.

To escape this problem of radical discontinuity, i.e., New Testament church vs. Old Testament prophecy, Ryrie appealed to Erich Sauer, but in fact Sauer's argument rests squarely on the arguments of postmillennial Calvinist critic O. T. Allis. The church was indeed founded at Pentecost; the events of Pentecost were merely transitional. No radical discontinuity should be assumed here, Ryrie insisted. So did Allis.[19] Ryrie also used Stam-type arguments—insisting on a radical discontinuity, church vs. Israel —against Allis. This theological juggling act was not a successful intellectual defense of traditional dispensationalism; it was nothing less than abject surrender. Ryrie in effect picked up a white flag and identified it as dispensationalism's regimental colors. He publicly gave away the farm.

Theologians inside the dispensational camp apparently recognized what Ryrie had done in the name of defending the traditional system. I think this is the reason why there was no subsequent attempted academic defense of dispensationalism until House and Ice, a generation later, wrote *Dominion Theology.* But they no longer defend original Scofieldism. Neither do their published colleagues at Dallas Seminary. (Professor Robert Lightner still carries the old white flag in the classroom at Dallas, but the Christian book-buying public has never heard of him.)

Quite frankly, no one is sure just what the "new, improved" dispensational theology looks like. There has been no public presentation of the revised system. Chafer's *Systematic Theology* has been pulled out of print by its publisher, Dallas Seminary. The old theological system was bled to death, drop by drop, by a thousand qualifications, but nothing has taken its place. There has been an embarrassed silence about this moribund condition for at least two decades. House and Ice have therefore opened a very dangerous can of worms.

---

19. Ryrie cites Sauer's argument that the "mystery" of Ephesians 3:1-12—the gentiles as fellow-heirs with the Jews in salvation—was not a radically new idea, but only comparatively new, i.e., no radical discontinuity. Ryrie, *Dispensationalism Today* (Chicago, IL: Moody Press, 1965), p. 201. This is of course Allis's argument against all dispensationalism: *Prophecy and the Church* (Philadelphia, PA: Presbyterian and Reformed, 1945), pp. 91-102.

House and Ice appear to be on the offensive in their book, but in fact they are on the defensive. Like a duck gliding rapidly across a lake, everything appears calm on top of the water, but underneath the surface there is a lot of rapid paddling going on. The fact is, when House and Ice are finished with their attack on Christian Reconstructionism, their targets are still intact — in fact, completely untouched — but House and Ice are out of ammunition. Worse: they have blown up the barrel of their lone remaining cannon. That they suspected that this might be the case was indicated by their refusal to allow Gary DeMar and me to see their book's pre-publication manuscript in early 1988, despite the fact that we were scheduled to debate Tommy Ice, who was not a published book author at the time. (A similar lack of confidence burdens Hal Lindsey, who also refused to allow me to read the pre-publication manuscript of *The Road to Holocaust*, despite my repeated written appeals.) People who are confident about their opinions will allow their targeted victims, upon request, to read the attacking manuscripts in advance. (Our responses get into print so rapidly anyway, why bother to play coy?)

Now comes the theonomists' counter-attack to House and Ice. If you are a dispensationalist, *House Divided* will not be pleasant reading. But it surely will be educational.

Tommy Ice

I do not remember my first meeting with Rev. Ice, but he does. He recalled for me and our audience the details of this 1974 meeting during our April 12, 1988 debate.[20] He says that I spoke to a small group of students attending Howard Payne College in Brownwood, Texas in 1974 (an evening meeting which I do remember), and at that time he challenged me to provide a single Bible citation to support postmillennialism, which I was unable to do (which I do not remember). He then went on to say that I have yet to provide him with a single Bible citation proving postmillen-

---

20. Gary DeMar and Gary North vs. Rev. Thomas Ice and Dave Hunt.

nialism.[21] He repeats this accusation in the Preface to *Dominion Theology*:

> My challenge is simply this: Since postmillennialism is on every page of the Bible, show me *one* passage that requires a postmillennial interpretation and should not be taken in a premillennial sense. After fourteen years of study it is my belief that there is not one passage anywhere in Scripture that would lead to the postmillennial system. The best postmillennialism can come up with is a position built on an inference.[22]

All right, Tommy, how about Psalm 110, verses 1 and 2? This psalm is quoted in the New Testament more than any other Old Testament passage. It was quoted during the first century of the early church more than any other passage.[23] Consider its words:

> A Psalm of David. The LORD said unto my Lord, Sit thou at my right hand, until I make thine enemies thy footstool. The LORD shall send the rod of thy strength out of Zion: rule thou in the midst of thine enemies (Psalm 110:1-2).

Who is ruling? Jesus. Where does Jesus sit? At God's right hand. Where is this located? In heaven. Stephen announced: "Him hath God exalted with his right hand to be a Prince and a Saviour, for to give repentance to Israel, and forgiveness of sins. . . . But he, being full of the Holy Ghost, looked up stedfastly into heaven, and saw the glory of God, and Jesus standing on [at] the right hand of God, And said, Behold, I see the heavens opened, and the Son of man standing on [at] the right hand of God" (Acts 5:31; 7:55-56). How long will Jesus remain in heaven? Until God has made a footstool of all Christ's enemies. Peter announced at Pentecost: "This Jesus hath God raised up, whereof we all are witnesses. Therefore being by the right hand of God exalted, and having received of the Father the promise of the Holy Ghost, he hath shed

---

21. Audiotapes and a videotape are available of this debate: Institute for Christian Economics, P.O. Box 8000, Tyler, Texas 75711.

22. Ice, "Preface," *Dominion Theology*, p. 9.

23. David M. Hay, *Glory at the Right Hand: Psalm 110 in Early Christianity* (Nashville, TN: Abingdon Press, 1973), p. 15.

forth this, which ye now see and hear. For David is not ascended into the heavens: but he saith himself, The Lord said unto my Lord, Sit thou on [at] my right hand, Until I make thy foes thy footstool" (Acts 2:32-35). And when will this be? When death is conquered at the end of history: "For he must reign, till he hath put all enemies under his feet. The last enemy that shall be destroyed is death" (1 Cor. 15:25-26).

There is no question that this is a postmillennial passage. Let me also assure the reader that there is no possible way for a premillennialist to explain this passage in terms of his system, let alone a dispensationalist. And so premillennialists rarely comment on it. It is one of those favorite neglected passages in the premillennial camp.

Rev. Ice is a very confident man. Consider, however, the justification for Rev. Ice's self-confidence in light of the fact that traces of postmillennial theology can be found in the writings of John Calvin.[24] Some historians would trace this eschatology back at least to the fourth century church historian, Eusebius. The postmillennial system was subsequently developed by the Puritans in the seventeenth century.[25] In contrast, Rev. Ice's own theological system — premillennial, pre-tribulational dispensationalism — was developed at the earliest in 1830.[26] Now, when someone tells you that there is not a single Bible verse that teaches a doctrine that has been held by a significant segment of the Puritans, plus Matthew Henry, Jonathan Edwards, Charles Hodge, A. A. Hodge, Benjamin B. Warfield, W. G. T. Shedd, and O. T. Allis, you are entitled to take such statements with more than a grain of salt. Such universal negative assertions — "Not a single verse!" — are made only by theological amateurs who are utterly unfamiliar

---

24. Greg L. Bahnsen, "The *Prima Facie* Acceptability of Postmillennialism," *Journal of Christian Reconstruction*, (Winter 1976-77), pp. 69-76.

25. *Ibid.*, pp. 77-88.

26. Clarence B. Bass, *Backgrounds to Dispensationalism: Its Historical Genesis and Ecclesiastical Implications* (Grand Rapids, MI: Eerdmans, 1960), Chapter 2. See also Dave MacPherson, *The Great Rapture Hoax* (Fletcher, NC: New Puritan Library, 1983).

with the history of dogmatic and exegetical theology. There has been a continuing debate over eschatology among church theologians for at least 1,800 years, and over postmillennialism since the sixteenth century. But Rev. Ice would have us believe that not one of these postmillennial arguments has ever penetrated his consciousness, an assertion which I am quite ready to believe.

One thing is certain: nobody debated pre-tribulational dispensationalism prior to 1830. It did not exist before then. This is one aspect of Rev. Ice's dilemma. There are others.

My Letter Apparently Triggers His Paradigm Shift

I had pointed some of this out to him in private correspondence two years before our public debate, but he was not persuaded. In fact, in 1986 he sent me a letter of about a dozen pages telling me in great detail how I needed to revise my published statements regarding the history of dispensationalism, since I had relied too heavily on Dave MacPherson's revisionism. He refers to this letter in his Preface,[27] though not that it was a computer letter, printed by a dot-matrix printer with a fading ribbon, and had been sent to me on uncut computer print-out pages. It unfolded like an accordion. I did not want to strain my eyes or my patience by reading it. So, I marked in its margins that I would be willing to read all this if he could get it published in book form, but not before. I reminded him that the dispensational camp had stopped writing books defending the system in the mid-1960's, and that the movement desperately needs modern books that can at least give the illusion of successfully defending the system. Maybe his could be such a book. Thus, we now have *Dominion Theology: Blessing or Curse?*, as he freely admits.[28]

My personal challenge had apparently triggered something in Rev. Ice's mind. Up until that time, he had steadfastly publicly proclaimed himself to be a Christian Reconstructionist. He had been the pastor of David Schnittger, the author of the excellent

---

27. Ice, "Preface," *Dominion Theology*, p. 8.
28. *Ibid.*, p. 9.

booklet, *Christian Reconstruction from a Pretribulational Perspective*, which was published by the Southwest Radio Church of Oklahoma City in 1986.[29] (The publisher no longer distributes this booklet.)[30] Rev. Ice had even attended a 1983 Christian Reconstructionist seminar in Tyler, Texas, where he videotaped the lectures. He has always claimed to be a Calvinist, presumably meaning Calvin's doctrine of absolute predestination, though not his doctrine of covenant theology. He says that he is a presuppositionalist, i.e., a follower of Cornelius Van Til.

Then, in 1986, virtually overnight, he switched his views on Christian Reconstruction. As he admitted in the 1988 debate, he and David Schnittger had "tried to put together a premillennial Reconstructionist ethic. I don't believe you can do it."[31] Ray Sutton and I had been telling him this for several years. This truth finally sank in about the time I refused to read his computerized print-out. (Personal paradigm shifts usually take place for reasons other than mere footnotes.)

What *House Divided* demonstrates is that he should have been content in filing away and forgetting about that print-out with my marginal notations. But some people learn slowly. Or not at all. (I should probably admit that my second choice for the title of this book was *Ice Breaker*. My third choice was *Ice Crusher*.)

Wayne House

In sharp contrast to Rev. Ice is his co-author H. Wayne House. Dr. House can be accurately described as a Christian activist. He pickets abortion clinics. He has co-authored a book on Christian activism.[32] House is not persuaded, as Ice is, that my

---

29. *Ibid.*, p. 7.

30. The booklet maintained that it is possible to maintain a dispensational version of Christian Reconstruction. Like the equally unlikely claim that there can be such a thing as optimistic amillennialism, the booklet provided no outline or suggestion of how this might be possible apart from scrapping the bulk of dispensational theology.

31. Cited by Gary DeMar, *The Debate over Christian Reconstruction* (Ft. Worth, TX: Dominion Press, 1988), p. 185.

32. Richard A. Fowler and H. Wayne House, *Civilization in Crisis* (2nd ed.; Grand Rapids, MI: Baker Book House, 1988).

strategy is dangerous to dispensationalism: getting dispensationalists to become social activists. I argue that if Christian Reconstructionists can get premillennial Christians to act like postmillennialists — i.e., become *operational postmillennialists* — then it will be far easier later on for us to bring them to a belief in postmillennialism. I have said this in print repeatedly throughout the 1980's, and Rev. Ice called attention to this fact during the debate, which I freely admitted.

In sharp contrast to Rev. Ice, Professor House still believes that dispensationalism can be successfully rewritten to allow for political activism without giving up its fundamental tenets, i.e., its denial of Old Testament law in this, the Church Age, and its denial of the possibility of earthly success for reform efforts during the Church Age. He believes that he should attempt to recruit large numbers of his theological peers into what has to be, from the point of view of original dispensationalism, a suicidal frontal attack against the entrenched forces of secular humanism. House is a founding member and official theologian of what he thinks is "Dispensational Activists for Jesus," but which has to be, from the point of view of Scofieldism, "Kamikazes for Christ."

What I really would like to see is a public debate between Rev. Ice and Professor House on this question: "Resolved: that the adoption of a Bible-based social program of social action plays into the hands of Gary North and the Reconstructionists."

After the 1988 debate, Professor House told Gary DeMar that he had decided to co-author *Dominion Theology: Blessing or Curse?* because he had grown tired of reading my continual jibes against dispensationalists: saying that their system cannot be defended intellectually and that such an attempt has not even been attempted since the mid-1960's. [33] This, I hope the reader will understand, is

---

33. Most notably, and most embarrassingly, by then-Dallas Seminary Professor Charles Ryrie, whose *Dispensationalism Today* is still published by Moody Press without revisions a quarter century later. Dr. Ryrie later left Dallas Seminary under unpleasant circumstances. Other departures: S. Lewis Johnson, who abandoned the original dispensational system, as did Bruce Waltke, who became a covenant theologian and who now teaches at Westminster Seminary. Ed Blum is also gone.

the main reason I had made such provocative accusations in the first place: to flush into the open some dispensational scholar — not just a Hal Lindsey or a Dave Hunt, but a true academic spokesman of the movement. It took years of continual verbal harassment on my part to pressure one of them to take up the challenge. For some reason, he then allowed Rev. Ice to join in this effort. He therefore bears equal responsibility for Rev. Ice's text — a responsibility that I surely would fear to share. Professor House unwisely took the bait and went into print. Now he gets to confront Dr. Bahnsen.

In 1988, he had also told Gary DeMar, my former book distribution manager David Dunham, and me that he was ready to debate any theonomist publicly, and he complained that none of us would take up his challenge.[34] He subsequently agreed to appear in a debate with one of us at the Simon Greenleaf School of Law in Orange County, California, in the spring of 1989. There was some question as to who would be his opponent. Then Dr. Bahnsen accepted the challenge, but he insisted that it be a full-scale debate, one on one, with cross-examination. Professor House immediately declined the offer and withdrew, specifically refusing to submit to cross-examination. He suggested instead a presentation of prepared speeches and a mutual sharing of views. Dr. Bahnsen refused to agree to this, and the whole project was dropped. Perhaps this book will persuade Professor House of the wisdom of his decision to decline. Then again, perhaps not.

What Professor House faced was the dilemma that the entire dispensational academic world has faced since Ryrie wrote *Dispensationalism Today*: How to meet the critics head-on without visibly losing the battle? On the other hand, how to maintain the illusion of being capable of meeting all intellectual challenges while remaining cooped up in the classroom, where non-dispensationalist scholars are never allowed to speak? The basic solution for a long time at Dallas Seminary was to allow Professor Lightner

---

34. This took place in July, 1988, at the Christian Booksellers Association's convention in Dallas.

to exercise his self-appointed task of refuting the critics' books in one-page reviews in *Bibliotheca Sacra*, where no one is likely to read them. A similar strategy has been adopted by Grace Theological Seminary. But then Dr. House "broke ranks" and went into the theological battlefield by writing a book. He was dragged into this by Rev. Ice, the Don Quixote of dispensational theology. They now face something more threatening to their reputations than windmills.

The Dispensational Memory Hole

Decade after decade, dispensational theologians cling to a version of church history which even their own students know is a series of preposterous falsehoods strung together with classroom polemics. Take, for example, a myth repeated by House and Ice, that the major promoter of postmillennialism was the early eighteenth-century Anglican theologian, Daniel Whitby. Dr. Gentry deals with this in his chapters on "The Exposition of the Kingdom" and "Documentation Inadequacies." Now, anyone with even a brief knowledge of the history of Puritanism knows that there were many postmillennialists in the seventeenth-century Puritan camp, including John Owen. Whitby was born in 1638 and did not write until the early eighteenth century. He is a minor figure in the history of the church, which is why the dispensationalist polemicists dwell on him as the originator: it makes postmillennialism appear to be a backwater eschatology. Dispensationalists comfort themselves with the thought that "real Bible-believers don't believe in postmillennialism," in the same way that Southern rednecks believe that "real men don't eat quiche." Only dispensational writers have ever proclaimed this Whitby myth, and they have done so generation after generation, *but never those who teach church history and who also hold a Ph.D. in the field.* Sadly, the church historians on dispensational campuses are apparently unwilling or psychologically unable to go to their less well-informed colleagues and say, "Look, fellows, this whole story was a myth our founders invented for polemical reasons, and we are making fools of ourselves by continuing to proclaim it." So the Whitby myth goes on, accepted dutifully by generations of C-average students who hate both church history and systematic theology, but who are "into" church growth.

Tommy Ice regurgitated this old myth in our debate in 1988; I promptly reminded him of the dating problem with Whitby, and then I reminded him that at least my eschatological system was developed as early as 1600; his was invented in 1830. He had nothing to say in response,[35] but a variation of this same old saw now appears in his book. Why would a man of academic integrity do this? Answer: a man of academic integrity wouldn't.[36]

Another example: the statement that the early church fathers were all premillennialists. House and Ice really compound the problem. They say that Daniel Whitby said that the first Nicene council was premillennial.[37] Whitby said exactly the opposite, as Dr. Gentry shows in his chapter on "The Exposition of the Kingdom." A Th.M. thesis written by a Dallas Seminary student in 1977 took to task Charles Ryrie's statement that the early church fathers were premillennialists. Not so, the student concluded; they did not hold a unified eschatological view.[38] But do you think any dispensational author is ready to go into print and admit that Ryrie's account is mythical? Not on your life! It was not just Ryrie's account; this myth has been taught by virtually all dispensationalists except those professionally trained in early church history.

A Movement Without an Official History

What has happened is this: each incoming class of eager seminary students is treated to a rehash of classroom lecture notes — notes that suppress the history of the church whenever this history comes into conflict with the "received truths" of the dispensation-

---

35. There is a record of his silence on tape, unlike my supposed silence at our 1974 meeting.

36. On the academic integrity of the two authors, see Part III.

37. House and Ice, *Dominion Theology*, p. 206.

38. Alan Patrick Boyd, "A Dispensational Premillennial Analysis of the Eschatology of the Post-Apostolic Fathers (Until the Death of Justin Martyr)," unpublished master's thesis, Dallas Theological Seminary, May, 1977.

alism of the 1920's through the 1950's. The students are not told of Dave MacPherson's discovery that Margaret Macdonald, a girl about twenty years old, went into trances in 1830 and announced the pre-tribulation doctrine. We are still waiting for Professor John Hannah, a competent and talented church historian, to go into print and show from original source documents that MacPherson's thesis is nothing but a sham. Strangely, he has decided to remain silent. Or not so strangely, as the case may be.

It is worth noting that no church historian on a dispensational seminary campus has been willing to write a documented official church history of the dispensational movement, for this would involve confronting the embarrassing fact of at least three generations of what had passed for official history, and what in Stalin's day was called "agitprop." We have in our midst an influential theological and ecclesiastical movement which is now a hundred and sixty years old, yet we do not yet have a single, footnoted, carefully researched history of the movement by any professor teaching in a dispensational seminary. What this means is that only anti-dispensationalists and non-dispensationalists have bothered to write the history of the movement. This, to put it mildly, is most peculiar.

I will put it bluntly: any intellectual-ideological-institutional movement which is incapable of producing its own official history is equally incapable of maintaining itself. It has lost the war in advance.

I will put it even more bluntly: the reason why dispensationalism has not produced a detailed, documented, publicly accessible history is because its adherents do not believe that they have a future. A record of the past, they believe, is hardly worth preserving because the earthly future for Christians will soon be cut short. Premillennialism strikes again!

Unrevised Lecture Notes

Dispensational seminary and Bible college professors (those not teaching church history) read their worn-out lecture notes to their students — notes copied from their own professors years ago.

The myths and outright lies get repeated, incoming class after class. The charade of academic integrity can go on for only as long as these students and graduates refuse to read serious works of scholarship. Understand, most graduates of most seminaries are perfectly content to avoid reading works of scholarship. Those dispensationalists who do read serious books, however, risk experiencing a trauma. They may discover that they had spent three or four years in seminary getting a pack of lies taught to them in the name of historical classroom continuity. Their professors had been equally misinformed by their professors, and so on, right back to the founding of the seminary. Nobody bothers to check the primary source documents, since this might require an updating of his lecture notes.

Dispensational theology is like a large stable that never gets swept out. Nobody wants to go in there with a shovel and broom to remove the accumulated filth, so it just gets deeper and riper. It becomes more obvious to their brighter students that they risk stepping in bad stuff every time they go into a classroom to hear the familiar Party Line. The brighter graduates very often depart from the Party Line. But still the classroom charade goes on. The facts of church history get dumped down the equivalent of the memory hole in Orwell's *1984*.

This academic practice identifies a dying movement. You cannot legitimately expect to move forward if your students are deliberately misinformed. This is the same crisis facing the Soviet Union and Red China today: ill-informed people make ill-informed decisions. Only those Christian leaders who believe that there is no future, that Jesus is coming again shortly to Rapture them out of their troubles — especially the Augean stables of dispensationalism's unpublished official history — would be so foolish as to refuse to cut their losses, admit the past lies, and do serious historical scholarship in terms of the movement's official theology. Once again, bad eschatology has produced suicidal results.

The Campus Black-Out

This is why dispensationalist seminary professors — that is, professors on dispensational seminary campuses who still actually take dispensationalism seriously in their classrooms (a rapidly declining number)—work so hard to keep their students from reading anything that is not on the required reading lists. They know what will happen to the best and the brightest of their students if the students start reading "off campus" books. The familiar defensive measure against this probability (i.e., near certainty) of "corruption" is the creation of a systematic academic black-out, especially the prohibition of debates on campus between the faculty and outside scholars. They know what will happen.

When Dr. Ray Sutton was a student at Dallas Theological Seminary in the mid-1970's, he was told again and again by his professors: "Don't read that book." Without exception, the forbidden books were written by Calvinistic authors. Predictably, he went to the library and read the books. The brighter students always did. By the time he was a senior, he was a Calvinist. So were a lot of his fellow students. When the best response a movement-oriented faculty member can offer to his movement's academic critics is "Don't read that book," that movement is close to death. (This is why I wrote *75 Bible Questions Your Instructors Pray You Won't Ask* in 1984.[39] Take advantage of every opportunity to shed a bit of light on campus, I always say.)

What is not so well known is that a variant of the dispensational black-out—admittedly the oldest and most successful of the seminary black-outs—has also been adopted by Calvinist seminaries with respect to the dreaded theonomists. It is just that it is less obvious on Calvinist seminaries, which do have a long tradition of academic excellence to maintain, unlike dispensational seminaries. The Calvinist version of the tactic is more sophisticated and more subtle.

Dealing with the Academic Black-Out

This leads us to the consideration of an important point. I have developed a reputation for being somewhat acerbic in my writings, especially in my introductions, forewords, and prefaces

---

39. Revised edition; Tyler, Texas: Institute for Christian Economics, 1988.

to books. There is a reason for my style. Both my outraged critics and my worried associates have failed to understood the extent to which I am self-conscious in what I do. You can date the appearance of these hostile introductions: the early 1980's.

I have tried to model my polemical writings after Martin Luther's tracts against his theological opponents, of whom there were many. Had he confined his criticisms to a strictly academic defense of his 95 theses, he would not be remembered by anyone today except a handful of specialists in church history, who would probably be Roman Catholics. (Have *you* ever read the 95 theses? Yes, I mean even you seminary professors.) Had Luther persisted stubbornly in a purely academic strategy, he would eventually have been burned at the stake. But he understood the possibilities for radical institutional change that were offered by the printing press, and he pioneered the polemical pamphlet. You can find few examples in subsequent history that match Luther's tracts for invective, vitriol, and contempt for one's opponents. I am only a pale imitation of Luther in this regard. Yet the heirs of Luther's Reformation click their tongues and shake their heads at my style, as if they did not owe their very freedom to criticize me to the social and political effects of Luther's pamphlets. They act as though they believe that the Reformation was little more than a scheduled debate in the faculty lounge.

Academic Suppression in the Name of Jesus

There has been method in my seeming madness. By 1980, I had waited patiently for over five years for scholars or polemicists in any Christian camp to respond to R. J. Rushdoony's monumental book, *The Institutes of Biblical Law* (Craig Press, 1973). His two dozen books, several of them classics,[40] were greeted with stony silence. This was especially obvious with respect to the *Institutes*. The only important exceptions were Harold O. J. Brown's 1974 *Christianity Today* essay on the major books of 1973, in which

---

40. I refer to *The Messianic Character of American Education*, *Freud*, *Foundations of Social Order*, and *The One and the Many*.

he said that Rushdoony's *Institutes* was the most important Christian book published in 1973, and John Frame's 1977 review of the book — notice the time lag — in the *Westminster Theological Journal*, which faculty member Frame had virtually forced the editor to accept, against the latter's strong recommendation to the contrary. Any future historian who attempts to trace the rise of the Christian Reconstruction movement will not be able to understand how it took place if he confines himself to the published academic reviews of Rushdoony's works by contemporary evangelical scholars. There were very few such reviews in the 1960's and 1970's.

I will once again put things bluntly: until I started tweaking their noses in public, their black-out was remarkably successful. But one by one, they are growing tired of being taunted by me in print, and I predict that they will eventually respond in print. The day they do, however, we've got them, as you will see in *House Divided*. It has taken almost a decade for me to begin to flush them out of the bushes.

I had also waited patiently for any academic figure of prominence to respond to Dr. Bahnsen's Westminster Seminary master's (Th.M.) thesis, *Theonomy in Christian Ethics* (Presbyterian and Reformed, 1977). Again, dead silence. With the exception of Meredith G. Kline's ill-conceived review essay and Paul B. Fowler's self-published response,[41] the entire Christian academic world failed to respond. The "guardians of the traditions" adopted that most popular of public academic strategies designed to deal with the opposition's arguments: "No comment, with reservations." Then, in the safety of their classrooms, they attacked the book as theologically untenable.

This is the seminary professor's equivalent of a Punch and Judy puppet show. He labels the puppet with the bat "orthodoxy" and the puppet without a bat "theonomy," and for a few minutes

---

41. Meredith G. Kline, "Comment on the Old-New Error," *Westminster Theological Journal*, XLI (Fall 1978). Dr. Bahnsen was denied access to reply to Kline in this in-house journal, so as the editor of the *Journal of Christian Reconstruction*, I published his response: "M. G. Kline on Theonomic Politics: An Evaluation of His Reply," *JCR*, VI (Winter 1979-80). Paul B. Fowler, "God's Law Free from Legalism" (privately distributed, 1980). Dr. Bahnsen replied to Fowler's response in a privately published paper.

each semester, the orthodoxy puppet beats the tar out of the the-onomy puppet.[42] The C-average students are impressed.

The noticeable absence of theonomists on seminary and Christian college faculties is another manifestation of this system-atic black-out. It is surely not our lack of academic credentials or our lack of publications.[43] The faculties are doing whatever they can to keep students from wandering into the dark forest of bibli-cal law and postmillennial eschatology.

There is a less noticeable consequence of this black-out, one which will be far more important in the long run: the continued attraction of "the best and the brightest" of their graduates to Christian Reconstructionism. Not all of them have permanently joined the theonomist ranks, but few of them have remained un-affected. There is something vaguely exciting about sneaking into a forbidden zone in the marketplace of ideas. Theonomy appeals to those students who can follow an argument and read a foot-note. It is this fact which has most disturbed the brighter tenured guardians, and for good reason. They instinctively recognize the truth of that old political slogan: "You can't beat something with nothing."

Bonfire of the Faculties

Thus, one of my strategies has been to appeal directly to semi-nary students by calling attention to the silence of their professors. To catch their attention, I have on occasion used a bit of sarcasm. It is my view that an effective way for an outsider to deal with an academic black-out is to build a bonfire on the outskirts of the campus and invite the students to a weenie roast. A lot of students show up, and a lot of weenies get roasted.

---

42. For those who remember the "Mr. Bill" segments of the old *Saturday Night Live* show, just substitute "Mr. Greg."

43. Bahnsen was Cornelius Van Til's first choice to replace him in the class-room, a fact widely known at the time. Bahnsen went off to earn his Ph.D. in philosophy from the University of Southern California. Who finally got Van Til's chair? The son of the then-president of Westminster Seminary, a young man who held an M.A. in philosophy from a minor university. This is how the academic game is played, and not just in the secular world.

Predictably, this practice has not won me Th.D.-holding friends or influenced tenured people. It has also embarrassed some of my colleagues within the Reconstructionist movement, who still hope that a place for them on campus lies ahead, if only I would substitute verbal pleasantries for my practice of calling a spade a spade — especially a spade that the user fully intends to dig theonomy's collective theological grave. They do not recognize the plain fact which our opponents do recognize: this is a war to the death of rival views of Christianity. No prisoners will be taken on this intellectual battlefield. Van Til took no prisoners either, which is why he was hated and feared.

A Theonomic Curriculum

I will tell you why this black-out cannot work forever: *home schooling and Christian day schools.* There, we do find theonomists teaching, and we will find more of them as time goes on. Our position does tend to make long-term strategists out of people. We clearly recognize the institutional soft underbelly of the non-theonomists: intellectually third-rate teaching materials. I intend to begin producing teaching materials aimed at high school students in home schools and day schools. The black-out strategy of the seminaries and colleges has rested on the presupposition that the entering freshman students have been given large doses of secular humanism in their textbooks, and that they will not be familiar with the basic tenets of Christian Reconstruction. Thus, silence seems sufficient. As times goes on, however, this strategy's bedrock assumptions will collapse. The theonomists will have captured the minds of many of the brighter students before they hit college, and surely before they hit seminary. And their professors will learn an important theonomic truth: one well-informed student can shed a remarkable amount of light in the midst of a black-out. The darker the black-out, the brighter the light appears to onlookers. (I have some other strategies of infiltration, but it is my view that one should not take bows before the fourth act is over.)

Gentlemen of the closed campus and monopolistic classroom, your free ride is just about over. Better get over to the library and do some intellectual calisthenics.

No More Subsidies

Because my business and my foundation have been graciously provided with sufficient funds, I have been given the opportunity, and therefore the moral responsibility, to break through this systematic black-out. It has taken a lot of money, a lot of books, and a lot of acerbic introductions. I decided years ago that I would have to depart from the tradition of American scholarly debate (though not the British tradition). Scholars in the U.S. are expected to deal gently with each other in print, a tradition, like tenure, which has become a kind of academically enforced subsidy of a vicious, well-entrenched, intellectually corrupt, humanistic, establishment academic community, so-called — a rag-tag collection of tenured pedants who have grown intellectually flabby over the years as a result of institutional and financial insulation.

The Christian academic world, while not equally corrupt, is analogously flabby. I decided in 1980 to taunt them publicly at every appropriate opportunity. I saw no other way to expose them and their charade of intellectual integrity, and no other way to get them to venture into the intellectual arena to defend themselves. Once in that public arena, I knew, we in the Reconstructionist camp would have an opportunity to prove our case.

And prove it Bahnsen and Gentry do. One by one, they very politely and graciously expose the arguments of House and Ice as half-baked, carelessly researched, insupportable, and intellectually dishonest. Part III by Dr. Gentry is gentlemanly almost to a fault (certainly not *my* style!); it is also devastating. It reveals to what depths desperate men will resort in order to defend a visibly lost intellectual cause. The desperation of dispensationalism today is available for public viewing by men of honest scholarship, point by point, in Part III. If House and Ice are the most competent defenders of dispensationalism today, then dispensationalism as a system clearly has no tomorrow.

What you are about to read should serve as a warning: *people who don't have the horses should stay out of the Derby.* They will only get trampled.[44] It will remind professors within the dispensational camp that there are definite risks in going public with the tenets of the dispensational position.

Baptizing Dave Hunt

This time, Dallas Seminary and its various undergraduate Bible college clones cannot take refuge by saying that "these people" — meaning Hal Lindsey, Salem Kirban, Constance Cumbey, and Dave Hunt — somehow "do not represent us." Tommy Ice is Dave Hunt's chosen debate team partner in their attempts to refute the dreaded Reconstructionists. Professor House "baptized" Rev. Ice intellectually when he decided to co-author *Dominion Theology* with him. Some of that "baptismal font water" has now splashed down on Mr. Hunt (although of course dispensationalists require total immersion rather than mere sprinkling). Professor House surely represents the dispensational academic world, and if no one is willing to help carry him off the intellectual battlefield and replace him, then his efforts and Ice's will have to serve as the best that dispensationalism can offer. This would clearly spell the end of dispensationalism as an intellectual system.

I will say it once again, just to be sure that everyone understands: *Dominion Theology: Blessing or Curse?* is a public admission of the death of dispensationalism. This is the first full-scale statement of the dispensational position — by way of critiquing theonomy — that we have seen since Ryrie's brief and ineffective book, *Dispensationalism Today.* That book failed to answer the critics of dispensationalism. *Dominion Theology: Blessing or Curse?* is far worse, from the point of view of Scofieldism: it raises even more

---

44. I am not referring here to the intellectual capacity of dispensational theologians. I am speaking rather of the specific details of the system they have chosen to adopt for distinctly non-intellectual reasons. I agree with Van Til's analogy: no matter how sharp the blade of a crooked buzz saw is, it will always cut crooked.

explosive questions, yet pretends that it has answers to the on-
slaught of the theonomists.

I will say it once again: *the theological debate is over.* Christian
Reconstructionism has not yet won the debate with every known
theological critic, but it surely has won the debate with the dispensationalists. And in engaging the dispensationalists directly, Dr.
Bahnsen and Dr. Gentry have brought up to date the work of
O. T. Allis. Allis inflicted mortal wounds on dispensational theology in 1945. Bahnsen and Gentry merely act as public coroners.
Their autopsy report is now on record. Ladies and gentlemen, the
cadaver is surely dead; rigor mortis has set in. It is time to give it a
decent Christian burial.

But first, read *House Divided*, the equivalent of an open-casket
funeral.

The Quiet Defection of the Seminaries

What few dispensationalists in the pews realize is that even
Dallas Seminary no longer emphasizes dispensational theology to
the degree that it once did. Ever since its accreditation in the
mid-1970's, it has emphasized such topics as Christian counselling
far more than 1950's dispensationalism. The departure of Charles
Ryrie from the Dallas faculty was symbolic of this shift in emphasis. Meanwhile, in the late 1980's, Talbot Theological Seminary
in La Mirada, California abandoned dispensationalism entirely.
For the sake of alumni donations, however, neither seminary discusses these changes openly. Only Grace Theological Seminary of
the "big three" still forthrightly preaches Scofieldism's "received
truths." (To its credit, Grace Seminary still teaches a literal six-
day creation, a doctrine which Dallas Seminary, like all the Calvinist seminaries except for Reformed Episcopal Seminary and
Mid-America Reformed Seminary, has carefully avoided defending. Dallas Seminary's self-proclaimed "literal hermeneutic"
begins only with Genesis 2.)

The problem is, the opponents of theonomy in all camps keep
such inside information bottled up. They refused to engage us in
open debate for over fifteen years. Then, in late 1988, the pub-

lished refutations began. My introductions and prefaces finally enraged some captains in the opposing army, and they went into print.

In short, like a good hunting dog, I finally flushed a pair of quail into the sky, where Dr. Bahnsen and Dr. Gentry had a field day. Lead pellets filled the sky and hit their marks. Next!

Coming soon: a gaggle of Westminster Seminary geese, and only a little over a decade and a half after the *Institutes* appeared.[45] (By Westminster standards, this was a rush job.) Please stay tuned!

Final Remarks

I address this to the inquisitive dispensational reader who is willing to consider the possibility of having to rethink his position. It is unquestionably painful to rethink one's position. I went through this experience. I was an ultradispensationalist in the early spring of 1964. Had it not been for John Murray's lectures on Romans 11, I might still be an ultradispensationalist.[46] Murray's view that the conversion of the Jews will inaugurate a wave of blessings during an earthly millennium was basically a detailed exposition of the nineteenth-century position of Robert Haldane and Charles Hodge — a fact that amillennialists at Westminster Seminary still gag on.[47] I learned from Murray that postmillennialism offers a way to deal with the future of Israel without spiritualizing away every prophecy regarding Israel's role in the coming of a glorious future in history and on earth.

---

45. We have heard about this elusive book for over three years.

46. John Murray, *The Epistle to the Romans*, 2 vols. (Grand Rapids, MI: Eerdmans, 1965), vol. 2, pp. 65-103.

47. They appeal to their notes of his classroom lectures on eschatology, which do sound more amillennial. I was auditing his eschatology class at the same time that I audited his Romans lectures, and I noted this discrepancy at the time. But Murray was never all that confident about his lecture notes on systematic theology, which is why he never published them. What he did publish was his commentary on Romans 11. That exposition is clearly postmillennial. Murray was a Scot, after all, not a Dutchman, and the Scottish Presbyterian position, unlike the Dutch, has always been postmillennial.

House Divided is a postmillennial book. It does not seek to fight
something (dispensationalism) with nothing (amillennialism).
You are *not* being asked to abandon hope in dispensationalism's
escape hatch in the future (the pre-tribulation Rapture) only to
take up residence in amillennialism's Fort Contraction, with a
tribe of howling Darwinian Indians circling it, all armed with repeating rifles. You are being asked instead to join a victorious
army led by Jesus Christ, who sits at God's right hand, and who will
remain seated there until He subdues all His enemies under His
feet. "Then cometh the end, when he shall have delivered up the
kingdom to God, even the Father; when he shall have put down
all rule and all authority and power. For he must reign, till he
hath put all enemies under his feet" (I Cor. 15:24-25).

*   *   *

P.S.   Neither Dr. Bahnsen nor Dr. Gentry is responsible for
my "unChristian, offensive, insensitive, uncharitable, confrontational, argumentative, arrogant, unscholarly" style, as it has been
described on occasion. They are both certified for seminary employment. As for me, I prefer off-campus bonfires.

PREFACE

WHY I COULD NOT
REMAIN A DISPENSATIONALIST

Rev. Kenneth L. Gentry, Th.D.

From 1966 until 1975 I was a dispensationalist. I was attracted to the movement because it boasted of a consistent biblical outlook, which could explain the times. I was saved by the grace of the Lord Jesus Christ at a dispensationalist youth camp in Boca Raton, Florida; I attended a dispensationalist church (Calvary Bible Church, Chattanooga, Tennessee) pastored by my dispensationalist uncle (Rev. John S. Lanham); I graduated from a dispensationalist college (Tennessee Temple University, Chattanooga, Tennessee) with a degree in Bible; I attended a dispensationalist seminary for two years (Grace Theological Seminary, Winona Lake, Indiana); and I even owned a loose-leaf *New Scofield Reference Bible*, filled with all the notes necessary to make and keep one a dispensationalist.

In many ways it was great being a dispensationalist, yet also frustrating. It was great to know that we had the reasons for the problems of modern society. It was frustrating that as a Christian I was not expected to have any hope of successfully promoting any biblical solution to those problems, even though I was taught that the earth is the Lord's and the gospel is the power of God unto salvation. At the age of twenty, I even turned down a life insurance policy because I was convinced that I would not be around long enough to have a family that would need it. My college days were lived "with anticipation, with excitement" because I thought "we should be living like persons who don't expect to be around much longer."[1] I wish I could take some of the courses over: I was around at least long enough for graduation day to come.

While studying at Grace Theological Seminary, two influences converged causing me to reject dispensationalism. The first was my researching a paper on the Lordship Controversy.[2] This led to my discovery of the significance of the Acts 2 enthronement passage, which shook my dispensationalism to its very foundation. The second was the discovery at about the same time of O. T. Allis's *Prophecy and the Church*. This work bulldozed the residue of my collapsed dispensationalism. A couple of friends of mine (Rev. Alan McCall and Mr. Barry Bostrom, Esq.) and I not only soon departed dispensationalism but transferred from Grace Seminary to Reformed Theological Seminary in Jackson, Mississippi. Previously we had been partial Calvinists, now we had become fully reformed, hence non-dispensational.

At Reformed Seminary I took two courses that initially seemed implausible and misguided extravagance. The courses were "History and Eschatology" (in which was defended postmillennialism) and "Christian Theistic Ethics" (in which was set forth theonomic ethics). Both of these courses were taught by my co-author, Dr. Greg L. Bahnsen.

Regarding the eschatological question, even though I was no longer a dispensationalist I had assumed Pentecost, Lindsey, and other dispensationalists were correct in affirming "postmillennialism finds no defenders or advocates in the present chiliastic discussions within the theological world."[3] Unfortunately, I still had dispensational blinders on my eyes, for in the very era in which Pentecost's book was published (1958) there were at least four notable works in defense of postmillennialism — one of them en-

---

1. Hal Lindsey, *The Late Great Planet Earth* (Grand Rapids, MI: Zondervan, 1970), p. 145.

2. This paper was eventually published. See Kenneth L. Gentry, Jr., "The Great Option: A Study of the Lordship Controversy," *Baptist Reformation Review* (Spring, 1976), pp. 49ff.

3. J. Dwight Pentecost, *Things To Come: A Study in Biblical Eschatology* (Grand Rapids, MI: Zondervan/Academie, [1958] 1964), p. 387; cp. Lindsey, *Late Great*, p. 176.

dorsed by the famed, orthodox Old Testament scholar, O. T. Allis: J. Marcellus Kik's, *Matthew Twenty-Four* (1948) and *Revelation Twenty* (1955), Roderick Campbell's *Israel and the New Covenant* (Introduction by O. T. Allis, 1954), and Loraine Boettner's *The Millennium* (1957).

And how could *anyone* believe in the applicability of Old Testament law to modern culture? The notion was even more far-fetched to me than the idea of victory of the Gospel in history. Dispensational constructs still haunted my mind.

In *both* of the aforementioned courses I continued in steadfast opposition to the professor through almost half of each of the courses. You might say that I "kicked against the pricks." But in both courses I was eventually swayed by the sheer force of biblical exegesis and consistent theological analysis. I went into these courses as an anti-theonomic amillennialist; I came out as a theonomic postmillennialist. I date my adherence to Christian Reconstructionism from 1977. My reformed theology was now complete; with the Westminster Divines I could cite Old Testament case laws alongside of New Testament passages for divine insight into the resolution of moral issues and I could turn to the Old and New Testament prophetic hope for a proper understanding of the Gospel Victory Theme of eschatology. In short, I could apply the whole of Scripture to the whole of life in confident anticipation of all glory being Christ's in His world.

Contrary to the analysis of House and Ice as to why most people become Reconstructionists, however, my interest in Christian Reconstructionism was related solely to the exegetical case in its behalf. Grace Seminary had trained me well in grammatico-historical analysis. It was just that sort of approach to the biblical material that drew me to Reconstructionism. In fact, I was already politically and socially "conservative" as a dispensationalist. Political and social concerns had *nothing* to do with my persuasion in eschatology or ethics; their consistent biblical grounding, which came with theonomic ethics, were happy side-effects. My becoming convinced of Reconstructionism was roughly analogous to Wayne House's refusing to meet Greg Bahnsen in formal debate allowing cross-examination: the position seems to be irrefutable from a biblical basis and it is humiliating even to try to refute it.

My interest in co-authoring this book is *not* to attack House and Ice. They are servants of the same Lord as I. My interest, rather, is to defend against unjust and misguided criticisms the theology that I and a number of my friends (and many others) hold. The distortions rampant in the Reconstruction debate are terribly frustrating. I am a full-fledged, bona fide Westminster Confessionist, yet to hear some discussions of the distinctives of Reconstructionism and some even regarding myself (!), I feel wrongfully accused and horribly misunderstood. One master's thesis at Calvin College even suggested my theonomic views damaged my first church, which I pastored for five years![4] That unfounded, wholly erroneous assault on my ministry was retracted and an apology written after my former church and I both wrote letters to the thesis writer informing him of his horrendous error.[5] It is just *that* sort of thing that compels me to co-write the present book: misunderstanding can be dangerous. I am thankful that *Dominion Theology* by House and Ice did not stoop to that sort of argumentation, but the misinformation promoted in the work still possesses the potential for both theological confusion and ministerial harm.

Theonomy in the PCA

I have even had acquaintances ask me if I were going to leave the Presbyterian Church in America (in which I hold my ordination) in search for a more theonomic environment. My answer has been and continues to be, "No!" My denomination is Bible-believing, Presbyterian, and Reformed in its confessional and

---

4. David Watson, "Theonomy: A History of the Movement and an Evaluation of its Primary Text" (Grand Rapids, MI: Calvin College Master's Thesis, 1985), pp. 21, 22, 24.

5. His apology to me read, in part: "I am sorry for the erroneous conclusion I drew from the raw data about your ministry. Please accept my sincerest apology for any hurt I may have caused you. I now realize that my understanding of the facts was inadequate. I have gone about correcting or appending letters of apology to the few copies which I've distributed outside the theonomic camp. . . . I trust that my previously misinformed work will not spread further" (David Watson to Ken Gentry, Sept. 3, 1985).

constitutional standards — and that is what provides the basis for both my pastoral ministry and my personal Reconstructionist views. Besides, the PCA has considered theonomic issues on a few occasions and has always allowed it[6] — even to the point of the General Assembly's rebuking a presbytery that slowed down a man's progress toward ordination on the sole basis of theonomy[7] and adjudicating another in a way favorable to a particular theonomist, Rev. Brad Fell, who was wrongly denied ordination solely due to his theonomic sympathies.[8]

On another occasion in which the General Assembly was asked about the contemporary applicability of Deuteronomy 13, the answer of the committee leaned toward a non-theonomic position. But this answer was immediately followed by a qualifier prohibiting an improper use of the information it provided the inquiring presbytery: "Since there are differences of opinion with regard to the application and 'general equity' of the various penal sanctions, this declaration shall not be used by the courts of the Church to bind the conscience of elders in the PCA."[9]

I trust my contribution to the present work will be helpful in the wider discussion.[10] The progress of the orthodox apprehension of truth almost always has been over sincere and spirited debate. It is important that Reconstructionist views be clearly heard and carefully understood.

---

6. "The General Assembly affirm[s] that no particular view of the application of the judicial law for today should be made a basis for orthodoxy or excluded as heresy," *Minutes of the Seventh General Assembly of the Presbyterian Church in America* (1979), p. 195 ("Report on Theonomy").

7. *Minutes of the Ninth General Assembly of the Presbyterian Church in America* (1981), p. 145, section 7 ("Review and Control of Presbyteries Report").

8. *Minutes of the Tenth General Assembly of the Presbyterian Church in America* (1982), pp. 107ff. ("Lee, et al. v. Gulf Coast Presbytery"). The antipathy by some toward theonomy is noted in that decision: "It is the judgment of the Commission that [Teaching Elder] Donald C. Graham has helped to aggravate the problem of dissension over 'theonomy' by circulating materials which contain intemperate language to certain members of Gulf Coast Presbytery" (p. 108).

9. *Minutes of the Eleventh General Assembly of the Presbyterian Church in America* (1983), p. 97 ("Advice of the Sub-Committee on Judicial Business").

10. Besides this Preface, I actually wrote Chapters 9-20 and Appendix B.

In closing, I would like to give special thanks to Bill Boney, Alan West, Ron Brown, Bob Nance, and Rev. Mark Duncan for their assistance in reading and interacting with my manuscript for my section of the present book. They were all dispensationalists once, but are now Reconstructionists. Their insights based both on their experience and knowledge were most helpful for the organizing of my material and the preparing of it for a general audience.

INTRODUCTION

We have discussed with Wayne House and Thomas Ice your request to review their manuscript on "Christian Reconstruction" [*Dominion Theology: Blessing or Curse?*] and have decided not to comply with that request.

We believe the authors have accurately represented the published views of leading Reconstructionist spokesmen and that their analysis of those views has been fair and irenic. To delay the book's release in order to subject it to additional prepublication critique is unwarranted.

—Rodney L. Morris
Editor, Multnomah Press

The first to plead his case seems just, until another comes and examines him.

—Proverbs 18:17, NASV

1

AN OPPORTUNITY FOR
CROSS-EXAMINATION

Introduction to the reason for this book and its aims.

This book might not have been necessary.

The authors of the present work are both "Reconstructionists" in their theological and ethical orientations. They believe that the entire Bible is ethically normative for us today, including the Mosaic law. They believe that the kingdom of Jesus Christ was established at His first advent, and that the Great Commission will see marvelous success before Christ returns. These two convictions lead them to expect and to seek the transformation of every area of life, including society and politics, according to the word of God. Such beliefs and practices are at the heart of what is labeled "Reconstructionism" today. Its ethical perspective is termed "theonomic,"[1] and its eschatological outlook is called "postmillennial."[2] In the past history of the Church, people who have endorsed these positions have often been called "Reformed" or "Puritan" (adhering to the theology of the Calvinistic Reformation as formulated in the Westminster Confession of Faith and Catechisms).

The authors of this book would just as soon be simply called "Christians." They are ordained presbyterian pastors and are active in the work of Christ's Church. They know very well that Christian faith centers on the saving work of Jesus Christ. They profess to

---

1. Cf. Greg L. Bahnsen, *Theonomy in Christian Ethics*, (ex. ed.; Phillipsburg, NJ: Presbyterian and Reformed, [1977] 1984).

2. We believe that Christ's return in glory will be subsequent ("post-") to the millennial period prophesied and promised in Scripture.

3

love the Savior with all their heart. They know that their new life
in Him, their new status of being right with God, and their hope
of eternal life have been granted to them by the grace of God.
They have nothing of which to boast (Eph. 2:8-9). With Paul they
would say, "Far be it from me to glory, save in the cross of our
Lord Jesus Christ, through which the world has been crucified
unto me, and I unto the world" (Gal. 6:14). Having been saved
from the world, their concern is to love their Lord with all their
heart, soul, strength and mind (Matt. 22:36-38). They now want
to walk in those good works which God intends for them (Eph.
2:10). They make a sincere effort to heed the words of Christ to
"seek above all the kingdom of God and His righteousness" (Matt.
6:33). They know that this kingdom, for which they pray regularly (Matt. 6:10), will not be consummated until after the return
of Jesus Christ and the final judgment, when all believers will
then rejoice in "a new heaven and earth wherein righteousness
dwells" (2 Peter 3:13). In the meantime they seek to perfect personal holiness in the fear of God (2 Cor. 7:1) and to make all the
nations disciples of their Lord and Savior, Jesus Christ (Matt.
28:18-20). It is only in the light and context of these beliefs and
practices that they see and understand their Reconstructionist position in ethics and eschatology.

The authors of this work are also educated Christians, each
with seminary training, an advanced masters degree and a doctoral degree. They make their mistakes, but they have been trained
well to try and avoid them. They approach their Christian convictions and theology with a zeal to pursue the truth wherever it
leads (Rom. 3:4). The ultimate standard of truth, in their estima-
tion, is the inspired word of God (John 17:17) found in the Scriptures of the Old and New Testaments. The authors have sought to
study and properly understand the Scriptures, giving their best
mental efforts to reaching the conclusions which they have. Because Scripture is the ultimate authority, not their own present
convictions, the authors hope to remain teachable and open to
correction in what they believe. They also want to be responsible

in their theological posture, being able and willing to offer a defense of the things that they confess to be true. Arbitrariness and subjectivity should be shunned when it comes to Christian theology.

Dispensationalism and Christian Reconstruction

The Reconstructionist understanding of Christian theology has proven to be controversial in some circles over the last two decades. Although disagreement (and disagreeableness) has shown up in Reformed circles over theonomic ethics and postmillennial eschatology, the most natural opponent of the Reconstructionist position is dispensationalism. The dispensational understanding of Scripture, advocated by many sincere and well-studied believers, emphasizes discontinuity with Old Testament ethics (particularly the Mosaic law) and emphasizes discontinuity between God's work in the present Church age and His work in the millennium. The dispensationalist contends that Christians are not under the law of Moses for their moral guidance, and that Christ must return prior to the millennium ("premillennial") in order for this world to enjoy significant transformation. Reconstructionism and dispensationalism, therefore, are clearly and diametrically opposed to each other on a few key distinctives in their theological systems.

Within the last couple of years two dispensationalists, Dave Hunt and Tommy Ice, have been particularly vocal in expressing criticism of the Reconstructionist outlook. They have both written about and publicly debated what they perceive to be not only weaknesses in Reconstructionist theology or biblical interpretation, but also a severe danger to the life and health of the Church. The accusations have not always been well-tempered, scholarly, or even accurate; but they have gained a hearing. Accordingly there have been answers published to these dispensationalist critics by Reconstructionists,[3] and we would recommend that the reader consult these works. In them one gets a well-balanced and biblically based presentation of the viewpoint and strengths of Reconstructionism.

---

3. Gary DeMar and Peter Leithart, *The Reduction of Christianity: A Biblical Response to Dave Hunt* (Ft. Worth, TX: Dominion Press, 1988); Gary DeMar, *The Debate over Christian Reconstruction* (Ft. Worth, TX: Dominion Press, 1988).

The dispute between dispensationalism and Reconstruction-ism has not abated, however. Tommy Ice and Wayne House of Dallas Theological Seminary have published what they call "the first book-length reply to the Christian Reconstruction movement,"[4] a 460-page volume entitled *Dominion Theology: Blessing or Curse?* The book aims to be thorough and appears to have been written by two authors who are familiar with much of the literature pub-lished by Reconstructionists (cf. their annotated bibliography). There is no doubt how the authors answer the question posed in the title of their book. They view Reconstructionism — in particular theonomic ethics and postmillennial eschatology — to be a curse. They find the position to be startling, upsetting, dangerous and unbiblical. They are concerned over its growing advocacy and in-fluence. Accordingly their book is hard-hitting. Despite occasional words of agreement and even praise for aspects of Reconstruc-tionism, authors House and Ice feel that the curse and theological error of Reconstructionism can be refuted and should be repudi-ated by Christians who wish to be faithful to Scripture.

Upon examination, however, the book by House and Ice seemed to the authors of this book to have fallen far short of its goals — and indeed of expected standards of scholarship. Reconstructionism had not been represented fairly and correctly at many places. The reasoning of House and Ice was weighed down with fallacies. The attempted exegetical rebuttal of Reconstructionist distinctives was flawed and ineffective. Nevertheless, the book set itself forth and was being hailed (by a number of prominent evangelical personal-ities) as the decisive answer to Reconstructionism which the Church sorely needed today.

The Debate That Never Was

It therefore pleased Bahnsen when the Simon Greenleaf Debate Society contacted him with a proposal that he debate one of the au-thors of *Dominion Theology*, Wayne House. In the early fall of 1988, Elias Hernandez of the debate society confirmed a date for this debate (May 13, 1989) and the commitment of House to meet Bahnsen in

---

4. H. Wayne House and Thomas Ice, *Dominion Theology: Blessing or Curse?* (Portland, OR: Multnomah Press, 1988), p. 9.

the public dialogue. This would have allowed an excellent opportunity to air, examine, and evaluate the reasoning set forth in *Dominion Theology*. It would have permitted a correcting of the record about what Reconstructionists do and do not really believe. The Christian public would have been given a serious look at the contrasts and relative strengths or weaknesses of the conflicting systems of thought: dispensationalism and Reconstructionism. It would have provided an occasion to examine and assess the reasoning and biblical exegesis employed by authors House and Ice, as well as to do the same with respect to the argumentation enlisted in support of Reconstructionism. Bahnsen was glad for the invitation and eager for the encounter.

But House apparently had second thoughts about the debate. Even though he had gone into print with a hard-hitting attack upon the alleged errors of Reconstructionism — and thus would have felt his work to be defensible (even important for the health of the Church) — House now felt that the nature and structure of the dialogue with Bahnsen should be altered. In fact, he said that his request for the change in the character of the debate was non-negotiable; he simply would not participate unless the change were made. He now wanted a "debate" *without* any direct cross-examination between the parties to the debate. That is, each side could bring their prepared remarks, but there must not be any interchange between the debaters on a one-to-one footing where direct questions and challenges would need to be entertained and answered. In short, a debate with its heart cut out. It was precisely cross-examination which would have made the debate valuable to the public and a true test of the two conflicting theological positions. Their relative strengths would then be open for inspection. Undoubtedly, House had his own good reasons for not wanting the debate with cross-examination a constitutive part of it.

Some other forum has needed to be sought in which the work of House and Ice can be publicly cross-examined. That explains why this chapter opened with the statement that this present book might not have been necessary, and it explains why it now is. The extensive discussion of Reconstructionism by House and Ice should not be ignored. It is seriously presented and serious in its charges. It deserves a serious reply. Reconstructionism should be publicly vindicated of the charges which *Dominion Theology* has made against it. Accordingly the two authors of this volume agreed to a joint project in order expeditiously to produce a book which would set forth the Reconstructionist outlook, answer the charges made against it by House and Ice, and rebut the contrary reasoning and theology upon which House and Ice relied. We are not out to make them appear to be heretics. We are, however, convinced that they can be shown to be in error.

The Purpose of "House Divided"

In the pages which follow we will address the two major distinctives which were challenged by House and Ice: theonomic ethics and postmillennial eschatology. Both of the present authors have influenced each other's contributions and stand behind each other's work. For the reader's information, though, the chapters found in the section entitled "The Ethical Question" were authored by Bahnsen, while the chapters found in the section entitled "The Eschatological Question" were composed by Gentry (as well as the section entitled "The Scholarly Question," the Conclusion, and Appendix B).

In the two sections of the book on ethics and eschatology we aim to juxtapose the dispensational and Reconstructionist views on particular issues. We offer biblical substantiation for the Reconstructionist perspective in ethics (theonomy) and for the Reconstructionist perspective on eschatology (postmillennialism). We also will give extended attention to the arguments which were published in *Dominion Theology* against both of these elements of the Reconstructionist system.

Our conclusion is that House and Ice are not persuasive and are demonstrably in error. Even further, as indicated in the chapters entitled "How Should We Then Decide?" and "The Failure of Accurate Portrayal" and in Part 3 entitled "The Scholarly Question" we have serious misgivings about the *repeated* misrepresentations of our sincerely held position and about the *kind* of reasoning which House and Ice often use to oppose that position. By the end of our analysis and answer, we humbly and teachably believe that the reader will understand well why the critique offered in *Domin-ion Theology* is not credible. We also hope that the reader will see what is at stake in the dispute and be encouraged to test all things by the infallible standard of God's holy word. If Reconstruction-ism comes up wanting, then it is unworthy of your support. If it communicates to you its biblical credentials and strength, then it poses an important challenge concerning your life and involve-ment as a Christian in this world.

"Prove all things; hold fast that which is good" (1 Thess. 5:21).

Part I
THE ETHICAL QUESTION

2

THE CONFLICT OF VISIONS

A comparison of the characteristic features of dispensational and Reconstructionist ethics.

"How should we then live?" The late Francis Schaeffer used that question as the title of his book (and film series) on the history of thought and culture.[1] The question is a good one for understanding and evaluating anyone's philosophy of life. The question is inevitable. Every view of reality, every view of man's nature and place in the cosmos, every view of God and His dealings with man — every view carries implications for our attitudes and conduct. We should ask that question about the various philosophical or theological positions that are adopted or advocated by people around us, including dispensationalism and Reconstructionism (or "theonomy").[2]

Let me begin by surveying the kind of lifestyle and ethic which is the natural result of a dispensational outlook on life, using it as a preface to analyzing *Dominion Theology: Blessing or Curse?*, the dispensational critique of Reconstructionism written by House and Ice.

If we could go back to the days prior to the appearance of dispensationalism in American Christianity, prior to the impact of

---

1. Francis A. Schaeffer, *How Should We Then Live? The Rise and Decline of Western Thought and Culture* (Old Tappan, NJ: Fleming H. Revell, 1976).

2. The Reconstructionist view of ethics is often termed "theonomy" and can be more fully pursued in two books: Greg L. Bahnsen, *Theonomy in Christian Ethics*, (ex. ed.; Phillipsburg, NJ: Presbyterian and Reformed, [1977] 1984), and *By This Standard: The Authority of God's Law Today* (Tyler, TX: Institute for Christian Economics, 1985).

dispensational thinking on the direction of evangelicalism, we would see that the thrust of evangelical ethics and social theory was Reconstructionist in its basic features. George M. Marsden puts it this way:

> From the time of the Puritans until about the middle of the nineteenth century, American evangelicalism was dominated by a Calvinistic vision of a Christian culture. Old Testament Israel, a nation committed to God's law, was the model for political institutions. Hence the Christian ideal was to introduce God's kingdom — a New Israel — not only in the lives of the regenerate elect, but also by means of civil laws that would both restrain evil and comprehensively transform culture according to God's will. . . . Jonathan Blanchard similarly spoke of "a perfect state of society," meaning that "the Law of God is the Law of the Land."[3]

The Reformed (and Reconstructionist) character of early evangelicalism emphasized the unity of Scripture and the comprehensive influence of Christian faith on every sphere of life. Consequently believers looked upon the whole Bible as their authority (when properly, contextually interpreted in terms of God's progressive outworking of redemption). Moreover, they did not hesitate to apply all of the moral instruction of Scripture, both Old and New Testaments, to the ethical problems of society and state (realizing that only the internal work of the Spirit could bring true conformity to God's will from the heart). In time, however, a fallacious line of thinking infected evangelical theology on these matters, suggesting that Christ's redemptive work and the Spirit's sanctifying work in the New Testament could be given their due place only if they were portrayed as standing in fundamental antithesis (rather than continuity) with God's previous work and revelation. Dispensational discontinuity came to color the reading of the Bible, leading to a disregard for the moral authority of the Old Testament and its relevance for social justice.

---

3. George M. Marsden, *Fundamentalism and American Culture: The Shaping of Twentieth-Century Evangelicalism, 1870-1925* (New York: Oxford University Press, 1980), p. 86.

By the 1870s when the dispensationalist movement began to take hold in America, holiness teachers already commonly spoke of "the Dispensation of the Spirit." This and similar phrases became commonplace within the premillennial movement, with the age of the Spirit sharply separated from the age of law. C. I. Scofield in his classic formulation called these two dispensations "Law" and "Grace". . . . The contrast between the present New Testament age of the Spirit and the previous Old Testament age of law did involve a shift toward a more "private" view of Christianity.[4]

It is clear from this historical observation, as well as from the need House and Ice felt to write a book-long criticism, that dispensationalism and Reconstructionism generate quite different conceptions of Christian ethics and the believer's involvement in the world. Let's set the two positions in contrast to each other by asking Schaeffer's question of each of them: how should we then live?

Dispensational Tendencies

Two fundamental, conflicting mindsets toward the questions of ethics are found in moral *absolutism* and moral *relativism*. Reconstructionists are moral absolutists who believe, along with the Christian Church in all ages, that the revelation of God's will for human life is not conditioned by situational qualifications or cultural limitations. If premarital sexual relations (or any other behavior) is deemed immoral by God, it is just as wrong in the twentieth century as in the first — just as wrong on the Samoan Islands as on the American mainland. Moral standards, according to the absolutist, are not fluctuating. To put it briefly, God's moral will, as revealed in His commandments, is not arbitrary but universally applicable — obligatory for all times and for all cultures.

Dispensationalists like House and Ice *want* to be moral absolutists, but their underlying theology poses a problem for them. The dispensational premise that God's moral will changes from one dispensation to another makes it a struggle to be an absolutist;

---

4. *Ibid.*, p. 88.

there is a natural, logical pull toward relativism which can be resisted only by an effort of will. Dispensationalism itself as a theology (or worldview) does not have the internal resources to avoid a situationally variable interpretation of God's moral commandments since God Himself (on this theory) changes the rules. What was immoral before Christ is not *as such* immoral after Christ; what was immoral in Israel is not *as such* immoral among the Gentiles.

Dispensationalist Charles Ryrie categorically dismisses the validity of Old Testament commands for non-Jews. Why? He writes: "The law was never given to Gentiles and is expressly done away for the Christian. . . . Neither are the words of Malachi 3 for the Christian" since the passage is addressed to the sons of Jacob.[5]

Dispensationalism becomes, ironically, a Christianized version of cultural relativism,[6] particularly in its view of fluctuating ethical standards throughout history:

> The Scriptures divide time . . . into seven unequal periods, usually called "Dispensations". . . . These periods are marked off in Scripture by some change in God's method of dealing with mankind, in respect of the two questions: of sin, and of man's responsibility.[7]

> A dispensation is a period of time during which man is tested in respect of obedience to some specific revelation of the will of God.[8]

---

5. Charles Caldwell Ryrie, *Balancing the Christian Life* (Chicago, IL: Moody Press, 1969), p. 88.

6. That is, the validity of moral standards is relative to the culture in which they are promulgated: "the very definition of what is normal or abnormal is relative to the cultural frame of reference" (M. J. Herskovits, *Cultural Relativism* [New York: Random House, 1973], p. 15). Dispensationalists would not agree, of course, that cultural acceptance (human agreement) constitutes the sole authority for the changing moral codes in different dispensations.

7. C. I. Scofield, *Rightly Dividing the Word of Truth* (Neptune, NJ: Loizeaux Brothers, 1896), p. 12 (emphasis mine).

8. *The Scofield Reference Bible*, ed. C. I. Scofield (New York: Oxford University Press, 1909), p. 5 (at Gen. 1:28).

Charles Ryrie draws the necessary conclusion that a "distinguishing characteristic" of each *different* dispensation is "a resultant change in man's responsibility."[9] This relativism is bluntly stated elsewhere: "What is law? The answer to that depends on what period of human history you are thinking about."[10]

How should we then live today? The answer necessitated by the dispensational theory is: "Not by the Old Testament law!"

> In this age the Christian is appointed to live by a new life-principle (cf. Rom. 6:4). The realization of the Spirit's presence, power, and guidance constitutes a wholly new method of daily living and is in contrast to that dominance and authority which the Mosaic Law exercised over Israel in the age that is past.[11]

> The Christian is not under the conditional Mosaic Covenant of works, the law, but under the unconditional New Covenant of grace. . . .[12]

Ryrie writes that law and grace are "opposites" when it comes to the "rule of life" under which people should live; the specific commands or moral code "were different under law from what they are under grace."[13] Elsewhere he refines this overstatement to allow for *some* overlap between Old and New Testament rules for life, while nevertheless rejecting the moral authority of the Old Testament. Ryrie insists that New Testament believers are bound to the law of Christ, and not to the commandments of the Old Testament *unless* they are *repeated* in the New Testament. The law of Moses is no longer binding, and we should presume discontinuity with it today.[14] "Dispensationalists," according to Lightner, "believe the Law of Moses in its entirety has been done away as a

---

9. Charles Ryrie, *Dispensationalism Today* (Chicago, IL: Moody Press, 1965), p. 37.

10. Ryrie, *Balancing the Christian Life*, p. 30.

11. Lewis Sperry Chafer, *Systematic Theology*, 6 vols. (Dallas, TX: Dallas Seminary Press, 1948), vol. 6, pp. 122-23.

12. *The Scofield Reference Bible*, p. 95 (at Exodus 19:5).

13. Ryrie, *Balancing the Christian Life*, pp. 151-52.

14. Charles Ryrie, "The End of the Law," *Bibliotheca Sacra* (1967), pp. 239-42.

rule of life." And why do they believe this radical premise? "The fact that God gave the Law to the people of Israel and not to the Church is the beginning point for dispensationalism's difference with theonomy. All other points of disagreement stem from this one."[15]

Accordingly, when it comes to ethics, dispensationalists are prevented by the nature of their theory from being "whole-Bible Christians." That portion of the Bible which they find "profitable for instruction in righteousness" is the New Testament only, excluding the Old Testament law. This mindset puts dispensationalism at odds with the Apostle Paul who spoke of "all scripture"—referring specifically to what we call the Old Testament—as profitable for instruction in righteousness and morally authoritative (2 Tim. 3:16-17). Antagonism to the Old Testament law ("antinomianism") also pits dispensationalism against the perspective of our Lord, who said that anyone who teaches the breaking of even the least commandment from the Law and the Prophets (i.e., the Old Testament) will be assigned the position of least in the kingdom of God (Matt. 5:17-19). Where Scripture stresses moral continuity with the Old Testament, dispensationalism stresses discontinuity.

Legalistic Antinomianism

What we have seen is that the dispensational answer to the question of how we should then live leans heavily toward (1) cultural *relativism* and toward (2) *antinomianism*. That is, dispensationalism is against the continuing authority of the Old Testament law, restricting it to the culture of Old Testament Israel. On the other hand, dispensational ethics also gravitates toward a form of (3) *legalism*—that variety of legalism which replaces God's commands with social traditions, human opinions, and subjective feelings (or manipulation). For instance, Charles Ryrie repudiates the requirement of tithing because it belongs to the Old Testament, and then replaces that standard with "giving in obedience to the still, small voice of the Spirit of God" which "on the basis of

---

15. Robert P. Lightner, "A Dispensational Response to Theonomy," *Bibliotheca Sacra* 143 (July, 1986), pp. 235-36.

the principles of the New Testament might mean *any* percentage," "may mean 8, 12, 20, 50 percent — any percent, depending on the individual case."[16]

Dispensational Churches and institutions usually preach and require that believers conform to a code of behavior which will outwardly avoid the appearance of *"worldliness,"* for instance a code prohibiting smoking, drinking,[17] and social dancing[18] — while on the other hand, these very same Churches will not enforce the dictates of God's word, such as those regarding interpersonal offenses and excommunication, charitable loans to those in financial need, keeping covenant with God in the education of our children (not in state-controlled schools), the observance of the Lord's Day, etc. For instance, some dispensationalists have no problem encouraging or allowing one to engage in his normal labors on the Lord's Day (which God forbids), but then forbidding the drinking of alcoholic beverage (which God allows).[19] Jesus excoriated this kind of legalism which observes human traditions, while making void the word of God (Matt. 15:3, 6, 9); Paul called adding human restrictions to God's all-sufficient word "will-worship" and the "doctrine of demons" (Col. 2:20-23; 1 Tim. 4:1-5).

Retreat from Culture Itself as "Worldly"

Let us return to our question: How should we then live, in light of dispensational theory? In the preface to *Dominion Theology,* Ice takes "the question" separating Reconstructionists and dispen-

---

16. Ryrie, *Balancing the Christian Life*, pp. 86-90 (emphasis mine). So adverse is Ryrie to the Old Testament that he writes: "If someone felt after prayer that the right proportion for him should be 10 percent, I would suggest that he give 9 or 11 percent just to keep out of the 10 percent rut."

17. Cf. Ryrie's high commendation of the policy that a believer should never invest in tobacco or liquor stocks: *Balancing the Christian Life*, p. 155.

18. Movies used to be on the list of prohibited activities earlier in this century, but pressures in our culture have forced an alteration in the prohibition here — showing signs of relativism, again.

19. Cf. Exodus 20:8-11; Mark 2:28; Hebrews 4:9. Also Psalm 104:15; Deuteronomy 7:13; 11:14; 14:26; Proverbs 3:10; 31:6-7. Cf. Kenneth L. Gentry, Jr., *The Christian and Alcoholic Beverages* (Grand Rapids, MI: Baker Book House, 1986).

sationalists to be this: "How and in what ways are we commissioned to be involved in this world?"[20] The answer to this question leads us to see another aspect or tendency in the lifestyle fostered by dispensationalism (in addition to the three we have seen above) — namely, (4) withdrawal from social involvement and from reform of education, economics, and politics. This attitude is sometimes termed "*pietism.*"[21] A Dave Hunt, for instance, castigates evangelicals "during the Reagan years" because they subordinated belief in an imminent (any-moment) rapture of believers to heaven. The deplorable result, he feels, is that "the Church succumbed once again to the unbiblical hope that, by exerting godly influence upon government, society could be transformed." He condemns "the false dream of Christianizing secular society," and holds that it may be as important as the Reformation itself for dispensationalists to divide from and oppose those "who believe it is our duty to Christianize society."[22]

Dispensationalism leans toward pietism for a couple of obvious reasons. The Old Testament revelation of God's moral will took into account numerous details of socio-political behavior, while the New Testament does not repeat the same emphasis. There is much more to be found in the Old Testament about the larger concerns of civil society than in the New. Reconstructionists find the explanation for this in the fact that God's Old Testament revelation was an expression of His perfect will, and once God has spoken to a subject, He does not need to repeat Himself. The New Testament focuses (though not exclusively) upon the

---

20. House and Ice, *Dominion Theology*, p. 9.

21. Herbert Schlossberg and Marvin Olasky write: "We need to understand the crucial difference between a vital component of authentic Christianity, piety, and a false ideology that we call pietism." They define 'piety' as "a reverence for God, as evidenced in prayer, Scripture reading, and doing mercy to others," while 'pietism' is taken as "a belief that the practice of piety is all the Christian has to do, and that it is alright to ignore larger concerns of the society." See *Turning Point: A Christian Worldview Declaration* (Westchester, IL: Crossway Books, 1987), pp. 25, 152; Chapter 2 is entitled "Piety vs. Pietism."

22. Dave Hunt, *Whatever Happened to Heaven?* (Eugene, OR: Harvest House, 1988), pp. 8-9.

personal redemptive transformation which needs to take place in each one of us before the larger worldview concerns found in the Old Testament model can ever be realized. [23]

Dispensationalists, by contrast, do not presuppose continuity between the moral standards of the Old and New Testaments, but rather restrict moral authority to what is said in the New Testament. Since the New Testament does not communicate extensive details about socio-political justice or explicitly call for Christian involvement in social reform, dispensationalists tend to have very little — or very little distinctively Christian — to offer in terms of dealing with socio-political problems. [24]

The second reason dispensationalists have eschewed social involvement and reform is that according to their eschatology, such efforts will ultimately be futile.

> The premillennial concept of the present age makes the interadvent period unique and unpredicted in the Old Testament.

---

23. Lest critics misconstrue my (Bahnsen's) words and paint me as one who hereby diminishes, undervalues, or obscures the surpassing importance of personal salvation, please notice that I am not for a moment suggesting that New Testament attention to the accomplishment and application of redemption for God's people (with a view to the individual's standing before God and eternal destiny) is "merely" an instrument to getting onto "what is really important," viz. social transformation. "God forbid that I should glory save in the cross of our Lord Jesus Christ, by whom the world is crucified unto me and I unto the world" (Gal. 6:14).

24. This observation reminds us that it is ethics, and not simply eschatology, that leads to divergent attitudes toward social involvement. Theonomic ethics points to moral obligations in the socio-political sphere which any Christian, regardless of eschatological convictions, should want and seek to obey. Ice and House do not seem to recognize this. Broaching the question "whether believers should be involved in this world," they simplistically speak of "the postmillennial root" of "the Reconstructionist agenda" (House and Ice, *Dominion Theology*, pp. 358-59). The ethical root independently produces the same agenda. Furthermore, many believers of Reformed persuasion believe that Christ calls us to the transformation of every area of life, including society and politics, and yet are not postmillennial in eschatology. One can in his theological reasoning very well be committed to the reconstructionist ethical vision and standards for Christian social reform without adopting postmillennialism — contrary to a statement made by Ice on page 9, but then contradicted on pages 354-55. (It is true that, as an encompassing *label* commonly used of *persons* — rather than a social *agenda* — "Reconstructionist" is a word denoting someone who is both a theonomist committed to social transformation *and* a postmillennialist.)

The present age is one in which the gospel is preached to all the world. Relatively few are saved. The world becomes, in fact, increasingly wicked as the age progresses. The premillennial view . . . presents no commands to improve society as a whole. The apostles are notably silent on any program of political, social, moral, or physical improvement of the unsaved world. Paul made no effort to correct social abuses or to influence the political government for good. The program of the early Church was one of evangelism and Bible teaching. It was a matter of saving souls out of the world rather than saving the world.[25]

"We will never be able to redeem society," say House and Ice.[26]

Dispensationalist Eschatology

Dispensationalism holds that world conditions must worsen continually until believers, far from being agents of social transformation, will be raptured away from the world in preparation for Christ's return. This has practical implications for how we should live now:

If Christ will come for His Church before the predicted time of trouble, Christians can regard His coming as an imminent daily expectation. From a practical standpoint, the doctrine has tremendous implications.[27]

[For instance:] Because of the relationship of the Church to governments in this age [viz., called to be in subjection; cf. Rom. 13:1-7] and because of the Satanic control of government in the seventieth week [the tribulation period; cf. Rev. 13:4], the Church must be delivered before this Satanic government manifests itself. The Church could not subject herself to such a government. Israel during the seventieth week will rightly call down the judgment of God upon such godless men, and cry for God to vindicate Himself, as is seen in the imprecatory Psalms. *Such is not the ministry nor the relationship of the Church to governments in this age.*[28]

25. John F. Walvoord, *The Millennial Kingdom* (Grand Rapids, MI: Zondervan, 1959), p. 134.
26. House and Ice, *Dominion Theology*, p. 343.
27. John F. Walvoord, *The Rapture Question* (rev. ed.; Grand Rapids, MI: Zondervan, 1979), p. 15.
28. J. Dwight Pentecost, in his discussion of the pretribulation rapture, in *Things to Come: A Study in Biblical Eschatology* (Grand Rapids, MI: Zondervan, [1958] 1964), p. 210 (emphasis mine).

Only after the rapture, tribulation, and return of Christ will the affairs of this world be straightened out — by military might (the battle of Armaggedon), *not* evangelism and education, as Reconstructionists think. In discussing the "righteous government of the millennium," Walvoord writes:

> The second important characteristic of the millennial rule of Christ is that His government will be absolute in its authority and power. This is demonstrated in His destruction of all who oppose Him. . . . No open sin will go unpunished. . . . Those who merely profess to follow the King without actually being saints . . . are forced to obey the King or be subject to the penalty of death or other chastisement.

Reconstructionists believe in the present power of Jesus Christ and His empowering through the Holy Spirit — a situation which the Bible teaches to be more advantageous than His physical presence (e.g., John 14:12-18; 15:7-10; 16:7-11). They believe that the resurrected Lord is present with His Church for the accomplishment of the Great Commission (Matt. 28:18-20). They believe in the transforming power of preaching, teaching, persuasion, charity, Christian nurture, and reform. Apparently House and Ice consider such an idea deplorable, inferring that it is improper for Reconstructionists to believe (in common with charismatics, alas) "that Christ's power can be drawn upon to vanquish worldly adversaries," including "social and political evils."[29]

Dispensationalists have a different vision, one which requires the military presence of Christ for conditions in the world to change: "As premillennialists, we much prefer to have the Lord Jesus Christ himself ruling over the nations directly. . . ."[30] "History needs the cataclysmic intervention of Christ for societal salvation."[31] House and Ice see in this a fundamental antithesis between the Reconstructionist and dispensationalist views of the Christian life and ethic:

---

29. House and Ice, *Dominion Theology*, p. 24.
30. *Ibid.*, p. 80.
31. *Ibid.*, p. 337.

A premillennialist believes that Christ's intervening judgment will destroy current society and then Christ will institute millennial conditions. Once I realized the antithesis of the two positions, I had to . . . leave behind Reconstructionism. These conflicting views impact the way believers are involved in this present society.[32]

If the Bible teaches premillennialism, then we should be involved in this present world in a different way than someone who is postmillennial.[33]

According to House and Ice, this current world is under "impending judgment"; after it comes,

Christ will take over control of the world and rule it. But until that happens, the message and activities for believers should be, 'Flee the wrath to come by finding safety in Jesus Christ' "—not [to] try to rebuild society . . . not . . . attempting to change society.[34]

House and Ice declare that "our calling is not to Christianize the world, but to evangelize the world"[35]—a revealing comment and false contrast, showing the narrow and incomplete view of evangelism (of the "Great" Commission) which is held by the dispensationalist. Christ called believers to "make disciples of" the nations (Matt. 28:19)—entailing faith in His saving work, but also following Christ as superior to and thus paramount over *all things* (Luke 14:26, 33). No area of life can be withheld from Him. He has "preeminence in all things" (Col. 1:18). All things are put in subjection under His feet for the sake of the Church (Eph. 1:22). Right now He is the "King of kings" (1 Tim. 6:15), not simply in some future millennial era. *So right now the nations are to become such disciples who follow Christ as Lord over all.* Accordingly they must be "taught to observe whatsoever" He has "commanded" (Matt.

---

32. *Ibid.*, p. 9.
33. *Ibid.*, p. 356.
34. *Ibid.*, pp. 356-57 (emphasis mine).
35. *Ibid.*, p. 342; cf. p. 356.

28:20). Evangelism in Biblical perspective does not end with a decision for Jesus (and the new hope of heaven); it extends to full discipleship — full "Christianizing" — of the convert's life, thoughts, attitudes, conduct and influence. Christ sent us to disciple the nations in this way. He taught us to pray: "Thy will be done on earth" (Matt. 6:10).

Nevertheless, Ice claims to "know" that God is not pleased to give to the Church the tools or graces presently necessary "for the kind of victory" envisioned by Reconstructionists.[36] "God has not given the Church a proper dose of grace to Christianize the world."[37] One gets the impression from the New Testament, however, that the "dose" of God's *grace* given with the redemptive work of Christ and the outpouring of the Spirit is not lacking in power! "This is the victory which overcomes the world, even our faith. And who is he that overcomes the world, but he that believes that Jesus is the Son of God?" (1 John 5:4-5). "Unto Him that is able to do exceeding abundantly above all that we ask or think, according to the power that works in us . . ." (Eph. 3:20). "I can do all things through Him who strengthens me" (Phil. 4:13). "Seeing that His divine power has granted unto us all things that pertain unto life and godliness" (2 Peter 1:3). "And the God of peace shall bruise Satan under your feet shortly" (Rom. 16:20). "The gates of hell shall not prevail against it [My Church]" (Matt. 16:18).

Yet according to Ice the study of Scripture will protect us from "the romantic attraction of changing the world." We should, instead, hope "that Christ will soon rapture his Bride, the Church, and that we will return with him in victory to rule and exercise dominion with him for a thousand years upon the earth."[38] Both dispensationalists and Reconstructionists have a vision for transforming society in history, then.

Of course, both theologies confess that the ultimate social state "wherein righteousness dwells" lies beyond history (and even the magnificent, but mixed, state of the millennium) in the consum-

---

36. *Ibid.*, pp. 7, 351.
37. *Ibid.*, p. 340.
38. *Ibid.*, p. 10.

mated "new heavens and earth" (2 Peter 2:13; cf. Rev. 21:1-22:5). Reconstructionists are committed to the present, Spiritual power of the gospel ("the sword of the Spirit"), while dispensationalists look to Christ's *future*, physical intervention with a sword of steel.[39]

Dispensationalist Pietism

Since dispensationalists do not seek Biblical answers to a number of pressing social concerns (and do not have such answers as might be afforded in the Old Testament), and since they do not have Biblical confidence that efforts at social transformation will be blessed by God (prior to the intervention of Christ in military might), they very naturally tend toward a pietistic understanding of the Christian life in this age which retreats from the outward affairs of the world and awaits the rapture. House and Ice want to "expose evil with the light"[40] — but insist that Christians should not offer to the world any *alternative* to its evil direction, like walking by the light of God's word where its course was once evil.[41]

Expose evil, says the dispensationalist, but don't redirect the behavior or attitudes which the light condemns, at least when they are matters pertaining to this world! The opinion of House and Ice is so bleak that they insist that striving to change and transform social institutions so that culture or civilization takes a more Christian direction "will only lead the Church astray," "will only result in the leaven of humanism permeating orthodox Christian-

---

39. Ironically, one of the criticisms of Reconstructionism which is frequently heard from dispensationalists is that theonomy is harsh, calling for use of the Mosaic penal sanctions. But theonomists expect social reform and civil statutes to be adopted through persuasion, using preaching and deeds of love and mercy, not physical force or coercion. Dispensationalism on the other hand openly endorses the notion — and rejoices in the prospect — that physical, despotic and destructive force will be used in the millennium to compel society to change and to get people to comply with Jesus. Which of these views is the more severe and tyrannical, really?

40. House and Ice, *Dominion Theology*, pp. 342, 344.

41. While dispensationalists want to expose evil by the light, Ice and House — through the faux pas of mixing metaphors — say that Reconstructionists by contrast wish "to take over the darkness" (*ibid.*, p. 344)! (The not-so-subtle presupposition here is that social institutions are by definition in moral darkness.) The truth is that light does not "expose" darkness, but "dispels" it, as incompatible with it (John 1:5; cf. Matt. 4:16; John 8:12; Eph. 5:8; 1 Peter 2:9; 1 John 1:5).

ity."[42] So cultural impotence becomes a mark of "separation" from the "world system" and of orthodoxy.

Summary

Dispensationalism is a view of God's work in history which (commendably) wants to take account of the redemptive discontinuities between the Old and New Testaments, such as the fact that we do not offer animal sacrifices today. Dispensationalists are motivated by a driving desire, as we all should be, to guard the principle of salvation by grace, which believers enjoy today, from the terrible error of seeking salvation through works of the law, as taught by the Jews both before and after the advent of Jesus Christ. However, the way in which dispensationalism attempts to accomplish these ends unnecessarily divides the Bible into different regimes of ethics and incorrectly separates Israel from the Church as the covenant people of God.

We have found that:

1. The dispensational answer to how we should then live comes to be characterized by cultural relativism, which jeopardizes moral absolutes.

2. The dispensational answer to how we should then live comes to be characterized by antinomianism, which jeopardizes the Scripture's unity.

3. The dispensational answer to how we should then live comes to be characterized by legalism, which detracts from the Scripture's sufficiency.

4. The dispensational answer to how we should then live comes to be characterized by pietism, which detracts from the Christian calling to social transformation.

---

42. *Ibid.*, pp. 335, 340.

3

THE RECONSTRUCTIONIST OPTION

Continuation of the comparison with dispensationalism.

When readers turn to *Dominion Theology* for a summary of the Reconstructionist view of ethics (theonomy), they do not get a balanced, refined or adequate explanation of the position. Perhaps this is not surprising. But without a better picture of what theonomic ethics actually maintains (and why it maintains it), the reader cannot fairly evaluate the position for himself or herself.[1] It would be more satisfactory to rehearse the Reconstructionist outlook in the following way,[2] beginning with the question of whether it is legitimate from a biblical standpoint to make contemporary use of the Old Testament revelation of God's law for human conduct.

On the one hand, to deny that dictates revealed in the Old Testament are unchanging moral absolutes is implicitly to en-

---

1. House and Ice gratuitously assert at one point that "Bahnsen has so modified some of his views" that the theonomic position is dying the death of a thousand qualifications (H. Wayne House and Thomas Ice, *Dominion Theology: Blessing or Curse?* [Portland, OR: Multnomah, 1988], p. 20). Absolutely no examples or substantiation is given, and I (Bahnsen) have no idea what they imagine has been modified. As far as I know, my publications and lectures subsequent to the appearance of *Theonomy in Christian Ethics* present nothing of any significance which contradicts the position taken earlier. Moreover, fuller explanation and consistent refinement of a thesis is not usually deemed a fault ("dying"), but a virtue. If I say "There is a cat on the mat," the truth of my thesis is not challenged if I qualify it further by saying, "There is a black cat on the mat."

2. The following synopsis, with slight changes and a few additional notes, is taken from Bahnsen's paper, "The Theonomic Position," found in *God and Politics: Four Views on the Reformation of Civil Government*, ed. Gary Scott Smith (Phillipsburg, NJ: Presbyterian and Reformed, 1989). The article goes on to apply what is rehearsed here to socio-political ethics, interacting with the opposing viewpoint of pluralism.

dorse the position of *cultural relativism* in ethics ("they were morally valid for that time and place, but invalid for other people and other times")—which is diametrically contrary to the testimony of Scripture (Mal. 3:6; Psalm 89:34; 111:7; 119:160; Eccl. 12:13; Rom. 2:11). *But* on the other hand, to affirm that the principles of ethics found in the Old Testament law are binding in our day and age might suggest to some people that no differences between Old and New Covenants (two different "dispensations" or administrations of the covenant of grace), or between an ancient agrarian society and the modern computer age, have been recognized. After all, in the Old Testament we read instructions for holy war, for kosher diet, for temple and priesthood, for cities of refuge at particular places in Palestine, for goring oxen and burning grain fields. Obviously there are *some kinds* of discontinuity between these provisions and our own day. We should stop to analyze them.

Some of these discontinuities are *redemptive-historical* in character (pertaining to the coming of the New Covenant and the finished work of Christ), while others are *cultural* in character (pertaining to simple changes of time, place or lifestyle). The latter are unrelated to the former. There are cultural differences, not only between our society and the *Old* Testament, but *also* between modern America and the *New* Testament (e.g., its mention of whited sepulchers, social kisses, and meats offered to idols)[3]— indeed, there are cultural differences even *within* the Old Testament (e.g., life in the wilderness, in the land, in captivity) and *within* the New Testament (e.g., Jewish culture, Gentile culture) themselves. Such cultural differences pose important *hermeneutical* questions—sometimes very vexing ones since the "culture gap"

---

3. Authors House and Ice seem to have completely overlooked this fact when they took it into hand to criticize the theonomic position for creating the difficulty of bringing the Old Testament into the twentieth century. They *object* that this cultural updating is a hard thing to do: "This raises questions of subjectivity and the danger of, in effect, adding to God's Word" (*Dominion Theology*, p. 39). From this standpoint it is just as difficult to apply the ancient culture of the New Testament to the twentieth century! If the objection by House and Ice against theonomy is to be taken seriously, then, we should really reject the use of the entire Bible today.

between biblical times and our own is so wide;[4] however, these differences are not especially relevant to the question of *ethical validity*.

That is, it is one thing to realize that we must translate biblical commands about a lost ox (Exodus 23:4) or withholding pay from someone who mows fields (James 5:4) into terms relevant to our present culture (e.g., about misplaced credit cards or remuneration of factory workers). It is quite another thing altogether to say that such commands carry no ethical authority today! God obviously communicated to His people in terms of their own day and cultural setting, but what He said to them He fully expects us to obey in our own cultural setting, lest the complete authority of His word be shortchanged in our lives.

Moreover, it should be obvious that in teaching us our moral duties, God as a masterful Teacher often instructs us, not only in general precepts (e.g., "Do not kill," Exodus 20:13; "love one another," 1 John 3:11), but also in terms of *specific illustrations* (e.g., rooftop railings, Deut. 22:8; sharing worldly goods with a needy brother, 1 John 3:17) — expecting us to learn the broader, underlying principle from them. Again, those biblical illustrations are taken from the culture of that day. After the New Testament story of the good Samaritan, Jesus said "Go and do likewise" (Luke 10:37). It does not take a lot of hermeneutical common sense to know that our concrete duty is not thereby to go travel the literal Jericho road (rather than an American interstate highway) on a literal donkey (rather than in a Ford) with literal denarii in our pockets (rather than dollars), pouring wine and oil (rather than modern antiseptic salves) on the wounds of those who have been mugged. Indeed, one can be a modern "good Samaritan" in a circumstance that has nothing to do with travel and muggers whatsoever. Unfortunately though, this same hermeneutical common sense is sometimes not

---

4. A critic like Rodney Clapp "Democracy as Heresy," *Christianity Today* (Feb. 20, 1987) is seriously misled to think that this question of culture gap is any more uncomfortable for — or critical of — theonomists than it is for any other school of thought committed to using the ancient literature of the Bible (whether Old or New Testament) in modern society. The alternative — which any believer should find repugnant — is simply to dismiss the Bible as anachronistic.

applied to the cultural illustrations communicated in Old Testament moral instruction.[5] For instance, the requirement of a rooftop railing (Deut. 22:8), relevant to entertaining on flat roofs in Palestine, teaches the underlying principle of safety precautions (e.g., fences around modern backyard swimming pools) — not the obligation of placing a literal battlement upon today's sloped roofs.[6]

Dispensational Differences

There are, then, *cultural* discontinuities between biblical moral instruction and our modern society. This fact does not imply that the ethical teaching of Scripture is invalidated for us; it simply calls for hermeneutical sensitivity. In asking whether it is theologically legitimate to make contemporary use of biblical (especially Old Testament) precepts — even those pertaining to civil law — then, our concern is more properly with *redemptive-historical* discontinuities, notably between Old and New Covenants. Clearly, the Scriptures teach us that a new day arrived with the establishment of Christ's kingdom, the New Covenant (Luke 22:20; Jer. 31:31-34; Heb. 8:7-13; 10:14-18), and the age of the Spirit (Acts 2:16-36; Luke 3:16-17) — a day anticipated by all the Old Covenant scriptures (Luke 24:26-27; Acts 3:24; 1 Peter 1:10-11).

---

5. Just here Christopher J. H. Wright has misconceived and thus badly misrepresented the "theonomic" approach as calling for a "literal imitation of Israel" which simply lifts its ancient laws and transplants them into the vastly changed modern world ("The Use of the Bible in Social Ethics: Paradigms, Types and Eschatology," *Transformation* [January/March, 1984], p. 17). The same kind of simplistic misrepresentation of theonomic ethics is found in Meredith Kline's "Comments on an Old-New Error," *Westminster Theological Journal* (Fall, 1978).

6. "But this is an easy example," complain House and Ice (House and Ice, *Dominion Theology*, p. 39). You see, on the same page, they are trying to criticize theonomic ethics for leaving it a "vague area" in determining "how literally case laws should be brought into our New Covenant era." They complain because having such "easy" examples available (and there are many more) makes it hard for House and Ice to prosecute their complaint or win the argument. Nobody denies, of course, that some case laws are more difficult than others to understand and apply. But the same thing could be said about all of Scripture (even the New Testament) — indeed, Peter said it (2 Peter 3:16)!

What differences with the Old Covenant era have been introduced? Only the King, the Lord of the Covenant, who speaks by means of the Holy Spirit is in a position to answer that question with authority, and thus we look, not to sinful speculation or cultural tradition, but to the inspired word of Christ to guide our thoughts regarding it. There we are taught that the New Covenant surpasses the Old Covenant in (1) power, (2) glory, (3) finality, and (4) realization. Such discontinuities must not be overlooked, and yet, in the nature of the case, they presuppose an underlying unity in God's covenantal dealings. The historical changes in outward administration and circumstance grow out of a common and unchanging divine intention.

The Old Covenant law as written on external tablets of stone accused man of sin, but could not grant the internal ability to comply with those demands. By contrast, the New Covenant written by the Holy Spirit on the internal tables of the human heart communicates life and righteousness, giving the *power* to obey God's commandments (Jer. 31:33; Eze. 11:19-20; 2 Cor. 3:3, 6-9; Rom. 7:12-16; 8:4; Heb. 10:14-18; 13:20-21). Although the Old Covenant had its glory, the sin-laden Jews requested Moses to veil his face when revealing its stipulations, for it was fundamentally a ministration of condemnation. But the New Covenant redemptively brings life and confidence before God (2 Cor. 3:7-4:6; Rom. 8:3; Heb. 4:15-16; 6:18-20; 7:19; 9:8; 10:19-20), thus exceeding in unfading *glory* (2 Cor. 3:9, 18; 4:4-6; Heb. 3:3). Moreover, unlike God's word to Old Covenant believers, special revelation will not be augmented further for New Covenant Christians; it has reached its *finalized* form until the return of Christ. This New Testament word brings greater moral clarity (removing Pharisaical distortions of the law, Matt. 5:21-48; 23:3-28, and unmistakably demonstrating the meaning of love, John 13:34-35; 15:12-13) and greater personal responsibility for obedience (Luke 12:48; Heb. 2:1-4; 12:25).

Finally, the New Covenant surpasses the Old in *realization*. To understand this, we must take account of the fact that the laws of the Old Covenant served two different purposes. Some laws defined the righteousness of God to be emulated by men (thus being moral in function), while other laws defined the way of salvation for the unrighteous (thus being redemptive in function).

To illustrate, the law forbidding us to steal shows what righteousness demands, whereas the law stipulating animal sacrifice shows what must be done by a thief to gain redemption. This distinction between justice-defining and redemption-expounding laws was proverbially expressed by the Jews: "To do righteousness and justice is more acceptable to Jehovah than sacrifice" (Prov. 21:3). It was evident in the prophetic declaration from God, "I desire goodness, and not sacrifice: and the knowledge of God more than burnt-offerings" (Hos. 6:6; cf. Matt. 9:13; 12:7). Accordingly, the New Testament teaches that there are some portions of the Old Testament law which were "shadows" of the coming Messiah and His redemptive work (Heb. 9:9; 10:1; Col. 2:17). They were deemed weak and beggarly rudiments which served as a tutor unto Christ and taught justification by faith (Gal. 3:23-4:10). Paul called them "the law of commandments contained in ordinances" which imposed a separation of the Jews from the Gentile world (Eph. 2:14-15).

These descriptions do not accurately apply to moral laws of the Old Testament which, for instance, forbid adultery or oppressing the poor. Such laws do not foreshadow the redemptive work of Christ, show us justification by faith, or symbolically set apart the Jews from the Gentiles. Laws pertaining to the priesthood, temple, and sacrificial system, etc., do accomplish those ends, however, and are to be considered "put out of gear" by the coming of that reality which they foreshadowed. This is the logic pursued by the author of Hebrews, especially in chapters 7-10. For instance, the coming of Christ has brought a change of law regarding the priesthood (Heb. 7:12), and the administrative order of the Old Covenant is vanishing away (8:13). By realizing the salvation foreshadowed in the Old Covenant, the New Covenant supercedes the details of the Old Covenant redemptive dispensation. We no longer come to God through animal sacrifices, but now through the shed blood of the Savior—in both cases, type and reality, acknowledging that "apart from the shedding of blood there is no remission" from the guilt of sin (Heb. 9:22).

The New Covenant People of God

In connection with the superceding of the Old Covenant shadows, the redemption secured by the New Covenant also *redefines* the people of God. The kingdom which was once focused on the nation of Israel has been taken away from the Jews (Matt. 8:11-12; 21:41-43; 23:37-38) and given to an international body, the Church of Jesus Christ. New Testament theology describes the Church as the "restoration of Israel" (Acts 15:15-20), "the commonwealth of Israel" (Eph. 2:12), the "seed of Abraham" (Gal. 3:7, 29), and "the Israel of God" (6:16). What God was doing with the nation of Israel was but a type looking ahead to the international Church of Christ. The details of the old order have passed away, giving place to the true kingdom of God established by the Messiah, in which both Jew and Gentile have become "fellow-citizens" on an equal footing (Eph. 2:11-20; 3:3-6).

It is important for biblical interpretation to bear this in mind because certain stipulations of the Old Covenant were enacted for the purpose of distinguishing Israel as the people of God from the pagan Gentile world. Such stipulations were not essentially moral in function (forbidding what was intrinsically contrary to the righteousness of God), but rather symbolic. This accounts for the fact that they allowed Gentiles to do the very thing which was forbidden to the Jews (e.g., Deut. 14:21). Accordingly, given the redefinition of the people of God in the New Covenant, certain aspects of the Old Covenant order have been altered: (a) the New Covenant does not require political loyalty to Israel (Phil. 3:20) or defending God's kingdom by the sword (John 18:36; 2 Cor. 10:4). (b) The land of Canaan foreshadowed the kingdom of God (Heb. 11:8-10; Eph. 1:14; 1 Peter 1:4) which is fulfilled in Christ (Gal. 3:16; cf. Gen. 13:15), thus rendering inapplicable Old Covenant provisions tied to the land (such as family divisions, location of cities of refuge, the levirate). (c) The laws which symbolically taught Israel to be separate from the Gentile world, such as the dietary provisions (Lev. 20:22-26), need no longer be observed in their pedagogical form (Acts 10, esp. v. 15; Mark 7:19; Rom. 14:17), even

though the Christian does honor their symbolized principle of separation from ungodliness (2 Cor. 6:14-18; Jude 23).

Therefore, the redemptive dispensation and form of the kingdom which was present in the Old Covenant has dramatically
changed in the age of the New Covenant. The New Covenant
surpasses the Old in power, glory, finality and realization. In
short, the New Covenant is a "better covenant enacted upon better promises" (Heb. 8:6). Even those aspects of the Old Covenant
law which typified the kingdom of God and the way of redemption
(e.g., priesthood, sacrifice, temple, promised land, symbols of
separation and purity) were speaking to the *promises* of God, preparing for and foreshadowing the salvation and kingdom to be
brought by the Messiah. Thus the discontinuities between Old
and New Covenants which we have been discussing actually point
to a more elementary, underlying *continuity* between them. At bottom, the two covenants are one, although they differed in administrative outworking according to their respective places in the history of redemption. All the distinctively Jewish covenants of the
Old Testament are "the [plural] covenants of the [singular] promise" (Eph. 2:12). However many were the Old Covenant promises
of God, they are all affirmed and confirmed in Jesus Christ (2 Cor.
1:20). Thus it was preposterous, Paul said, to set the Mosaic covenant of law against the Abrahamic covenant of promise (Gal.
3:15-22). So then, we find in the Scripture a substantial, covenantal continuity of promise which underlies the important
administrative or formal discontinuities between Old Covenant
anticipation (shadows, prophecies) and New Covenant realization (fulfillment).

Perfection and Continuity of Moral Demand

Regarding the promises pertaining to redemption, then, we
may rightly speak of the "better promises" of the New Covenant.
They *differed* from the Old Covenant provision by being the fulfillment of that to which it looked ahead, giving both covenants the
same intention and objective. The differing covenantal administrations of God's *promise* are due precisely to the historical charac-

ter of His redemptive plan. However, regarding God's *law*, one nowhere reads in Scripture that God's moral stipulations share the same historical variation or anything like it. The Bible never speaks of the New Covenant instituting "better commandments" than those of the Old Covenant. Far from it.

Instead, Paul declared that "the [Old Testament] law is holy, and the commandment is holy, and righteous, and good" (Rom. 7:12). He took the validity of the law's moral demands as a theological truth which should be obvious and presupposed by all, stating without equivocation: "We know that the law is good" (1 Tim. 1:8). That should be axiomatic for Christian ethics according to the Apostle. Contrary to those today who are prone to criticize the Old Testament moral precepts, there must be no question whatsoever about the moral propriety and validity of what they revealed. It should be our starting point — the standard by which we judge all other opinions — that the law's moral provisions are correct. "I esteem *all* Thy precepts concerning *all things* to be right" (Psalm 119:128).

Accordingly, James reminds us that we have no prerogative to become "judges of the law," but are rather called to be doers of the law (4:11). And when Paul posed the hypothetical question of whether the law is sin, his immediate outburst was "May it never be!" (Rom. 7:7). God's holy and good law is never wrong in what it demands. It is "perfect" (Deut. 32:4; Psalm 19:7; Jas. 1:25), just like the Lawgiver Himself (Matt. 5:48). It is a transcript of His moral character. It so perfectly reflects God's own holiness (Rom. 7:12; 1 Peter 1:14-16) that the Apostle John categorically dismissed anyone as a *liar* who claimed to "know God" and yet did *not* keep His commandments (1 John 2:3-4). God's law is a very personal matter — so much so that Jesus said "If you *love* Me, you will keep My commandments" (John 14:15; cf. vv. 21, 23; 15:10, 14). It is characteristic of the true believer to have the law written upon his heart and delight inwardly in it (Jer. 31:33; Rom. 7:22; Psalm 1:1-2) — just because he so intimately loves God, his Redeemer.

The Universality of the Law

Paul teaches elsewhere that *all men* — even pagans who do not love God and do not have the advantage of the written oracles of

God (cf. Rom. 3:1-2) — nevertheless know the just requirements of God's law. They know what God, the Creator, requires of them. They know it from the created order (1:18-21) and from inward conscience, the "work of the law" being written upon their hearts (2:14-15). Paul characterizes them as "knowing the ordinance of God" (1:32) and, thus, being "without excuse" for refusing to live in a God-glorifying fashion (1:20-23). This discussion indicates that the stipulations of God's moral law — whether known through Mosaic (written) ordinances or by general (unwritten) revelation — carry a universal and "natural" obligation, appropriate to the Creator-creature relation apart from any question of redemption. Their validity is not by any means restricted to the Jews in a particular time-period. What the law speaks, it speaks "in order that *all the world* may be brought under the judgment of God" (3:19). God is no respecter of persons here. "*All* have sinned" (3:23), which means they have violated that common standard of moral integrity for all men, the law of God (3:20).

A good student of the Old Testament would have known as much. The moral laws of God were never restricted in their validity to the Jewish nation. At the beginning of the book of Deuteronomy, when Moses exhorted the Israelites to observe God's commandments, he clearly taught that the laws divinely revealed to Israel were meant by the Law-giver as a *model* to be emulated by all the surrounding Gentile nations:

> Behold I have taught you statutes and ordinances even as Jehovah my God commanded me, that you should do so in the midst of the land whither ye go in to possess it. Keep therefore and do them; for this is your wisdom and your understanding in the sight of the peoples, that shall hear all these statutes and say, Surely this great nation is a wise and understanding people. . . . What great nation is there that hath statutes and ordinances so righteous as all this law which I set before you this day? (Deut. 4:5-8).

"All the peoples," not just the Israelites, should follow the manifestly righteous requirements of God's law. In this respect, the justice of God's law made Israel to be a light to the Gentiles (Isa. 51:4).

Unlike many modern Christian writers on ethics, God did not have a double standard of morality, one for Israel and one for the Gentiles (cf. Lev. 24:22). Accordingly, God made it clear that the reason why the Palestinian tribes were ejected from the land was precisely because they had violated the provisions of His holy law (Lev. 18:24-27). This fact presupposes that the Gentiles were antecedently obligated to obey those provisions. Accordingly, the Psalmist condemned "all the wicked of the earth" for departing from God's statutes (119:118-119). Accordingly, the book of Proverbs, intended as international wisdom literature, directs all nations to obey the laws of God: "Righteousness exalts a nation, but sin is a disgrace to any people" (14:34). Accordingly, the Old Testament prophets repeatedly excoriated the Gentile nations for their transgressions against God's law (e.g., Amos, Habakkuk, Jonah at Ninevah). Accordingly, Isaiah looked forward to the day when the Gentile nations would stream into Zion, precisely that God's law would go forth from Jerusalem unto all the world (2:2-3).

Two premises about the law of God are thus abundantly clear if we are faithful to the infallible testimony of Scripture: (1) The law of God is *good* in what it demands, being what is natural to the Creator-creature relation. And (2) the demands of God's law are universal in their character and application, not confined in validity to Old Testament Israel. Consequently, it would be extremely unreasonable to expect that the coming of the Messiah and the institution of the New Covenant would alter the moral demands of God as revealed in His law. Why, we must ask, would God feel the need to change His perfect, holy requirements for our conduct and attitudes? Christ came, rather, to atone for our transgressions against those moral requirements (Rom. 4:25; 5:8-9; 8:1-3). And the New Covenant was established precisely to confirm our redeemed hearts in obedience to God's law (Rom. 8:4-10; 2 Cor. 3:6-11). Should we sin because we are under the grace of God? Paul declared "may it never be!" Being made free from sin we must rather now become the "servants of righteousness" (Rom. 6:15-18). The grace of God has appeared and Jesus Christ has given Himself to "redeem us from all lawlessness and purify unto Himself a people . . . zealous of good works" (Titus 2:14; Eph. 2:8-10).

While the New Testament condemns any legalistic (Judaizing) use of God's law to establish one's personal justification or sanctification before God, and while the New Testament rejoices in the fact that the work of Christ has surpassed the legal foreshadows and rituals of the Old Covenant, we never find the New Testament rejecting or criticizing the *moral demands* of the Old Testament law. They are at every point upheld and commended.[7] Thus Paul firmly taught that "every scripture" (of the inspired Old Testament) was "profitable for instruction in righteousness" that we might be equipped perfectly for every good work (2 Tim. 3:16-17). James is equally clear that if someone is guilty of breaking even one commandment of the law, he has broken them all (2:10) — indicating our obligation to every one of them. Jesus rebuked Satan (and many modern ethicists) by declaring that man should live "by every word that proceeds from the mouth of God" (Matt. 4:4). This is the uniform New Testament perspective and presumption regarding the laws of the Old Testament. God certainly has the prerogative to alter His commandments. His word teaches, however, that we should countenance such change in particular cases *only* when God Himself teaches such. We are not arbitrarily to assume that His commandments have been repealed, but only where, when, and how He says so.

Jesus and the Law

The decisive word on this point is that of our Lord Himself as found in Matthew 5:17-19. Since the moral demands of God's law continue to be deemed good and holy and right in the New Testament, and since those demands were from the beginning obligatory upon Jews and Gentiles alike, it would be senseless to think that Christ came in order to cancel mankind's responsibility to keep them. It is theologically incredible that the mission of Christ was to make it morally acceptable now for men to blaspheme, murder,

---

7. The antitheses of Matthew 5:21-48 are not an unfair *ex post facto* condemnation of the Pharisees by a higher standard than that which they already knew. They prove to be a series of contrasts between Jesus' interpretation of the law's full demand and the restrictive, external, distorted interpretations of the law by the Jewish elders (cf. 5:20; 7:28-29; e.g., 5:43, which does not even appear in the Old Testament).

rape, steal, gossip, or envy! Christ did not come to change our evaluation of God's laws from that of holy to unholy, obligatory to optional, or perfect to flawed. Listen to His own testimony:

> Do not begin to think that I came to abrogate the Law or the Prophets; I came not to abrogate but to fulfill. For truly I say to you, until heaven and earth pass away, until all things have happened, not one jot or tittle shall by any means pass away from the law. Therefore, whoever shall break one of these least commandments and teach men so shall be called the least in the kingdom of heaven (Matthew 5:17-19).

Several points about the interpretation of this passage should be rather clear. (1) Christ twice denied that His advent had the purpose of abrogating the Old Testament commandments. (2) Until the expiration of the physical universe, not even a letter or stroke of the law will pass away. And (3) therefore God's disapprobation rests upon anyone who teaches that *even* the *least* of the Old Testament laws may be broken.[8] The underlying ethical principles or duties which are communicated in the minute details (jot and tittle) of the law of God, down to its least significant provision, should be reckoned to have an abiding validity — until and unless the Lawgiver reveals otherwise.

Of course, nothing which has been said above means that the work of Christian ethics is a pat and easy job. Even though the details of God's law are available to us as moral absolutes, they still need to be properly interpreted and applied to the modern world. It should constantly be borne in mind that no school of thought, least of all the theonomist outlook, "has all the answers." Nobody should get the impression that clear, simple, or uncontestable "solutions" to the moral problems of our day can be just

---

8. Attempts are sometimes made to evade the thrust of this text by editing out its reference to the moral demands of the Old Testament — contrary to what is obvious from its context (5:16, 20, 21-48; 6:1, 10, 33; 7:12, 20-21, 26) and semantics ("the law" in v. 18, "commandment" in v. 19). Other attempts are made to extract an abrogating of the law's moral demands from the word "fulfill" (v. 17) or the phrase "until all things have happened" (v. 18). This, however, renders the verses self-contradictory in what they assert.

lifted from the face of Scripture's laws. A tremendous amount of homework remains to be done, whether in textual exegesis, cultural analysis, or moral reasoning—with plenty of room for error and correction. None of it is plain and simple. It must not be carried on thoughtlessly or without sanctified mental effort.

Moreover, in all of it we need each other's best efforts and charitable corrections. Only after our ethical senses have been corporately exercised to discern good and evil by the constant study and use of God's law—only after we have gained considerably more experience in the word of righteousness (Heb. 5:13-14)—will we achieve greater clarity, confidence, and a common mind in applying God's law to the ethical difficulties which beset modern men. Nevertheless, even with the mistakes that we may make in using God's law today, I prefer it as the *basis* for ethics to the sinful and foolish speculations of men. It would be absurd for a man to resign himself to poison just because medical doctors occasionally make mistakes with prescription drugs!

Transformationalism

As Christians we have been entrusted with God's prescriptions for how men should live their lives so as to bring glory to the Creator and to enjoy loving, peaceful relations with other men in this world. God's prescriptions counter the destructive tendencies of sin, and those destructive tendencies are felt in all areas of life, from private and personal matters of the heart to the public matters of socio-political affairs. God's prescriptive guidance is needed, therefore, in all areas of life. Moreover, the Christian acknowledges that Jesus Christ is Lord in every aspect of human experience and endeavor. In every walk of life a criterion of our love for Christ or lack thereof is whether we keep the Lord's words (John 14:23-24) rather than founding our beliefs upon the ruinous sands of other opinions (Matt. 7:24-27).

Thus Christians who advocate Reconstructionism reject the social forces of *secularism* which too often shape our culture's conception of a good society. The Christian's political standards and agenda are not set by unregenerate pundits who wish to quarantine religious values (and thus the influence of Jesus Christ, speaking in the Scripture) from the decision-making process of those who set public policy. Reconstructionists repudiate the *sacred/secular dichotomy* of life which implies that present-day moral standards for our political order are not to be taken from what the written word of God directly and relevantly says about society and civil government. This stance is a theologically unwarranted and socially dangerous curtailing of the scope of the Bible's truth and authority (Psalm 119:160; Isa. 40:8; 45:19; John 17:17; Deut. 4:2; Matt. 5:18-19).

We beseech men not to be conformed to this world, but to be transformed by the renewing and reconciling work of Jesus Christ so as to prove the good, acceptable and perfect will of God in their lives (2 Cor. 5:20-21; Rom. 12:1-2). We call on them to be delivered out of darkness into the kingdom of God's Son, who was raised from the dead in order to have pre-eminence in *all* things (Col. 1:13-18). We must "cast down reasonings and every high thing which is exalted against the knowledge of God, bringing *every* thought into captivity to the obedience of Christ" (2 Cor. 10:5) in whom "*all* the treasures of wisdom and knowledge are deposited" (Col. 2:3). Thus believers are exhorted to be holy in all manner of living (1 Peter 1:15), and to do whatever they do for the glory of God (1 Cor. 10:31). To do so will require adherence to the written word of God since our faith does not stand in the wisdom of men but rather in the work and teaching of God's Holy Spirit (1 Cor. 2:5, 13; cf. 1 Thess. 2:13; Num. 15:39; Jer. 23:16). That teaching, infallibly recorded in "*every* scripture" of the Old and New Testaments, is able to equip us "for *every* good work" (2 Tim. 3:16-17) — thus even in public, community life.

In light of the Biblical truths discussed above, Reconstructionists are committed to the *transformation* (Reconstruction) of every area of life, *including* the institutions and affairs of the socio-political realm, according to the holy principles revealed *throughout* God's inspired word (theonomy).

Summary

Like dispensationalism, the Reconstructionist or theonomic position is a view of God's work in history which wants to take account of the redemptive discontinuities between the Old and New Testaments, such as the fact that we do not offer animal sacrifices today. Reconstructionists, just as much as dispensationalists, want to guard the principle of salvation by grace, which believers enjoy today, from the terrible error of seeking salvation through works of the law, as taught by the Jews both before and after the advent of Jesus Christ. However, the way in which Reconstructionism attempts to accomplish these ends does not impose artificial divisions upon the Bible or upon the people of God, but rather allows Scripture to speak for itself by establishing those internal assumptions and qualifications which should operate in our system of theology and biblical interpretation. Accordingly:

1. Reconstructionism maintains an ethic of "higher law" which is absolute, *universal* or trans-cultural — in opposition to cultural relativism and situationism.

2. Reconstructionism at the same time guards the ethical unity of Scripture, finding its unchanging moral standard revealed throughout the whole Bible — in contradistinction from an antinomian rejection of the Old Testament.

3. Reconstructionist ethics insists upon the sufficiency and sole authority of God's word for defining right and wrong — thereby rejecting the legalism which adds human traditions and interpretations to the standards revealed in Scripture.

4. Reconstructionism vigorously maintains that Jesus Christ is Lord over all areas of life and calls His followers to exercise transforming influence in everything, including the outward concerns of society — in conflict with the vision of the Christian life adopted by pietism.

4

HOW SHOULD WE THEN DECIDE?

An assessment of the theological reasoning employed by House and Ice.

Dispensationalism produces one kind of orientation or perspective in ethics. Reconstructionism produces another. It is not impossible for the two positions to agree on particulars here and there (and happily they do), but it is evident from the above discussion that dispensationalism and Reconstructionism represent a conflict of visions regarding the Christian life and involvement in the world. Their respective approaches to ethics are in tension with each other at fundamental points — viz., the moral unity of Scripture, the absolute authority and sufficiency of God's law, and the present scope of Christian responsibility in the world.

Betraying the Supreme Judge

The authors of *Dominion Theology* are dispensationalists who feel that the Reconstructionist view of ethics is mistaken. Why? Sometimes they offer the opinion that Reconstructionism is mistaken because there is no "scriptural basis . . . exegetical proof" for the position[1] — it is not supported by the Bible and is actually contrary to it. At other times, though, they suggest a *different standard* for judging Reconstructionism to be in error:

> Christian Reconstructionism argues for a way of thinking about God's law, his plan for the future, and the role of the church fundamentally different from that commonly accepted among mainstream evangelicals. . . . We shall describe the two major areas

---

1. H. Wayne House and Thomas Ice, *Dominion Theology: Blessing or Curse?* (Portland, OR: Multnomah, 1988), p. 8.

45

that are in primary deviance from contemporary evangelicalism and Protestant Christianity in general—theonomy and postmillennialism. . . .[2]

These views, they claim, are "shocking to some and questioned by most of the evangelical theological community."[3] But this kind of criticism, of course, is:

- unsubstantiated (House and Ice are not acquainted with most evangelicals, even contemporary ones),

- self-serving (who determines who will count as a "mainstream" evangelical?),

- contrary to historical fact (simply forgetting two centuries of Puritan influence and even nineteenth-century evangelicalism),[4]

- and above all, *anything but* Protestant in character.

---

2. *Ibid.*, pp. 16-17.
3. *Ibid.*, p. 20.
4. Although the evidence is rather clear and has been presented a number of times, House and Ice waver regarding it (pp. 90-98). Actually, they stumble into downright self-contradiction in expressing their own view about historical precedence: "it is true the Puritans were generally theonomistic in outlook" (House and Ice, *Dominion Theology*, p. 94)—but on the next page: "the movement as a whole was never in wholehearted agreement" [with theonomy] (p. 95). Well, which is it? (The reader may pursue this subject in the "Symposium on Puritanism and Law," *The Journal of Christian Reconstruction* [Winter, 1978-79], passim.)

House and Ice likewise betray how unstudied they are in this subject when they categorically state "Calvin opposed implantation of the Mosaic law into civil life" (p. 93), apparently basing this opinion on a remark in the *Institutes* about a certain "perilous and seditious" view—when in fact Calvin was not referring to endorsement of the Mosaic civil law, but the using of it as a pretext for revolutionary repudiation of the powers that be by Anabaptist radicals (cf. Jack W. Sawyer, Jr., "Moses and the Magistrate: Aspects of Calvin's Political Theory in Contemporary Focus," unpublished masters thesis, Westminster Theological Seminary, 1986). Calvin wrote "Absurd is the cleverness which some persons but little versed in Scripture pretend to, who assert that . . . the obligations under which Moses laid his countrymen are now dissolved" (commentary at Lev. 28:6). One needs to read Calvin's sermons on Deuteronomy or consult the biblical defense of his conduct in Servetus affair (where he calls the Mosaic judicial law "a perpetual rule"), etc. Because of such indications as these, House and Ice are forced to call the evidence on Calvin "mixed," and they accuse Calvin's thinking of being "confused" (pp. 91, 93). But I (Bahnsen) find the Genevan scholar far more clear and consistent in his thinking than his current detractors.

The Protestant (and biblical) standard of theological truth, over against appeals to tradition or group opinion (as we find in Romanism), is *sola Scriptura.* Scripture alone should be the source of our theological convictions and the final judge in all disagreements. Critics of Reconstructionism like House and Ice tend to forget that standard, in practice not being loyal to it. They want to look around to see who in the social circle with which they are comfortable will agree or disagree with certain ideas. The way in which they vacillate between group opinion and biblical exegesis as the criterion for evaluating Reconstructionism betrays a failure (in practice, not profession) to let Scripture function as their supreme authority.

Horrid Consequences

This same failure is evident when House and Ice attempt to sway their readers away from the Reconstructionist perspective in ethics by asking "What Would a Christian Reconstructed America Be Like?" (the title of Chapter 4 in their book). They offer a couple of opening "scenarios" purporting to represent what would happen if the Reconstructionist view in ethics came to be widely adopted — imaginary cases intended to make the reader recoil from Reconstructionism in shock or dread. The *implicit* line of reasoning is that, whether or not Reconstructionism is *biblical*, the *consequences* are so uncomfortable that readers will not want to accept it anyway.

We could, if we wished, pause here to expose the artificiality, contrivance, and downright fraudulence of the alleged illustrations offered by House and Ice for what would happen in a Reconstructed America.[5] They resort to attacking straw men. However,

---

5. If we were to go into detail, high on the list would be the two preposterous suggestions made by House and Ice that (1) theonomic ethics is incompatible with the Bill of Rights, and (2) a theonomic civil magistrate would apply criminal sanctions against anyone holding dispensational beliefs. Such statements display inexcusable ignorance of the First Amendment of the U.S. Constitution, as well as of the actual requirements of God's law. About the former, John W. Whitehead observes: "Thus the philosophical base of the First Amendment was that of

no detailed reply is required since they *themselves* admit that they are not setting forth the actual truth about Reconstructionism, but their own projections — which is a notorious type of sophistry: not criticizing what your opponent actually says, but what he might say (you think). After spending an entire chapter suggesting that readers would not want the horrible consequences which will come with Reconstructionism, House and Ice (amazingly) concede at the end of their discussion: "No one really knows what a country controlled by Reconstructionists would be like"![6]

However, what should concern us much more than the contrivance in the line of criticism found here is the underlying nature of *this kind* of theological thinking which: — indirectly insults God for His ethical errors (implying that what He required in His law, at least for Old Testament Israel, was disgusting or horrible, not perfect, righteous and desirable: cf. Psalm 19:7-10), and — subordinates the authority of God's word to the feelings, thinking, and preconceptions of sinful men.

Reconstructionists have offered a perspective in ethics which they believe to be biblical — authorized by God speaking in His holy word. House and Ice suggest to their readers, however, that if this ethical perspective would lead to certain "horrible consequences," then the position should be discarded as unacceptable. Implicitly there is some standard having higher authority and value than God's own word, then. The subtle and unstated impli-

denominational pluralism — a healthy coexistence between the various Christian denominations. Such practical denominational pluralism is not to be confused with the new concept of pluralism, which commands complete acceptance of all views, even secular humanism" (*The Second American Revolution* [Elgin, IL: David C. Cook, 1982], p. 96). About the law of God, it should have been noticed that what the civil magistrate is called to punish is blasphemy (public cursing of God), not errors in doctrine. In the Old Testament the task of kings was not the same as priests (e.g., 2 Chron. 26) who were responsible for orthodoxy (cf. Mal. 2:7-8), even as in the New Testament the "keys" of the kingdom are separated from coercive "sword" of the state (Matt. 16:19; 2 Cor. 10:4; Rom. 13:4). There is no biblical warrant for thinking that the civil magistrate has either the competence or the divinely-given authority to judge heretics or resolve theological disputes between different Christian schools of thought.

6. House and Ice, *Dominion Theology*, p. 80.

cation is that if you are personally displeased with a particular interpretation of Scripture proposed to you, you should automatically consider it untrue to God's word. Don't betray your own comfortable ideas or ways of thinking!

But is this the way evangelicals are supposed to do theology? Liberals do. They trim down the Scriptures according to their own preconceptions; they "reform" the Bible, rather than letting the Bible reform their thinking or feelings. When one accepts the supreme authority of God's word, however, he is committed to believing its teachings, regardless of the consequences (and how his own outlook or feelings must change). I know people who will not accept biblical inspiration because they would then have to adopt the ("outlandish") doctrine of blood atonement — a consequence too horrible for them. I know people who will not accept the doctrine of biblical inerrancy because their thinking would then clash with ("respectable") secular scholarship in history or science — a consequence too horrible for them. I am sure that House and Ice would immediately reject such reasoning when it comes to inspiration or inerrancy. We must be true to biblical teaching and accept the consequences (cf. Rom. 3:4)! However, House and Ice turn around and use *the very same line* of criticism against Reconstructionism ("you wouldn't want these horrible things to happen in America, would you?"), thereby abandoning *in practice* the supreme authority of God's word to which Reconstructionists have appealed for their teaching.

The only question we should have before us is whether the Reconstructionist view of ethics (or the dispensationalist view) is based upon and faithfully conforms to the teaching of God's infallible word in the Bible. It is to this question that we will turn in a further chapter. At this point we have simply paused to observe that House and Ice, as critics of theonomic ethics, do not consistently practice a commitment to the supreme, sole and unchallengeable authority of Scripture. That is a fatal defect, but it is not the only one. We would also challenge a number of the types of arguments pressed into service by House and Ice in their effort to refute Reconstructionism. Unfortunately, their book is freighted with fallacious thinking and logical shortcomings which considerably weaken the effort and value of *Dominion Theology*. The cautious reader will, consequently, not find their reasoning trustworthy.

"You're Wrong Because You Might Be"

Of all the complaints which are brought against Reconstructionism in *Dominion Theology*, by far the most strained and scurrilous is the argument that the position, although innocent of some fault, is nonetheless guilty because it might lead to that fault. Over and over again House and Ice indicate that Reconstructionism should be rejected because there is in it "the possibility" or "the danger" or "the tendency" or "the temptation" or "the potential" for some specified transgression to result from it.

The title of Chapter 15 in *Dominion Theology* is "The Dangers of Christian Reconstruction." The list of things heretical and wicked which are laid at the feet of Reconstructionists is catastrophic: moralism,[7] [yet] a spirit of compromise which abandons veracity for unprincipled pragmatism,[8] leading the Church astray into apostasy,[9] permeating Christianity with humanism,[10] intermingling Christianity with non-Christian thinking or merging with the world's system,[11] making the preaching of the gospel secondary,[12] bringing destructive non-Christian thought and influence into the Church,[13] creating anti-Christian institutions,[14] [yet] intermingling Church and state,[15] synthesis with the world,[16] [yet] encouraging a severe backlash against Christianity.[17]

---

7. *Ibid.*, p. 338.
8. *Ibid.*, p. 341.
9. *Ibid.*, pp. 335, 342; cf. pp. 374-75, 377.
10. *Ibid.*, pp. 340, 349.
11. *Ibid.*, pp. 341, 344; cf. p. 390.
12. *Ibid.*, p. 356.
13. *Ibid.*, p. 344.
14. *Ibid.*, p. 340.
15. *Ibid.*, p. 339.
16. *Ibid.*, pp. 342, 344.
17. *Ibid.*, p. 338.

The reader should notice that, in their baseless diatribe against potential sins of Reconstructionism, House and Ice cannot even get straight on what they want to accuse Reconstructionism of; they fail to develop a *consistent* list of speculative dangers inherent in the system. These self-contradictions generated by House and Ice are denoted in the preceding list by the editorial insertion of "[yet]." Just look at the last one. On the one hand Reconstructionism will give into, compromise and synthesize with worldly attitudes, *but* on the other hand Reconstructionism is so opposed to and will diverge so sharply from worldly attitudes that the world will backlash against it! Well, which is it? Our imaginative authors have Reconstructionism simultaneously *diminishing* and *increasing* the antithesis between Christianity and the world. Likewise, having blasted Reconstructionism for tolerating mutual influence of believers and unbelievers (synthesis), House and Ice turn around and blast them for *failing* to tolerate the peaceful coexistence of wheat and tares![18] Are Reconstructionists *too* tolerant or *not* tolerant *enough*? House and Ice have reduced themselves to erratic pot-shots which fly at cross-purposes with each other in their book.

At some points House and Ice speak of these terrible things being what "could" happen, things Reconstructionists would be "tempted" to do, things for which there is a "tendency," "possibility," or "potential danger" in Reconstructionism.[19] At other points, however, they more arrogantly assert that Reconstructionism "will only lead to [result in]" these things, is "in effect" these very things, "will always end up [result]" with these defects, or that these defects "cannot be avoided."[20]

However, *at no point whatsoever* do House and Ice for any of these cases offer the slightest hint of evidence that Reconstructionists are in actual fact guilty of even one of the horrible crimes laid at their feet. The reader must appreciate the significance of this startling situation. House and Ice have leveled the most grievous

---

18. *Ibid.*, p. 338.
19. *Ibid.*, pp. 338, 341, 344.
20. *Ibid.*, pp. 335, 340, 341, 342, 344, 349, 350.

accusations imaginable against their Reconstructionist brothers, yet without bothering to adduce for any accusation even one shred of substantiating evidence. In fact, the only thing like evidence to which they allude[21] disproves the very criticism they are trying to lay on Reconstructionism. Far from allowing "destructive non-Christian thought and influence" to be brought into Christian circles—as the authors allege—the quotation from Chilton shows that Reconstructionists themselves are opposed to such a thing happening, are sensitive to detect it, and resist it openly. How can they cite a Reconstructionist's criticism of something as proof that Reconstructionism (the position) itself is guilty of it? From the standpoint of Christian morality (Old *and* New Testaments) this is unspeakably perverse and vicious. "At the mouth of two or three witnesses every word [must] be established" (Matt. 18:16). "Do not witness against your neighbor without cause and (thereby) deceive with your lips" (Prov. 24:28). "Put them in mind . . . to speak evil of no man" (Titus 3:1-2). "You shall not take up a false report" (Exodus 23:1). "Putting away falsehood, speak the truth each one with his neighbor" (Eph. 4:25). The authors of *Dominion Theology* have stooped to leveling accusations without concern for substantiation—and in the very face of acknowledging that there is no *actual* truth to what they are saying anyway, but simply what *might* (or will) *become* true. Even unbelieving scholars would not try to get away with publishing such shabby thinking and pretense at "rebuttal."

Ungrounded Speculation

But further: House and Ice have taken a prophetic mantle upon their own shoulders and presumed to predict evil resulting from Reconstructionist theology. Yet neither author claims (or would claim) the inspiration of God's Spirit for their dire predictions. The source and authority for their projections, then, is simply human opinion and speculation, which, in the nature of the case here, means they have indulged in what the Bible condemns as "evil suspicion" (1 Tim. 6:4). They have not read Reconstructionists in the best light possible, given the available evidence.

---

21. *Ibid.*, p. 344.

They have rather read them in the worst light, without any evidence at all. They have sought to discredit fellow believers without textual, logical, or observational warrant.[22] They have formed and communicated personal opinions without the restraint of objective evidence, and thus with a negative and uncharitable attitude toward Reconstructionists. If they had proof, that would be one thing. Without it, they should have honored God's direction that "Love . . . is kind . . . rejoices not at unrighteousness, but with the truth . . . believes all things, hopes all things" (1 Cor. 13:4-7).

Special attention is warranted for Appendix B in *Dominion Theology*, as it is an extended indulgence in this same kind of criticism as we have seen here, accusing Reconstructionists of the "potential for anti-Semitism."[23] In this case the charge is especially preposterous, given the postmillennial commitment to the latter day, widespread revival of the Jews (Rom. 11) and given remarks like those of converted Jew, Steve Schlissel, in a short essay on this very subject.[24] Nevertheless, House and Ice insist upon making the defamatory claim. The moral demand of both Old and New Testaments teaches: "He who would love life and see good days, let him refrain his tongue from evil and his lips that they speak no guile" (1 Peter 3:10; Psalm 34:12-13). It is cunning deceit to publish the epithet of "anti-Semitic" against people who do and say *nothing* "against" the Jews, but rather condemn racial hatred directed against the Jews, defend them against persecution, and pray for their conversion. How do House and Ice justify this sham? Well,

---

22. We should be very clear here. The objection does not stem from the notion that Christians should never speak critically of one another's thinking or conduct. Criticism which is properly grounded and communicated can cultivate each other's goodness as Christians and be edifying (Rom. 15:14; Eph. 4:29); it is often required in order to be faithful to God (Rom. 16:17; Titus 1:9; Rev. 2:2, 6, etc.). However, such criticism must be tethered to objective evidence (e.g., eye-witnessed facts, documented statements) and cogent reasoning (e.g., pinning on an author what his words actually infer by good and necessary consequence).

23. House and Ice, *Dominion Theology*, pp. 397-406.

24. "To Those Who Wonder if Christian Reconstruction is Anti-Semitic," an appendix to Gary DeMar's *The Debate over Christian Reconstruction* (Ft. Worth, TX: Dominion Press, 1988), pp. 256-61.

since postmillennialists have a *positive* hope for the future of the
Jews which is somewhat different from the dispensationalist's
positive hope for the future of the Jews, House and Ice feel they
are allowed to conclude that postmillennialists are actually *negative*
about the Jews ("anti"-Semitic) — so that a word with extreme,
emotive and horrible connotations of Jewish hatred may be applied to them. The authors ought to be ashamed of themselves for
talking this way. They should also realize that the same line of
fallacious thinking could just as easily (and fallaciously) be used
by postmillennialists to accuse *them* of "anti-Semitism." That is,
since House and Ice do not agree with the postmillennialist's
positive hope about the future of the Jews, the dispensational view
is not really positive at all, but actually negative. Dispensationalists are thus "anti-Semitic." What is sauce for the goose is sauce for
the gander.

A Taste of Their Own Medicine

Perhaps by means of a few more "counter-examples" we can
drive home the extremity of the inappropriateness and insult involved in the kind of criticism ("potential dangers") House and Ice
have taken up against Reconstructionism. "For with what judgment you judge, you shall be judged; and with the measure you
mete it out, it shall be meted out to you" (Matt. 7:2).

Notice, first, the general *form* of this reasoning, taking the ab-
breviation MUD for any monstrous unbiblical doctrine or practice you choose. "(a) Our theological opponents say nothing in
their writings which indicts them of MUD, are not actually guilty
of MUD, do not endorse MUD, work to avoid MUD in themselves, and actually take a public stand against MUD in others.
(b) However, their theological system does not render it absolutely, personally impossible for some individual holding it to be
later persuaded to depart from the position and be 'tempted' into
the MUD. (c) Indeed, a few of the characteristics or beliefs of
those who promote MUD can also be found in our opponents,
despite their opposition to MUD. (d) It is then 'possible' that our
opponents are not really, completely clean of MUD. (e) Moreover,

there must be a 'tendency' or 'potential danger' that the position of our opponents 'could possibly' be 'in effect' the same as MUD. (f) Therefore, readers should reject the position of our opponents, watching out for its MUD." We can designate this line of reasoning the mud-slinging fallacy.

Let us apply the form of this fallacious thinking to the authors of *Dominion Theology*. They are not theological liberals and would actually oppose liberalism. However, dispensationalism is not a personal prophylactic against moving into liberalism; some people have done it. In fact, in tune with the liberals, House and Ice have been known to urge *extra*-biblical reasons for rejecting some position which is presented *as* biblical. Bahnsen has pointed this out at the beginning of this chapter. Moreover, liberals are notorious for rejecting the authority of the Old Testament (ridiculing the ethical code that allowed for holy war or capital punishment or slavery, etc.)—just as dispensationalists are against the ethical perspective of the Old Testament (cf. the "antinomianism" in dispensationalism which Bahnsen observed in Chapter 2 above). It is possible that dispensationalism is not free of liberalism, then. The tendency in dispensationalism is to produce liberal thinking and attitudes. In effect, dispensationalism is liberalism. Therefore, readers, if you oppose liberalism, you will want to reject dispensationalism too!

But then, this same line of thinking can be applied to the "potential danger" of Romanism in dispensationalism. At the beginning of this chapter Bahnsen has shown that House and Ice have, in practice and at points, done what a Romanist would do: urge against a theological position that it is out of accord with tradition or with the agreement of their religious group. Looks like "possible" Romanism to me! And if it might be, then it probably is. At least, we have to say that there is a tendency toward Romanism in dispensationalism. Oh, but that's not all. No, no. In Chapter 2 Bahnsen has observed and documented the general tendency for dispensationalists to be pietists who deny that the Christian is called to engage in reforming society, politics, education, etc. Pietists emphasize personal holiness, but withdraw from cultural transformation, knowing that it is impossible to effect any genuine change before the violent intervention of Christ. Since House and Ice are dispensationalists, they would both have to agree with author, Dave Hunt, that trying to change society through Christian activism is not biblical (rather a sign of the New Age heresy). Moreover, some pietists in the history of the Church have renounced society *altogether* and retreated to the cloistered holiness of a monastery. Now House and Ice do not actually say Christians should exclusively promote personal piety, reject worldly society, and stay in monasteries. But it is "possible" for a dispensationalist to do so. There are some things which pietistic dispensationalists have in common with monks. So the tendency toward a monastic life cannot be denied. And just remember the *legalism* which Bahnsen noted as a dispensationalist tendency in Chapter 2! Since its the Roman Catholic Church which has fostered legalistic, monastic living, we have a further indication that dispensationalism shares Romanist sympathies.

What? You say that dispensationalism is notorious for its stands against theological liberalism and Roman Catholicism? That makes no difference whatsoever. Dispensationalists must be "unwitting" liberals and Romanists. They are guilty, because they might be guilty. Sure, I cannot produce any actual evidence of actual endorsement of the actual distinguishing marks of liberalism or Romanism in the actual authors, House and Ice. The potential danger alone is enough to condemn them. House and Ice should be shunned as liberal Roman Catholics should be shunned!

In fact, things are far worse than we imagined. In terms of conceptual structures and analysis, the dispensationalism of House and Ice shows definite parallels to the reasoning of cultural relativists, as revealed by Bahnsen in Chapter 2. House and Ice would, of course, openly repudiate cultural relativism, despite their being conceptual brothers under the skin. House and Ice believe that what is right and wrong changes on the basis of temporal and ethnic changes — that morality is relative to the dispensation (law/grace) and the race (Jew/Gentile) of the society about which one is thinking. Cultural relativists say the same thing (and are simply more thorough and consistent in carrying it out). The potential danger of cultural relativism can thus be seen in dispensationalism. It would always be a temptation to move right on over from dispensationalism into full-fledged moral relativism. In time it simply cannot be avoided.

Dispensationalism must be rejected, then, before the Church is dragged down into the mud of lawless, licentious relativism by the likes of dispensationalists House and Ice! And speaking of licentious moral relativism, there are some other "possibilities" that need to be considered about authors House and Ice. You will notice that they are friends, see each other socially, are both of the same sex, and both oppose the Old Testament penal sanction of death for homosexuality. The same can certainly be said of most practicing homosexuals. The mud-slinging fallacy would lead us to warn the reader, then, against the "possibility" that our authors are moral perverts, and lead us to conclude that such immorality is the constant danger of dispensational thinking.

Enough. The course of discussion in this section has been purposely facetious, not at all seriously meant, and completely without merit (except as a *reductio ad absurdum*). I know very well that authors House and Ice are not liberals, Romanists, or perverts. But can you imagine how offended they would be, and how outlandish my scholarship would be, if my published critique of their dispensational position included claims like "There is the potential danger of liberalism and perversion in dispensationalism"? I would hope never to treat them in that fashion or to try to pass off such comments as a serious analysis and critique of generic dispensationalism. Our common Lord, in calling us to observe the morality of "the Law and the Prophets," said: "All things therefore whatsoever you would have men do unto you, even so do you also unto them" (Matt. 7:12). In that spirit, I wish to repudiate the kind of criticism which has been used (for purposes of illustration) in this section — and call upon brothers House and Ice to do likewise. None of us gets treated fairly with the mud-slinging fallacy. Likewise, I exhort the serious reader to disregard the unfortunate sections of *Dominion Theology* which utilize this baseless line of

criticism in order to dissuade him or her from adopting Reconstructionism.

Guilt by Association

A close cousin to the mud-slinging fallacy is the rhetorical
device of imputing guilt by association, suggesting that a position
is objectionable because of other positions (or people) which are
associated — or may be made to *appear* to be associated — with the
position. House and Ice did not pass up the opportunity to press
this strained and fallacious line of criticism into service against
Reconstructionism. They attempt to tar Reconstructionism with
the same brush which might be used against the charismatic
movement, in particular the Positive Confession and Manifest
Sons of God branches, and Bishop Earl Paulk, not to mention liberalism's social gospel and secular "can-do" optimism.[25] Such discussion accounts for just under ten percent of the entire effort put
into their book. And it is all for nothing.

Guilt by association and tribute by association are simply
different sides of the same coin. From the logical standpoint there
is no way to tell in advance whether the coin is bogus or not. Let
me illustrate. If a school of thought which you reject agrees on
some point with a school of thought which you favor, is that a
tribute to the former (since they are not as mistaken as they might
be) or a matter of *guilt* for the latter (since they are more mistaken
than you hoped)? Of course there is no way of saying *until* you
have independently examined that one area of agreement and determined whether *it* represents something true or false. You cannot tell in advance, just by looking at those who agree with it! The
reader can see from this that House and Ice are trying to take an
illegitimate shortcut in their critique of Reconstructionism. Instead
of examining the position's theological theses on their own merits
(or demerits), the authors cut to an evaluation based simply on
the observation that those theses are *also* endorsed (or appear to be

---

25. *Ibid.*, pp. 22, 23, 336, 339-40, 341, 348, and the entirety of Appendix A:
pp. 367-95.

endorsed) by some group which is in disfavor with House and Ice. That procedure simply begs the question as to whether those beliefs are true or false — thus being a matter of credit or of guilt.

The rhetorical device of guilt by association is also very easy to turn around against dispensationalists like House and Ice themselves. For instance, the game of showing parallels with the Manifest Sons of God on particular points of doctrine[26] can be used to show (as does Gentry in Chapter 19 below) that dispensationalism agrees with the Jehovah's Witnesses at numerous points! If House and Ice found such agreement to be a sufficient basis for condemning Reconstructionism, then they must be prepared for a dose of the same medicine. They should have realized, even apart from this embarrassing *faux pas*, that arguing guilt by association is logically unacceptable and dangerous. As Philip Hughes noted more than a decade ago:

> No more impressive is it to cite the names of liberals, romanists, and unitarians whose outlook has been other than premillennial, as though this suffices to demonstrate that premillennialism and soundness of faith belong inseparably together. The device of guilt by association proves nothing and can readily become a boomerang, since it is easy to retort that the premillennial position has also been that of heretics and deviant sects, from Cerinthus in the time of the apostles to the Mormons and Jehovah's Witnesses in our day.[27]

Indeed, if a theological position is to be rejected for its association with a heretical group or cult, then (as Gentry again illustrates in Chapter 19 below) we would need to reject dispensationalism itself for its points of contact with the Jehovah's Witness cult. If House and Ice now attempt to resort to special pleading, their scholarship cannot be taken seriously. They should have thought out in advance the implications and pitfalls of their chosen line of argumentation. As it stands, they must now admit to fallacious reasoning or to the guilt of cultic theology.

---

26. Played by House and Ice on pp. 385-89.
27. Philip Edgcumbe Hughes, *Interpreting Prophecy* (Grand Rapids, MI: Wm. B. Eerdmans, 1976), p. 102.

Intramural Disagreements and Past Failures

In their book, *Dominion Theology*, authors House and Ice display a penchant for utilizing lines of argument against Reconstructionism which prove to be two-edged swords — criticisms which cut two directions, to the chagrin of the authors. If their weapons hurt Reconstructionism at all, they are even more fatal to dispensationalism. We have seen ample evidence of this already in the present Chapter. Two further illustrations can be given, again pointing to the polemical short-sightedness of House and Ice.

At a number of points in their book, the authors fault Reconstructionists for not agreeing on all aspects and applications of their position.[27] Apparently that is supposed to be an embarrassment — "no clear-cut answers," "many unanswered questions," "divergence of opinion," "significant issues remain uncertain" — rather than a sign of healthy inquiry, honest independence of thought, growth, and humble recognition that nobody "has all the answers." Scripture would lead us to expect that believers will need more and more "experience in the word of righteousness" before they become mature and, "by reason of use have their senses exercised to discern good and evil" (Heb. 5:11-14). The Church itself strives to grow in its knowledge of God's Son "unto a full-grown man" that is "no longer tossed to and fro" by every wind of doctrine, but rather "attaining the unity of the faith" (Eph. 4:13-15). The Christian life (and the history of the Christian Church) is one of developing and improving our ability to grasp and to live according to the precious truth of God's revelation; sanctification is progressive. Thus perfect doctrine and perfect obedience are not attained at the outset. This is just as much true for Reconstructionists as it is for any other Christian, and so I fail to see how it is any special fault in Reconstructionism that there are as yet unresolved disagreements on certain points regarding it.

If intramural doctrinal disagreement is itself a basis for discrediting some school of thought, then we should consider two consequences. (1) The application of this criterion to Christianity

---

28. House and Ice, *Dominion Theology*, pp. 39, 40, 43, 64, 80.

as a religion would lead to the discrediting of the faith itself. Is not this one of the arguments urged by many unbelievers against Christianity? ("There are so many denominations, so many different interpretations of the Bible.") The apologetical answer with which we would respond to that attack is in its general principles one which likewise applies to the problem House and Ice have raised with Reconstructionist disagreements. If House and Ice are not proposing to abandon *Christianity* on this basis, they should not propose that their readers abandon Reconstructionism on it either. Consistency is hard to come by.

(2) Dispensationalists should be about the last ones in the evangelical community to raise a fuss over the doctrinal or interpretive disagreements found in other camps! Have House and Ice forgotten the history of debate, dissension, splintering and mutual condemnation within the ranks of dispensationalists themselves? When will the rapture be? (pretribulational, midtribulational?) When did the Church begin? (Pentecost? Acts 9? Acts 13? Acts 28?) How many different dispensations are there? (four? seven? eight?) Who is the antichrist? (you name a wicked well-known leader, and some dispensationalist has probably tagged him!) What was the basis of Old Testament salvation? Was the New Covenant for Israel or the Church? Is the rapture datable as a generation from the return of Israel to the land? etc., etc. Intramural debates and disagreements (not only in doctrine, but in ethics and Christian living) have always marked dispensationalism. "Significant issues remain uncertain!" In light of this, it was a stroke of good sense for House and Ice to back off from needling Reconstructionists with that kind of remark and to come around three hundred pages later and admit: "This is not to say that Reconstructionists need to agree on every point. There are always differences between people within any framework"![29]

Similar good sense would have been appropriate and applicable elsewhere in *Dominion Theology* when House and Ice take to pointing to the (alleged) past failures of groups which were basically

---

29. *Ibid.*, p. 352.

Reconstructionist in conviction and practice.[30] Reconstructionists are said to be "haunted by the past failures of previous generations of postmillennialists to Christianize the world."[31] House and Ice jump to the only conclusion they apparently care to consider: A "major objection to Reconstructionism is that it just does not work."[32] Once again, their theological reasoning betrays to the reader its own shortcomings.

First, about this alleged haunting, three things. (1) I do not think that House and Ice even approximate a fair-minded assessment and appreciation as historians of the godly, helpful, and influential successes (even in the midst of struggle and mistakes) of such past groups of believers; the prejudice of our authors is showing through here. (2) House and Ice commit here a fallacy often made by those unfamiliar with historiography: viz., making generalizations over a disparate and changed group as though it were one continuous party of people in history. Some say "the Puritans failed," when what they are really talking about is not the Puritans at all, but rather the errors of a later community (e.g., New England Unitarians) which had generational or social ties with the Puritans, but had abandoned crucial Puritan convictions — in which case it was *not* "the Puritans" (but non-Puritans) creating the problems being considered.

(3) Further, if any group should be "haunted" by their past failures, the authors should have been a bit more objective and worried about *dispensationalism's own* ghosts. How many times have we endured false (but confident) identifications of the antichrist? How many times has it been preached that things are degenerating so quickly that in this generation (i.e., that of the particular preacher) there is no time or reason for long-term projects or investments? "The end" has been "soon" *so many* times! How many times has the Church been embarrassed by those who have declared on the date of Christ's return? (One just recently was widely published and insisted that 1988 *had* to be it! He had 88

---

30. *Ibid.*, pp. 92, 95, 336, 345, 347-48.
31. *Ibid.*, p. 347.
32. *Ibid.*, p. 335.

reasons.) As a follower of Calvin, the Puritans, and the Westminster Confession I would be glad to sit around and *compare* "past failures" with a dispensationalist any day.[33]

Second, there is another wrinkle on the polemic about "past failures" which needs to be ironed out. If postmillennialism were true, suggest House and Ice, then we should see success for the kingdom-building efforts of past Reconstructionist-type groups. Since we do not, the "pattern" is clear that Reconstructionism is false. "In fact, the church has not been able even to come close to the conditions Reconstructionists say will exist over the face of the globe before Christ returns."[34] Now, do House and Ice weigh and *then* reject the possibility that this (biased) observation of theirs maybe proves *something else*: viz., that we might not be close to the time when Christ will return? No, they simply beg that question. Apparently the fallacious nature of the rebuttal of *any* millennial school on the basis of "present historical conditions" eludes our authors here. (For instance: The distinctive, biblical, precursor signs of Christ's return as conceived by *dispensationalism* were not really present in 1850 — since Christ did not in fact return at that point — and "therefore" in 1850 a believer could have correctly observed the characteristics of his particular age and drawn the "obvious" conclusion that dispensationalism was false!)

---

33. House and Ice taunt Reconstructionist efforts to take seriously past problems and to understand what corrections are needed: "There has always been some excuse," the authors say (House and Ice, *Dominion Theology*, p. 348). But offering an explanation ("excuse") is in the nature of the case — for any school of thought — the only alternative to repudiating the position. Given their long list of past embarrassments and failures, do dispensationalists House and Ice abandon dispensationalism or try to account for the mistakes made with it? Do they taunt themselves now with "there's always some excuse"?

But now what do dispensationalists do in response to their long list of past failures and embarrassments? Apparently, unless they are willing to repudiate the theological position, they examine and explain how they feel the mistakes came about. That is only natural. Does it make sense to taunt them now, saying "oh yeah, there's always some excuse"?

34. House and Ice, *Dominion Theology*, p. 336.

Bad Personalities

By this point the reader has been given a pretty good idea of the general kind of failure in reasoning which attends so much of the argumentation by House and Ice against Reconstructionism. Over and over again in *Dominion Theology* they jump into some effort to discredit their opponents, only to find that they themselves (or dispensationalists) are easily and *equally* discredited by similar considerations. As polemicists House and Ice have not made application to their logical reasoning of the axiom that one should first take the log out of his own eye before removing the speck from the other's eye (cf. Matt. 7:5).

This is a glaring fault when House and Ice stop to criticize the personal failings or incautious language of particular Reconstructionist writers. On a *personal* level, I believe that their rebuke of adherents of the Reconstructionist *position* for not showing greater humility, for not getting along with each other, for displaying a churlish lack of love, etc.,[35] is entirely appropriate and needs to be heeded. At some places, however, their personal attacks are so exaggerated as to border on slander: E.g., "Some Reconstructionists champion obedience as the only concern of true Christianity," in distinction from others who are sympathetic to inward, personal piety as well.[36] No Christian can be proud of or defend a failure to show the fruit of God's Holy Spirit. Moreover, Reconstructionists are not always careful to avoid possible misunderstanding of the way they express themselves (e.g., "take-over" language, noted in Appendix C: pp. 407-15); this too is a helpful criticism.

Such personal criticisms have little place or relevance, however, in a critique of the Reconstructionist position. It is just here that House and Ice have fallen into another notorious logical fallacy (viz., arguing *ad hominem*). Its fallacious nature can be seen from a number of angles. (1) The Reconstructionists who are

---

35. *Ibid.*, pp. 347, 351-52, 359-61.
36. *Ibid.*, p. 94.

being criticized by House and Ice for their bad personalities (or for using careless expressions) are also professing Christians. If their bad personalities were proper grounds for House and Ice to reject Reconstructionism as a position, they would likewise be proper grounds for House and Ice to reject the Christian faith altogether — which would be absurd for them to do.

(2) Reconstructionists *themselves* have been critical of other Reconstructionists for the harshness or carelessness about which we are thinking here. Indeed, House and Ice make note of the in-house exhortation and rebuke on these very points which have taken place among Reconstructionists.[37] Obviously it is not the theological position *itself* which is the culprit, then, since adherents of that position both display *and* decry the bad personal traits or habits which are in view here.

(3) Indeed, you find this to be the case among *dispensationalists* as much as you do with Reconstructionists. Both camps contain individuals who fall short of the mark in Christian maturity or sanctification. Both have "embarrassing advocates" as well as models of Christian grace and love. Hopefully House and Ice recognize that it would be too easy a task (and unedifying) for me to amass a list of the pugnacious, arrogant, divisive and churlish behavior or remarks of various dispensationalist writers and preachers. Hopefully House and Ice recognize that such a personal laundry-list would not have anything to do with refuting dispensationalism as a theological position. It might only be hoped, however, that House and Ice had applied the *same* restraint in their critique of Reconstructionism. Logs and specks, you know.

Summary

In this chapter we have assessed the theological reasoning employed by authors House and Ice in their book, *Dominion Theology.* Recognizing that there is a fundamental difference in outlook between dispensationalism and Reconstructionism, we have wondered how, then, a person should decide *between* the two systems.

---

37. *Ibid.*, pp. 360-61, 407.

Should a Christian decide on the basis of the reasoning or the kind of reasoning which is found throughout *Dominion Theology*? Upon examination and reflection, we cannot draw anything other than a negative answer. The book is rebutted by its own doctrinal and logical failures:

1. House and Ice have in practice resorted at points to false standards for judging the theological acceptability of Reconstructionism, betraying a commitment to *sola Scriptura*.

2. Beyond that, a large portion of their book resorts to venomous speculation ("potential dangers") and notorious logical fallacies in trying to discredit their opponents — inconsistencies, short-sightedness, guilt by association, irrelevant personal chiding, etc.

3. In evangelical scholars, these kind of failures in theological reasoning are disappointing.

4. If House and Ice fell into one such line of fallacious reasoning, it would not commend their book. But because they repeatedly fall into these fallacious lines of thought, their polemic against Reconstructionism has lost its credibility and value.

5

THE FAILURE OF ACCURATE PORTRAYAL

A survey of ways in which House and Ice mislead their readers by misrepresenting Reconstructionism.

Before moving on to the only relevant question in the dispensationalist dispute with Reconstructionism — the question of Biblical credentials — we must pause briefly to register a complaint against the way in which House and Ice deprive their readers of a clear picture of Reconstructionist aims and beliefs. Because they are so often off target in describing Reconstructionism as a position, one can have little confidence in their personal commentary or critique.

This objection does not arise from any party spirit or defensiveness about Reconstructionism. It is merely the application of a generally recognized standard of scholarly integrity. No book is worth publishing which contains repeated failures to portray accurately what it is discussing. No book can be taken seriously which has not been adequately researched. No book can be deemed a relevant critique of another position when the object under review is regularly misrepresented or examined only in its weakest formulations. For these reasons *Dominion Theology* is, simply from the standpoint of scholarship, nearly pointless. It may work as propaganda or diatribe, but it fails as analytical reflection and assessment. Let me use a variety of different kinds of illustrations from the book.

Incoherent Description

It is expected that a reviewer, taking all of the available evidence into account and reading statements in the best light, will portray a position as consistently and faithfully as possible. It simply misleads the reader, while providing no basis for criticism, when the reviewer cannot get straight on what he says about the position — and reads avoidable contradictions into *his own restatement* of the position. This is exactly what House and Ice do with theonomic ethics, though.

On the one hand they *summarize* theonomy's "central thesis" as advocating that the laws of Moses down to the last jot and tittle "should be applied directly to American life," wanting modern society to "adhere rigidly" to the Old Testament code.[1] Note the important adverbs "directly" and "rigidly." Theonomists are said to require the case laws "to be literally performed by Christians in this age."[2] Yet *on the other hand*, the authors *criticize* theonomy for getting into problems over "how literally case laws should be brought into the New Covenant era," for leaving unanswered questions in its "progressive recodification" of Old Testament laws[3] — questions about "how specific points of the Mosaic law should be transferred from the ancient Hebrew culture" — and for placing "pragmatism" over God's law by showing flexibility regarding such questions![4] The authors actually quote Bahnsen as saying that the particular cultural expression found in a case law is irrelevant to contemporary application of it.[5]

So which way is it? Does theonomy advocate *rigid, direct* application of Old Testament laws, or does it advocate *flexible, progressive* recodification of them? It is not hard to tell from a reasonable reading of Reconstructionist literature, but House and Ice have given a pejorative formulation of the position, reading an unnecessary incoherence into it. Their early characterization of rigid, direct application of every detail of the Old Testament is misrepresentation having nothing but emotive value for the critic (but no

---

1. H. Wayne House and Thomas Ice, *Dominion Theology: Blessing or Curse?* (Portland, OR: Multnomah, 1988), pp. 15, 20.
2. *Ibid.*, p. 37.
3. *Ibid.*, p. 39.
4. *Ibid.*, p. 76.
5. *Ibid.*, p. 98.

truth value for the reader).[6]

Thus when House and Ice later suggest that what Reconstructionists want to do is "to codify the Mosaic law as the law of the land,"[7] they are badly misleading their readers and wasting time by setting up a straw man to knock down (as they should realize from what they say elsewhere). The law as "codified" in a modern country will apply the same moral principles as are revealed in the codified law delivered through Moses, but the codes will not read exactly the same way. See Chapter 3 above.

Unrepresentative Selection

House and Ice further mislead their readers when they portray some particular opinion as being "the Reconstructionist view" on a given subject — when in fact there are honest *differences* between Reconstructionist writers on that subject which are not duly noticed by the authors or pointed out to the reader.[8] This happens repeat-

---

6. Another example of House and Ice not working to understand clearly and describe correctly the thinking of their opponents is found on page 99. They cite as theonomic a suggestion for justifying the immutability of "special imperatives" such as the particular command for Abraham to sacrifice Isaac, and then quickly dismiss it with a shallow, disparaging question. (How would Abraham know "when those identical conditions recurred?" Obvious answer: when God told him.) The inadequate and poor scholarship here is conspicuous. What House and Ice have cited is not a suggestion by a theonomist, but rather a proposal made by a critic of theonomy, imagining what a theonomist might say. Further, House and Ice footnote this critic's article, but make absolutely no reference to (or show any awareness of) Bahnsen's rebuttal of that article in the very same journal! Readers can consult it for themselves: "Should We Uphold Unchanging Moral Absolutes?" (*Journal of the Evangelical Theological Society* [September, 1985], pp. 309-15).

7. House and Ice, *Dominion Theology*, p. 133.

8. This problem stems from the mistaken notion that there is something in the world corresponding to terminology about the Reconstructionist "movement" (e.g., *ibid.*, pp. 16, 17, 359). Such a term is simply inappropriate (and makes Reconstructionism seem more ominous than it really is). There is no organizing, planning, agreed upon agenda, internal regimenting, central authority structure, commonly accepted leader(s), community of method, uniformity of application, etc. among those considered Reconstructionists. In short, none of the characteristics of a "movement" are present, and some of the very opposite traits are more than obvious — conflicting priorities, different interests, divergent set-

edly in *Dominion Theology.*

The authors make it a theonomic distinctive that non-Christians "must be excluded from a government" or from "citizenship,"[9] when in fact there are a variety of views on that question held by leading theonomists. Reconstructionism is portrayed as precluding constitutional monarchy;[10] in actuality, various theonomists hold differing opinions on that question. Not all theonomists would "outlaw" thirty-year mortgages or put "tight limitations on debt,"[11] but you get the very opposite impression from reading House and Ice. Nor do all theonomists expect every social sphere to "have its own court system."[12] House and Ice state as fact that theonomists take the family as the "first governing institution";[13] however, there is debate among some Reconstructionists as to what this means and whether it is true. It is said categorically that the Reconstructionist view calls for the Church to turn over to the

---

tings, disagreements over application, debates about method, personal disunity.

"Reconstructionism" does not represent a movement, but a set of fundamental theological convictions of a distinctive yet general nature, and held by an unorganized group of individual Christians — held in differing ways, for differing reasons, and with differing ramifications. To properly deal with generic Reconstructionism, then, instead of with a particular author or two, House and Ice should have limited themselves to the commonly accepted, underlying theological distinctives of those called "Reconstructionists" (things like eschatological optimism, the normativity of the whole Bible, etc.). They have confused themselves and their readers by repeatedly shifting between species and genus. Even though they are aware of strong disagreements between different Reconstructionists (e.g., my critique of Sutton's alleged covenantal model, pp. 347-48, or the Tyler departure from theonomy, p. 364), they continue to survey, speak of, and treat "Reconstructionism" like a monolith. They also muddy the picture by including in the Reconstructionist circle someone like James Jordan who no longer identifies himself as being a Reconstructionist. Because of Jordan's departure from standard Reformed hermeneutics (the historical, grammatical, Biblico-theological method) for the eccentric and imaginative approach of "interpretive maximalism," other Reconstructionists would be hesitant to acknowledge him as adhering to the underlying, crucial convictions of Reconstructionism any longer.

9. House and Ice, *Dominion Theology*, pp. 71, 74.
10. *Ibid.*, pp. 74-75.
11. *Ibid.*, pp. 76-77.
12. *Ibid.*, p. 69.
13. *Ibid.*, p. 71.

state unrepentant sinners who are civil offenders,[14] when in fact theonomists continue to debate whether and when that might be true.

Choosing the Weaker Version

By now the reader can get the point: *The way* in which House and Ice portray Reconstructionism is neither well thought out, adequately researched, nor reliable. To make their misleading representations even worse, however, the authors sometimes — in full knowledge of scholarly and theological disagreement among Reconstructionists — choose the weaker or more easily faulted opinion to illustrate Reconstructionism to their readers. This is irresponsible, cheap scholarship.[15] If you are going to do a worthwhile job in criticizing a school of thought, you must choose the best formulations and least controversial versions of it so that you are accurate and your criticisms go to the heart of the matter. House and Ice take the low road here. For instance, although they acknowledge in these cases that theonomists hold contrary opinions (House and Ice thus admit that they are not dealing with the generic position, anyway), the authors choose to report and focus upon Rushdoony's idiosyncratic view of the continuing validity of the laws regarding diet and mixed-fibre clothing, and on North's endorsement of stoning as the method of capital punishment even today.[16] It is hard to find other theonomists who agree with Rushdoony on this point (although that does not make him wrong),

---

14. *Ibid.*, p. 72.

15. Remember, since they made the choice to deal with generic Reconstructionism — as though it were a "movement" — rather than dealing with particular writers, each on his own, House and Ice ought to stick to the central, agreed upon convictions of recognized Reconstructionist scholars. When they (ill-advisedly) depart from that operating procedure, reporting instead on a position peculiar to some writer(s) over against others, they are responsible to select that position which shows the generic school of thought at its best. The generic dispensationalist position would be a sitting duck for pejorative presentation, having someone choose to introduce and illustrate "dispensationalism" by pointing to the more controversial ideas of its crank advocates!

16. House and Ice, *Dominion Theology*, pp. 39, 73-74.

and it is easy to find other theonomists who can present cogent counter-arguments to North (although his position might be right).

Distortion by Tailored Expression

Another variety of misrepresentation employed by House and Ice is to put a *slant* on their account of Reconstructionist beliefs which edits out the true intent or meaning of those beliefs. This is conspicuous when they assert that "theonomists center God's commands for today on Old Testament law."[17] Incredibly, the authors attempt in their very next sentence to substantiate this charge of Old-Testament-preoccupation by quoting a Rushdoony statement which does not even mention the Old Testament as such! ("Thus, Rushdoony flatly states that '. . . the law is the way of sanctification.'") The authors are so obsessed with their preconceived criticism of theonomists that they read it into theonomist statements without the slightest textual warrant. Such overbearing bias is not flattering, especially when the authors elsewhere contradict (and refute) their own charge that theonomists narrowly stress the Old Testament! Contrary to the impression they try to communicate to their readers by comments and expressions used elsewhere, they quote Rushdoony: "The Biblical concept of law is broader than the legal codes of the Mosaic formulation. It applies to the divine word and instruction in its totality."[18] An honest report would be that theonomists teach that we are to follow the moral norms revealed by God throughout the Bible, "*including*" those found in the Old Testament (cf. 2 Tim. 3:16-17) — but House and Ice turn this into an obsessive "*centering on*" the Old Testament. Such twisting of what theonomists mean borders on deceit. Notice how they do it again. Theonomists uphold the justice of God found in the Old *and* New Testaments (in fact, maintaining that the Old must be interpreted in light of the New). But listen to how House and Ice put it. "The Reconstructionists believe that the Law of God, or Biblical Law, as codified in the Old

---

17. *Ibid.*, p. 29.
18. *Ibid.*, p. 35.

Testament should be instituted as the law of the United States and every nation on earth."[19] They say that theonomists pursue a civil government which is "under biblical (mainly Mosaic) law,"[20] a "minister of God's Old Testament justice";[21] "theonomists define standards of good and evil in term of the Old Testament law."[22] The false slant is given in these remarks by inserting the qualifier "Old Testament" (which is really unnecessary to the truth of the statements), thereby purposely *editing out* the theonomist commitment to the controlling authority of the New Testament.

The misconstruing of theonomy as fixation upon the Mosaic law is made explicit by House and Ice: "The basic contention of theonomy"—note how this is made *the* foundational point for everything else—"is that God's covenant has been expressed as a full social program only in the revelation to Moses."[23] "*Only*"! This is outrageous and inexcusable. God's "full" social program must be found and properly interpreted in the entire Bible, from cover to cover; no theonomist would say otherwise.[24]

House and Ice misrepresent Reconstructionism by tailored (truncated) reporting of its beliefs elsewhere as well. On the very first page of Chapter 1 in their book, they portray the concern of the early Puritans and later Reconstructionists for the kingdom of God as *reduced* to a concern for a "civil code."[25] Listen to them again on the same page, misleading their readers by describing Reconstructionists as those "who believe that only"—only—"through the establishment and enforcement of Old Testament"—Old Tes-

---

19. *Ibid.*, p. 27.
20. *Ibid.*, p. 65.
21. *Ibid.*, p. 29.
22. *Ibid.*, p. 30.
23. *Ibid.*, p. 32.
24. "Why do they, then, so often argue for the validity of the Mosaic law?" Because it is so often openly denied by people in our day and age. "Why do they give so much attention to the Mosaic law?" Because there is so much there from which to learn. In defending and interpreting the Mosaic law theonomists never deny the validity, necessity and importance of the New Testament, nor do they ignore (at least purposely) the content of any other part of Scripture, especially the New Testament.
25. House and Ice, *Dominion Theology*, p. 15.

tament — "civil law can . . . the world be saved from destruction."
Later they assert: "The means which theonomists advocate for exercising dominion and fulfilling the covenant is to institute the
civil laws given to Moses"[26] — note: *"the* means" (suggesting "the
only" or "the most important" means).[27] If House and Ice are this
desperate to *create* some appearance of heresy, their critique of
Reconstructionism is a shameful waste of time.

False Characterization or Inference

On top of the various kinds of misrepresentation employed by
House and Ice which have been surveyed above, we can add a list
of downright errors: statements about Reconstructionist (theonomic) ethics which are simply false.

• Reconstructionists do not believe that God's pre-fall covenant
with man "finds its paramount expression in the Mosaic law."[28]
Indeed, the Mosaic law is not even the paramount expression of
the *post*-fall covenant. Moreover, the Mosaic law dealt with matters which "from the beginning had not been so" (Matt. 19:8).
Thus the claim by House and Ice is not only mistaken, it is also
muddled.

• Reconstructionists do *not* seek "to make a modern Israel in
America," though that is the false and misleading impression that
House and Ice want to leave with their readers on page 100.

• Theonomic thought does *not* endorse, encourage or argue
for "interpreting the New Testament strictly in light of the older
revelation."[29] As amply illustrated in Chapter 3, theonomy calls

---

26. *Ibid.*, p. 32.
27. On page 28 of House and Ice, *Dominion Theology*, we read, "Theonomists
present law-keeping to be imperative in two widely encompassing areas. These
are Christian living and civil government." Do they mean to suggest "in only two
areas"? Why did they not report that theonomists find obedience to God's word
imperative in every area: family, economics, schooling, medicine, the arts, industry, science, etc. The implication by House and Ice that theonomists hold
some special or heightened imperative for obedience in civil government is misleading.
28. House and Ice, *Dominion Theology*, p. 30.
29. *Ibid.*, p. 30.

for the very opposite of what House and Ice charge here — calls for interpreting the Old Testament according to the New. The whole Old Testament must be seen and interpreted in light of Christ (Luke 24:27; John 5:39; 2 Cor. 1:20), who is the climax of God's revelation of Himself (Heb. 1:1-2).

Ironically, it is precisely dispensational theology which extracts an interpretation from Old Testament passages in isolation and then clings to them despite the different interpretation (and different way of interpreting them) found in the New Testament![30]

This procedure elicits the following comment by Hughes:

> But we fear that the dispensationalist method of interpretation does violence to the unity of Scripture and to the sovereign continuity of God's purposes, and cavalierly leaves out of account a major portion of the apostolic teaching — that, chiefly, of the Acts and the Epistles — as unrelated to the perspective of the Old Testament authors [due to seeing the kingdom as postponed and the Church as a parenthesis in God's plan].[31]

What we see here parallels the dispensationalist disruption of the *unity* of Scripture with respect to God's law and the dispensationalist resistance to the *continuity* of God's moral purposes.

• Furthermore, "every jot and tittle" is *not*, as claimed by House and Ice, "Bahnsen's phrase" — but rather that of our Lord Jesus Christ Himself (Matt. 5:18).

• Theonomic ethics does not maintain that Old Testament

---

30. For an instructive example, notice how dispensationalist interpreters struggle with Peter's appeal to Joel 2:28 in his Pentecost address (Acts 2:16-21). Contrary to Peter's interpretation — viz., that Pentecost fulfilled Joel's prophecy ("this was that which was spoken through the prophet Joel") — dispensationalists insist on holding to their own interpretation of Joel in isolation from the control of the New Testament. They still insist that Joel was "literally" referring to ushering in the as-yet-future earthly millennium (for many of the things mentioned by Joel and repeated by Peter "obviously" did not occur on Pentecost). Peter thus only meant that pentecost was a "foreshadowing" of the millennium (Paul Lee Tan, *The Interpretation of Prophecy* [Winona Lake, IN: BMH Books, 1974], pp. 183-85).

31. Philip Edgcumbe Hughes, *Interpreting Prophecy* (Grand Rapids, MI: Wm. B. Eerdmans, 1976), p. 104.

law stands "until explicitly abrogated."[32] Many of the things which
theonomists believe have been laid aside on the authority of the
New Testament (e.g., breakdown of levitical orders and duties,
prohibition of mixed-fiber clothing, the levirate institution) are
not "explicitly" abrogated in the New Testament, but rather dis-
continued on the basis of what is inferred by other statements.[33]

● It is a complete *reversal* of the truth to allege that theonomists
maintain "that Israel was not, in any unique way, a theocracy."[34]
In reply to the same kind of incredible misrepresentation made by
M. G. Kline, Bahnsen pointed to over fifty places in *Theonomy*
where the unique status and history of Israel were mentioned and
acknowledged, going on to say:

> In conclusion, it must be clear by now that *Theonomy* never said
> or even implied what Kline attributes to it. I do not deny, but
> gladly affirm, the typological value of Israel's king and political
> laws, nor do I overlook the distinction between Israel as a holy
> nation and the other political entities as common nations.[35]

Kline's misrepresentation and its easy refutation were also explicitly
mentioned in the preface to the expanded version of *Theonomy*.
Furthermore, Bahnsen was unmistakably clear in *By This Standard*:

> The magistrate in Old Testament Israel was in various ways
> unique. . . .

---

32. House and Ice, *Dominion Theology*, p. 36.

33. Admittedly, this might disturb our authors since they disparage the use of
"inference" in theology, but that betrays a poor understanding of the nature of inference, as well as of its necessity in doing theology (e.g., the doctrines of the
Trinity or the hypostatic union). House and Ice only fool themselves if they think
that dispensationalism really evades the use of inferences from Scripture! The
Westminster Confession correctly teaches that "the whole counsel of God, concerning all things necessary for his own glory, man's salvation, faith, and life, is
either expressly set down in scripture, *or by good and necessary consequence may be
deduced* from scripture" (I.6, emphasis mine). Of course, not all alleged deduc-
tions are in fact good and necessary.

34. House and Ice, *Dominion Theology*, p. 100; cf. pp. 341-42 where Kline is
cited.

35. "M. G. Kline on Theonomic Politics: An Evaluation of His Reply," *Journal
of Christian Reconstruction* (Winter, 1979-80), p. 209.

Of course there were many unique aspects to the situation enjoyed by the Old Testament Israelites. . . .

The redemptive history and national covenant enjoyed by Israel certainly set the Old Testament Jews apart from modern nations as significantly unique.[36]

How, in the face of such open, clear and repeated statements by theonomists of the "unique" character of Israel, can House and Ice rationalize their bald statement to the very opposite? How can they be taken seriously when they apparently do not understand what they are criticizing? It is simply culpable to tell readers that your opponents believe the very *opposite* of what they actually say — and say often.[37]

Theonomy and the Civil Magistrate

• Theonomic ethics does *not* call for every magistrate to "institute the entirety of God's law."[38] That would be a horrifying abuse of political authority, turning every sin (e.g., lust, laziness, discourtesy, coveting, backbiting, impatience) into *civil* crimes! No theonomist endorses such overwhelming authority for the state — and authors House and Ice very well *know* this since they themselves elsewhere quote Bahnsen as teaching "It would be vain for [the civil magistrate] to assume the prerogative of judging and punishing any and all sins"![39] How can they justify this blatant contradiction in their description of what theonomists believe? The truth is that theonomic ethics holds that civil magistrates may enforce only those provisions of God's law which authorize penal sanctions against narrowly defined kinds of outward misbehavior.[40] God's law sets an objective limit upon the magistrate beyond

---

36. Bahnsen, *By This Standard: The Authority of God's Law Today* (Tyler, TX: Institute for Christian Economics, 1986), pp. 223, 288, 324.

37. Note can be made of the analysis of different ways in which theologians use the word "theocracy" in *Theonomy*, pp. 427-32. In the glossary to *By This Standard*, Bahnsen notes that some people use "theocracy" as "a code word for the uniqueness of Old Testament Israel," whatever that is taken to be.

38. House and Ice, *Dominion Theology*, p. 30.

39. *Ibid.*, pp. 91-92.

40. See Bahnsen's discussion of the theonomic limitation upon political power in *God and Politics: Four Views on the Reformation of Civil Government*, ed. Gary Scott Smith (Phillipsburg, NJ: Presbyterian and Reformed, 1989).

which he may not go, whereas other schools of thought have no way of arguing against the state growing into a "beast" that "lawlessly" claims every area of life as its jurisdiction (cf. 2 Thess. 2:3, 7; Rev. 13:15-17).

• Theonomy most assuredly does not endorse capital punishment for rebellious "adolescents."[41] The Old Testament law—which Jesus explicitly upheld (Matt. 15:3-6)—dealt with an individual old enough to be a drunkard who can beat up his father (Exodus 21:15; Deut. 21:18-21). Nor do theonomists believe that the death penalty should be imposed by the civil magistrate for "apostasy."[42] *Neither* does theonomic ethics hold that in the later days of gospel prosperity (what House and Ice call "the final state of global conquest") some who are now deemed heretics will be "reclassified from targets for conversion to targets for prison."[43] As footnoted above, the law of God does not authorize civil magistrates to judge or punish either *heresy* or the spiritual condition of a person's heart (not in the past, much less now or later).

• Reconstructionists do not in practice need a "fusion of church and state"[44] or "require the state to be . . . intermingled with the church"[45]—becoming "merely an extension of . . . the visible church"[46]—by expecting the state to punish heresy or to "punish what the church condemns."[47] This is groundless nonsense since theonomists do not believe the state has the right or duty to punish heresy in the first place. Nor would theonomists require the officials of the state automatically to submit and kowtow

---

41. House and Ice, *Dominion Theology*, p. 16.

42. *Ibid.*, pp. 40, 73, 78.

43. *Ibid.*, p. 65.

44. *Ibid.*, p. 95.

45. *Ibid.*, p. 339.

46. *Ibid.*, p. 93.

47. *Ibid.* House and Ice are so blinded by this false and groundless projection of how a theonomic state would operate that they find it "astounding" that a theonomist has no problem whatsoever with the 1788 revision of the Westminster Confession which clearly removed any hint of state interference in ecclesiastical matters (p. 97)—but it is true (notice that the authors offer no refutation or pointed interaction whatsoever with the detailed analysis and argumentation regarding this issue in Bahnsen, *Theonomy in Christian Ethics*, pp. 526-37, 541-43).

to the preaching of the institutional Church on *any* issue (even those pertaining to its legitimate duties), rather than being ultimately responsible to interpret God's revelation for themselves and act in accordance with their consciences before God. House and Ice try to twist theonomy into a version of *ecclesiocracy* (even though they indicate elsewhere that they should know better).[48]

• Furthermore, Reconstructionist ethics does *not* propose "the elimination" of political pluralism,[49] does not seek "to abolish" pluralism for some "monolithic form of government,"[50] and does not believe "democratic societies are considered contrary to the enforcement of biblical law."[51] Reconstructionists have been badly misrepresented here. They enthusiastically champion democratic procedures within the state (e.g., open debate, competing parties, free elections). And they would not abolish pluralism as such, but simply seek the redefinition of its limits. *Everyone* places *some* limit upon the plurality of politically acceptable options. Even House and Ice would not say child molestation must be tolerated when practiced in subservience to a satanic religion. Theonomists wish to define those limits according to Scriptural teaching, while others use other ethical standards to set the limits. The question here, as always, is what should be the source of our ethical authority and direction, in politics and every other area.

• In their view of expected, eventual social transformation, Reconstructionists do *not* "become Arminian in the view of man" by stressing "what the unregenerate man can do" or forgetting "man's depravity."[52] They rather maintain the sovereignty *of God*

---

48. *Ibid.*, p. 71.
49. *Ibid.*, p. 16.
50. *Ibid.*, p. 133.
51. *Ibid.*, p. 131. The comment about "democracy" is particularly remiss, not only because the word is susceptible to numerous different meanings, but because the authors themselves go on to recognize the particular sense in which it is being used and to "concur" with Rushdoony's criticism of "democracy," understood as the idea that there is no absolute moral standard except the whim of the people (pp. 132-33)! Why, then, the implied criticism of Reconstructionism for being contrary to the very thing House and Ice also repudiate ("democracy" in this stipulated sense)?
52. *Ibid.*, pp. 337, 351.

(as consistent Calvinists): "Is anything too hard for Jehovah?" (Gen. 18:14). And talk of trusting *un*regenerate man's ability is utter misrepresentation. Reconstructionists hope for social reform precisely because they expect God's sovereignty to bring widespread revival — making many men regenerate. Moreover, those who will be agents of social transformation according to the Reconstructionist outlook will *not* be the unregenerate, but the regenerate!

Van Til and Christian Reconstruction
   • Reconstructionism is not at all "incompatible" with the apologetics of Cornelius Van Til.[53] Van Til constantly taught that both the Christian and non-Christian ultimate principles were "imperious," seeking to expand their authority into all areas. He taught that "the covenant idea" is not properly maintained in theology unless its application is "all inclusive," so that we do *all* things to the glory of God (not simply in worship). "In all of men's activities . . . men are either covenant keepers or covenant breakers."[54] He taught that man's thinking ought to be "receptively Reconstructive," interpreting all things in light of God's revelation.[55] So: "The Bible sheds its indispensable light on everything we as Christians study." Christians should interpret everything "self-consciously as an act of re-interpretation of God's revelation."[56] Accordingly Van Til declared: "Failing to make [this] clear . . . leads to a serious weakening of the Christian testimony. A typical example of such a weakening of the Christian testimony is found in Lewis Sperry Chafer's *Systematic Theology*."[57] It is ridiculous, then, for House and Ice, later followers of the dispensationalist Chafer, to pretend to be "more consistent with" Van Til's approach[58] and to be the champions of Van Til against advocates of the covenant idea who desire an all-inclusive Reconstruction of

---

53. *Ibid.*, pp. 340-44.
54. See Chapter 2, "The Christian Philosophy of Life," in Van Til's unpublished classroom syllabus, *Apologetics* ([1935] 1966), p. 26.
55. See *The Defense of the Faith* (Philadelphia PA: Presbyterian and Reformed, 1955), pp. 65-66.
56. See Van Til's syllabus, "An Introduction to Systematic Theology" ([1937, rev. 1947] 1966), p. 15.
57. *Ibid.*
58. *Ibid.*, p. 342.

life in terms of God's revelation.[59]

• The *way* in which House and Ice try to set Van Til's "apologetics at odds with the postmillennial spirit"[60] is equally fraudulent.[61] In attempting to give an appearance of discrepancy, the authors resort to attributing things to Reconstructionism which are utterly false, thereby doing nothing more than tripping over *themselves*. Postmillennialism does *not*, as House and Ice assert, involve "improper synthesis with the world"[62] or require us to do anything like "intermingle with non-Christian systems."[63] That surely would be contrary to Van Til's emphasis upon antithesis. But the remarks are utterly baseless — just as baseless as the claim that "Van Til believed that orthodox Christians are to separate from . . . world systems, institutions, and, to some extent, society itself."[64] *Where* is Van Til supposed to have said such an isolationist thing? *Where* does Reconstructionism "intermingle its Christianity with non-Christian thinking" or "mix the holy with the common"?[65]

---

59. Van Til commended and approved of the theonomic lectures delivered by Bahnsen at Westminster Seminary in March of 1980, and later Van Til wrote these words about Bahnsen's extensive tape series giving a postmillennial interpretation of the book of Revelation: "I have greatly profited spiritually and my knowledge of Scripture expanded by the hearing of the lectures on 'Revelation' by Greg Bahnsen. . . . These tapes will be a comfort to all those that hear them" (Supplement Catalog of Mt. Olive Tape Library, p. 3). Apparently he did not see or have concerns about any fundamental incompatibility.

60. House and Ice, *Dominion Theology*, p. 340.

61. It should be added that, in my (Bahnsen's) evaluation, Gary North's attempt to set Van Til's view of common grace at odds with postmillennialism (*Dominion and Common Grace* [Tyler, TX: Institute for Christian Economics], 1987) is also misconstrued, but this is not the place for a detailed analysis and critique of that book also. (North's own words are that Van Til "builds his whole theory of common grace in terms of his hidden eschatology [an undeclared amillennialism], probably never realizing" that this was the case [*ibid.*, p. 15]. North's examination is a drawn-out verbal dispute over talk about God's "favor" and "earlier grace.") The important thing to observe here, though, is that the criticism of one aspect of Van Til's writings by one Reconstructionist cannot cogently be turned into Van Til expressing by his apologetical system wholescale incompatibility with postmillennialism.

62. House and Ice, *Dominion Theology*, pp. 342, 344.

63. *Ibid.*, p. 340.

64. *Ibid.*, p. 344.

65. *Ibid.*, p. 341.

House and Ice have taken to propagating pure fabrications. Does this sound anything like synthesis with the world?

> It should be rather clear, therefore, that genuine Christian ethics must not align itself with the autonomous methodology and systems of unbelieving philosophy. The Christian should never attempt to find out principles of morality outside of God's revelation and direction. . . . It is all or nothing, ethic or non-ethic, obedience or sin.[66]

> For the Christian, this [Mosaic laws of separation] now requires separation from any ungodliness or compromising unbelief anywhere they may be found (2 Cor. 6:14-18).[67]

I am afraid that House and Ice arrived at their distortions of Reconstructionism here by falling into the all too common mistake of equivocating on the word "world"—confusing the general *place* where we find people, houses, schools, businesses, capitols, etc. (e.g., 1 Cor. 5:10) with the specific *spiritual* attitude, arena and populace which rebels against God (e.g., 1 John 2:16; 5:19; James 4:4).[68] Hear our Lord: "I pray not that You should take them out of the world. . . . They are not of the world. . . . As You did send Me into the world, even so I sent them into the world" (John 17:15-18). Jesus likewise prayed regarding this "unworldly" mis-

---

66. Bahnsen, *Theonomy in Christian Ethics*, pp. 305-6.
67. Bahnsen, *By This Standard*, p. 166.
68. This same kind of error (though not using the word "world") is especially evident on page 390, where House and Ice condemn the postmillennialist expectation of major "revival" in history and active "kingdom" work before Christ's return. According to them: "Reconstructionists will influence a large segment of the church to set its mind on the things that are on the earth and not on things above (Colossians 3:2)." But this entails a tremendous misreading of Paul, as though he were calling us to renounce life and involvement in things "on the earth" in favor of complete "otherworldliness"—contrary to his other injunctions (3:18-4:1). "Things above" represents Christ as the ascended Lord over all (see v. 1 for context). We "set our minds" on Him rather than any earthly authority because we are spiritually united to Him (vv. 3-4). Now whatever thoughts we have (2:3, 8) and whatever work we do (3:23) are controlled, not by anything of this creation, but by Christ reigning from God's right hand. And His Lordship gives Him "preeminence in all things"—"whether things upon the earth or things in the heavens" (1:18, 20).

sion "into the world" (in contrast to "otherworldliness") that we would be "sanctified" — set apart (antithesis) — by the truth (v. 17).

Civil Law and the Kingdom of God

• Theonomy does not hold that adopting the Old Testament *civil* code would "thereby" create a model of "the kingdom of God on earth,"[69] Greg Bahnsen does *not* describe the "world" in its political ordering (republics, etc.) as " 'the Kingdom of God, an international community of faith,' which 'comes . . . through evangelistic preaching.' "[70] It is God's kingdom, not the geopolitical world, that Bahnsen describes in that way.[71] Indeed, on the very page from which House and Ice quote, Bahnsen goes on to say that members of God's *kingdom* will want to obey God in the areas of "home, church, and even state," thus making it all the more obvious that he distinguishes the kingdom of God from the political order itself where (like home and Church) the *effects* of God's reign are experienced.

There are a number of other errors we could highlight, but we must conclude.[72]

---

69. House and Ice, *Dominion Theology*, p. 15.

70. *Ibid.*, pp. 65-66.

71. To see how badly the authors skew things, the reader is encouraged to check their portrayal of what Bahnsen is saying with the actual quotation (*Theonomy in Christian Ethics*, p. xx) — which ironically appears on a page with the subheading "Misrepresentations by Critics."

72. A further indication of negligent scholarship is found at a number of places in *Dominion Theology* which, to be sure, do not bear on the theological issues which separate Reconstructionists and dispensationalists; they do illustrate again carelessness with the facts, however. Gary DeMar is not head of "the Institute of Christian Government in Atlanta" (p. 21), nor does an institution with that name even exist there. Greg Bahnsen is (and was) not "dean of the graduate school of a local teacher's college" (p. 20). He was not "forced to resign from Reformed Seminary's faculty because of his book" (p. 27), nor was he "dismissed . . . because of propagation of his theonomy views" (pp. 20, 443) — which are conflicting stories, anyway. Further, he has never lectured for Joe Kickasola "at CBN University" (p. 383). And it is utterly apocryphal that he "read some of Rushdoony's works as a boy" (p. 19). Where do the authors get this stuff? (An elder in Bahnsen's church corrected a page proof for the book before House and Ice falsely published that Bahnsen is married to a daughter of Rushdoony!) North's doctorate is not "in economics" (p. 18), but history. His split with Rushdoony was not over an article he "wanted to publish in *The Journal of Christian*

Summary

1. Carefulness and accuracy of portrayal are incumbent upon those who would seek to critique any system of thought.

2. The large number, and especially extreme character, of House and Ice's reports about the alleged teachings of Reconstructionist ethics are more than sufficient to impeach House and Ice as critics of the position.

3. Though House and Ice say, "it is absolutely critical to eliminate any margin for misunderstanding,"[73] they have turned around and *widened* that margin by miles.

4. House and Ice have created a credibility gap regarding their role as reviewers. One can hardly avoid becoming disenchanted with their scholarship.

5. The authors of *Dominion Theology* are either unable or unwilling to portray Reconstructionism fairly. In Christian charity, I do not know which is the least severe conclusion to draw here.

Reconstruction" (pp. 18-19), but in the "Chalcedon Report." In 1965 Rushdoony did not establish the Chalcedon Foundation "in Vallecito, California" (p. 18), but in Canoga Park (hundreds of miles away). One or two of these factual bloopers would be embarrassing enough. One after another destroys credibility.

73. House and Ice, *Dominion Theology*, p. 35.

6

THE THEOLOGICAL CONCEPT OF LAW

A reply to House and Ice regarding God's character and its bearing on the concept of moral law.

Ice speculates that "most" people who are Reconstructionists are attracted by its commitment to transforming the world, "rather than [coming to the position] through the front door of biblical study."[1] That certainly was not true for me. Even though, at the time, I had some personal doubts about the gospel's influence and victory in the world (postmillennialism), it was continuing, detailed study of Scripture — biblical exegesis — which drove me to theonomic conclusions in ethics.[2] To use Ice's words, I came to this conviction "through the front door." That is why I have always welcomed fellow Christians examining and questioning theonomy from a biblical standpoint, but have never been very much swayed by the extra-Scriptural criticisms which are usually urged against the position.

In replying to *Dominion Theology* by House and Ice, then, the most important thing I can do is to offer a response to their cri-

---

1. H. Wayne House and Thomas Ice, *Dominion Theology: Blessing or Curse?* (Portland, OR: Multnomah, 1988), p. 10. A proclivity for fallacious and groundless argumentation is illustrated here again. By psychologizing their opponents and imputing improper motives for coming to beliefs which do not agree with those of House and Ice, the authors speak uncharitably and with absolutely no objective justification for their accusation.

2. In time it also drove me, of course, to adopt a postmillennial eschatology and to do detailed work as a theological teacher in that area. An extensive study of the book of Revelation, other key texts about the future of God's kingdom, and theological analysis and discussions of the millennial question are available from Covenant Tape Ministry, 24198 Ash Court, Auburn, CA 95603 (catalogues available).

tique where it attempts to argue on a biblical basis. As we saw in
Chapter 4, they have not always challenged theonomic ethics
from that standpoint, and their reasoning has too often taken a
fallacious or mistaken direction. And as we saw in Chapter 5,
House and Ice have extensively misrepresented what the Reconstructionist position in ethics really is. (I have summarized the
theonomic approach to ethics and its treatment of the validity of
Old Testament law in Chapter 3 above, offering extensive Biblical
substantiation for the major premises advanced.) However, when
critics House and Ice charge that Reconstructionist ethics is not
biblical (or that dispensationalist ethics is), they deserve to be
heard and answered. Speaking of Reconstructionists, House and
Ice boldly assert: "A proper exegesis of God's Word will not produce their most basic ideas."[3] Has their book demonstrated that
conclusion? I believe that sober analysis of their argumentation
constrains a negative answer.

The Unchanging Character of God

In Chapter 5 of *Dominion Theology* House and Ice begin their
attempted rebuttal of the theonomic position on ethics by addressing
the theonomic argument from God's unchanging moral character.
It is hard to tell what, if any, rebuttal is actually offered, though.

We may cogently derive the basic *presumption* of *continuity* of
God's moral demands in all ages and for all people from the biblical
truths that: Those demands reflect His character, and His character is immutable.[4] House and Ice are willing to grant the legitimacy of such theological reasoning:

> Tying the law to the nature of God is an important emphasis of
> theonomy and one we readily accept. . . . It is agreed, as men-
> tioned, that God's character never changes, and his law for man

---

3. House and Ice, *Dominion Theology*, p. 335.
4. Cf. Greg L. Bahnsen, *Theonomy in Christian Ethics* (ex. ed.; Phillipsburg,
NJ: Presbyterian and Reformed, [1977] 1984), Chapter 5; *By This Standard: The
Authority of God's Law Today* (Tyler, TX: Institute for Christian Economics, 1985),
Chapter 6. House and Ice give their summary on pp. 32-33.

at any time flows from his perfect character. . . . Revealed law contains many instructions—both principles and specific directives—which remain the same despite changes in temporal factors such as time, place, dispensation, or immediate divine purpose. These are continuities.[5]

This continuity of moral character (in God and thus in His revealed moral principles) does not preclude different *expressions* or different *applications* of God's moral demands suited to the situation or culture which is addressed (e.g., self-giving love to my neighbor can be expressed in terms of the specific details of an overloaded donkey as well as someone mugged on the Jericho road: Exodus 23:5; Luke 10:30-37). Theonomists recognize this, as is evident in the detailed exposition found in Chapter 3 above. They also, as acknowledged by House and Ice,[6] teach that God's immutable character does not prevent "changes in God's instructions," where He so orders (e.g., the sacrificial cultus and temple: Heb. 9-10). Nor do theonomists deny that in terms of His immediate purposes, God the Lawgiver is free to make exceptions to His ordinary requirements (e.g., sparing Cain or David).[7]

House and Ice say that there have been "different manifestations" of God's moral character revealed to different groups in different ways, mentioning as examples: general revelation, the garden, divine visitations, communication with Abraham, and the Mosaic law.[8] Theonomists could say the same. They would also be able to endorse the statement that:

> Every revelation of God's law reflects his character, regardless of when it was given. Moreover, there is a basic consistency in God's law, with variations based only on cultural factors and God's purposes for mankind at the time the law is given.[9]

Given such agreement between our two authors and theonomists, what is the nature of their *objection* to theonomic reasoning

---

5. House and Ice, *Dominion Theology*, pp. 86, 87-88.
6. *Ibid.*, p. 88.
7. *Ibid.*, p. 89.
8. *Ibid.*, pp. 86-87.
9. *Ibid.*, p. 87.

from the unchanging moral character of God? It is not at all clear from what they have written, unless they are simply misconstruing (again) what theonomists actually teach. They declare: "The idea that the unchangeableness of God requires that the specific details of the Mosaic code be transferred to all times and cultures simply does not follow."[10] But of course, as these authors themselves acknowledge elsewhere (and is clear from Chapter 3 above), *theonomists do not* argue for transferring "the specific details" of the Mosaic code to all other cultures (e.g., the specific detail of rooftop railings is not relevant to much of modern American culture.) At a different point House and Ice declare: "The issue is . . . to which manifestation of his law are [Christians] to be obedient."[11] But as we have already seen, *theonomists do not* require that God's moral demand be approached *only* according to the "manifestation" (or form) of it found in the Mosaic code; all of its manifestations — in the garden, to Abraham, through the Proverbs and prophets, in the New Testament epistles, etc. — are all to be consulted by believers to learn the principles of holy living. "All scripture" is profitable for "instruction in righteousness" (2 Tim. 3:16-17), for all of the manifestations of God's word to men are expressions of His unchanging moral will and character.

When House and Ice imply that they are objecting to theonomic reasoning, then, it is very obscure just what they are arguing. The key may be found in the way they juxtapose the words "expression" and "provision" — as in the sentence: "The later Mosaic covenant became a more specific expression of many provisions of God's will observed in the patriarchal period."[12] Note well: "specific expression *of* many provisions." "Provision" will then denote the underlying moral demand (principle) of God, while "expression" will denote the manner of communication and degree of detail with which the provision is revealed at a particular time and place in history. Accordingly, "each expression of his law," they say, "is perfectly suited to the unique period and circumstances into

---

10. *Ibid.*, p. 87.
11. *Ibid.*, p. 86.
12. *Ibid.*, p. 87.

which he speaks it. . . . Scripture shows God revealing different expressions of the law appropriate for different times."[13]

We can add to this analysis the observation that House and Ice appear to state their disagreement with theonomic thinking by using the words that the Gentile nations "are not under the provisions of" the Mosaic manifestation of God's law.[14] It is in that sense they later speak of "varying laws [which] flow from God's eternal purposes."[15]

Bringing together all of the above, it would seem that what House and Ice are trying to say amounts to this claim:

> It does not follow from God's unchanging moral character that His moral demands — i.e., the "provisions" or principles which are given different, specific "expressions" at different times and places — are required in all ages and cultures.

On that interpretation, however, House and Ice have rather obviously contradicted themselves. The presumption of continuing and universal validity for the moral *provisions* (underlying demands, not specific cultural details) of God's law does indeed "follow" from their reflection of His essential and unchangeable character. They may be "expressed" in different ways, but God's moral requirements (e.g., self-giving love to one's neighbor) are the same everywhere.

---

13. *Ibid.*, p. 88.
14. *Ibid.*, p. 86.
15. *Ibid.*, p. 88. Actually, at this point House and Ice have slipped from one theological concept (God's essential "character") into a logically different one (God's "eternal purposes"). The second denotes God's good pleasure which is not constrained or necessary (and thus could have been otherwise), while the first denotes what is always and necessarily true of God. (It is conceivable that their inexact vacillating between different theological concepts contributes to the obscurity of their reasoning and ambiguity in what they are trying to say.) The prohibition of stealing stems from God's unchanging character (it is not an open question whether God would choose to condemn or to commend stealing), whereas the provision of atoning sacrifice stems from God's eternal purpose (necessity did not constrain, but God graciously chose it in His good pleasure). That is why God could purpose to change the way of atonement (Christ's cross fulfills the anticipatory animal sacrifices), but could not purpose to violate His character and now commend stealing to us.

The moral provisions or principles of God's law which are revealed to some particular individual or group (e.g., Noah, Abraham, Israel, etc.) are *not* different from the moral provisions of His law for anyone else, *unless* we have some *revealed basis* for thinking so in particular cases (e.g., Cain, the laws of sacrifice). Given God's character, our operating presumption about God's revealed will is moral continuity, and that *presumption* cannot logically be defeated *simply* by observing that some moral demand from God was revealed or addressed to group A *rather than* group B.

Removing Vagueness Regarding "Law"

What emerges from the preceding analysis is the observation that House and Ice are not conceptually clear on the multiform use of the word "law" in discussions of theological ethics. Since they have not adequately sorted out and systematized the various possible concepts marked by the word and its related terms (nor have taken account of the different intended meanings and the personal variation of linguistic expression from writer to writer), they end up being not very clear in their own thinking about "the law," nor do they have a basis from which to gain a clear or adequate understanding of what others are saying about it. This seems to explain the careless contradictions into which they fall (as above), as well as the unnecessary bewilderment they feel about alleged "vagueness" or "vacillation" or "potential contradiction" in what theonomists mean by their use of the term "law."[16]

It is rather commonplace for biblical scholars to point out the many different ways in which the Hebrew and Greek words for

---

16. E.g., House and Ice, *Dominion Theology*, pp. 34, 35, 36, 38, 39, 134. More self-induced confusion comes into the picture when House and Ice themselves inject contradictions right into their restatement of the theonomic position — alleging that it admits of a "few" legitimate New Testament revisions of the Old Testament law (p. 36), but then alleging that it "never" views the New Testament as abrogating Old Testament requirements (p. 38). Similarly, without any warrant, they distort theonomic teaching as saying that the "perfect" law of God is "improved" (p. 36). New Testament revisions are never deemed improvements of a previously defective law by theonomists. Such a construction must be blamed on the critics.

"law" are employed throughout the Bible.[17] We do not need to repeat their work here. We should add to the list they come up with, however, the overlapping and distinct uses of the word "law" found in Christian ethicists and writers. We end up with ripe conditions for ambiguity, equivocation, miscommunication, and verbal dispute. But for the purposes of working out the differences between dispensationalists and theonomists, it is not all that difficult to narrow our scope and regiment the relevant concepts used in the debate.

The verbal token "God's law" could be used for any number of concepts, among which we will mention:

(1) any communication of God to man [we will stipulate for present purposes that the English word "*revelation*" be used for this notion],[18]

(2) any divine communication which serves to deliver an order or command to someone [stipulating "*imperative*" for this notion],

(3) any divine command addressed and restricted to a particular person or group and applicable to a particular situation or point of time [stipulating "*directive*" for this notion],

(4) any divine command which expresses God's will in terms of a specific cultural setting and is obligatory for classes of individuals or over some extended period of time [stipulating "*code*" for this notion],

(5) any linguistic generalization about the detail(s) of a code [stipulating "*regulation*" for this notion],

---

17. This complexity is complicated even further by the fact that "the law" is sometimes used, not for what is objectively communicated by the law (whether God's written word in general, the Pentateuch specifically, some statute in particular, etc.), but for how the law is subjectively appropriated and applied—for instance, the Jewish legalistic interpretation and teaching about the law ("Israel, following after a law of righteousness did not arrive at the law because they sought it not by faith, but as it were, by works," Rom. 10:31-32).

18. No special significance or necessity is claimed for this and the following stipulations. Different ways of assigning the linguistic tokens is possible and equally acceptable.

(6) any command which expresses God's will in generic, axiomatic or abstract terms not tied to any particular culture, but expressed in some particular natural language [stipulating *"precept"* for this notion],

(7) any moral standard, guideline, or demand arising from the essential nature of God and conceived extra-linguistically — that is, not expressed in some particular natural language but expressible in any [stipulating *"principle"* for this notion].

In light of this linguistic scheme, we can try to state precisely the conflict between dispensationalists and theonomists.

Both schools of theology love God's revelation, wishing to be guided by it and obey it, especially as it is clearly and savingly articulated in Scripture. Thus they both take notice of Scriptural imperatives, sorting out those which have no continuing authority for our practice or conduct today (like directives)[19] from those which do. Neither maintains that the codes revealed in the Bible are as such to be obeyed today.[20] Both would agree, moreover, that (whether in the Old and/or New Testaments) the moral obligation of people living outside of the biblical cultures is to the regulations arising from the details of these codes, as well as to the precepts of Scripture;[21] when properly derived, the regulations carry the same force as the precepts and can either be expressed in the very words of the precepts or help to further define and apply those precepts.

Theonomists maintain that the Mosaic[22] code and regulations contain some items which are not based upon necessary moral principles, but rather God's sovereign good pleasure; as such they

---

19. E.g., Christ's instruction for Peter to go find a coin in the mouth of a fish (Matt. 17:27).

20. E.g., "Greet one another with a holy kiss" (Rom. 16:16); women are not to have braided hair or gold jewelry (1 Peter 3:3), etc.

21. E.g., "Servants, obey in all things them that are your masters according to the flesh," with "whatsoever you do, work heartily as unto the Lord, and not unto men" (Col. 3:22-23).

22. I (Bahnsen) focus on the Mosaic code here, not out of preoccupation, but simply because this is the crux of the debate.

are not binding in all ages and upon all cultures — items which must be distinguished and identified on the basis of Scriptural teaching.[23] The other Mosaic regulations and precepts communicate God's unchanging moral principles — and indeed are identical to those precepts which correspond to the divine moral principles learned through general revelation.[24]

Dispensationalists disagree with this perspective at a few crucial points. *First*, they claim that *none* of the Mosaic regulations or precepts are *as such* universally obligatory, but were binding only on Old Testament Israel. Christians today are under the regulations and precepts only of the Adamic covenant, the Noahic covenant, and the New Testament.[25] House and Ice assert that "the Mosaic law given to Israel" is not binding upon "any other nation not under the [Mosaic] covenant."[26] This means that "the law of God . . . and the law of Moses are two *different things*."[27]

Second, dispensationalists claim that all of the details or regulations of the Mosaic code are of the same character. They all *"reflect the character of God,"* and the entire Mosaic code "stands or falls as a whole."[28] *Third*, the precepts learned in general revelation are not equivalent *to the regulations and precepts of the Mosaic* revelation. House and Ice speak of "the written law given to Moses" being different from "the law written on the hearts of the Gentiles."[29]

Back to the Law and God's Character

What should we make of the dispensationalist perspective elaborated here? House and Ice maintain that the law of God is "different" from the law of Moses. (1) Obviously the Mosaic code

---

23. E.g., the laying aside of animal sacrifices (Heb. 9) and dietary restrictions (Acts 10).

24. E.g., the prohibition of homosexuality learned in the Mosaic law (Lev. 18:22; 20:13), written epistle (1 Cor. 6:9; 1 Tim. 1:8-10), as well as general revelation (Rom. 1:24, 26-27, 32).

25. House and Ice, *Dominion Theology*, p. 119.

26. *Ibid.*, p. 100.

27. *Ibid.* (emphasis mine).

28. *Ibid.*, p. 89 (emphasis mine).

29. *Ibid.*, p. 129.

is a different *kind* of thing from the divinely authorized regulations and precepts (see the distinctions drawn above). House and Ice mean *more* than this, however. (2) They also mean that the *regulations and precepts themselves* which were revealed through Moses are *not coextensive* with those revealed through Adam, Noah, and Christ. The moral demands are to some extent different from each other, *and* the regulations and precepts revealed through Moses are not universally obligatory. But then the Mosaic law is "different" from God's law in yet another way. (3) The regulations and precepts revealed through Moses were not based upon God's unchanging moral *principles*. That is just to say that they did *not* reflect the essential moral character of God (even at the level of precept).

This inference is confirmed by the assertion of House and Ice that the Mosaic law is not equivalent to the law delivered in special revelation. The difference between the two laws for dispensationalists is much more than a difference in "specificity" (the point mentioned by House and Ice)[30] — a claim made without the slightest Biblical substantiation for such a contrast, by the way. Even more, the difference is that the precepts of general revelation reflect God's unchanging moral *principles* (and thus His essential character), whereas the precepts of Moses do not.

We are now in a position to see why the dispensational perspective of House and Ice is theologically unacceptable. *First*, it is now evident that, when the linguistic ambiguity and equivocations are cleared up, leaving us to see the conceptual scheme of dispensationalism for its true character, House and Ice have roundly contradicted themselves. They fully believe that the Mosaic law was ordained by God, of course; it is *from* God ("law" in the sense of revelation). From the standpoint of conceptual analysis they have taught that the *precepts* of the Mosaic revelation are not "law" in the sense of reflecting the moral *principles* of God's unchanging character (just because they change and are not universally valid). *Yet on the other hand*, they elsewhere state that the Mosaic law in its entirety *does* reflect the character of God.

---

30. *Ibid.*, p. 129.

They really cannot have their cake and eat it too. For this reason it is not surprising that within the very same paragraph in which they assert that "the codes of Israel reflect the character of God," they go on to say that "the whole" of that law has *fallen* with the coming of Christ![31] This is tantamount, were House and Ice to be logically consistent, to saying that the character of God has fallen.

The *second* reason why the conceptual scheme of dispensationalism is theologically unacceptable is that it runs counter to the teaching of Scripture itself. Are the regulations and precepts of the Mosaic law to be called "God's law" only because He sovereignly ordained them and they came from Him? Scripture says much more.[32]

The righteousness and perfection toward which the "commandments" of "the Law and the Prophets" (Matt. 5:17-19) guide us was identified by Jesus when He said, "you shall therefore be perfect as your heavenly Father is perfect" (v. 48). God is morally perfect (Deut. 32:4; Psalm 18:30) and His law is declared to be the same (Psalm 19:7; cf. James 1:25). Both Moses and Peter concur in their inspired teaching that the commandments lead us to emulate the very holiness of God Himself: "You shall be holy, for I the Lord your God am holy" (Lev. 19:2; 1 Peter 1:15-16). The regulations and precepts of the Mosaic law are properly conceived of as God's holy character coming to expression. Those regulations and precepts can no more change or be cancelled than the essential and immutable holiness of God could be altered.

---

31. *Ibid.*, p. 89.

32. House and Ice say emphatically that we must differentiate "God's law" from "the law of Moses" (House and Ice, *Dominion Theology*, p. 100, etc.). However, when we read the Old Testament Scriptures, we find that God shows a special jealousy and is adamant to maintain that the law given through Moses is His law. The law of Moses is identified over and over again as the law of Jehovah (e.g., Deut. 30:10; Josh. 24:26; 2 Kings 10:31; 17:13; 21:8; 1 Chron. 22:12; 2 Chron. 6:16; 31:21; Ezra 7:6, 12, 14, 21; Neh. 8:8, 18; 9:3; 10:28, 29; Psalm 78:1; 81:4; 89:30; 119:34, 77, 92, 97, 109, 174; Isa. 1:10; Jer. 6:19; 9:13; 16:11; 26:4; 31:33; 44:10; 22:26; Dan. 6:5; Hos. 4:6; 8:1).

The Bible teaches us that God alone is holy (Rev. 15:4) and that God alone is good (Mark 10:18). But Paul had no hesitation in attributing these exclusive divine attributes to the law of God as well: "So the law is holy, and the commandment is holy, and righteous, and good" (Rom. 7:12). The holiness and goodness of God refer to His essential character, not simply to the pleasure of His will. And it is this essential character which comes to expression in "the law," according to Paul. Now to which law was Paul referring? Regardless of the claim of House and Ice that the law of Moses is different from the law of God, the law of God about which the Apostle Paul was speaking was precisely the well-known law of Moses — that law which was the special pride and advantage of the Jews (Rom. 2:17-18; 3:1-2) and whose precepts are quoted by Paul right out of the Mosaic revelation (e.g., 2:21-22) and called "the law" (7:7-8). This is the law which is holy, just and good — displaying God's own unchanging and absolute righteousness.

Dispensational theology has not yet come to grips with the essentially godly (Godly) character of the law which was revealed by Moses, the absoluteness of God's moral nature, and the immutability of the Lord. This failing is, upon analysis, manifest in *Dominion Theology* by House and Ice. Undoubtedly the authors' hearts move one direction on those issues, while their theological constructs would logically lead them another.

Case-Law and Ceremonial-Law Categories

It is commonplace in the history of theology to draw distinctions between the moral law, judicial (case-) law, and ceremonial law as found in the Mosaic revelation. This way of schematizing the Old Testament commands can be found in many of the creeds and theologians of the past. House and Ice recognize that many Christians accept these internal distinctions in the Old Testament law.[33] It is not some novel device dreamed up by theonomists to rescue them from a theological bind in their system.

---

33. House and Ice, *Dominion Theology*, p. 42.

Theonomists accept the general breakdown of the Mosaic law into the categories of moral, judicial, and ceremonial — despite having some reservations about misleading terminology (e.g., "ceremonial" might better be called redemptive or restorative) and having strong objection to the *a priori* way in which some people impose the scheme upon the Old Testament text. Essentially, this category-scheme will be of no genuine help to the interpreter as he approaches any particular text; its value is simply that of a retrospective summary device, after doing the necessary exegesis and application of specific passages in the law.

House and Ice raise some objection to the theonomic use of this outline of the law's divisions, however, and we should pause to respond to those misgivings before ending this chapter. With respect to the category of judicial law (or the case-laws), the authors complain that the distinction between it and the moral law is vague, that it is not always clear why some judicial laws are changed today, and (generally) that the attempt to apply them to our culture today is sometimes pretty difficult and potentially cumbersome.[34] The last complaint can hardly be given much weight since it would bear equally against doing any serious biblical interpretation or systematic theology at all.

As for the clarity of the distinction, the reader can reflect again upon the difference between "code," "regulation," and "precept" as explained earlier in this chapter (remembering that different verbal tokens could be used), as well as upon the fuller exposition of discontinuities with the law which is given in Chapter 3 above — where I also try to make it clear how and on what basis the code or precepts of the Mosaic law have changed today. Undoubtedly the-

---

34. *Ibid.*, pp. 35, 39, 74, 76, 81, 99. On a related note they also call the theonomic understanding of the phrase "general equity" in the Westminster Confession of Faith 19:4 "unusual" and "controversial" (pp. 97-98). They do not offer any reason for saying so, though, which must be rather unconvincing to the studied reader in light of the vast historical evidence and examples which have been adduced for seeing "general equity" as the underlying moral principle which is illustrated in the judicial law's wording (e.g., James Jordan, "Calvinism and 'The Judicial Law of Moses'," *Journal of Christian Reconstruction* [Winter, 1978-79], pp. 17-48).

onomists do from time to time make mistakes in their understanding, revising, codifying or applying the judicial laws. That does not count as a fundamental reason to reject the distinction altogether — any more than other theological distinctions ("dispensations," maybe) should be scuttled because theologians do not always make proper use of them. The dictum about babies and bathwater still makes common sense.

The objection raised by House and Ice to the ceremonial categorization of the law (redemptive-restorative provisions) is more serious — and more seriously wrong. The same (overly broad) complaint is voiced which we heard above: namely, that drawing this distinction in general, or in particular cases, can be difficult.[35] Granted. However, the necessity of drawing just such a distinction in order to preserve evangelical theology is more than an offsetting counter-weight to this objection.

It has to be obvious even to House and Ice that what is called the moral and judicial law did not serve *the same* soteriological *function* as did the laws which are retrospectively called ceremonial, and for instance, did not "foreshadow" the work of the Messiah *in the same way* that the sacrificial laws did so. To think otherwise is exegetically groundless and theologically misleading. The civil laws of Old Testament Israel did not, as was characteristic of the ceremonial laws, expound the way of gaining redemption or symbolize the setting of God's people redemptively apart from the world.

Now the word "redemption" can certainly be used *broadly* enough by a theologian to cover both *the means* of redemption (Christ's sacrificial, substitutionary death) as well as the *effects* of that redemption (the holy conduct of His people). But to intermingle or confuse those two different senses of "redemption" would be a grave theological mistake which is bound to obscure the purity of the gospel. We are not saved *by* our righteous behavior, but rather saved *unto* righteous behavior (e.g., Eph. 2:8-10; Rom. 3:28; 8:4). One overlooks that very gospel truth in the Old Testament if he says the moral and ceremonial laws are not separable

---

35. House and Ice, *Dominion Theology*, pp. 38-39.

from each other, stand or fall together, or reflect the character of God in exactly the same ways.[36] The authors of *Dominion Theology* unwittingly make a serious theological mistake, then, when they argue that all of the Mosaic laws should be treated in the same way that we treat the ceremonial laws[37] as though they were all equally redemptive in nature. It is precisely in order to eschew that theological equivocation that the Church has discriminated between laws which display the way of redemption (ceremonial) from laws which define the righteousness of God (moral, civil) pointing to my *need* of a Savior and showing me the moral character which is to be emulated as an *effect* of redemption.

Moral, Judicial, and Ceremonial Law

Finally, we can entertain the complaint of House and Ice that the moral, judicial, and ceremonial laws of Moses are "inseparable," or "were not always strictly separated" in the Old Testament, or "are not easily divided" today.[38] This kind of remark, though not uncommon in our day,[39] is a bit exaggerated. It is simply untrue to the text of the Old Testament, for instance, to think that ancient Israel did not distinguish religious cult from political affairs. The functions and the qualifications for office were recognizably different for priests and civil leaders in Old Testament Israel. Regardless of the form of civil government Israel had at any particular time in her national history, there was still a differ-

---

36. *Ibid.*, pp. 89, 100, 134.

37. *Ibid.*, pp. 42-43. House and Ice show a fundamental misunderstanding of this issue when they claim that Christ "fulfilled" the moral law for us just as He fulfilled the ceremonial, and that therefore we are equally "relieved of the requirement" of them both. (1) Christ "fulfilled" the laws about atoning sacrifice by becoming the sacrificial victim, antitype replacing type; the moral precepts which He obeyed (which is important to His becoming my Savior) were not typological in nature. (2) His fulfilling the laws of atoning sacrifice means that I may disregard them in practice. It would be absurd to say that His fulfilling of the moral laws (e.g., "Thou shalt not commit adultery") means that believers may now disregard those laws in practice.

38. *Ibid.*, pp. 89, 100, 134.

39. For example it is repeated in Paul Schrotenboer's response to my (Bahnsen's) paper on "The Theonomic Perspective," found in *God and Politics: Four Views on the Reformation of Civil Government*, ed. Gary Scott Smith (Phillipsburg, NJ: Presbyterian and Reformed, 1989), from which I borrow my answer.

ence between laws which God revealed for political rulers to obey
and those which were revealed for the priests to follow.

Furthermore, the moral, judicial and ceremonial (redemptive-
restorative) categories of law did not need to be written out in *de-
lineated* literary subsections in order for them to be, nevertheless,
clearly and conceptually *distinguishable* by the Israelites. A category
distinction is unmistakable in God's declaration, "I desire faithful
love, not sacrifice" (Hosea 6:6). That statement would have made
no sense whatsoever if Israel could not tell the difference between
the laws demanding sacrifice (which we call "ceremonial") and the
laws demanding faithful love (which we call "moral" and "civil").
Are we to believe that the ancient Israelites lacked the mental
acumen to catch the contrast between laws which bound Jews and
Gentiles *alike* (e.g., the death penalty for murder, Lev. 24:21-22)
and those which bound Jews but *not* Gentiles (e.g., the prohibition
of eating animals that died of themselves, Deut. 14:21)? Whether
they used the verbal labels of "civil" and "ceremonial" (as we do) is
beside the point. The category difference was hardly beyond an
Israelite's mental discernment. The common objection about the
moral/judicial/ceremonial breakdown invents a major difficulty
where only a minor one exists.

Using rhetorical questioning as a form of criticism, House and
Ice ask: "What standards must one use to decide which [laws] are
to be continued . . . ?"[40] The theonomic answer has always been:
not some a priori principle imposed from outside the text of Scripture, but precisely painstaking and detailed Scriptural exegesis.
We do have, after all, the great advantage of the New Testament
and its commentary upon the Old. With the coming of New Covenant revelation which helps us understand even better the meaning and purpose of Old Covenant commands, the cogency and
necessity of something like the moral/judicial/ceremonial distinction becomes *all the more* apparent. It accounts for Paul's insistence on submission to case-law ("civil") provisions of the Old
Testament (e.g., 1 Tim. 5:18), but refusal to see other ("ceremonial")

---

40. House and Ice, *Dominion Theology*, p. 134.

laws as obligatory (e.g., Gal. 2:3; 5:2, 6). *Even if* these distinctions were somehow obscured in the Old Testament, theonomists believe that New Testament revelation provides the criterion and guide by which we can see with adequate clarity today the difference between laws that have been put out of gear (by Christ's redemptive work) and laws whose validity is reinforced by Christ (whether expressed in terms of broad principle or cultural illustration).

Summary

In this chapter we have found no cogent argument from dispensationalists House and Ice against the theonomic conception of God's law (in its various forms) or against the theonomic use of the judicial and ceremonial categories of the Mosaic law. We have found upon analysis that:

1. There is an inherent contradiction within the dispensational conception of different "laws of God."

2. Dispensationalism does not adequately appreciate and deal with the fact that the law of God, even the Mosaic revelation thereof, is a reflection of God's essential and unchanging, moral character.

3. Dispensationalism exaggerates the difficulties involved in distinguishing between — and making modern application of — the moral, judicial, and ceremonial distinctions within the law.

4. Dispensationalism jeopardizes the doctrine of salvation of grace by failing to distinguish between the functions of the ceremonial and moral (judicial) laws in the Old Testament, suggesting that all were redemptive and all were put aside by the work of Christ.

THE JURISDICTION OF THE LAW

A reply to the argument that the nations and New Testament believers are not under the law.

In Chapters 6 and 7 of *Dominion Theology* House and Ice argue against the theonomic understanding of the law of God, which holds that the moral regulations and precepts of the Mosaic law (along with the rest of Scripture's revelation of moral duty) are binding upon the New Testament Christian, just as they were binding upon the Gentiles of the Old Testament era. Biblical evidence and exposition for this conviction can be reviewed in Chapter 3 above. In their attempt to offer a biblically based reply to the theonomic position about the universality of God's moral principles (wherever and however they are expressed in the Bible), House and Ice hope to do two kinds of things: to *undermine* the apparent biblical support which is enjoyed by the theonomic thesis, and to prove the contrary conclusion on the basis of separate considerations. With due respect for their sincere involvement in the biblical text, we cannot see that their efforts have met with success on either score.

The Argument over Matthew 5:17-20

Does the New Testament teach that the commandments of the Mosaic law continue to have moral authority in the New Testament era unless revised or set aside by the authority of God Himself? Theonomic ethics answers "yes," and it sets forth a large assortment of biblical and theological arguments in support of that conviction.[1] The abiding validity of God's law is examined in terms of the character of God, the life and example of the Messiah, the sanctifying work of the Holy Spirit, the blessings promised for conformity to the law, the underlying unity of God's covenants, the nature of God's word as a norm, the ethical relevance of the entire Bible, New Testament concepts of grace and faith and love, New Testament ethical themes like kingdom righteousness or holiness or the fruit of the Spirit, numerous particular passages in the New Testament which assume or state the authority of the Old Testament law, repeated New Testament ethical judgments on particular issues which apply the Old Testament law, a host of particular texts and teachings of Jesus or the Apostles, and Matthew 5:17-20.

Of all of these mutually supportive and independently challenging lines of reasoning, House and Ice examine only one in *Dominion Theology*: the exposition of Matthew 5:17-19. The other texts of Scripture elaborated upon in the many other theonomic arguments are not given specific attention as such. Therefore, although Matthew 5 is the literary center of attention on the question before us, the opinion of House and Ice is premature and strained when they comment: "If Bahnsen's view on this passage is wrong, then his *entire* thesis *is in doubt*."[2] The fact is that the dispensational rebuttal of theonomic ethics would have considerably more work to do before House and Ice would be home free. As it is, however, even the theonomic support gained from Matthew 5:17-20 is not left "in doubt" by their discussion of the text.[3]

---

1. The following list touches only on the lines of argumentation found in *Theonomy in Christian Ethics* (ex. ed.; Phillipsburg, NJ: Presbyterian and Reformed, [1977] 1984) and *By This Standard: The Authority of God's Law Today* (Tyler, TX: Institute for Christian Economics, 1985), out of the many which could be mentioned and which have been set forth by Reformed scholars for centuries.

2. H. Wayne House and Thomas Ice, *Dominion Theology: Blessing or Curse?* (Portland, OR: Multnomah, 1988), p. 104 (emphasis mine).

3. For an extensive analysis of the text and theology of this passage, see Bahnsen, *Theonomy*, Chapter 2.

Think not that I came to destroy the law or the prophets: I came not to destroy, but to fulfil. For verily I say unto you, Till heaven and earth pass away, one jot or one tittle shall in no wise pass away from the law, till all things be accomplished. Whoever therefore shall break one of these least commandments, and shall teach men so, shall be called least in the kingdom of heaven: but whosoever shall do and teach them, he shall be called great in the kingdom of heaven. For I say unto you, that except your righteousness shall exceed the righteousness of the scribes and Pharisees, ye shall in no wise enter into the kingdom of heaven. (ASV)

House and Ice begin by giving reasons to think that the "tone" of Matthew 5:17-20 is more that of a prophetic statement than a legal one; even "the Law" in verse 17 is taken to have "prophetic import."[4] Jesus is allegedly emphasizing His continuity with the flow of redemptive history revealed in Old Testament. This does not really harmonize with the immediate literary context and purpose of Christ's teaching, however. Christ addresses the lifestyle, attitudes and conduct of His followers (vv. 3-15) and speaks of their "good works" (v. 16); He goes on to apply his words to "the commandments" (v. 19), the "righteousness" of the scribes and Pharisees (v. 20), and the proper interpretation of the Old Testament precepts (vv. 21-48). Be that as it may, the interpretation of House and Ice does not exclude reference being made to the moral instruction of the Old Testament, anyway: "This is not to deny that the ethical demands of the law are included within this statement."[5] With that concession, we need not linger over disputes about emphasis.

Fulfilling the Law

House and Ice next claim that "the way in which Jesus came to fulfill" the Old Testament "is different from" the view advanced by Bahnsen.[6] Does this different "way" of fulfillment contradict the

---

4. House and Ice, *Dominion Theology*, pp. 106, 107. The authors' portrayal of Bahnsen as insisting that "Law" in v. 17 refers (only?) to "ethical stipulations" is a distortion. It actually denotes a literary portion of the Old Testament canon ("the Law or the Prophets"), and what Bahnsen says is that the focus of this pericope is upon the commands of the Old Testament (*Theonomy*, pp. 49-52).

5. House and Ice, *Dominion Theology*, p. 107.

6. *Ibid.*, p. 107.

theonomic thesis? That is the real question if House and Ice are aiming to refute the theonomic view (rather than simply offering an alternative interpretation). The theonomic theological conclusion drawn from this text still stands on most of the credible interpretations of the word "fulfill," although *Theonomy* proposes the precising definition of "confirm in full measure" for the word. House and Ice do not think that all of the examples adduced for giving this sense to the word "necessarily" mean "confirm," but they have to grant that the word can mean something like "substantiate."[7]

They do not think the Greek word "but" always takes a strong adversative sense; however, their alleged counterexample (Matt. 6:13) does not help them in the least (since "leading into" temptation is indeed the exact opposite of "delivering from" evil).[8] Their proposal[9] is that "but" in Matthew 5:17 functions as part of an idiom conveying the force of relative negation ("not so much this, but rather that," e.g., Acts 5:4) — which is by far not the usual way Matthew treats expressions of the form "not . . . but."[10] Moreover, the expression as used in Matthew 5:17 lacks the paradoxical (or dialectical) introductory schema which is a customary mark of relative negation elsewhere (e.g., "whoever receives me does not receive me," Mark 9:37; "the one who believes on me does not believe on me," John 12:44), setting up the tension which is then

---

7. *Ibid.*, p. 109. There are a large number of scholars who could be cited in support of giving "fulfill" the sense suggested in *Theonomy.* To take one example: "The word translated 'fulfill' can mean to 'establish, confirm, cause to stand' and need mean only that Jesus asserted the permanence of the Law and his obedience to it" (George Eldon Ladd, *A Theology of the New Testament* [Grand Rapids, MI: Wm. B. Eerdmans, 1974], p. 124). The word "confirm" is used to exposit this text by John Murray, Herman Ridderbos, W. C. Allen, Hans Windisch, David Brown, George Campbell, etc. — even the dispensationalist scholar A. C. Gaebelein (*The Gospel According to Matthew* [New York: Our Hope Publication Office, 1910], p. 120)! See also: Zane Hodges, *The Gospel Under Seige* (Dallas, TX: Redencion Viva, 1981), p. 31.

8. It is odd that they would miss something this clear, but they do it again on the next page (House and Ice, *Dominion Theology,* p. 110), incredulously claiming that peace and the sword are not exact opposites in their literary use (cf. Lev. 26:6; Jer. 4:10; 12:12; 14:13; Rev. 6:4).

9. House and Ice, *Dominion Theology,* pp. 109-10.

10. See Matthew 5:15; 7:21; 8:8; 9:12, 13, 24; 10:34; 13:21; 15:11; 16:12, 17, 23; 17:12; 18:30; 19:11; 20:23, 26, 28; 22:32.

relieved by the clause which begins with "but" — e.g., "whoever receives me does not receive me, but (even more) the One who sent me." In contrast to this, Matthew 5:17 does not begin with a paradoxical remark, but with a repeated denial of something.

House and Ice argue that the emphatic denial by Jesus that He had come to abrogate the law cannot be taken in an "absolute sense" because even theonomists admit that some parts of the Mosaic law (ceremonial) passed away in the New Testament.[11] Now this is certainly true. The emphatic declaration of Christ is to be qualified and applied according to the rest of New Testament teaching. However, as discussed in *Theonomy*[12] and missed by House and Ice, the literary fact is that Jesus spoke *categorically* in Matthew 5:17, not drawing any distinctions or making any exceptions. His reference as found in Matthew 5:17 was to the entire law (cf. "every jot and tittle," v. 18; "the least commandment," v. 19), even including the ceremonial provisions; our knowledge of their being set aside is based on *other* texts of Scripture, not this one.

Presumption of Continuity

This observation leads us to the fundamental hermeneutical difference separating theonomists and dispensationalists. Just because of Christ's firm and categorical declaration of the total Old Testament law's continuing validity in Matthew 5:17-19, theonomists teach that theologians of the New Testament must *presume* that any precept of the Old Testament is morally authoritative *until and unless* they have biblical warrant for revising or setting aside that precept. Theonomists readily say that such warrant is indeed given at many points in the New Testament. But without such justification (based on textual exegesis and good reasoning), the presumption must be that of continuing validity, or else we have not seriously heeded and submitted to the categorical thrust of

---

11. House and Ice, *Dominion Theology*, p. 110. Although it is somewhat unrelated, House and Ice observe here: "Bahnsen's contention that the setting aside of the law in Romans 10:4 is setting aside the law as a way of righteousness does not follow since the law was never a means of attaining righteousness" (p. 110; cf. p. 114). I must agree with this criticism. See further the excellent study by Daniel P. Fuller, *Gospel and Law: Contrast or Continuum?* (Grand Rapids, MI: Wm. B. Eerdmans, 1980), pp. 82-88.

12. Bahnsen, *Theonomy in Christian Ethics*, pp. 48-49.

Christ's teaching on the law in Matthew 5:17-19. Dispensationalism presumes the very opposite: namely, that the Mosaic precepts are not binding, unless they happen to be repeated in the New Testament. Matthew 5:17-19 settles this conflict between theonomic and dispensational hermeneutics, resolving the issue on the theonomic side.

Not surprisingly, then, we find that House and Ice[13] attempt to derive from their dispensational interpretation of Matthew 5:18 something which at least suggests the passing away of the entire law, thus countering the appearance of a categorical endorsement of its continuing moral validity.[14] They give verse 18 this sense: Within the general framework of all time, not the smallest detail of the law will pass away until all things (the details of God's law) are realized. The exegetical defense of this rather strange way of taking the Greek is defended in a long footnote.[15] But the reasoning employed there is strained, illogical and grammatically inaccurate.[16]

---

13. House and Ice, *Dominion Theology*, p. 112.

14. It needs to be noted that House and Ice (p. 111) criticize Bahnsen's treatment of Matthew 5:18 by saying that he incorrectly translates the (common) Greek verb *genetai* as "invalid" [sic: "become invalid"?]. But Bahnsen nowhere does that. In fact, on the very same page, House and Ice quote Bahnsen's treatment of Matthew 5:18 and it is quite evident that he translates the Greek verb as "take place."

15. House and Ice, *Dominion Theology*, pp. 120-21.

16. House and Ice make "one jot or tittle" (v. 17) the supposed antecedent to the Greek term "all things," but the two expressions do not agree in either number or gender. Far from being considered collectively as a plural, "one jot or one tittle" are presented disjunctively with the emphatic repeating of the adjective "one" (instead of using it only once to cover and group together "jot" and "tittle"). Our authors are simply reading into the text what their interpretation will necessitate. The plural conception is not true to Matthew's sense and syntax. Furthermore, if the neuter word "all" were intended to refer back to "one jot or one tittle," its gender would ordinarily have agreed with the last-mentioned item in the complex antecedent—but it does not (cf. the feminine word "tittle"). By a violent abuse of logic applied to the Pindaric construction in Greek, the authors now "reason" that since a neuter plural word can sometimes take a third singular verb, therefore the third singular verb attached to phrase "one jot or one tittle" turns that phrase into a neuter plural! The usage of the Pindaric construction, by the way, had been greatly weakened by the time of the New Testament, was not invariable, and applied to words not nominal expressions—much less to complex nominal expressions! The fallacious and forced reasoning here is readily refut-

If this is the only way in which a dispensationalist can save his theory from biblical refutation, then the position is desperately weak in the first place. In light of the mental gymnastics attempted by House and Ice in interpreting Matthew 5:18, dispensationalism is a tenuous theological theory indeed.

Now aside from the technical matters of interpretation over which scholars can debate regarding Matthew 5:17 and 5:18, the theonomist realizes that everyone has to come to terms with the application of these two verses by Christ in the teaching of verse 19. This verse alone substantiates the theonomic attitude toward the Old Testament law of God: "Therefore, whosoever shall break one of these least commandments and shall teach men so shall be called least in the kingdom of heaven." Christ warns us that our approach to the precepts of the Old Testament — even the least of them — must be a submissive one which acknowledges that they are valid and should be obeyed. To say otherwise (even if you do not yourself break these commandments) is itself culpable and leads to being assigned the position of least in the kingdom of heaven. It light of this straightforward endorsement of a theonomic approach to Christian ethics and living in Matthew 5:19, it is noteworthy that the only verse which House and Ice do not

---

able: anything that is a crow is black, my black shoe is therefore a crow. A further mistake made by House and Ice is their taking "until heaven and earth pass away" as simply stating a general framework within which the second temporal clause, "until all things happen," gives the particular terminus for the jots and tittles of the law passing away. One would have thought that the two temporal clauses were rather parallel to each other, judging from their similarities and from the fact that they have no logical connective supplied to show their relationship. Besides, why would Jesus need to use such an artificial introductory device to what He specifically meant to say? Notice the emphasis He places upon it. (The mortgage company does not usually express itself in this way: "Until the twenty-first century has taken its course, your house payment is due on the first of next month.") This imaginative interpretation of the text of Matthew 5:18 founders finally on the fact that the clause which is taken to have the precising function ("until all things happen") within the more general framework ("until heaven and earth pass away") is actually less precise semantically than the clause it is qualifying. In Luke's version of this saying (Luke 16:17), there is no mention whatsoever of the (allegedly) qualifying phrase "until all things happen" — leaving only the (allegedly) framework clause standing all by itself.

touch upon or discuss in their treatment of Matthew 5:17-20 is precisely verse 19. The reader can understand why.

We conclude that the exegesis of Matthew 5:17-20 offered by House and Ice in *Dominion Theology* has not refuted or weakened the theonomic understanding of the passage. We have found, rather, that their own interpretation is fraught with fatal defects. Furthermore, Matthew 5:17-20 clearly establishes the presumption of continuing validity and moral authority of the Old Testament law, thereby coming into direct conflict with, and forcefully refuting, the key operating premise of dispensational hermeneutics and ethics. Christ declares with divine authority that His advent did not have the purpose or effect of abrogating the moral authority of Old Testament ethical regulations and precepts. The coming of Christ has, by His own declaration, not cancelled the moral jurisdiction of the law.

The Argument that Paul Set Aside the Law's Authority

Dispensationalism finds no support in the teaching or ministry of Jesus for its view of the Old Testament law. In the second part of Chapter 6 in *Dominion Theology*, authors House and Ice turn to various teachings of the Apostle Paul to see if it might be found. Here too they will be disappointed. Upon examination, the texts to which they appeal will be found to misconstrue what Paul actually says and to offer no support for the idea that the moral authority of "the law of Moses has been set aside."[17]

Romans 6:14

House and Ice begin with a favorite verse of dispensational polemicists, Romans 6:14, where Paul states: "For sin shall not have dominion over you: for you are not under law, but under grace."[18] House and Ice allude to Galatians 3:23, thus interpreting Paul's words in Romans 6:14 to mean that "Christians are not

---

17. House and Ice, *Dominion Theology*, p. 113.

18. House and Ice fall into another unfortunate contradiction in the presentation of their views. According to them, Old Testament Israel is not said to be "under grace," if we wish to be biblically precise (House and Ice, *Dominion Theology*, p. 113). On page 128, however, they turn around and say "the stipulations of Sinai were . . . to a people under grace."

'under the law' as a rule of life."[19] This is a serious misreading. Unlike Galatians 3, Romans 6:14 does not refer to "the law" of Moses (cf. Gal. 3:19) or to the Mosaic law as a particular administration of God's covenant (cf. Gal. 3:17, 24). There is nothing like this in the immediate textual context of Romans 6:14 to supply a specifying sense to Paul's words, and to be technically precise, one should observe that Paul there does *not* speak of being under "the law" — but rather to being "under law" (generically, without any definite article). He teaches that those whose personal resources are merely those of law, without the provisions of divine grace, are for that reason under the inescapable dominion of sin; "there is an absolute antithesis between the potency and provisions of law and the potency and provisions of grace."[20] The "dominion of law" from which believers have been "discharged" is forthrightly explained by Paul to be the condition of being "in the flesh [the sinful nature]," being "held in" by "sinful passions which bring forth fruit unto death" (7:1-6). From this spiritual bondage and impotence, the marvelous grace of God through the death and resurrection of Jesus Christ has set the believer free. It has not set him free to sin against God's moral principles.

Now then, when Paul speaks of not being "under law," even House and Ice cannot consistently interpret him to mean "law" in the sense of a "rule of life" (moral demands) since *they* themselves *insist that believers* are *under a law in that sense*, "the law of Christ."[21] Their interpretation would have Paul denying that the believer has any such "law" (= rule of life), thus contradicting themselves. Moreover, "law" in Romans 6:14 *cannot* refer to the *Mosaic* administration or dispensation in particular, for as we have seen, "under law" is equivalent to being under the dominion of sin. House and Ice would have to say that all those saints who lived under the law of Moses, then, were under sin's dominion — which is absurd and

---

19. *Ibid.*, p. 118.
20. John Murray, *The Epistle to the Romans*, 2 vols. (Grand Rapids, MI: Wm. B. Eerdmans, 1959), vol. 1, p. 229. The reader is also recommended to study Murray's fine discussion of "Death to the Law (7:1-6)" for as excellent an exegetical treatment as can be found (pp. 239-47).
21. House and Ice, *Dominion Theology*, pp. 85, 179, etc.

unbiblical. One last point. It is clear to all schools of interpretation that Paul in Romans 6:14 teaches that believers should *not* be controlled by "sin" (cf. vv. 1-2, 6, 11-13, 15-18). How, then, did Paul himself understand what sin was? "I had not known sin except through the law" (7:7). Consequently, far from dismissing the authority of the law, Romans 6:14 teaches that believers should not transgress the law (and thereby sin). It is precisely the mind of the sinful flesh which is "not subject to the law of God" (8:7). But Christians have the mind of the Spirit, who leads and enables them to "fulfill the ordinance of the law" (8:4).

Dispensationalism finds no footing for its theology in the teaching of Paul in Romans, then, much less in Romans 6:14. House and Ice now turn to 1 Corinthians 9:19-23, claiming that "Bahnsen deals little with this passage."[22] They apparently cut short their research in preparing to write their book. Bahnsen gives special attention and offers a detailed analysis of this very passage in *By This Standard*, pages 187-89. A note of review can be mentioned in passing. When Paul spoke of himself as "not being myself under the law," yet being willing to act "as though under the law" *for the sake* of those under the law, he is clearly referring to his relations with the Jews. "And to the Jews I became as a Jew, that I might gain Jews" (v. 20). But he was *just as willing* to act "as though without law" in dealing with "them that are without law" (v. 21), a reference to the Gentiles. "I am become all things to all men that I may by all means save some" (v. 22).

Clearly then, the law which Paul could adopt or ignore, depending upon whether he was among Jews or Gentiles, could not at all have been "the whole Mosaic law" as alleged by House and Ice.[23] Even they recognize that much of the Mosaic law enshrined moral principles (learned through general revelation) which bind the Gentiles as much as the Jews. Nor can we imagine that Paul is confessing to acting with duplicity, according to a double standard of *morality* ("law as a rule of life," say House and Ice). It would be

---

22. *Ibid.*, pp. 114-15.
23. *Ibid.*, p. 115.

unthinkable to think he was saying that he committed blasphemy and bestiality among those who did such things, but refrained from such behavior among others who did not favor such conduct! The only "law" which distinguished Jews from Gentiles, yet without involving inherent moral principle, was what we call today the ceremonial law. Now the passage makes sense. When ministering among the Jews, Paul would conform to certain ceremonial provisions which had been set aside (e.g., purification rites and vows, cf. Acts 18:18; 21:20-26), even though it was not antecendently obligatory for him to follow those regulations — but while ministering among the Gentiles there was no need for him to do so.

The Law in Galatians

House and Ice proceed to look at Galatians 4:4-5[24] which in turn leads them to consider Ephesians 2:14-22 and Colossians 2:14-17 (but without giving the citation).[25] Bahnsen had previously expounded and applied the Galatians passage (incorporating Colossians 2) in *By This Standard*,[26] and he had responded to the Ephesians 2 passage in *Theonomy*.[27] Since House and Ice took it into hand to write a rebuttal of theonomic ethics, and in the process they have chosen to deal with these same texts, we would have expected them to interact in some detail with the theonomic discussion of these texts and show what they believe to be mistaken about them. Instead, they completely *bypass* the treatment of the Galatians passage (showing no awareness of it) and make merely a passing *assertion* (no argument) that the Ephesians passage does

---

24. *Ibid.*, p. 116. Actually, they stop at Galatians 2:19-3:5 first, thinking to correct the supposed theonomic mistake of seeing the law as the dynamic power of sanctification. This is a terrible misrepresentation which could have been easily avoided if they had read Chapter 7 of *Theonomy* in Christian Ethics or Chapter 8 of *By This Standard*. In fact, in their own quotation of Bahnsen's view, House and Ice have before them the statement that the law is to be kept "as a pattern of sanctification" — not the power thereof! Also, no theonomist would disagree with the remark that "an adoption of the Jewish cycle of feasts and fasts . . . as the pattern for sanctification is totally out of place," although House and Ice seem to think that it counters theonomic ethics.

25. House and Ice, *Dominion Theology*, p. 117.

26. Bahnsen, *By This Standard*, pp. 189, 309-10.

27. Bahnsen, *Theonomy*, pp. 209-10.

not imply what Bahnsen said. This is not serious scholarly interaction with their opponents. Are readers supposed to choose the
dispensational approach over the Reconstructionist approach
simply on the say-so of House and Ice? We need reasons, not simply reactions. Short of offering some kind of detailed interaction,
the authors cannot deceive themselves that what they are doing
amounts to refutation.

As for Galatians 4 and Paul's allusion to the law in terms of
childhood, slavery, and "weak, beggarly principles," our authors
correctly interpret him as warning against any return to such conditions. But what is it against which Paul warns exactly? House
and Ice cite the opinion of A. J. Bandstra that the "elements of the
world" pertains in part to "the law . . . as . . . [a] fundamental
cosmical force," and the only example given of which is circumcision. It is hard to say whether House and Ice have seriously considered and understood the bizarre metaphysical notion cham-
pioned by Bandstra (law as fundamental cosmical force), but it is
doubtful that they adopt it. One way or the other, the fact remains
that the example of circumcision readily harmonizes with the
theonomic interpretation of the passage, rather than detracting
from it.

Old Testament Israel was under "the law" as a schoolmaster or
tutor which has in some sense passed away now that Christ has
come. Detailed exegesis discloses that Paul's specific denotation
was the ceremonial character of the law.[28] The language (semantics) of Paul, the illustrations used in literary context, the historical setting, and the very way Paul described the law as a "tutor
unto Christ" all point to the fact that he was not speaking of the
moral law, but rather the ceremonial law. He spoke of those "rudiments" (Gal. 4:3, 9) which Colossians 2:16-17 says were a fore-

---

28. House and Ice evidence again that they have not understood the theonomic position when they claim that Acts 10:9-16 shows that the ceremonial law
"was not the only segment which was abolished" with the coming of Christ
(House and Ice, *Dominion Theology*, p. 117). From their research, they should have
been aware that theonomic ethics views the abrogated dietary laws as a prime example of one aspect of the ceremonial (redemptive-restorative) system of laws!
See *Theonomy*, pp. 209, 228; *By This Standard*, p. 166.

shadow of things to come, the body of which is Christ. He spoke in the historical context of a contest with the Judaizers who insisted upon circumcision for salvation (Gal. 2:3-4), and he used the illustration of the ceremonial calendar (4:10). It was the ceremonial law which was a tutor for those in their spiritual minority that pointed to Christ and taught justification by faith (Gal. 3:24); the moral law itself contained no such gospel, but only the demand which convicts sinners and brings them under judgment.

Finally, we can note the textual support afforded by Scripture itself for the theological concept of an interrelated *system* or subsection of redemptive-restorative ("ceremonial") commands. Notice Paul's phraseology in Ephesians 2:15. He speaks not simply of the Mosaic commandments, but rather of "the law of commandments"—the policy, order or principle which binds these commandments together. He says that the *particular* stipulations which are selectively in mind here are those "commandments contained in *ordinances*"—the term used in Colossians 2:14 for regulations which were a "shadow of things to come" (v. 17, noticing the example of circumcision in v. 11). Paul saw this system of commandments contained in foreshadowing ordinances as separating and imposing enmity between the Jews and Gentiles (e.g., Acts 10:13, 14, 19, 28) and symbolized by the temple's middle wall of partition (v. 14). Through Christ's redemptive death on the cross, says Paul, such ordinances and that to which they pointed have been "abolished" (vv. 15-16).

Therefore, the Pauline texts to which House and Ice have drawn our attention have not helped them show the theonomic position to be unbiblical. Just the opposite has occurred. These texts have rather provided an opportunity to see in even more exegetical depth the warrant and value of theonomic ethics as the outlook of the New Testament writers, Paul in particular. Jesus affirmed the continuing moral jurisdiction of the Old Testament law for the New Covenant age. Paul's teaching did not conflict with that of Christ. Rather, Paul recognized the continuing moral jurisdiction of the Old Testament law in the life of New Testament believers. He also targeted the setting aside of the ceremonial (redemptive-restorative) law along with the drawbacks of the Mosaic covenantal administration. The New Covenant is far more glorious than anything available in the Old, but it does not resist the perfect and holy precepts of God revealed therein. Their moral jurisdiction over mankind continues into and through this age, both Jesus and Paul being witness.

The Argument Regarding the Nations

Chapter 7 of *Dominion Theology* has House and Ice moving on to argue that the Mosaic law — the law included within the Mosaic covenant — was unique to Israel. The Gentile nations were not under obligation to the moral demands revealed through Moses. "The stipulations of Sinai were not for the nations in general but to [sic] a people under grace."[29]

We cannot work through this section of our authors' book, unfortunately, without encountering two fundamental conceptual confusions which flaw and invalidate their reasoning. The *first* is their misunderstanding of the theological concept of law which we treated in Chapter 6 above. Using for a moment the stylized and stipulated vocabulary scheme proposed there (to help prevent misunderstanding), we would say that House and Ice continue to miss the fact that the *same* moral *principle* from God can be expressed in the form of a specific *code*, a related *regulation* (generalization), or a general precept. The verbal expressions may differ, but the moral requirement (the principle) is the same in them all. For instance, the *code* "You shall not muzzle the ox," the *regulation* "The worker is worthy of his hire" (1 Tim. 5:18), and the *precept* "You shall not steal" (Exodus 20:5) — just like the further *precept* "You shall love your neighbor as yourself" (Lev. 19:18), etc. — all require the *same thing* in a particular situation. They may all be deemed "God's law" because they all give expression to the same underlying moral principle reflecting God's character. The specifics of the Mosaic code, then, may very well communicate the same *moral*

---

29. House and Ice, *Dominion Theology*, p. 128.

content (precepts, principles) as is found in another code which utilizes a different *literary* form.

The *second* fundamental conceptual confusion in the discussion by House and Ice is their failure to distinguish a set of moral *commands* from the *covenantal form*, circumstances, purposes, and trappings in which they are found. The moral commands revealed by Moses are not one and the same (though intimately related to) the covenant administered by Moses. They are both distinct and separable. Even the dispensationalist ordinarily recognizes that the New Covenant and the Mosaic covenant can both enunciate the same moral requirement (e.g., "honor your father and mother," Deut. 5:16; Eph. 6:2) without thereby becoming the same dispensation (the same covenantal administration). Take a hypothetical, imaginary example. Pretend we have a gracious, loving, interpersonal covenant between a father and son which is such that the son wants very much to please his father, and among the things expected by the father is compliance with the maxim: "Honor your parents." Pretend we have a different interpersonal covenant between a father and son, one where the child legalistically aims to earn favor with his father in order to manipulate goodies from him, and among the things expected by this second father is also the maxim: "Honor your parents." Do the two children share a common moral *requirement* [30] to honor their parents? Yes. Do they have the same *covenant* with their respective fathers? No. The first child is not under the same covenantal administration as the second child, but the first child is responsible to the same moral requirement as the second.

Moses and the Nations

Notice, now, how the authors House and Ice betray conceptual confusion over the above two points. (1) In replying to the fact that the Canaanites were punished for disobeying the law of

---

30. It is the same or common as far as it goes itself. Obviously there are other implied conditions which affect the way in which compliance is given to this common requirement (e.g., the one father wishes willing obedience from the heart). I wish to make very clear that my illustration does not mean to suggest that in Scripture we find both of the kinds of covenant pictured here. There are no legalistic covenants of self-merit in God's gracious word.

God (Lev. 18:24-27), House and Ice retort that such responsibility extended as far back as Abraham's time (which is not really relevant to the point) and then: "Never were they judged for direct violation of a Mosaic code."[31] Well, of course, the Canaanites who had never received any communication (much less a law-code) from Moses himself were not judged by God for violating such a communication — for violating the Mosaic codification of His law. This is a trivial observation. Why do our authors feel that it has any strength as an answer to the theonomic use of Leviticus 18:24-27? Because they fail to distinguish a particular code (with its historical circumstances, trappings and expression) from the *moral requirements revealed through* that code — requirements to which others can very well be held responsible even though they have not received or read that "code" as such (cf. Rom. 2:12-15). The very same abominations forbidden by the Mosaic precepts were the abominations committed by the Canaanites which brought them under God's curse (Lev. 18:26-27) — despite the fact that the Canaanites did not possess the Mosaic code as such.

House and Ice make the same kind of mistake when they incorrectly hold that "the nations have a law written in their hearts even though they do not have the stipulations of the Mosaic law."[32] The Bible never suggests that general and special revelation represent two different laws of God, the former being a smaller set of the larger. The Bible does not suggest that the "specific regulations" differ between the two revelations, or that one is "more detailed" than the other.[33] This may very well be the heart of the problem in the dispensational opposition to the theonomic thesis. House and Ice appear to have an inadequate understanding of general revelation (the law written on the heart of every person). The content of that law is identical in substance, though not in form (or manner of communication), with the moral content of biblical law (including the Mosaic precepts).

---

31. House and Ice, *Dominion Theology*, p. 136.
32. *Ibid.*, p. 130.
33. *Ibid.*, pp. 130-31.

Commands and Covenants

(2) The second conceptual confusion by House and Ice is evident from what they think theonomists must demonstrate: namely "that the Sinaitic Covenant was intended to be primarily applicable to more than just Israel"; they wish to disprove the notion that "the covenant made with Israel, with its accompanying commandments, should still be practiced by Christians."[34] But of course it should have been obvious to them that theonomists would be horrified at the thought of placing a contemporary believer under "the *covenant* made with Israel" — with its high priesthood, tabernacle, sacrifices, feasts, rituals, Palestinian plots and commonwealth, dietary restrictions, spiritual weakness, and keeping at a distance from God! It is not at all the Mosaic *administration* of the covenant that theonomists promote today (cf. Westminster Confession of Faith 7:5-6), but rather the moral regulations and precepts which were revealed by Moses (in conjunction with the Mosaic covenant, of course).

Moral requirements, then, should be clearly distinguished from their literary formulation (code, precept, etc.) and from the covenantal administrative form in which they are expressed or found. When that fact is realized, the dispensational effort to counter theonomic ethics by arguing that the Gentile nations were *not* under the Mosaic law (its moral precepts) faces an insurmountable obstacle in the text of Scripture itself. Clearly the Gentiles were obligated to the *same* moral requirements as the Jews, even though the Jews *alone* enjoyed the privileges of a special covenantal relationship with Jehovah. On the one side the Old Testament indicated that Israel had a special, redemptive relationship to God, for He Himself said "You alone of all the families of the earth have I known" (Amos 3:2). On the other side, the nations of the world were morally bound to God's commandments, just as were the Jews. Thus Isaiah 24:5 reads, "The earth also is polluted under the inhabitants thereof; because they have transgressed the laws, violated the statutes, broken the everlasting covenant." About this verse E. J. Young commented:

---

34. *Ibid.*, p. 124.

Just as Palestine itself, the Holy Land, had become profane through the sin of its inhabitants (Num. 35:33; Deut. 21:19; Jer. 3:9; and Psa. 106:38), so also the entire earth became profane when the ordinances given to it were violated. . . . Transgression is against the law of God, and this is expressed by the terms law, statute, everlasting covenant. The laws which God has revealed to His people bind all mankind; and hence, the work of the Law of God written on the human heart, for example, may be described under such terms.

The Law was not specifically revealed to the Gentiles as it was to the Jews at Sinai. Nevertheless, according to Paul, the Gentiles do by natural instinct those things which are prescribed by the Law . . . and this fact shows that the work of the Law is written on their own hearts. In transgressing those things prescribed in the Law, however, it may be said that the Gentiles were actually transgressing the Law itself. Here, the plural is used to show that the Gentiles had transgressed divine commands and ordinances, and also that their sins were many and varied. We may say that the Gentiles transgressed specific items of the Law, a thought which the plural form of the noun would also support.[35]

Young here disputes the idea expressed by House and Ice that "the law written on the hearts of the Gentiles does not have the specificity or clarity of the law written on tables of stone."[36] The opinion of House and Ice also runs afoul of the teaching of Paul, who said that God's moral demands were so clear in general revelation that men are "without excuse" for their unrighteousness (Rom. 1:20). Paul also taught that general revelation was specific in its communication of the "ordinance of God" and the "things" or "works" of "the law" (1:32; 2:12-15) — so much so that idolatry (1:23), sexual impurity (1:24), homosexual conduct and desires in particular (1:26-27), backbiting, haughtiness, envy etc. (1:29-31) can be mentioned as illustrations.

It was a transgression of the divine will generally, or as Calvin puts it, "all the instruction contained in the Law."

---

35. E. J. Young, *The Book of Isaiah*, 3 vols. (Grand Rapids, MI: Wm. B. Eerdmans, 1969), vol. 2, pp. 156-57.
36. House and Ice, *Dominion Theology*, p. 129.

The mention of "statute" is perhaps intended for the sake of specificity, for inasmuch as both commandment and promise are included in the Law, this word stresses the commandment. . . .

Lastly, we are told that men frustrated or made void the everlasting covenant. . . . It must be noticed, however, that those who have frustrated the eternal covenant are not merely the Jews but the world generally. The frustrating of the covenant is something universal. For this reason we may adopt the position that the eternal covenant here spoken of designates the fact that God has given His Law and ordinances to Adam, and in Adam to all mankind. . . . Isaiah uses the language which is characteristic of the Mosaic legislation, and thus describes the universal transgressions of mankind.[37]

House and Ice disclose the conceptually unreliable and unbiblical nature of their reasoning, then, when they assert "Since the nations around Israel were not called to adopt the *Mosaic Covenant*, it seems evident that the pagan nations would not be judged by *the law* of Moses."[38] The Bible repeatedly illustrates that the pagan nations were judged by the same moral standard as the Mosaic law, however. The Creator of all mankind did not have a double standard of ethics. The law which would later be revealed through Moses (Lev. 18:22; 20:13) expressed the same divine moral principle by which the Sodomites were *earlier* condemned for their "lawless works" (Gen. 19:15; 2 Peter 2:9). Had they violated the Mosaic law? Yes and no.

They violated a law which corresponds to and is revealed through Moses, but Moses had not yet even given the law.[39] "All the wicked of the earth" who stray from God's "statutes" are condemned (Psalm 119:118-119), and in context this cannot credibly exclude the Mosaic moral precepts. God declares His intention to "judge among *the nations*" on the basis of "the law" which shall "go

---

37. Young, *Isaiah*, pp. 157-58.

38. House and Ice, *Dominion Theology*, pp. 128-29 (emphasis mine); cf. p. 130.

39. House and Ice seem to miss the startling significance of this fact (*ibid.*, p. 136). So obvious is it in Scripture that the Mosaic moral commands are universally binding that the standards of the Mosaic law do not await the historical event of his promulgating them for God to begin enforcing them.

forth *out of Zion*" (Isa. 2:3-4). Amos, Nahum, and Habakkuk all declared Jehovah's judgment upon Gentile nations for violating moral standards found in the law of Moses — for example, pertaining to matters as mundane and specific as slave trafficking (Amos 1:6; Exodus 21:16; Deut. 24:7), witchcraft (Nahum 3:4; Exodus 22:18; Lev. 19:21), and loan pledges (Hab. 2:6; Exodus 22:25-27; Deut. 24:6, 10-13). John the Baptist declared the moral standard of the Mosaic law to Herod, saying "it is not lawful" for him to have his brother's wife (Mark 6:18). The moral standards of the Mosaic law were not unique to Israel, even though the Mosaic covenantal administration was.

Conclusion

The Bible is decisive on this point at Deuteronomy 4:6-8, where Moses declared that "all these statutes . . . all this law"[40] which he had delivered to the nation would be the conspicuous "wisdom" and "righteousness" of Israel in the sight of the surrounding peoples. This passage pointedly contradicts the statement by House and Ice that "the nations surrounding Israel were never called upon to adopt the law of Moses."[41] To rescue themselves they can only try to tone down the implications of the passage by saying it merely says the nations would be "attracted" to Israel and deem it wise.[42] Such is the contrivance to which dispensationalism is driven. Scripture says that the nations would also perceive the "righteousness" of the Mosaic precepts (Deut. 4:8). Yet House and Ice are trying to hold that the nations were not thereby "called to adopt" those precepts! Such thinking founders on the presupposition either that righteousness is not something obligatory in the sight of God but optional (one choice among many, a matter of preference), or that righteousness is variable (being different things from culture to culture).

---

40. Notice how this emphasis contradicts the opinion expressed by House and Ice that Israel's status as a "model" to the nations did not require the nations to follow "all or most of the commands given to Israel" (House and Ice, *Dominion Theology*, p. 131).

41. *Ibid.*, p. 128.

42. *Ibid.*

Summary

1. Dispensationalists House and Ice have not offered in their book, *Dominion Theology*, any significant rebuttal to the theonomic view of God's law.

2. House and Ice's exegesis of Matthew 5:17-19 was logically and grammatically flawed.

3. Their appeal to Paul fell short of showing him to set aside the Old Testament law.

4. Their discussion of the nations not being under the law of Moses rested upon fundamental conceptual confusions and ran directly up against the text and teaching of Scripture.

5. Our examination of their arguments has given us opportunity to see again part of the biblical basis for the conviction that the jurisdiction of God's law is universal.

6. The moral requirements revealed in the Mosaic law are not unique to the Old Testament era or to the Jewish people in that period.

7. The law of God, even as revealed through Moses, continues to have abiding validity in the New Covenant, and its authority extends to the Gentile nations. Listen to Paul. "Now we know that whatever things the law says, it speaks to those who are under the law" (Rom. 3:19). Who is it to whom the law speaks, and who thereby comes under its scrutiny and judgment? Paul answers our question immediately, teaching that the law is addressed to all men "in order that . . . all the world may be brought under the judgment of God." The world, we conclude, is under the jurisdiction of God's law, even its Mosaic revelation of its requirements.

8

THE CIVIL AND CULTURAL USE OF THE LAW

A reply to the argument that God's Law has no moral authority in politics and society.

The opposition of dispensationalists House and Ice to the Reconstructionist vision of ethics and the Christian life comes to a head over the issue of applying God's law (including the Mosaic revelation of its precepts) to modern society and the civil magistrate. This seems to be the thing which dispensationalists find especially controversial about Christian Reconstruction. Were it not for this, it is likely the criticism would be toned down, and the effort put into refuting Reconstructionist ethics would be less intense. However, given the theonomic understanding of the universal and perpetual authority of God's law, it would be arbitrary special pleading to exempt society and its civil leaders from moral obligation to the provisions of God's law which speak to them, provide guidance for them, and pose an absolute ethical standard by which to evaluate them.

It remains for us, then, to defend the Reconstructionist position against the complaints and arguments of House and Ice pertaining to the civil magistrate and social transformation. As it turns out, much of what needs to be said in response to the critique of *Dominion Theology* as it addresses these subjects has already been written in previous chapters. The major drawbacks faced by critics House and Ice are that they so extensively misrepresent the Reconstructionist position (see Chapter 5 above) and employ false standards and numerous kinds of fallacious argumentation throughout their book (see Chapter 4 above).

Once those matters are cleared away, there is considerably less to deal with in their critique of Reconstructionist ethics. Of what remains, the greater part of their argument is directed at the foundational premises of theonomic ethics which lead to the disputed application of God's law to modern society and politics. The Biblical credentials of these premises have been defended in Chapters 6 and 7 above. One should recognize, we have argued, that the law of God, even the Mosaic revelation of it, reflects God's essential and unchanging, moral character; the principles of His law are sometimes communicated in terms of concrete cultural circumstances (judicial or case-law forms), in which case it is the underlying moral requirement which binds all men in all cultures.

There is also in the Mosaic law a ceremonial code (redemptive-restorative provisions) which rests upon God's good pleasure to save His people; such commands as these have been set aside in the New Covenant (with the coming of the reality which they foreshadowed). With these things in mind, we have found that Matthew 5:17-20 establishes a presumption in favor of the continuing validity of Old Testament commandments. Although Paul the apostle does lay aside the ceremonial system of ordinances, he never removes believers from the authority of the moral precepts of the Old Testament or Mosaic law. According to Scripture, the jurisdiction of God's moral requirements is not at all limited to Old Testament Israel, but is universal and thus extends to the nations. The law is addressed to the entire world.

With the establishment of these things, the Reconstructionist view of ethics is in a strong position to draw the general conclusions which it does about the validity of the law in guiding modern societies and states. What are the remaining arguments advanced by House and Ice to oppose those ideas? We turn to give them a response.

Direct Interaction with Theonomic Argumentation

At a few points House and Ice directly challenge aspects of the argumentation offered by theonomists for the view that civil magistrates are bound to the law of God as revealed through Moses.[1] For instance, they agree with theonomists that in Romans 13 Paul states that rulers have the function of being avengers of His wrath. They immediately add: "But he never ties it into the law of Moses."[2] Their rebuttal is itself rebutted, however, by looking at 1 Timothy 1:8-10. There Paul very clearly ties the restraint of evil men to the law of God, and "the law" to which he refers is certainly the law of Moses (or at least includes it). "The law" would be the well-known law, and Paul's insistence upon its goodness takes as its background disputes over the status and value of the law of Moses in particular. Furthermore, returning to Romans 13, House and Ice should have noticed that the word "evil," which is used for what the civil magistrate is to punish (v. 4), is also mentioned in verse 10, where it has been defined in terms of "the law." This law is quoted in verse 9, where again it cannot be denied that Paul was thinking of the Mosaic law.

House and Ice agree that David desired to bring the nations under his kingship, but they say that David did not want to "rule over them" but simply defeat them.[3] Provided that some clearer sense can be made of this claim, we would have to dispute its accuracy. David wished to see his dynasty rule the nations (e.g., Psalm 72). The authors go on to assert, "nowhere is there a statement of seeking to impose the Mosaic code on the nations." This too is inaccurate. In Psalm 119, which indisputably includes reference to the law of Moses, David spoke of his desire to speak God's testimony and commandments before kings (v. 46), where these must be Gentile kings.

In response to the biblical evidence that the Old Testament prophets condemn the nations for moral infractions of the Mosaic law, House and Ice claim that "all of the judgments of the nations mentioned in the prophets may be seen . . . long before Sinai."[4]

---

1. In particular they attempt to rebut lines of argument offered in *Theonomy in Christian Ethics* (ex. ed.; Phillipsburg, NJ: Presbyterian and Reformed, [1977] 1984), with special attention on Chapters 18 and 19.

2. H. Wayne House and Thomas Ice, *Dominion Theology: Blessing or Curse?* (Portland, OR: Multnomah, 1988), p. 135.

3. *Ibid.*, p. 136.

4. *Ibid.*, p. 137.

Once again they have spoken prematurely. The reader may simply consult the examples of this sort of thing which are adduced in Chapter 7 above: things such as the prohibitions about slave trafficking, witchcraft, and loan pledges. We invite House and Ice to offer a convincing substantiation that these prohibitions were specifically revealed prior to Moses.

The counter-claims made by House and Ice to the biblical evidence and reasoning of theonomists do not carry any validity, then. The theonomic argument about the civil magistrate in the Gentile nations and in the New Testament has not been damaged at all.

The Argument from the Noahic Covenant

House and Ice propose that the world at large is not under moral obligation to the provisions of the Mosaic law. However, due to the nature and recipients of the covenant made with Noah, all nations today are bound to the moral instruction of the Noahic covenant.[5] The nations are judged under the Noahic, not Sinaitic, covenant according to them.[6] They would say that the civil magistrate's duty to deter evil and honor the good today (Rom. 13:1-4) is simply the duty which is laid out in the Noahic covenant.[7] Likewise, "Paul in Romans 13:1-2 states that rulers have this function [avenging God's wrath], but he never ties it into the law of Moses."[8]

---

5. *Ibid.*, pp. 86, 119, 127, 130, 135, 137, 339.

6. *Ibid.*, p. 137.

7. *Ibid.*, p. 135. House and Ice note that several passages are adduced by Bahnsen for the view that magistrates must deter evil and honor the good (such as from Proverbs), "but none of these passages are directed to Gentiles" (p. 136). This remark is wrong on two counts. (1) One of the passages adduced for this point is precisely Romans 13:3, which is most certainly directed to Gentiles! (2) The passages from the book of Proverbs are also applicable to the Gentiles when one remembers the nature and function of the Hebrew wisdom literature which was aimed to be international in influence and scope. This is noted in *Theonomy* (p. 343), but House and Ice to not interact with it, which they will need to do before their categorical remark above can carry any weight.

8. House and Ice, *Dominion Theology*, p. 137.

What is defective with this position ought to have been noticeable when House and Ice were thinking it through. Upon reflection, few people today would really want the moral standards for civil government limited to the revelation of God's will to Noah. First, the revelation to Noah does not cover many (indeed, most) of the matters which have to be dealt with by civil magistrates in order to protect their citizens; for instance, the revelation to Noah says nothing about stealing and fraud, nothing about rape and kidnapping, nothing about perjury and contracts, nothing about compensation for damages, etc. House and Ice unduly restrict the function and authority of the civil government by tying its powers solely to the Noahic covenant.

Second, the one major civil provision made in the Noahic covenant deals with the punishment of murder. However, most people would prefer to have the advantage of progressive revelation, looking to the Mosaic law for the explanations and qualifications which are necessary to apply the law about murder. For instance, the Noahic revelation takes no account of the difference between accidental and premeditated homicide. If the moral authority of the civil magistrate today were limited to the Noahic covenant, as House and Ice say, then we would be prevented from applying such a qualification in our courts today. It simply is not wise for us to turn away from the help which God's revelation makes available to us after the time of Noah.

Third, it is obvious that the apostle Paul did not think of the civil magistrate's authority in the limited terms proposed by House and Ice. When Paul spoke of the legitimate powers of the state in Romans 13, he chose the example of collecting taxes (v. 7). However, there is absolutely no hint of such a thing in the Noahic covenant. Paul was either consciously supplementing the Noahic standards for civil rule (taxes would have been morally illegitimate prior to that point), or he did not adopt the artificial restriction of civil prerogatives and responsibilities to the Noahic covenant.

Fourth, we might imagine that House and Ice begin now to work hard and creatively in order to devise some way to justify civil taxes, manslaughter distinctions, and prohibitions about loan pledges, slave trafficking, etc. — all on the basis of Scriptural revelation only up to and through the time of Noah. This task is lacking in plausibility, but let us imagine that it were somehow accomplished. The theonomist would simply at that point take the very same kind of (creative) hermeneutical approach which had been used by House and Ice and show that any and all the other provisions of the Mosaic law could equally be discovered by this way of treating the biblical text. More likely, House and Ice would not try to go through gymnastics with the text at all, but would rather appeal to a moral knowledge which general revelation has given all men concerning slave trafficking, taxes, manslaughter distinctions, etc. The theonomist would simply reply that all of the Mosaic provisions are equally contained in general revelation. Either way, the approach to difficulties taken by House and Ice will prevent them from rejecting the theonomic commitment to the law of Moses (along with the rest of God's word).

The Argument from Silence

Many times in *Dominion Theology* the authors argue that the penal sanctions of the Mosaic law are not binding after the Old Testament because they are not repeated or their enforcement is not called for by New Testament writers.[9] This is akin to the reasoning that says the penal sanctions of the Mosaic law were not extended to the Gentile nations and are thus variable.[10]

What can we say to this line of reasoning? Well the obvious thing is simply that arguing from silence is a notorious logical fallacy. (E.g., I have not been told or shown that House and Ice paid their income taxes last year; therefore, they did not pay their taxes.) There are numerous reasons why the civil sanctions of the Old Testament law may not or could not be enforced (or even

---

9. *Ibid.*, pp. 89, 111, 118. Some of the examples offered by House and Ice that Jesus did not endeavor to have the Mosaic penal sanctions enforced actually rest on their own misunderstanding of the law (e.g., what crimes called for the death penalty, and under what conditions) or of the New Testament (e.g., that Matt. 13:27-30 deals with false prophets), etc.

10. House and Ice, *Dominion Theology*, pp. 89-90.

mentioned) at certain points in the New Testament (e.g., John 18:28-32). Given those alternative explanations, one cannot automatically conclude that the civil sanctions were deemed abrogated. Why does the New Testament not explicitly condemn bestiality? To follow the reasoning of House and Ice, we would be led to answer that the prohibition has been abrogated — which shows the absurdity of arguing from silence.

Why did Paul not direct the Church to apply the Mosaic penal sanction to the man guilty of incest?[11] A number of reasons may be relevant, but perhaps the most important that we can imagine is that God has not authorized the Church to function in that way; only the civil magistrate bears not the sword in vain. Besides, the actual civil government at the time would not likely have cared to punish the individual in this case, anyway. House and Ice respond to this second consideration by saying that Christians should have raised a prophetic voice against the unrighteousness of their civil government.[12] Well, let us assume that this is so. Do we know that they did not raise that prophetic voice? The absence of any mention of (or call for) it in the text cannot tell us the answer to our question. Do we know that they raised a prophetic voice to rebuke the unrighteousness of their civil leaders for failing to punish rape? Well, there is no indication of it in the text, and surely the city of Corinth had people who were guilty of this crime. Should we conclude now that rape is not to be a punishable offense in the New Testament?

The fact is that House and Ice are indulging in all too easy fallacious reasoning when they conclude that Paul set aside the enforcement of the Mosaic law simply because he did not urge the application of its penal sanctions when dealing with situations within the Church. *When* Paul did speak to the subject of the public restraint of criminal behavior, he quite openly commended the goodness of God's law (1 Tim. 1:8-10; cf. Heb. 2:2). Silence cannot reasonably outweigh his definite statements elsewhere, nor does it

---

11. *Ibid.*, p. 118.
12. *Ibid.*, pp. 121-22.

have the power to overcome the presumption of the Old Testament law's continuing authority (cf. Matt. 5:17-19).

The Wisdom Approach to Civil Law

Although it is the burden of House and Ice to argue in *Dominion Theology* against the theonomic view that it is morally obligatory for all men in all ages to obey the precepts of God's law (even as revealed through Moses), they would not take the position that people are forbidden to follow the law of Moses today. According to them, you may choose to follow the provisions of the Mosaic law for reasons which seem persuasive to you, but there is no moral obligation for you or anybody else to do so.[13] Indeed, the nations may look at the precepts of Moses and gain wisdom from them.[14] The laws of Moses may be helpful to us today as examples.[15] "Certainly many of the practical expressions of the law God gave to Israel, and the particular penalties, may be used as a model for establishing civil laws for society, but there is no requirement to do so."[16] "Wisdom is advice with no legal penalties attached," for consideration is given instead to "certain benefits" which will come from following the law's suggestion.[17]

In comparing their "wisdom" approach to the law of God and the theonomic approach, House and Ice end up saying "There is not much difference in how one approaches the Old Testament case laws."[18] Each school of thought feels there is a sense in which these laws are applicable, and each makes some modifications for modern culture. Both approaches love the law of God and follow it because they walk in the Spirit. Nevertheless, it must be said that the Mosaic commandments "are wrongly taken as law binding on us today."[19]

---

13. *Ibid.*, pp. 86-87.
14. *Ibid.*, p. 100.
15. *Ibid.*, p. 119.
16. *Ibid.*, p. 137.
17. *Ibid.*, p. 186.
18. *Ibid.*, p. 187.
19. *Ibid.*, p. 188.

What should we make of this "wisdom" approach to the law of God? It may sound good, convenient or relevant to many people, but ultimately the real question is whether it represents a biblical mentality and a biblical approach to responding to God's holy word. The question is whether this approach really reflects *the biblical concept of wisdom itself*, or rather represents a concept devised in an extrabiblical fashion and is now being imposed upon the Bible from outside. We must be careful of any subtle (even well-meaning) influences which would lead us to diminish from God's word what He Himself has not taken away (Deut. 4:2).

The book of Proverbs is calculated to teach and instill in us the virtue of true wisdom (1:2). The wisdom which it gives encourages insightful and faithful application of God's word to the practical details of life — thus involving some flexibility, a large dose of teachability, and proper appreciation for the general and long-term consequences of one's conduct and attitudes. So then, wisdom brings a nimble *application* of God's law. The question we must ask, though, is about the character of *God's law* itself. Does it have the nature of helpful suggestion or advice which we are free to take or leave? Is law ever presented in the Bible as something less than obligatory? Precepts, commandments, statutes are things which the Bible sets forth as demanding *obedience* (although there is plenty in Scripture which speaks of the consequentialist advantages or blessings which attend obedience). They are marked by "Thou shalt" and "Thou shalt not." What is the attitude and approach of true *wisdom* to these commands from God? Proverbs tells us:

The wise in heart will receive commandments (10:8).

He that fears the commandment shall be rewarded (13:13).

He that keeps the commandment keeps his soul, but he that is careless of his ways shall die (19:16).

They that forsake the law praise the wicked, but such as keep the law contend with them (28:4).

Whoever keeps the law is a wise son (28:7).

Where there is no revelation the people cast off restraint, but he that keeps the law, happy is he (29:18).

Looking at things through biblical eyes, then, we see that it is the epitome of foolishness to depart from the path laid out in God's word. It is never *wise* for us to disagree with or act contrary to the divine *wisdom* which is set forth in the word of God, including His obligatory law. Where would we ever get the *greater wisdom* necessary to decide against compliance with the wisdom set forth in a commandment from God? By *what standard* would a sinful human being look at the demand of God's law, compare it with some other (uninspired) suggestion, and then choose the latter *over* the former? "The ordinances of Jehovah are true and righteous altogether. . . . Moreover by them is thy servant warned. . . . Who could discern His errors?" (Psalm 19:9-12). "O the depth of the riches both of the wisdom and the knowledge of God! . . . For who has known the mind of the Lord? or who has been His counselor?" (Rom. 11:33-34). "Who has known the mind of the Lord that he should instruct Him?" (1 Cor. 2:16).

The whole "wisdom approach" of House and Ice is theologically and biblically wrong-headed, as we can see from a consideration of the biblical texts set forth above. God has supreme wisdom, and nobody can presume to correct His ordinances or instruct Him. The wisdom which He graciously grants His people leads them to accept His commandments, not only as their absolute obligation but also as supremely rewarding to their lives. The wise son is not the one who at times decides he can disagree with his heavenly Father or sees his Father's prescriptions as mere suggestions, but the one who keeps his Father's commands. He knows that there is no wiser way to get along in this world. In fact, the commandments of God — every statute of them — *constitute* his wisdom in this world (Deut. 4:6-8).

Summary

1. House and Ice have proven to be unsuccessful in challenging the biblical support for the Reconstructionist approach to ethics and politics.

2. House and Ice have not negated the force of the biblical support which the theonomic position can enlist.

3. House and Ice have done little more than fallaciously argue from silence against the modern application to politics of God's law as revealed through Moses.

4. House and Ice have proven unsuccessful in devising a cogent alternative to political ethics which enjoys the support of God's written word.

5. Their suggestion to follow the Noahic covenant instead of the Mosaic revelation is both artificial ("all scripture . . . is profitable for instruction in righteousness," 2 Tim. 3:16-17) and inadequate to meet the practical problems of political order.

6. They have suggested that we need not look upon the judicial laws of the Old Testament as genuine laws (obligatory), but simply as optional suggestions or examples, thereby presuming to be wiser at some points than God Himself and to act contrary to true wisdom by not submitting to the wisdom of God's people in this world, the divine law which has been delivered to us.

7. To call House and Ice's view the "wisdom approach" is a misnomer of startling proportions.

8. To employ this subtle form of autonomy when it comes to guiding the civil magistrate is not to heed true Wisdom which says, "By Me kings reign, and princes decree justice. By Me princes rule, and nobles, even all the judges of the earth" (Prov. 8:15-16). "Now therefore be wise, O ye kings: Be instructed, ye judges of the earth. Serve Jehovah with fear, and rejoice with trembling. Kiss the Son, lest he by angry, and ye perish in the way, For his wrath will soon be kindled. Blessed are all they that take refuge in him" (Psalm 2:10-12).

Part II
THE ESCHATOLOGICAL QUESTION

9

THE CONFLICT OF EXPECTATIONS

Accurately defining postmillennialism in terms of the Gospel Victory theme.

The following chapters will be given over to a consideration of the various criticisms that House and Ice have brought against Reconstructionist eschatology — particularly its dominant post-millennialism. Unfortunately, our inquiry necessarily will have to be merely summary, due to space limitations. This is quite disappointing for at least two reasons: (1) With their shotgun attack upon Reconstructionism, a great number of issues were sprayed across their pages, many of them in a superficial manner.[1] (2) Contrary to the simplistic impression left by their book, the eschatological locus of systematic theology is exceedingly broad, deep and involved. Certainly no "one passage"[2] should lead to any eschatological system.

As will be illustrated in survey fashion, the material of eschatology begins at the genesis of universal history and extends to the consummation.[3] Thus its breadth encompasses the whole of time and the entirety of the biblical record. It is a deep inquiry in that it involves God's unsearchable, infinite, and eternal will and pur-

---

1. See Part III below where a number of their scholarly lapses are pointed out.

2. H. Wayne House and Thomas Ice, *Dominion Theology: Blessing or Curse?* (Portland, OR: Multnomah, 1988), p. 9. See quotation on pp. 141-42 below.

3. House and Ice recognize this: "David Chilton once offered me the following exegetical support for postmillennialism: 'That's why my book started in Genesis. I wanted to demonstrate that the Paradise Restored theme (i.e., postmillennialism) is not dependent on any one passage, but is taught throughout Scripture. . . . The fact is, postmillennialism is on every page of the Bible' " (*ibid.*, p. 9). "To understand Reconstructionist views of the end, we must go back to the beginning" (*ibid.*, p. 47).

pose. It is involved in that it incorporates both personal and cosmic eschatology and a number of redemptive, spiritual, ethical, and cultural matters flowing from them. Furthermore, it draws upon revelational language and concepts from all eras of revelation: the pre-Mosaic, Mosaic, Prophetic, and Christic-Apostolic eras.

This leads to a practical necessity for limiting our inquiry due to the designedly compressed nature of our study. We will focus on just a few themes related to cosmic eschatology that have been woefully misunderstood by House and Ice and neglected by many contemporary evangelicals. One particular theme — the Gospel Victory Theme — is quite dominant in the entire prophetic Scriptures; its omission in much modern eschatology is to be lamented. Its replacement with a defeatist scheme for Christian activity has paralyzed the Christian cultural enterprise, emptied the Christian worldview of practical significance, and given the Christian a sinful comfort in lethargy. It has left the earth (which "is the Lord's," Psalm 24:1) to a conquered foe and the enemy of our Lord and Savior. This paralysis is all the more lamentable in that it has caused the forfeiture of great gains made by the tireless and costly labors of our Christian forefathers, particularly from the Reformation era through the early 1900s.

Furthermore, this Gospel Victory Theme of postmillennialism — an eschatology thought moribund for much of the present century — is receiving renewed attention and debate in our era, as House and Ice's work so clearly demonstrates. The topic is quite relevant since the mid-1970s. Let us begin with a definition of the system to which the writers of this book adhere.

Definition of Postmillennialism

Postmillennialism is that system of eschatology which understands the Messianic kingdom to have been founded upon the earth during the earthly ministry and through the redemptive labors of the Lord Jesus Christ in fulfillment of Old Testament prophetic expectation. The fundamental nature of that kingdom is essentially redemptive and spiritual, rather than political and corporeal. Because of the intrinsic power and design of Christ's redemption, this kingdom will exercise a transformational socio-cultural influence in history as more and more people are converted to Christ. Postmillennialism, thus, expects the gradual, developmental expansion of the kingdom of Christ in time and on earth. This expansion will proceed by means of the full-orbed ministry of the Word, fervent and believing prayer, and the consecrated labors of His Spirit-filled people, all directed and blessed by the ever-present Christ, Who is now at the right hand of God ruling and reigning over the earth. It confidently anticipates a time in earth history (which is continuous with the present) in which the very gospel already operative in the world will have won the victory throughout the earth in fulfillment of the Great Commission. During that time, the overwhelming majority of men and nations will be Christianized, righteousness will abound, wars will cease, and prosperity and safety will flourish. After an extended period of gospel prosperity, earth history will be drawn to a close by the personal, visible, bodily return of Jesus Christ (accompanied by a literal resurrection and a general judgment) to introduce His blood-bought people into the consummative and eternal form of the kingdom, and so shall we ever be with the Lord.

Our Concern

We will begin with a quick biblico-theological overview of the revelatory progress of eschatology in Scripture. From there we shall move on to consider several of the more significant questions raised by House and Ice — questions regarding the nature, presence, mission, and victory of the Messianic kingdom; the rise of postmillennialism in ecclesiastical history; and the legitimacy of a preteristic approach to certain prophecies.

In doing this we will be answering their concern:

At best, the Reconstructionist system is built upon a theological inference, from which they try to develop a large body of Scripture.[4]

---

4. What kind of statement is this? No Reconstructionist attempts to develop a large body of Scripture from a theological inference. Surely they mean it the

If certain things are assumed about the Bible, a Reconstructionist can make his system appear to work within the biblical framework, especially to the naive. However, this system can never be
derived from specific biblical passages.

What passages do Reconstructionists base their eschatology
upon? Where does the Bible teach that we, not Christ, are the
instruments to establish Christ's earthly kingdom? Where does
the Bible say that we are to be involved in the social, political,
and economic aspects of society during the church age in the way
Reconstructionists affirm? Failure to answer such questions reveals the weakness of Christian Reconstructionist dogma when
examined under the light of the Scriptures alone.[5]

Ice is quite aghast at the assertion of a postmillennial expectation and is confident that it is wholly baseless:

My challenge is simply this: Since postmillennialism is on every
page of the Bible, show me *one* passage that requires a postmillennial interpretation and should not be taken in a premillennial
sense. After fourteen years of study it is my belief that there is
not one passage anywhere in Scripture that would lead to the
postmillennial system.[6]

Still further in this direction we may note the following (apocryphal?)[7] story:

While in college in 1974, Tommy spent an evening in the home
of a professor who was hosting Gary North. . . . Toward the

---

other way around, i.e., Reconstructionists seek to develop a *theological inference*
from a *large body of Scripture*. In fact, a more accurate statement in this regard is
found elsewhere in their book: "Tommy . . . was quite interested in how postmillennialism could be developed from the Bible" (*ibid.*, p. 335). Their frequent
carelessness in wording betrays their carelessness in theological method, as well.
    5. House and Ice, *Dominion Theology*, pp. 149-50.
    6. *Ibid.*, p. 9 (emphasis his).
    7. Gary North has absolutely no recollection of such an event as outlined by
Ice. And such an episode is wholly out of character for such a person as North,
who, according to House and Ice, "evidences a profundity of thought" (p. 19), is
"brilliant" (p. 335), and is one who enjoys "gleefully attacking ideological foes"
(p. 18).

end of the evening, Tommy, who was quite interested in how postmillennialism could be developed from the Bible, asked North what passages of Scripture he appealed to for his eschatology. Tommy recounts North's reaction: "I will never forget his response. He just looked down at the floor and stared, not answering. I prompted him, but he continued to stare at the floor."

This incident serves as a microcosm of our first criticism, not just of postmillennialism, but of many features of the entire Christian Reconstruction movement.[8]

What are we to make of such boldness? After fourteen years of study has Ice not been able to find "one passage" which would suggest even the possibility of postmillennialism and protect the theological standing of such postmillennial theologians as Matthew Henry, John Owen, Jonathan Edwards, David Brown, Charles Hodge, A. A. Hodge, J. A. Alexander, Albert Barnes, J. H. Thornwell, W. G. T. Shedd, Robert L. Dabney, Augustus H. Strong, B. B. Warfield, J. Gresham Machen, O. T. Allis, Loraine Boettner, J. Marcellus Kik, John Murray, Iain Murray, and John Jefferson Davis, to name but a few?[9] Have these biblical scholars squandered their considerable labors and endangered their theological reputations by building monumental systems without even "one passage" of support? In the three centuries covered by these scholars, have they failed to produce even "one passage" to suggest their views? This is not to say that simply because these notables held to postmillennialism, therefore it is true. But Ice's assessment

8. House and Ice, *Dominion Theology*, p. 335.
9. Matthew Henry, *Matthew Henry's Commentary* (1714); John Owen, *The Works of John Owen*, vol. 8 (first published 1850-1853); Jonathan Edwards, *The Works of Jonathan Edwards* (first published 1834); David Brown, *Christ's Second Coming: Will It Be Premillennial?* (1849); Charles Hodge, *Systematic Theology* (1871); A. A. Hodge, *Outlines of Theology* (1860); J. A. Alexander, *Commentary on Isaiah* (1847); Albert Barnes, *Isaiah* (1860); J. H. Thornwell, *Collected Writings*, vol. 4 (1871); W. G. T. Shedd, *Dogmatic Theology* (1888); Robert L. Dabney, *Lectures in Systematic Theology* (1878); Augustus H. Strong, *Systematic Theology* (1907); B. B. Warfield, *Selected Shorter Writings* (first published 1970); J. Gresham Machen's view is referenced in Gary North, *Common Grace*; O. T. Allis, "Preface" to Roderick Campbell, *Israel and the New Covenant* (1954); Loraine Boettner, *The Millennium* (1957); J. Marcellus Kik, *An Eschatology of Victory* (1955); John Murray, *Romans*, vol. 2 (1965); Iain Murray, *The Puritan Hope* (1971); John Jefferson Davis, *Christ's Victorious Kingdom* (1986).

is such that not even "one passage" has ever been discovered that could suggest postmillennialism!

Dispensationalist Follies

And is postmillennialism "naive"? How soon we forget! Was it not in the same year that House and Ice wrote their book that fundamentalism was in a frenetical uproar over Edgar Whisenant's best-selling *88 Reasons Why the Rapture Is in 1988*? And consider the lament of an endorser of House and Ice's book: In dispensationalist Dave Hunt's 1988 work he pointed to the disappointment of many (naive) dispensationalists in the 1980s: "Needless to say, January 1, 1982, saw the defection of large numbers from the pretrib position. . . . Many who were once excited about the prospects of being caught up to heaven at any moment have become confused and disillusioned by the apparent failure of a generally accepted biblical interpretation they once relied upon."[10]

Has not dispensationalist pop-theologian (another endorser of House and Ice's book) Hal Lindsey written *The 1980's: Countdown to Armageddon*, suggesting the real possibility of the rapture in that decade? "*The decade of the 1980's could very well be the last decade of history as we know it.*"[11] What of premillennialist Dwight Wilson's penetrating exposé of numerous miscalculations of the Rapture by noted dispensationalists and premillennialists throughout this century?[12] Thus, who presents a "danger" of "false hopes"?[13]

And what is more "naive" than to expect "one passage" to lead to a whole "system" of eschatology? Do dispensationalists have "one passage" that leads to their "system" of an offer of an earthly, political, Jewish kingdom in the days of Christ, only to have it postponed for millennia after the Jews rejected it,[14] with the pres-

---

10. Dave Hunt, *Whatever Happened to Heaven?* (Eugene, OR: Harvest House, 1988), p. 68.

11. Hal Lindsey, *The 1980's: Countdown to Armageddon* (New York: Bantam, 1980), p. 8 (emphasis is his); cf. pp. 12, 15.

12. Dwight Wilson, *Armageddon Now: The Premillenarian Response to Russia and Israel Since 1917* (Grand Rapids, MI: Baker Book House, 1977). This book is scheduled to be reprinted by the Institute for Christian Economics.

13. House and Ice, *Dominion Theology*, cf. pp. 344-45.

14. J. Dwight Pentecost, *Things to Come: A Study in Biblical Eschatology* (Grand Rapids, MI: Zondervan/Academie, [1958] 1964), p. 201. Despite their trying forcefully to make Him king (John 6:15)!

ent era being an intercalation in the plan of God,[15] but all the while expecting an imminent, secret rapture[16] and secret resurrection of saints only (the first resurrection), followed by a seven year tribulation in which the Jewish temple will be rebuilt and Jewish evangelism without the baptism, sealing, indwelling, and filling power of the Holy Spirit[17] will be more successful in seven years than 2,000 years of Holy Spirit-empowered Church evangelistic labor,[18] followed by the visible, glorious Second Coming of Christ "to the earth,"[19] at which point saved Jews of the Old Testament era and the Tribulation saints will be resurrected (a second resurrection),[20] to establish a 365,000-day[21] literal, earthly, political kingdom with Jews[22] reigning at the highest levels (over their servants, the saved Gentiles),[23] which kingdom will be over an earthly population composed also of unresurrected mortals, while a heavenly city will "be made visible above the earth" for 1,000 years in which dwell glorified, resurrected saints,[24] and will witness the divinely approved reinstitution of memorial animal sacrifices,[25] followed eventually by the second humiliation of Christ, when His personally administered kingdom revolts against Him

---

15. *Ibid.*, pp. 133-38, 201.

16. *Ibid.*, p. 203. One of the most remarkable phenomena exists in regard to this "secret rapture." The very verse it is based most solidly on is 1 Thessalonians 4:16, which is the noisiest verse in Scripture! "For the Lord himself shall descend with a *shout*, with the *voice of the archangel*, and with the *trump of God.*"

17. *Ibid.*, p. 263.

18. *Ibid.*, p. 269 speaks of the salvation of "a multitude that defies enumeration" in the Tribulation. See also pp. 273-74.

19. *Ibid.*, pp. 206, 280, 478. "There is no question but that the Lord Jesus Christ will reign in the theocratic kingdom on earth . . ." (p. 498).

20. *Ibid.*, pp. 410-11.

21. One thousand years times 365 days (it *must* be "literal," they say). *Ibid.*, pp. 491ff.

22. House and Ice, *Dominion Theology*, pp. 145, 169, 174, 400-5.

23. Pentecost, *Things to Come*, pp. 507-8.

24. Pentecost speaks of unresurrected people in the millennium (*ibid.*, pp. 489, 503ff.), as well as glorified people, although the resurrected people will be floating above the earth in a heavenly Jerusalem (Chapter 31) and "casting its light, which is the shining of the effulgence of the Son, onto the earth so that 'the nations of them which are saved shall walk in the light of it' " (pp. 577ff.).

25. *Ibid.*, pp. 512ff.

in an attempt to "destroy the seat of theocratic power and the subjects of the theocracy"[26] (despite the heavenly city, populated with
millions of indestructible men, floating above the earth), ending
up with the resurrection of the unsaved (a third resurrection,
which leaves in limbo the question of the resurrection of the dead
who were converted but died during the Millennium)[27] and the
Great White Throne Judgment?

Really, now, is it not "naive" to expect "one passage" to lead to
a whole "system"?

And what of the unwarranted charge regarding the postmillennial cultural hope as held by Reconstructionists? House and
Ice assert: "Failure to answer such questions reveals the weakness
of Christian Reconstructionist dogma." Have Reconstructionists
really *failed* to answer the questions in the eighty-five books listed
in House and Ice's "Annotated Bibliography of Dominion Theology"
spanning pages 425-440?

But then what are we to make of their other statements, in light
of this alleged failure? Did not they themselves say, Reconstructionist "arguments are too forceful to be lightly disregarded" and
"evidence a profundity of thought which merits consideration in its
own right"?[28] Did they not marvel over Rushdoony's "remarkable
output" of thirty books, including even his "massive (1600-page)
study."[29] Were they not impressed with "the challenging and prolific
writers who constitute the leadership of the Christian Reconstruction . . . ?"[30] The problem comes down to a familiar refrain: "He
who has ears, let him hear."

The story of Ice's episode with North is embarrassingly anachronistic. Even judging it to be true, how can a charge based on an
alleged silence of North to answer a theological question in 1974
serve "as a microcosm of our first criticism, not just of postmillennialism, but of many features of the entire Christian Reconstruc-

---

26. *Ibid.*, p. 551, cf. pp. 549, 578.
27. *Ibid.*, p. 411.
28. House and Ice, *Dominion Theology*, pp. 28, 19.
29. *Ibid.*, pp. 17-18.
30. *Ibid.*, p. 21.

tion movement"[31] in 1988? Hundreds of thousands of dollars have been invested in the publication of scores of Reconstructionist books in the decade and one-half since that date.

Engaging the Relevant Issues

The Table of Contents of *Dominion Theology: Blessing or Curse?* suggests a well-organized critique of Reconstruction thought. But looks are deceiving. The approach of the book tends to wander in two serious respects: (1) It is supposed to be critiquing the distinctive theology of Christian Reconstructionism. The title itself warrants this conclusion: "Dominion Theology: Blessing or Curse? An Analysis of Christian Reconstructionism." Instead, much of the work assaults Reformed theology in general.[32] (This should serve as a lesson in not judging a book by its cover — or at least its Table of Contents.) (2) There is a constant, frustrating meandering of thought in the argument as presented. Instead of focusing on distinctives of Reconstruction thought and firing toward the target in a focused manner, the tendency of the book is to stray off onto rabbit trails, well off from the hunt. This makes our task somewhat difficult: when being fired upon by a shotgun, it is hard to duck!

Hopefully our response to House and Ice will not suffer from such pandemonium. Having carefully read their analysis and having searched out the salient points of their arguments, we propose to deal especially with the following matters of significance in the debate over eschatology.

---

31. *Ibid.*, p. 335.

32. As one perceptive review put it: "The authors have drawn the lines for a stimulating debate between opposing sides, but *where* they have drawn the line tends to confuse the basic issues. Dispensationalism is on one side as a theological structure, but the opposite of that structure is *not* Reconstructionism. The opposite is the structure of Reformed theology — within which Reconstructionism is but one *application* from that structure. Since the authors do not make this clear, they tend to argue as if refuting Reconstructionism will necessitate adopting dispensationalism. The real debate is between the application of dispensationalism to modern Christian life and the application of Reformed theology." Robert Drake, "What Should the Kingdom of God Look Like?" *World* (February 11, 1989), p. 13.

Summary

1. Eschatology is a deep and involved aspect of Christian theology that may not be approached in a simplistic manner. No one passage may be expected to present an entire eschatological system.

2. The Gospel Victory Theme dominates the entire prophetic Scriptures, from Genesis 3:15 on.

3. The substitution of a defeatist scheme regarding Christian endeavor for the Gospel Victory Theme has paralyzed Christian endeavor in this century.

4. Postmillennialism holds that the prophesied kingdom of Christ was established in the first century and will victoriously spread throughout the earth by means of the propagation of the Gospel of the saving mercies of Jesus Christ.

5. There is coming a time in earth history, continuous with the present and resultant from currently operating spiritual forces, in which the overwhelming majority of men and nations will in salvation voluntarily bow to the Lordship of Jesus Christ, thus ushering in an era of widespread righteousness, peace, and prosperity.

6. Christ will not return to the earth until after His Spirit-blessed Gospel has won the victory in history (His coming is *post*-millennial).

7. Postmillennialism has been held by a great number of stalwart, evangelical and Reformed scholars in history.

10

THE EXPECTATION OF THE KINGDOM

A survey of the Biblical material revelational of the Gospel Victory theme.

The pre-dominant and distinguishing theme of Biblical eschatology is that of a sure expectancy of gospel victory in time and on earth. This can be seen in various ways in the Old Testament revelational record.

The Edenic Expectation of Victory

In order to understand a thing aright, it is always helpful to seek to understand its purpose according to its designer and builder. Eschatology[1] is a theological discipline that is concerned with discovering the divinely revealed, long range purpose[2] of the world and of history. It is concerned with the consummational direction of history: What will the consummation be? What are its precursors? How will it be brought about? When will it occur? By necessity, then, eschatology must be concerned with creation, for it is the divinely decreed fruition of creation as we know it — the end is tied to the beginning (Isa. 46:10; Rev. 21:6; 22:13).

God has created the world — and for a purpose. Despite the confusion brought into the question by certain leading dispensationalists, Reformed theology has as the ultimate goal of universal

---

1. All references to "eschatology" should be taken to refer to cosmic eschatology (e.g., the coming of Christ), rather than personal eschatology (the state of the believer at death).
2. The very question of "purpose" immediately draws a distinction between Christian eschatology and secular eschatology. Secularism disdains discussion of purpose, because it wholly undermines it with its fundamental irrationalism (in that it is rooted in Chance).

history, the glory of God.[3] His creational intent in bringing the world into being was for the manifestation of His own glory (Rev. 4:11; Rom. 11:36; Psalm 8:1; 19:1).

Furthermore, at the very beginning of history and before the Fall of man into sin, God created man in His own "image and likeness" (Gen. 1:26). One vital aspect of that image is that of man's acting as ruler over the earth and under God. This is evident in the close connection between the interpretive revelation regarding man's being created in God's image and His command to exercise rule over the creation order (Gen. 1:26-28).

Man lives up to His creational purpose as He exercises righteous dominion in the earth. God has implanted within man the drive to dominion.

The Creational (or Dominion) Mandate was given at the very creation of man, distinguishing man from the animal, plant, and protist kingdoms and defining His task in God's world in accordance with God's plan.[4] Not only was it given at creation *before* the Fall, but it remains in effect even *after* the entry of sin. This is evident in many ways, two of which will be mentioned. In the first place the revelational record of man's beginnings show man acting as a dominical creature and without disapprobation, subduing the earth and developing culture — even after the entry of sin. Indeed, from the very beginning and continuing into the post-Fall world, Adam and his descendants exercised dominion. And this

---

3. Dispensationalists attempt to construe covenantal theology as suggesting that redemption (narrowly considered) is the Bible's and history's overall goal, whereas dispensationalism has a more comprehensive goal: the glory of God. See Charles C. Ryrie, *Dispensationalism Today* (Chicago, IL: Moody Press, 1965), pp. 46, 98-105. This is erroneous in that: (1) It confuses a proximate goal (redemption) with an ultimate goal (God's glory); (2) it implies that there cannot be more than one goal (i.e., it is either glory or redemption); and (3) it is contrary to historic Reformed theology's glory emphasis as expressed in its most basic, covenantal creed: the Westminster Standards, including the Confession of Faith (3:3, 7; 4:1; 5:1; 6:1; 16:2, 7; 18:1; 33:12), the Larger Catechism (QQ. 1, 12, 13, 190), and the Shorter Catechism (QQ. 1, 2, 7, 47, 66, 101, 102, 107).

4. The Christian view is of at least a three-fold division in the natural realm: man, animal, and plant. This is contrary to the modern evolutionary division that includes man in the animal kingdom.

dominion impulse operated at a remarkably rapid rate, contrary to the primitive view of man held by modern anthropologists (Gen. 4:17-22).[5] Any primitiveness that may be found in earth cultures is a record of the developmental *consequence of sin* and of estrangement from God, not of *original creational status*. In the second place, the Creation Mandate is specifically repeated in Scripture in both testaments (Gen. 9:1ff.; Psalm 8; Heb. 2:5-8).

As will be demonstrated, the Gospel Victory Theme of postmillennialism comports well with God's creational purpose. It highlights the divine expectation of the true, created nature of man qua man. It expects the world as a system (or *kosmos*)[6] to be brought to submission to God's rule under the active, sanctified agency of redeemed man, who has been renewed in the image of God (Col. 3:10; Eph. 4:24). *Postmillennial eschatology expects what God originally intended.* It sees His plan as maintained and moving toward its original fruition.

The Post-Fall Expectation of Victory

The first genuinely eschatological statement in Scripture occurs very early: in Genesis 3:15. In keeping with the progressively unfolding nature of revelation, this eschatological datum lacks a specificity of the order of later revelation. At this stage of revelation the identity of the coming Redeemer is not sharply exhibited; it will take later revelation to fill out the picture, a picture not perfectly full until Christ actually comes at his First Advent. Yet the broad outlines drawn by this original eschatological statement are clear enough, particularly in light of the fuller New Testament revelation.

Orthodox Christians recognize the Genesis 3:15 reference as pointing to the coming and the redemptive labor of Christ as the Promised Redeemer. He is promised as One coming to crush His

---

5. That apes, lemurs, and monkeys are called "primates" (from the Latin *primus*, "first") is indicative of the evolutionary view of man.

6. *Kosmos* ("world") is the Greek word (used in the New Testament) which is expressive of the orderly system of the world; it is contrary to *chaos*. See pp. 201-7.

great enemy — undoubtedly Satan, the head of a nefarious kingdom. This passage portrays a mighty struggle between the woman's seed (Christ and His kingdom, cp. Rom. 16:20; cf. 1 Cor. 12:12-27; John 15:1-7; Matt. 25:40, 45) and the serpent's seed (Satan and his kingdom). This, then, is the theological explanation of struggle in history. It must not be overlooked that the point of this poetic *protoevangelium* is *victory*. A victory won by Christ. Later revelation in the New Testament shows that this prophecy began its fulfillment at the death-resurrection-ascension of Christ (1 John 3:8; Heb. 2:14; Col. 2:14,15; cp. Rev. 20:1-3), it is not awaiting some distant beginning of its fulfillment.

Thus, here we have at the very inception of prophecy in Scripture the certainty of victory. Just as the Fall of Adam has a worldwide negative effect, so is God's salvation, on the basis of the resurrection of Christ, to have a world-wide positive effect.[7] The crushing of Satan (Gen. 3:15) is not awaiting a consummative, catastrophic victory of Christ over Satan at the penultimate moment of present history. The idea (as will be more fully seen later) is that Satan the Destroyer, his nefarious kingdom, and its evil effects will be overwhelmed by the superior strength and glory of Christ the Lord, Who has already come (i.e., His First Advent). The specific means of its fulfillment must await later revelation.

The Patriarchal and Early Mosaic Expectation of Victory

As the redemptive cord grows stronger and the scarlet thread is woven more distinctively into the fabric of Scriptural revelation and history, the eschatological hope of redemptive victory trails right along, becoming itself more evident and more specific. The post-Adamic era of the patriarchs and the early Mosaic era are demonstrative of this fact. A list of a few of the more significant references in these eras will illustrate this truth.

Genesis 12:2-3; 13:14-16; 15:5; 16:10; 22:17-18; 26:4 promise that "all the families of the earth" will be blessed through the out-

---

7. Gary North, *Is the World Running Down?: Crisis in the Christian Worldview* (Ft. Worth: Dominion, 1988).

working of God's covenant with Abraham. Included in that seed by redemptive grace are people from "all the families of the earth." The New Testament informs us that Abraham has become "the father of circumcision to them who are not of the circumcision only, but who also walk in the steps of that faith of our father Abraham. . . . Therefore it is of faith, that it might be by grace; to the end the promise might be sure to all the seed; not to that only which is of the law, but to that also which is of the faith of Abraham; who is the father of us all" (Rom. 4:12, 16). We find the same truth taught in Paul's treatment of Abraham's seed in Galatians:

> Know ye therefore that they which are of faith, the same are the children of Abraham. And the scripture, foreseeing that God would justify the heathen through faith, preached before the gospel unto Abraham, saying, In thee shall all nations be blessed. So then they which be of faith are blessed with faithful Abraham. . . . That the blessing of Abraham might come on the Gentiles through Jesus Christ; that we might receive the promise of the Spirit through faith. . . . And if ye be Christ's, then are ye Abraham's seed, and heirs according to the promise (Gal. 3:7-9, 14, 29).

The land promised in the Abrahamic Covenant was merely a token of the inheritance of the whole earth, according to Paul's New Testament explication. "For the promise [was] that he should be the heir of the *world*" (Rom. 4:13). This will be made more clear as the prophets expand the horizons in later revelation.

The seed is promised victory in accordance with the original *protoevangelium* mention of the seed. Abraham's seed is to "possess the gates of the enemy" (cp. Gen. 22:17 with Matt. 16:18). Genesis 49:8-10 promises that Judah will maintain the scepter of rule until Shiloh [Christ] will come and then to Him "shall be the obedience of the peoples." Here is the first express mention of a personal redeemer. The redeemer is promised rule over all the peoples.

In Numbers 14:16-21 God promises to Moses, "Indeed, as I live, all the earth will be filled with the glory of the Lord." In Numbers 24:17-19 Balaam harkens back to Jacob's prophecy in Genesis 49:10. He foresees an all-powerful, world-wide dominion for the Messiah: "A star shall come forth from Jacob, and a scepter shall rise from Israel, and shall crush through the forehead of Moab, and tear down all the sons of Sheth. And Edom shall be a possession, Seir, its enemies, also shall be a possession, while Israel performs valiantly. One from Jacob shall have dominion, and shall destroy the remnant from the city."

The Prophetic Era Expectation of Victory

In the prophetic era we find a continuing and expanding development of the plan of redemption, and with it the promise of victory for the redeemed. Again, a list of biblical references will be ushered before the reader.

Particularly significant in this regard are the Messianic Psalms. In Psalm 2, Jehovah God laughs at the opposition of man to Him and to His Messiah. The Messiah is promised the "nations" and "the ends of the earth" as His "possession." On the basis of this promise, the kings and judges of the earth are exhorted to worship and serve the Son (Psalm 2:10-12).

In Psalm 22, it is prophesied that "all the ends of the earth will remember and turn to the Lord, and all the families of the nations will worship before Thee" (v. 27; cp. Psalm 66:4; 68:31-32; 82:8; 86:9). This obviously anticipates the fruition of the covenant of God given to Abraham and expanded in Moses and David.

In Psalm 72, this Messianic Gospel Victory Theme is tied to pre-consummative history, before the establishment of the eternal New Heavens and Earth. "Let them fear Thee *while the sun endures*, and *as long as the moon*, throughout all generations. May he come down like rain upon the mown grass, Like showers that water the earth.[8] In his days may the righteous flourish, and abundance of peace till the moon is no more, may he also rule from sea to sea, and from the River to the ends of the earth (vv. 5-8)."

---

8. The imagery of pouring rain here reflects the spiritual presence of Christ in the Person of the Holy Spirit (Rom. 8:9; John 14:16-18) being poured out upon the world from on high (Isa. 32:15; 44:3; Eze. 39:29; Joel 2:28-29; Zech. 12:10; Acts 2:17-18). Christ is "in" us via the Holy Spirit, which is poured out upon us since Pentecost.

The prophets greatly expand the theme of victory under the Messiah. Isaiah 2:1-4, 17-20 promise that in the "last days[9] . . . all nations shall flow to the house of the Lord" (v. 2), issuing forth in international peace (v. 4). In Isaiah 9:1-7 we learn that the Messiah's kingdom, once established, will ever increase. It is terribly important to notice the close connection between "the son" being born (His humiliation at the incarnation) as the one upon whom universal government devolves (v. 6) and his kingdom (His exaltation at the resurrection/ascension) growing and bearing peace (v. 7). In Isaiah 11:9, the future of the earth is seen prophetically as "full of the knowledge of the Lord as the waters cover the sea." Even the arch-enemies of God and His people, Egypt and Assyria, will be healed and will on an equal footing worship with Israel (Isa. 19:22-24).

Jeremiah foresees the day when the ark of the covenant will no longer be remembered, but in which "all the nations will be gathered before" the "throne of the Lord" (Jer. 3:16-17). The New Covenant (initiated by Christ, Luke 22; 1 Cor. 11) will issue forth in worldwide salvation (Jer. 31:31-34). Enemies of God's Old Testament people will be brought to blessing in the last days: Moab (Jer. 48:47), Ammon (Jer. 49:6), Elam (Jer. 49:39), and the Philistines (Zech. 9:7).

With Isaiah Daniel sees the expansion of the kingdom to the point of dominion in the earth (Dan. 2:31-35, 44-45; cp. Isa. 9:6-7). The Messiah's ascension and session will guarantee that "all people, nations and languages should serve Him" (Dan. 7:13-14). It must be noticed that Daniel 7:13-14 speaks of the Christ's ascension to the Ancient of Days, not His return to the earth. It is from this ascension to the right hand of God[10] that there will flow forth universal dominion.

Days of prosperity, peace, and righteousness lie in the future, according to Amos 9:11-15; Micah 4:1-3; 5:2-4, 16-17; 7:16-17;

---

9. I.e., in the times initiated by Christ at His First Advent (Acts 2:16, 17, 24; 1 Cor. 10:11; Gal. 4:4; Heb. 1:1-2; 9:26; James 5:3; 1 Peter 1:20; 1 John 2:18; Jude 18).
10. See later discussion of His present Kingship in Chapter 12.

Habakkuk 2:14-20; Haggai 2:7ff.; Zechariah 9:9-10; Malachi 1:11; 3:1-12.[11]

The New Testament Expectation of Victory

The Gospel Victory Theme of eschatology continues in various ways in the New Testament revelation. At this juncture we will briefly summarize just one type of evidence of the New Covenant victory expectation. This will bring the Old Testament expectations over into the New Testament and will be supplemented with a topical study in the following chapters.

Luke, in his first chapter, draws upon and arranges the Old Covenant expectations that were uttered in response to announcement of the coming of Christ's birth. He brings the rephrased prophecies to bear upon their New Covenant fruition. Interestingly, most of these are in poetic-song format, indicating the joyousness of the expectations.

In the angelic annunciation to Mary, Mary's Son, the promised Messiah, is promised the Davidic throne of rule (v. 32). His reign will know no end (v. 33).

Mary's Magnificat (Luke 1:46-55) is replete with the Victory Theme. In verses 47 and 48, she exalts the Lord as Savior, recognizing a universally resounding blessing upon her: "From this time on all generations will count me blessed." Why this universal homage? Because "the Mighty One" (v. 49) has begun to move in

---

11. These and many other such passages refer to the inter-advential age, not to the Eternal State (as per the amillennial view), for the following reasons: (1) Some prophetic language is inappropriate to the eternal state, such as the overcoming of active opposition to the Kingdom, the conversion of people, death, sin, and national distinctives and interaction, Isaiah 65:17ff. (2) Some prophetic language indicates the continuance of the curse, despite the dominance of victory, Isaiah 65:25. (3) Some prophetic language is indisputably applied to the First Advent of Christ, Isaiah 9:6; Daniel 2:35ff. (4) Some prophetic language ties the expectation to the present, pre-consummative order of things, such as the continuance of the sun and the moon, Psalm 72. (5) Hermeneutically, prophetic figures should not be figures of figures. That is, the nations' breaking their bows and spears is a figure of peace. Would the breaking of bows and spears be a figure of peace which is a figure of salvation?

history, using Mary for His glory. The prognostication is guided by the Victory Theme, not despair and lamentation. She recognizes that in the soon coming birth of Christ God will do "mighty deeds with His arm," He will "scatter the proud" (v. 51). He will "bring down rulers" and "exalt those who are humble" (v. 52). He will fill "the hungry with good things" (v. 53). He will do it through His people (v. 54) in keeping with the Abrahamic Covenant (v. 55). There is absolutely no intimation of defeat here, nor of a postponed millennial reign.

Zacharias's prophecy continues the glad tidings. He sees Christ's birth as bringing tidings of victory for God's people over their enemies (vv. 68-71). This, again, is in fulfillment of the Abrahamic Covenant (v. 73). Christ is the sunrise that will "shine upon those who sit in darkness and the shadow of death" (vv. 78-79). Elsewhere this refers to the Gentiles (Isa. 9:1,2; Matt. 4:16). This light is later seen as a positive force, dispelling darkness in the present age (Rom. 13:11-13; 1 John 2:8).

Summary

1. There is a strand of victorious expectation of the spread of righteousness, which begins in the Old Testament and continues into the New Testament.

2. At the creation of man, God so designed and commissioned man as to expect the worldwide operation of righteous cultural endeavor (Gen. 1:26-27). The Gospel Victory Theme of eschatological expectation comports well with God's creational purpose.

3. A vital aspect of the image of God in man has to do with his drive to dominion, a drive that must be governed by godly principles in order to fulfill its true intent (Gen. 1:26-27).

4. The first prophecy in Scripture, Genesis 3:15, expects a history-long struggle between Christ and Satan, with Christ ultimately winning the victory in history.

5. The Abrahamic Covenant promises the spread of salvation to "all the families of the earth" (Gen. 12:1ff.). The Gospel is the tool for the spread of the Abrahamic blessings (see Gal. 3:8, 29).

6. Patriarchal and Mosaic era prophecies foresee a time in earth history, issuing forth from the first Advent of Christ, in which God's glory and righteousness will cover the earth (Gen. 22:17; 49:10; Num. 24:17-19).

7. The prophets of the Old Testament continue the hope of the Gospel Victory Theme when they urge kings and judges to bow to Christ and promise that the ends of the earth will turn to God in salvation (Psalms 2; 22; 72; Isa. 2:1-4; 9:1-7).

8. The Gospel Victory era will be gained apart from Jewish exclusiveness and Old Testament ceremonial distinctives and all saved people will be on an equal footing with God through Jesus (Jer. 3:16-17; 31:31-34; 48:47; 49:6, 39).

9. The beginning of the Gospel Victory fruition is with the ascension of Christ to the right hand of God (Dan. 7:13-14).

10. The New Testament record of Christ's birth reflects on the Gospel Victory Theme of the Old Testament expectation, showing that Christ's first coming began the fruition of the promises (Luke 1).

11

THE NATURE OF THE KINGDOM

A Biblical analysis of the spiritual nature of the Messianic kingdom in contrast to the dispensationalist's political view.

One of the difficulties dispensationalists have in understanding the Messianic kingdom promised by the prophets is with regard to its fundamental nature. Several major misconceptions lead them astray in this regard. We highlight but three: they assert that the Messianic kingdom will (1) be a future, earthly, Armageddon-introduced, political system, (2) require the physical presence of Christ on earth, and (3) be fundamentally Jewish in purpose and character.

For instance, House and Ice write "that Christ will soon rapture his Bride, the church, and that we will return with him in victory to rule and exercise dominion with him for a thousand years upon the earth."[1] Emphatically this kingdom will not be "until Christ rules physically from Jerusalem."[2] A proper understanding of the Messianic kingdom requires "a consistent distinction between the Bible's use of Israel and the church" that leads "dispensationalism to distinguish God's program for Israel from his program for the church,"[3] hence the Jewishness of the Messianic kingdom.

The Spiritual Nature of the Kingdom

Despite House and Ice's confusion, the Scripture is quite clear regarding the spiritual nature of the kingdom. It is a distinctive of dispensationalism that asserts Christ offered to Israel a literal,

---

1. H. Wayne House and Thomas Ice, *Dominion Theology: Blessing or Curse?* (Portland, OR: Multnomah, 1988), p. 10.

2. *Ibid.*, p. 160.

3. *Ibid.*, p. 419. See especially pp. 400-5.

political, earthly kingdom, but that the Jews rejected it, thus causing its postponement.[4] This view of the kingdom is totally erroneous. As a matter of fact, it was just that sort of kingdom that the
first-century Jews wanted and that Christ refused: "When Jesus
therefore perceived that they would come and take him by force,
to make him a king, he departed again into a mountain himself
alone" (John 6:15).

The disciples themselves missed His point for the most part,
while He was on earth.[5] This is evidenced in the Emmaus Road encounter after the crucifixion, where these disciples lament: "But
we trusted that it had been he which should have redeemed Israel:
and beside all this, to day is the third day since these things were
done" (Luke 24:21). We should note that Jesus rebuked them for
such foolishness: "Then he said unto them, O fools, and slow of
heart to believe all that the prophets have spoken: Ought not Christ
to have suffered these things, and to enter into his glory? And beginning at Moses and all the prophets, he expounded unto them in
all the scriptures the things concerning himself" (Luke 24:25-27).
They expected political deliverance and glory to come to Israel
through this Messiah.[6] But Jesus spoke to them of the true meaning of the prophecies of the Old Testament, showing them that He
must suffer and then enter His resurrected, heavenly glory.[7]

In response to the Pharisees, Christ specifically declared that
the kingdom does not come visibly and gloriously (as the dispensational construction would have it!): "And when he was demanded of the Pharisees, when the kingdom of God should come,
he answered them and said, The kingdom of God cometh not with

---

4. *Ibid.*, pp. 173, 279. Cp. J. Dwight Pentecost, *Things to Come: A Study in Biblical Eschatology* (Grand Rapids, MI: Academie/Zondervan, [1956] 1964), pp. 456-66.

5. In another connection House and Ice admit this problem with the disciples: "But as was almost always the case, they were wrong" (House and Ice, *Dominion Theology*, p. 271).

6. Cp. their hope that He would "redeem Israel" with the Old Testament dec-laration that God "redeemed" Israel by delivering them from Egypt to become an independent nation (Deut. 7:8; 9:26; 13:5; 15:15; 24:18; 1 Chron. 17:21; Mic. 6:4).

7. Surely it cannot be denied that at the resurrection and ascension Christ "en-tered His glory," which was evidenced by Pentecost (John 7:39; 12:16; 12:23; Acts 3:13). He is now the "Lord of glory" (cf. James 2:1; 1 Peter 1:11; 2 Peter 3:18; Heb. 2:9).

observation: Neither shall they say, Lo here! or, lo there! for, behold, the kingdom of God is within you" (Luke 17:20-21). Obviously a spiritual conception of the kingdom is here demanded, in contradiction to an Armageddon-introduced, earthly, political kingdom.

This is why Christ went about preaching what is termed the *"gospel* of the kingdom" (Matt. 4:23; 9:35; 24:14; Mark 1:14-15). He proclaimed a redemptive, spiritual kingdom. Hence His being exalted to His throne[8] leads to a spiritual effusion of grace, not the political establishment of an earthly government (Luke 24:44-49; Acts 2:30-35; 3:22-26; 8:12; Eph. 4:8-11).

A major accusation against Jesus was that He promoted a political kingdom in competition with Caesar's empire. This explains why Jesus was concerned to discover the source of the accusation — He knew of the misconception of the Jews in this regard. His answer indicates that His is a spiritual kingdom:

> Then Pilate entered into the judgment hall again, and called Jesus, and said unto him, Art thou the King of the Jews? Jesus answered him, Sayest thou this thing of thyself, or did others tell it thee of me? Pilate answered, Am I a Jew? Thine own nation and the chief priests have delivered thee unto me: what hast thou done? Jesus answered, My kingdom is not of this world: if my kingdom were of this world, then would my servants fight, that I should not be delivered to the Jews: but now is my kingdom not from hence. Pilate therefore said unto him, Art thou a king then? Jesus answered, Thou sayest that I am a king. To this end was I born, and for this cause came I into the world, that I should bear witness unto the truth. Every one that is of the truth heareth my voice (John 18:33-37).

Had He not presented His kingship in terms of meekness and lowliness and not of a conquering, political entity? "All this was done, that it might be fulfilled which was spoken by the prophet, saying, Tell ye the daughter of Sion, Behold, thy King cometh unto thee, meek, and sitting upon an ass, and a colt the foal of an ass" (Matt. 21:4-5). In illustration of the Emmaus Road confusion,

---

8. See the next chapter.

John adds regarding this triumphal entry in fulfillment of prophecy that "these things understood not his disciples at the first: but when Jesus was glorified, then remembered they that these things were written of him, and that they had done these things unto him" (John 12:15-16).

Paul picks up on and promotes the spiritual nature of the kingdom, when he writes that "the kingdom of God is not meat and drink; but righteousness, and peace, and joy in the Holy Ghost" (Rom. 14:17). He disavows any carnal conception of the kingdom. Likewise does he speak of attaining an inheritance in the spiritual kingdom (the heavenly aspect of the kingdom) for those who are righteous (1 Cor. 6:9-10; 15:50; Gal. 5:21). He even says very plainly of the heavenly aspect of the kingdom: "Now this I say, brethren, that flesh and blood cannot inherit the kingdom of God; neither doth corruption inherit incorruption" (1 Cor. 15:50). How could it be that an earthly, political kingdom would hold forth no inheritance for flesh and blood people? It is in salvation that we are "delivered from the power of darkness, and translated into the kingdom of his dear Son: In whom we have redemption through his blood, even the forgiveness of sins" (Col. 1:12-13).

The Spiritual Presence of Christ in His Kingdom

Regarding the necessity of Christ's physical presence for His kingdom to come, House and Ice write: "Within the Reconstructionist framework, Messiah is in heaven and only present mystically in his kingdom. His absence from the earth during his kingdom reign robs Messiah of his moment of earthly glory and exaltation. It is a truncated reduction of the true reign of Christ. Since the first phase of Christ's career, his humiliation, was spent physically upon the earth, it follows that there should be a corresponding display of his great glory through his reign on the earth."[9]

Though not intended as such, this statement is really quite demeaning to Christ for several reasons. *First*, it diminishes the absolute glory and majesty that is His as He is now enthroned at

---

9. House and Ice, *Dominion Theology*, p. 240.

the right hand of God's throne on high. The New Testament Church looks to its heavenly king as one enthroned in awe-inspiring majesty, far above all rule and authority and power.[10] Shall we say that His rule from heaven is a robbery of the glory due His Name? Is it the case that His present session in heaven is "a truncated reduction" of His reign?

Second, it speaks rather condescendingly of Christ's rule. It offers to Christ but a "moment of glory" and speaks of His wondrous mystical presence as if it were meager: He "is *only* present mystically." But His kingdom is an eternal kingdom, not a momentary one (Isa. 9:7; Luke 1:33; 2 Peter 1:11; Rev. 11:15; 22:5). The indwelling presence of Christ is one of the rich blessings that flow forth from His glorious exaltation (John 7:39; Rom. 8:9; 1 Cor. 3:16; 6:19; 2 Cor. 6:16; Gal. 4:6; 1 John 3:24; 4:4). Shall we say He "is *only* present mystically"?

Third, this statement forgets that a major aspect of His humiliation was the fact that He came to earth,[11] hence it overlooks the fundamental consequence of His exaltation: His return to heaven to take up His manifest glory. In His High Priestly prayer we read:

> I have glorified thee on the earth: I have finished the work which thou gavest me to do. And now, O Father, glorify thou me with thine own self with the glory which I had with thee before the world was. . . . As thou hast sent me into the world, even so have I also sent them into the world. . . . Father, I will that they also, whom thou hast given me, be with me where I am; that they may behold my glory, which thou hast given me: for thou lovedst me before the foundation of the world (John 17:4-5, 18, 24).

Why should it be necessary that Christ's kingdom require His physical presence on earth? Does not Satan have a kingdom on earth, though he is only spiritually present (Matt. 12:26; Luke 4:6)?

Fourth, what kind of glory is it that teaches that Christ personally and corporeally rules on earth over a political kingdom that

---

10. Matthew 28:18; Acts 2:30-36; Romans 8:34; 1 Corinthians 15:23, 24; Ephesians 1:20; Colossians 3:1; Hebrews 1:3, 13; 10:13; 12:2; 1 Peter 3:22.

11. Romans 8:3; Hebrews 2:14; 10:5.

revolts against Him at the end (Rev. 20:7-9)?[12] This involves a second humiliation of Christ.[13]

As will be shown in the next chapter, Christ's rule has already been established; He does presently rule spiritually over His kingdom.

The Pan-Ethnic Character of His Kingdom

A distinctive feature of dispensationalism is that the Millennial kingdom will be fundamentally Jewish in character, even to the point of rebuilding the temple, setting up David's tabernacle, re-instituting the Jewish sacrificial system, and exalting the Jews: "This is the point: once Israel is restored to the place of blessing and the tabernacle of David is rebuilt, then will follow the third phase in the plan of God. That period will be the time of the millennium, when the nations will indeed be converted and ruled over by Christ."[14]

Dispensationalism surprisingly teaches such things as: "The redeemed living nation of Israel, regenerated and regathered to the land will be head over all the nations of the earth. . . . So he exalts them above the Gentile nations. . . . On the lowest level there are the saved, living, Gentile nations."[15] "The Gentiles will be Israel's servants during that age. . . . The Gentiles that are in

---

12. Pentecost, *Things to Come*, pp. 547-51.

13. One endorser of House and Ice's work has even brazenly stated: "In fact, dominion — taking dominion and setting up the kingdom of Christ — is an *impossibility*, even for God. The millennial reign of Christ, far from being the kingdom, is actually the final proof of the incorrigible nature of the human heart, because Christ Himself can't do" it. Dave Hunt, "Dominion and the Cross," Tape 2 of *Dominion: The Word and New World Order* (Ontario, Canada: Omega-Letter, 1987). See also Dave Hunt, *Beyond Seduction: A Return to Biblical Christianity* (Eugene, OR: Harvest House, 1987), p. 250.

14. House and Ice, *Dominion Theology*, p. 169. Regarding the rebuilding of the temple and the reinstituting of the sacrificial system, House and Ice exercise a wise silence, although their system as presented clearly allows for such (cf. pp. 142, 169, 174, 175). For more detail, see Pentecost, *Things to Come*, Chapter 30.

15. Herman Hoyt, "Dispensational Premillennialism," in Robert G. Clouse, *The Meaning of the Millennium: Four Views* (Downer's Grove, IL: Inter-Varsity Press, 1977), p. 81.

the millennium will have experienced conversion prior to admission."[16] "Israel will be a glorious nation, protected from her enemies, exalted above the Gentiles. . . ."[17] House and Ice concur: "God will keep his original promises to the fathers and will one day convert and place Israel as the head of the nations."[18] The "saved" (who are those "for whom Christ died," Rom. 14:15) will "be on the lowest level" in Christ's rule! They will be servants! Surely this is a Zionism of the worst sort in that on the mere basis of race, saved Israel is to be exalted over the saved Gentiles.[19]

To hold the historic Christian view of the Church as a new Israel forever, over against dispensationalism is not in any way suggestive of a Reconstructionist "charismatic connection" with the cultic Manifest Sons of God, as they suggest.[20]

Yet in Scripture Christ's kingdom is distinctly represented as being pan-ethnic, rather than Jewish. This misreading of Scripture is a crucial error of dispensationalism that makes it distasteful to many evangelicals. In defense of the Reconstructionist viewpoint that "the Bible does not tell of any future plan for Israel as a special nation"[21] we offer the following.

*The Setting Aside of **National** Israel*

While on earth Christ clearly and forthrightly taught that God would set aside *national* Israel as a distinctive, favored people in the kingdom. In Matthew 8:11-12 in the context of the Gentile centurion's faith, He expressly says that the "sons of the kingdom

---

16. Pentecost, *Things to Come*, p. 508.

17. John Walvoord, *The Millennial Kingdom* (Grand Rapids, MI: Zondervan, 1959), p. 136, cf. pp. 302-303.

18. House and Ice, *Dominion Theology*, p. 175.

19. It is difficult to see how they handle such passages as Isaiah 19:20-25, which teach that "In that day shall Israel be the *third* with Egypt and with Assyria, even a blessing in the midst of the land" (Isa. 19:24). This seems to comport well with the New Testament principle of equality (Gal. 3:28).

20. House and Ice, *Dominion Theology*, Appendix A.

21. *Ibid.*, p. 51.

shall be cast out" while "many from the east and west" shall enjoy the Abrahamic blessings. In Matthew 21:43 He parabolically teaches the rejection of national Israel when He says: "Therefore I say to you, the kingdom of God will be taken away from you, and be given to a nation producing the fruit of it." In Matthew 23-24 He prophesies the removal of the spiritual center, the temple. He says it will be left "desolate" (Matt. 23:38) during the Great Tribulation (Matt. 24:21) when men should flee Judea (Matt. 24:16). He emphatically noted that "all these things shall come upon this generation" (Matt. 23:36; 24:34).

It is true that racial Jews in great mass will be saved later in the development of the kingdom in history (Rom. 11:11-25), per postmillennialism.[22] The rub comes with their being exalted over and distinguished from saved Gentiles, and the turning back of the redemptive progress to "the weak and beggarly elements" of the sacrificial system. As mentioned above, Isaiah 19:19-25 expressly alludes to Israel's eventual equality in the kingdom: In verse 23 Isaiah says: "In that day Israel will be the third party with Egypt and Assyria, a blessing in the midst of the earth" (v. 23). Here the former enemies are seen receiving an equal share of God's favor. In Zechariah 9:7 God speaks of His future favor upon other enemies of Israel. He refers to Ekron, one of the five chief cities of Philistia: "I will remove their blood from their mouth, and their detestable things from between their teeth. Then they also will be a remnant for our God, and be like a clan in Judah, and Ekron like a Jebusite." This Philistine enemy is to become like "a clan in Judah."

In a surprising query, House and Ice favorably cite Hunt: "At what point did her sins become so bad that God had to go back upon His Word, nullify His promises, and reject Israel?"[23] The point they are looking for is without question the crucifying of the Messiah, the greatest sin of all history! Jesus makes this the point of the parable mentioned above (Matt. 21:33ff.). The constant ap-

---

22. *Ibid.*, p. 51. For a discussion of the place of Israel in postmillennialism see pp. 216-17 below and Gary DeMar, *The Debate over Christian Reconstruction* (Ft. Worth, TX: Dominion Press, 1988), Appendix B.

23. *Ibid.*, p. 174.

ostolic indictment against the Jews was this gross, conclusive act of rebellion. Although it is true that the Romans were responsible for physically nailing Christ to the cross (John 18:30-31), nevertheless, when covenantally considered, the onus of the divine curse falls squarely upon those who instigated and demanded it: many of the Jews of Jesus' day. The biblical record is quite clear and emphatic: *Jews* were the ones who sought His death (Matt. 26; 27; John 11:53; 18; 19). This most heinous sin of all time committed by the Jewish nation (represented by its leadership) is a constant refrain in the New Testament (Acts 2:22-23, 36; 3:13-15a; 5:30; 7:52; 1 Thess. 2:14-15).

The dispensational disavowal of covenantal ethical cause-and-effect blinds them to the reality of God's rejection of national Israel.[24] The very fact that it could be assumed that Israel's rejection as a nation is a "going back on His word" and a "nullifying of His promises" is evidence of this. Deuteronomy 28:15ff. is the classic statement of the reality of covenantal curse, but it is constantly brought before Israel (Deut. 6:14-16; 11:26-28; 30:15; Lev. 26:14-33). God's curse upon Israel, rather than representing a going back on His promise, was a fulfilling of His own publicly stated (Deut. 4:26; 31:19, 21, 26), Israel-affirmed (Exodus 19:8; 24:3, 7) covenantal threat.

---

24. In an anti-Reconstructionist, straw-man *hypothesis* (p. 398) as blind to history as it is to theology, House and Ice suggest a latent anti-Semitism in Reconstructionist theology! See House and Ice, *Dominion Theology*, Appendix B. Actually the dispensationalist statements above appear almost anti-Gentilic, for the Jews will dominate saved Gentiles in the "Millennium"! The historic recognition of the destructive role of the Jews in the crucifixion of Christ and their consequent disestablishment can be seen in the following Church fathers, some of whom are premillennial: Barnabas, *Epistle* 5, 13, 16; Ignatius, *Magnesians, Trallians*; Justin Martyr, *Apology* 35, 38, *Dialogue with Trypho the Jew* 24, 25, 72; Irenaeus, *Against Heresies* 3:12:2, 13; Melito of Sardis; Tertullian, *Apology* 21, 26, *On Idolatry* 7, *Answer to the Jews*, *Against Marcion* 3:6; Hippolytus, *Treatise on the Antichrist* 30, 57, *Expository Treatise Against the Jews*; Cyprian, *Treatises* 9:7, 10:5, 12; Lactantius, *On the Manner in Which the Persecutors Died*, 2. As dispensationalist Boyd has admitted of the Church fathers up to the death of Justin Martyr (A.D. 165): "The majority of the writers/writings in this period completely identify Israel with the Church" (Alan Patrick Boyd, "A Dispensational Premillennial Analysis of the Eschatology of the Post-Apostolic Fathers [Until the Death of Justin Martyr]," unpublished master's thesis, Dallas Theological Seminary, 1977, p. 47).

The Church as the "Israel of God"

House and Ice are correct to point out that "Reconstructionists appropriate for the church (seen as the new Israel) the material blessings for obedience—and curses for disobedience—originally promised by God to defunct national Israel."[25] How they could possibly set this forth as a "Reconstructionist" distinctive is beyond us, however. The dispensational view is the one with the distinctive element! Dispensationalist John Feinberg writes: "It is clear that holding a distinctive future for ethnic Israel is essential to Dispensationalism."[26] Ryrie states that "this is probably the most basic theological test of whether or not a man is a dispensationalist, and it is undoubtedly the most practical and conclusive."[27] Indeed, this has been a dispensational distinctive since dispensationalism first arose 150 years ago![28]

Let us survey the Scripture evidence for the Church's being the continuation—or better, the fruition—of Israel.

Christians individually considered and the Church as a collective body are called by distinctively Jewish names: "For he is not a Jew, which is one outwardly; neither is that circumcision, which is outward in the flesh: But he is a Jew, which is one inwardly; and circumcision is that of the heart, in the spirit, and not in the letter; whose praise is not of men, but of God" (Rom. 2:28-29). Hence, it may be dogmatically and, dare we say, *eternally* proclaimed: "God is no respecter of persons" (Acts 10:34; Rom. 2:11; Gal. 2:6; Eph. 6:9; Col. 3:11; 3:25; 1 Peter 1:17).[29]

Christians are called "the circumcision": "For we are the circumcision, which worship God in the spirit, and rejoice in Christ

---

25. House and Ice, *Dominion Theology*, p. 29, cp. p. 166.

26. John S. Feinberg, ed., *Continuity and Discontinuity: Perspectives on the Relationship Between the Old and New Testaments* (Westchester, IL: Crossway Books, 1988), p. 81.

27. Ryrie, *Dispensationalism Today*, p. 45.

28. See its prevalence in such dispensationalists as Ryrie (*ibid.*, pp. 43-47), Pentecost (*Things to Come*, pp. 199-205), and Hoyt (in Clouse, *The Meaning of the Millennium*, pp. 77ff.).

29. The Jews' "eternal place in the heavenly Jerusalem is certain, and in that heavenly state they are distinguished from the Church! Distinction is maintained even though the destiny is the same. To sum up: the earthly-heavenly, Israel-Church distinction taught by dispensationalists is true . . ." (Ryrie, *Dispensationalism Today*, p. 147). And this is despite Ephesians 2:14-15!

Jesus, and have no confidence in the flesh" (Phil. 3:3). We are called "the children" and "the seed of Abraham": "Know ye therefore that they which are of faith, the same are the children of Abraham. . . . And if ye be Christ's, then are ye Abraham's seed, and heirs according to the promise" (Gal. 3:7, 29). We are of the "Jerusalem which is above" and are called the "children of the promise" (Gal. 4:24-29). In fact, Christians compose "the Israel of God" for we are a "new creature" regarding which "circumcision availeth nothing" (Gal. 6:16).

James designates Christians as "the twelve tribes which are scattered abroad" (James 1:1). Peter calls the Christians to whom he writes, the "*diaspora*" (Gk., 1 Peter 1:1). Paul constantly calls the Church the "Temple of God" which is being built in history as men are converted (1 Cor. 3:16-17; 1 Cor. 6:19; 2 Cor. 6:16; Eph. 2:21).

Peter follows after Paul's thinking, when he designates Christians as "stones" being built into a "spiritual house" (1 Peter 2:5-9). But he does more; he draws upon several Old Testament designations of Israel and applies them to the Church: "a chosen generation, a royal priesthood, an holy nation." (1 Peter 2:9-10; Ex. 19:5-6; Deut. 7:6). He, with Paul, also calls Christians "a peculiar people" (1 Peter 2:10; Titus 2:14), which is a common Old Testament designation for Israel (Deut. 14:2; 26:18; Psalm 135:4).

The Work of Christ Unites Jew and Greek

The New Testament-era Church is not a distinct body of people for a time, but a newly organized fulfillment of the old body for all time. This Church is one with the Jewish forefathers, being grafted into the Abrahamic root and partaking of its sap (Rom. 11:17-18). Because of the redemptive work of Christ "there is neither Jew nor Greek . . . for ye are all one in Christ Jesus" (Gal. 3:28).

In Ephesians Paul is quite emphatic on this matter. Though in the past the Gentiles (Eph. 2:11) were "strangers to the covenants of promise" (2:12), Christ has brought them "near" (2:13) by breaking down the wall of separation between Jew and Gentile "through" redemption (2:14-15). This makes one people of two

(2:16-17), who worship one God (2:18), making the Gentiles "fellowcitizens with the saints, and of the household of God" (2:19), being built upon one foundation (2:20-22). House and Ice are aware of this passage, but somehow oblivious to its deleterious effect on dispensationalism: "In Ephesians 2:14-22, Paul reminds the Gentiles that they were once excluded from Christ, citizenship in Israel, and the covenants. What kept them on the outside was the 'dividing wall of hostility' caused by 'the law with its commandments and regulations.' "[30]

Specific "Jewish" Promises Are Applied to the Church.

Space constraints forbid an extensive development of this matter; one example will suffice. The well-known and vitally important "new covenant" is originally framed in Jewish terminology: "Behold, the days come, saith the LORD, that I will make a new covenant with the house of Israel, and with the house of Judah" (Jer. 31:31). But despite the contortions through which dispensationalists go to avoid the obvious,[31] this new covenant specifically comes to existence in the days of Christ. The Lord clearly establishes the new covenant as he appoints the sacrament of the Lord's Supper for His Church (Matt. 26:28; 1 Cor. 11:25; 2 Cor. 3:6; Heb. 8:6-13).

Many of the early church fathers — even those claimed as premillennialists by modern dispensationalists — understood the Church to be the recipient of Israel's promises. Let us show this by quoting Dallas Seminary dispensationalist Alan Patrick Boyd: "The majority of the writers/writings in this period [A.D. 70-165] completely identify Israel with the Church."[32] He specifically cites Papias, 1 Clement, 2 Clement, Barnabas, Hermas, the Didache,

---

30. House and Ice, *Dominion Theology*, p. 117. See below Chapter 12.

31. Though they do not go into the matter in detail, House and Ice do mention the new covenant in the context of their dispensationalist theology, pp. 146, 174. See Ryrie, *The Basis of the Premillennial Faith* (Neptune, NJ: Loizeaux Bros., 1953), Chapter 6 and Pentecost, *Things to Come*, Chapter 8, for more detail.

32. Boyd, "Dispensational Premillennial Analysis," p. 47.

and Justin Martyr.[33] Boyd notes that "In the case of Barnabas, . . . he has totally disassociated Israel from the precepts of the Old Testament. In fact he specifically designates the Church to be the heir of the covenantal promises made to Israel (4:6-7; 13:1-6; 14:4-5)."[34] Elsewhere he writes: "Papias applied much of the Old Testament to the Church."[35] Of Hermas he notes "the employment of the phraseology of late Judaism to make the Church the true Israel. . . ."[36] Of Justin Martyr, "he claims that the Church is the true Israelitic race, thereby blurring the distinction between Israel and the Church."[37]

A Common Objection

Perhaps one major objection to the Reconstructionist view ought to be considered, since it is often expressed. House and Ice write in regard to the disciples' question in Acts 1:6:

> It is important to notice that their question assumes that it is a matter of *when* the kingdom would be restored to Israel, not *if* it would be restored. . . . If God had taken the kingdom from Israel and not just postponed it, then surely such an important point would have been covered by our Lord when he taught the apostles about the kingdom of God during their forty day learning period. Yet, their view that a future in the kingdom remains for Israel as a nation is clearly unshaken.[38]

The possible contrary interpretive responses are numerous: *First*, the argument is one from silence. Absolutely nothing in either the question or the answer demands the notion that *national* Israel would be restored to a *political*, earthly kingdom.

---

33. Papias, *Fragment* 6; 1 Clement 3:1; 29:1-30:1; 2 Clement 2:1-3; 3:5; Barnabas 2:4-6, 9; 3:6; 4:6-7; 5:2, 7; Hermas, *Similitudes* 9:16:7; 9:15:4; 9:12:1-13:2; the *Didache*, 14:2, 3, and Justin Martyr, *Dialogue*, 119-20, 123, 125. See Boyd, "Dispensational Premillennial Analysis," pp. 46, 60, 70, 86.
34. Boyd, "Dispensational Premillennial Analysis," p. 46.
35. *Ibid.*, pp. 60-61.
36. *Ibid.*, p. 70.
37. *Ibid.*, p. 86.
38. House and Ice, *Dominion Theology*, p. 166.

Second, the disciples could have been mistaken. House and Ice admit the disciples were often in error.[39] Jesus constantly had to demand: "He that has ears to hear, let him hear" (Matt. 11:15; 13:9, 15, 16, 43; Mark 4:9; 4:23; 7:16; Luke 8:8; 14:35). For example, did they not for a long time after Christ's departure think John would live to the Second Coming because of something Jesus taught them, which they misunderstood (John 21:22ff.)? Were not they constantly mistaken about the necessity of His death (John 2:22; 12:16; 16:4; Luke 24:7-8)? If they sought an earthly, political kingdom in Acts 1:6, may it not be reasonably supposed that they were mistaken — especially since they desired places of prominence in it (Matt. 20:21-23)?

As a matter of fact, Jesus specifically told them there would be things they could not learn until the coming of the Spirit at Pentecost: "I have yet many things to say unto you, but ye cannot bear them now. Howbeit when he, the Spirit of truth, is come, he will guide you into all truth: for he shall not speak of himself; but whatsoever he shall hear, that shall he speak: and he will shew you things to come" (John 16:12-13). And Acts 1:6 is before Pentecost. Could this have been one of the things they did not understand, especially in light of their hesitancy at accepting Gentiles into the Church (Acts 10-11)?

Third, the emphasis of the question is overlooked. In the Greek of Acts 1:6 the question emphasizes "this time." A strong case (which we accept) may be made for an alternative understanding of the passage to both the dispensationalist one and the immediately preceding one. In light of the abundance of evidence we have presented above regarding Israel's demise, and in light of the data to be brought up in the next chapter regarding the presence of the kingdom, there is a viable alternative construction to this episode. May we not just as legitimately conclude that the disciples *did* understand the true conception of the spirituality of the pan-ethnic kingdom of Christ, and thus that they were here merely asking the Lord, "Is it *now* time for Israel to be converted

---

39. *Ibid.*, p. 271.

to You and enter the kingdom, which You have established?" This would fit well within the semantic, theological, and psychological framework of the episode: These were (theologically) postmillennialists and (psychologically) devout Jews (Acts 10-11; Rom. 9:1-2). In addition, Christ's answer would speak to this question.

Summary

1. The kingdom of Christ is not a future, Armageddon-introduced earthly, political kingdom.

2. The first-century Jews wanted a political kingdom to overthrow Rome and when Christ did not offer them such, they rejected Him (John 6:15), and even his disciples were disappointed (Luke 24:21-27).

3. The basic power of the kingdom is the "gospel of the kingdom" (Matt. 4:23; 9:35; Mark 1:14-15), the basic function of the kingdom is the promotion of God's truth (John 18:37), and the basic operation of the kingdom is via humility (Matt. 21:4-5).

4. The kingdom of Christ is essentially a spiritual kingdom (Rom. 14:17) that operates from within the heart (Luke 17:20-21).

5. We enter the kingdom of Christ by means of salvation (Col. 1:12-13; John 3:3).

6. Christ rules His kingdom by His mystical presence from heaven (John 18:36) and through the indwelling of the Holy Spirit (John 7:39; Rom. 8:9; 1 Cor. 3:16).

7. Israel as a nation has once for all been set aside as the specially favored nation of God (Matt. 8:11-12; 21:43), because of their prominent role in crucifying Christ (Acts 2:22-23, 36; 3:13-15; 5:30; 7:52; 1 Thess. 2:14-15).

8. Christ's kingdom includes people of all races on an equal basis (Isa. 19:19-25; Zech. 9:7; Eph. 2:12-17), even great numbers of Jews will eventually enter it (Rom. 11:11-25).

9. The New Testament-phase Church is "the Israel of God" (Gal. 6:16), "the circumcision" (Phil. 3:3), "the seed of Abraham" (Gal. 3:7, 29), the "Jerusalem above" (Gal. 4:24-29), the "temple of God" (Eph. 2:21), "a royal priesthood" and a "peculiar people" (1 Peter 2:9-10). Consequently, Jewish promises are applied to the

Church (Jer. 31:31-34; Matt. 26:28), as many of the early fathers recognized (Papias, Clement, Barnabas, Hermas, and Justin Martyr).

10. The question of the disciples in Acts 1:6 revolved around a concern as to "when" the Jews would re-enter the favor of God, i.e. re-enter God's redemptive purpose in the Church.

12

THE PRESENCE OF THE KINGDOM

A demonstration from the biblical evidence of a first-century establishment by Christ of the Messianic kingdom.

Anyone familiar with pre-1960s dispensationalism (e.g., Scofield, Ironside, Chafer) should recognize the drift toward a slightly more covenantal view of eschatology that Ryrie and 1960s-era dispensationalists effected on a number of questions. The very title of Ryrie's important book is an indicator of change: *Dispensationalism Today.* But he has not up-dated his book since its publication in 1965, though it radically needs it. Still further it should be noted that since the late 1970s many dispensationalists have continued in an evolution toward a more covenantal approach to the kingdom, due to the unrelenting pressures exerted upon the system by non-dispensational theology.[1]

One area of interest regarding changes within dispensational circles has to do with the very question before us in the present chapter. One noted dispensationalist scholar, John S. Feinberg, has commented:

---

1. Such pressure, as a matter of fact, was the motive behind the publication even of Ryrie's 1965 book (Frank E. Gaebelein, "Foreword" in Charles C. Ryrie, *Dispensationalism Today* [Chicago, IL: Moody Press, 1965], p. 7). This is also noted more recently by dispensationalist John S. Feinberg: "Generally, systems that move toward absolute continuity fit more in the mold of Reformed or covenantal theologies. Systems that move toward absolute discontinuity fit more in the mold of dispensational theologies" (John S. Feinberg, ed., *Continuity and Discontinuity: Perspectives on the Relationship Between the Old and New Testaments* [Westchester, IL: Crossway Books, 1988], p. 64). "In comparing my discontinuity/dispensational system to other more traditional ones, one would probably think it much closer to continuity systems than dispensational systems usually are, and I agree" (p. 85).

175

The basic distinction here among dispensationalists is that older ones tended to see the kingdom relegated entirely to the future. More contemporary dispensationalists hold that the full realization of the kingdom for Israel and the world awaits the future, but currently spiritual aspects of the kingdom are operative in the church.[2]

House and Ice admit this change, and they resist it. In fact, in keeping with their eclectic brand of dispensationalism (as opposed to some strains of dispensationalism[3] and all historic premillennialism,[4] amillennialism, and postmillennialism) House and Ice are quite adamant in their determination to keep the Messianic kingdom entirely future: "This present age is not the kingdom."[5] "Christ did not set up the kingdom during his first coming; it awaits his return."[6] They lament what they view to be "the mistaken notion that we are now in the kingdom."[7] In fact, in rebuttal to dispensationalist Robert L. Saucy and other advocates of an "already, not yet" view of the kingdom they assert:

> In recent years there has been a trend for some dispensationalists to adopt a conservative version of an "already, not yet" approach to the kingdom. . . . Saucy is saying that some form of the Messianic kingdom is present, although the theocratic aspects are yet future. However, we believe that whatever dynamic God has given believers today does not mean that the Messianic kingdom is here. We see it as totally future.[8]

Hence, "Christians are to pray that Christ will return and bring with him the kingdom. Then God's will in heaven will be brought to earth. But not until Christ rules physically from Jerusalem."[9]

---

2. Feinberg, ed., *Continuity and Discontinuity*, p. 82, referencing Robert L. Saucy, "Contemporary Dispensational Thought," *TSF Bul 7* (March-April 1984), pp. 10-11.
3. House and Ice, *Dominion Theology*, p. 220.
4. *Ibid.*, p. 219.
5. *Ibid.*, p. 159.
6. *Ibid.*, p. 229.
7. *Ibid.*, p. 160.
8. *Ibid.*, p. 220.
9. *Ibid.*, p. 160, cp. pp. 140, 167, 168, 229, 267.

Not only are House and Ice out of kilter with the bulk of evangelicalism on this matter (even some dispensational varieties!), but they attempt to equate the view that the kingdom is now in history with heretical tendencies, since it is held by a group they call the Manifest Sons of God cult.[10] It makes one wonder if this cult (which I know virtually nothing about) wrote such "kingdom now" hymns as: "We Gather Together to Ask the Lord's Blessing" (1625), "Now Thank We All Our God" (1636), "Ye Servants of God, Your Master Proclaim" (1744), "I Love Thy Kingdom, Lord" (1800), "Crown Him with Many Crowns" (1851)! Do they not realize that the 1647 Westminster Confession of Faith, to which they refer, teaches: "The visible Church . . . consists of all those throughout the world that profess the true religion; and of their children: and is the kingdom of the Lord Jesus Christ" (25:2)?[11]

Thy Kingdom Came

Let us survey various clear evidences from the New Testament regarding the coming of the kingdom. In the process of this study we will note there are different senses in which the kingdom comes.

The question before us is:

So then, is this present age the kingdom? This is really one of the most crucial questions which divides the premillennialists from both the postmillennialists and most amillennialists.

We equate the mediatorial kingdom with the kingdom in general. We believe that when the Bible speaks of Christ's kingdom, it is the mediatorial kingdom. "Every time the term kingdom is used theologically . . . it refers to the same thing, the kingdom yet to come on this earth inaugurated and governed by the Messiah."[12]

To truly be a ruling king one must meet certain minimal requirements: (1) He must possess regal authority, (2) he must exer-

---

10. *Ibid.*, p. 385.
11. *Ibid.*, pp. 96-97.
12. *Ibid.*, p. 224, citing dispensationalist Stanley D. Toussaint.

cise active rulership, and (3) he must have a kingdom, or domain over which to rule. Also we must recognize the multi-dimensional significance of the "kingdom." Christ's kingdom is both spatially and temporally vast, including both heaven and earth (cp. Matt. 28:18) and involving a progressive development of it in history.[13] The source-throne of His kingdom is heaven (John 18:36), and thus the kingdom is in heaven, as well as on earth. In one respect it requires the new birth and sanctification to enter it (John 3:3; Matt. 7:21; 18:3) and precludes the unrighteous (Matt. 5:20; 1 Cor. 6:9-10; Eph. 5:5). Yet, in another respect it contains even the wicked (Matt. 13:41ff.). Contrary to the dispensational view, which sees the kingdom coming after the resurrection of the saints, Jesus even teaches that the "kingdom" may be entered into by one who has an amputated foot or hand, or a gouged eye (Mark 9:43, 45, 47) — surely not a resurrected individual. Thus, at times the theological "kingdom" refers to the visible church; at other times to the invisible church; at other times to heaven, all of which are ruled by the King of kings, Jesus Christ.

That Christ presently is a king and is even now ruling over His kingdom is evident upon the following considerations.

The Approach of the Kingdom

It is evident from Scripture that with the coming of Christ (particularly after His formal, public manifestation at His baptism) the Kingdom has drawn near. There is a repeated emphasis on the proximity of the kingdom in His ministry. In Mark 1:14-15 we read: "Now after that John was put in prison, Jesus came into Galilee, preaching the gospel of the kingdom of God, and saying, The time is fulfilled, and the kingdom of God is at hand: repent ye, and believe the gospel" (cp. Matt. 4:12-17). Several aspects of this passage bear closer scrutiny.

First, notice carefully that He asserts "the time" is fulfilled. Of what "time" does He speak? Obviously the prophetic time which

---

13. See the Chapter 14, "The Victory of the Kingdom," where the gradual development of it is treated.

awaited the coming of the kingdom, for he immediately adds, *"the kingdom of God is at hand."* Indeed, Jesus was sent by the Father in "the fulness of time" (Gal. 4:4), thus we may take comfort in the fact that "now is the accepted time; behold, now is the day of salvation" (2 Cor. 6:2), because the prophecies of "the acceptable year of the Lord" had begun to be fulfilled (Luke 4:16-21; cp. Isa. 61:1).

Second, Christ clearly asserts that the time "is fulfilled." Actually a better translation of the verb tense and voice here (the perfect passive) would be: "The time has been fulfilled." Apparently John the Baptist is significant for Christ as a sort of line of demarcation separating the fading kingdom-expectation era from the kingdom-fulfillment era, which begins dawning with John's demise. Earlier John noted of Jesus: "He must increase, but I must decrease" (John 3:30). Jesus observes of John: "Verily I say unto you, Among them that are born of women there hath not risen a greater than John the Baptist: notwithstanding he that is least in the kingdom of heaven is greater than he. And from the days of John the Baptist until now the kingdom of heaven suffereth violence, and the violent take it by force. For all the prophets and the law prophesied until John. And if ye will receive it, this is Elias, which was for to come" (Matt. 11:11-14; cp. Mark 2:18-19; Luke 16:16).[14]

Third, Christ clearly and pointedly says the kingdom is "at hand," signifying "near, soon." The root term (*eggus*) literally means "at hand." The word is derived from the compounding of *en* (in, at) and *guion* (limb, hand).[15]

It would seem that in order to escape the obvious conclusion to which we have pointed, House and Ice would have to approach

---

14. Incredibly, one of the endorsers of House and Ice's book, Dave Hunt, is so adamant against Christian influence on government and society that he suggests John's death came unnecessarily early and was prompted by his unwarranted involvement in political affairs. That involvement was through John's exposure of the evil of Herod Antipas's marrying his half-brother's wife! (Dave Hunt, *Whatever Happened to Heaven?* [Eugene, OR: Harvest House, 1988], p. 82.)

15. Joseph H. Thayer, *A Greek-English Lexicon of the New Testament* (2nd ed.; New York: American Book Co., 1889), p. 164. For a fuller discussion of imminence terminology, see my *The Beast of Revelation* (Tyler, TX: Institute for Christian Economics, 1989), pp. 21-28.

the passage in either one of two ways: [16] (1) They might attempt to apply the dispensational hermeneutical equivalent of the *deus ex machina*: the "imminence" concept. That is, this "at hand" statement may merely speak of the kingdom's readiness to break forth into history at any moment.[17] But to stretch such a nearness out for almost 2000 years (thus far!), would vacate the term of all significance. In addition we should note that on another occasion Christ specifically promised His hearers "there be some of them that stand here, which shall not taste of death, till they have seen the kingdom of God come with power" (Mark 9:1). Some of those very persons *standing* before him would not *die* before the event! Which one of them is still alive today? Or (2) they might bring in the "new hypothesis" of dispensationalism: the postponement concept.[18] But this runs counter to the idea of "the time is fulfilled." Jesus never says, "The time is postponed," as per dispensationalism.[19] Does not God determine the times (Dan. 2:21; Acts 1:7)? Do not Ice and House vehemently argue that "Matthew presents Jesus as the fulfillment and realization of *all* that the Old Testament anticipates."[20]

Thus, the Gospels emphasize on several occasions the nearness of His kingdom (Matt. 3:2; 4:12, 17; 10:7; 16:28; Mark 1:14-15; 9:1; Luke 21:31). After the Gospels there is no longer any preaching of the kingdom as at hand because:

The Kingdom Was Established During Christ's Ministry

Clear and compelling evidence exists that the kingdom did in fact come in Christ's ministry. Perhaps one of the clearest state-

---

16. The older dispensational ploy of distinguishing between the "kingdom of heaven" and the "kingdom of God" cannot be brought in to assist. Dispensationalist Walter C. Kaiser observes: "In the past the usual way that this distinction was demarcated was by designating the eternal kingdom as the kingdom of God and the earthly program as the kingdom of heaven. It is a joy to note that we are now well beyond this state in argument" (in Feinberg, ed., *Continuity and Discontinuity*, p. 294). It is recognized as a false construct even by such dispensationalists as Ryrie, *Dispensationalism Today*, pp. 170ff. and Pentecost, *Things to Come*, pp. 443-44.

17. House and Ice, *Dominion Theology*, pp. 231-32, 420; see Chapter 14 below on the Victory of the Kingdom for further discussion of this doctrine.

18. See *ibid.*, pp. 173, 229.

19. *Ibid.*, p. 166.

20. *Ibid.*, p. 104 (emphasis mine).

ments in this regard is Matthew 12:28: "But if I cast out devils by the Spirit of God, then the kingdom of God is come unto you." The truth is, Jesus *did* cast out demons by the Spirit of God. The protasis of this "if/then" statement being true, then the apodosis follows: "The kingdom of God is come." The very fact that Satan's kingdom is being invaded and his possessions (demoniacs) are being carried off by Christ (Matt. 12:25-29) is proof that the kingdom has come, even though the king was not formally installed as king until Pentecost (Acts 2:30ff.).

House and Ice cite favorably a statement from Andrews: "Had it been the purpose of God to set the Son at His ascension as the King of the nations, He would in some way have made His kingship so plain that the nations could not have been ignorant of it, and of the duty of allegiance and homage."[21] This shows the shallowness of their argument. Have they never considered the related question, often hurled at us by the atheist: Why was not His death made known to all the world, since the world is condemned for not accepting it? We agree with Athanasius (A.D. 296-372): "For by His becoming Man, the Saviour was to accomplish both works of love; first, in putting away death from us and renewing us again; secondly, being unseen and invisible, in manifesting and making Himself known by His works to be the Word of the Father, and the Ruler and King of the Universe."[22]

In addition, such a statement as this regarding the kingdom is based on a radical oversight, for in Luke 17:20-21 we read: "And when he was demanded of the Pharisees, *when* the kingdom of God should come, he answered them and said, The kingdom of God cometh not with observation: Neither shall they say, Lo here! or, lo there! for, behold, the kingdom of God is within you." Christ answered their question almost 2000 years ago! Notice that to the Pharisees' question as to "when" the kingdom should come, Christ spoke in the present tense: The kingdom *is* present. It is not awaiting a future, Armageddon-introduced manifestation; it exists now

---

21. *Ibid.*, p. 236.
22. Athanasius, *The Incarnation of the Word*, Sec. 16.

and among them, says Christ. Hence, even in Christ's ministry men were pressing into it (Luke 16:16).

Paul speaks to the Colossians in a way quite agreeable to the reformed view of the coming of the kingdom: Colossians 1:12-13: "Giving thanks unto the Father, which hath made us meet to be partakers of the inheritance of the saints in light: Who hath delivered us from the power of darkness, and hath translated us into the kingdom of his dear Son." Inarguably He is speaking of Christ's kingdom, for He calls it "the kingdom of his dear Son." Just as clear is the fact that the "translation" of those saints nearly 2000 years ago was considered a past fact, not a future prospect. Paul uses aorist tense verbs when he speaks of their being "delivered" and "translated." He does the same in 1 Thessalonians 2:12. He even speaks of those who were his helpers in the ministry "for the kingdom of God" (Col. 4:10).

Thus, John follows suit in Revelation 1:6 and 9: "And [Christ] hath made us kings and priests unto God and his Father. . . . I John, who also am your brother, and companion in tribulation, and in the kingdom and patience of Jesus Christ." In these verses John speaks of the Christians of the Seven Churches of Asia (Rev. 1:4, 11; 2-3) as already "made" (aorist tense) to be "a kingdom" (literally). In fact, John is already a fellow with them in the "kingdom" (Rev. 1:9). Clearly the kingdom came in its initial stages during Christ's ministry. Just as clearly can we assert: That it was *not* postponed is evident from the biblical record.

Christ Presented Himself as King

The Triumphal[23] Entry of Christ is interesting in this regard: The people cried, "Hosanna: Blessed is the King of Israel that cometh in the name of the Lord. And Jesus, when he had found a

---

23. We hesitate to use the term "Triumphal" of His entry for two reasons: (1) House and Ice seem to find such terminology indicating triumph distasteful (see their Chapter 8 and Appendix C). (2) In the dispensational view Christ was in no way *triumphal* in His entry, for He was rejected in His presentation of Himself as an earthly-political king and had to postpone the kingdom, which He had declared was "at hand" (House and Ice, *Dominion Theology*, pp. 173, 279). See Chapter 14, note 36.

young ass, sat thereon; as it is written, Fear not, daughter of Sion: behold, thy King cometh, sitting on an ass's colt" (John 12:12-15). Here Christ is not only declared to be "king," but He accepts the public lauding of Himself as king in that it was in fulfillment of prophecy (Zech. 9:9) and despite Pharisaic rebukes (Matt. 21:15-16).

During His trial and at the inquiry of Pilate, Christ specifically admits His kingship and the presence of His kingdom: "Jesus answered, My kingdom is not of this world: if my kingdom were of this world, then would my servants fight, that I should not be delivered to the Jews: but now is my kingdom not from hence. Pilate therefore said unto him, Art thou a king then? Jesus answered, Thou sayest that I am a king. To this end was I born, and for this cause came I into the world . . ." (John 18:36-37a; cp. Matt. 27:11; Mark 15:2; Luke 23:3).

Although He defines His kingdom as something otherworldly, rather than essentially political (as was Caesar's kingdom),[24] He nevertheless indicates His kingdom is present: He speaks of "my kingdom" (v. 36a). He claims to have His own "servants" (even though they do not fight with sword to defend Him, v. 36b). He clearly states "I am king" (v. 37a). And, as we might expect, given our previous study of Mark 1:14-15, He states that it was for that very purpose He was born into the world (v. 37b)!

Christ Was Enthroned as King

The very first of the enthronement passages in the post-resurrection age associates Christ's enthronement with His exaltation, which began with His resurrection and culminates with His session at the right hand of God. Of David's prophecy anticipating his seed's sitting upon the Davidic throne, Peter proclaims:

> Therefore being a prophet, and knowing that God had sworn with an oath to him, that of the fruit of his loins, according to the flesh, he would raise up Christ to sit on his throne; he seeing this before spake of the resurrection of Christ, that his soul was not left in hell, neither his flesh did see corruption. . . . Therefore

24. See Chapter 11 on "The Nature of the Kingdom."

being by the right hand of God exalted, and having received of the Father the promise of the Holy Ghost, he hath shed forth this, which ye now see and hear. For David is not ascended into the heavens: but he saith himself, The Lord said unto my Lord, Sit thou on my right hand, Until I make thy foes thy footstool. Therefore let all the house of Israel know assuredly, that God hath made that same Jesus, whom ye have crucified, both Lord and Christ (Acts 2:30-31, 33-36).

Here we learn that David's prophecy regarding One Who was to sit on his throne was a prophecy of the "resurrection." Thus, Christ suffered ultimate humiliation on the Cross and in the tomb. But then His resurrection began His exaltation in preparation for His ascension to the right hand of the throne of God, the place of universal rule and authority. There He was "crowned with glory" (Heb. 2:9) to begin His rule (Rom. 8:34; Eph. 1:20; Col. 3:1; Heb. 12:2; 1 Peter 3:22; Rev. 3:21)[25] by wielding "all authority and power" (Matt. 28:18).[26] The Matthew 28:18-20 passage is much in contrast to His earlier reservation and humility. No longer do we hear the familiar, "I can do nothing of Myself" (John 5:19, 30; 8:28; 12:49; 14:10). Rather do we hear a resoundingly powerful: "All authority has been given Me in heaven and on earth." A mighty transformation has taken place in the ministry of Christ as a direct result of His resurrection. His first exercise of regal authority was the pouring out of the Spirit (Acts 2:34-36). This is a celebration of His coronation by the distribut-

---

25. Contrary to Walvoord (*The Revelation of Jesus Christ* [Chicago, IL: Moody Press, 1966], pp. 98-100), Revelation 3:21 does not require a millennial throne for Christ, which both is entirely future and separate from God the Father's throne. It no more does so than Jesus' statement to Mary in John 20:17 requires two distinct persons being referred to by "my Father and your Father." The throne of God and of Christ is *one* throne (Rev. 22:1, 3).

26. Athanasius writes of Acts 2:36: "Therefore the Word Himself became flesh, and the Father called His Name Jesus, and so 'made' Him Lord and Christ, as much as to say, 'He made Him to rule and to reign'" (*Discourses Against the Arians*, 2:15:16). Of Peter's Great Confession he writes: "He knew Him to be God's Son, confessing, 'Thou art the Christ, the Son of the Living God'; but he meant His Kingdom and Lordship which was formed and came to be according to grace, and was relatively to us" (*ibid.*, 2:15:18).

ing of gifts to His subjects, in the manner of a warrior-king returning triumphantly to his capital city upon his victory over the enemy (Acts 2:33; Eph. 4:7-12).[27] It promises His divinely royal assistance to His people (Rom. 8:34). In fact, He is there at the throne even now awaiting the collapse of all His enemies under that majestic and gracious rule (1 Cor. 15:23, 24; Heb. 1:3, 13; 10:13).[28] This is why there is so much "kingdom of God" proclamation in the New Testament.[29]

Early Christians Considered Him King

In Acts 3:15 Peter preaches Christ as the "prince of life." In Acts 5:31 he asserts his obligation to disobey civil authority when it demands that he cease preaching Christ. His rationale is important: "Him hath God exalted with his right hand to be a Prince and a Saviour." The word "prince" here can literally be translated "leader, ruler, prince."[30] He was exalted to become Prince or Ruler.

In Acts 17:7 we learn of the civil turmoil the early Christians were causing. The charge against them is most interesting and must be based in reality, even if largely misunderstood by the unbelieving populace. Just as the Jews accused Jesus of claiming to be a king,[31] so we read of the charge against His followers: "These all do contrary to the decrees of Caesar, saying that there is another king, one Jesus." Just as Jesus did in fact teach that He was a king (though in a non-political sense, John 18:36-37), his followers did the same.

The Apostle John clearly declared that Jesus was even then in the first century ruling and reigning: "Jesus Christ, who is the faithful witness, and the first begotten of the dead, and the prince

---

27. Cp. Genesis 14; 1 Samuel 30:26-31; Judges 5:30. See Isaiah 53:12.

28. See Chapter 14 on "The Victory of the Kingdom."

29. See Acts 8:12; 14:22; 19:8; 20:25; 28:23, 31; Romans 14:17; 1 Corinthians 4:20; 6:9-10; 15:50; Galatians 5:21; Ephesians 5:5; Colossians 1:13; 4:11; 1 Thessalonians 2:12; 2 Thessalonians 1:5; 2 Timothy 4:1; 4:18; Hebrews 1:8; 12:28; James 2:5; 2 Peter 1:11. See Chapter 11 on "The Nature of the Kingdom."

30. Arndt and Gingrich, *Lexicon*, p. 112.

31. See Matthew 27:29, 37; Mark 15:12, 26; Luke 23:3; John 18:33; 19:12, 15, 21.

of the kings of the earth" (Rev. 1:5). Notice how he applies
descriptive titles affirming Christ's present role as prophet, priest,
and king: He is just as much the ruler (literally) of the kings of the
earth as He is the faithful witness (i.e., prophet) and the firstborn
of the dead (i.e., priest).

According to Paul, God "*put* all things under his feet" (Eph.
1:22). God *gave* Him a title/name higher than any that is named
(Phil. 2:9). In both of these places Paul employs aorist tense
verbs, which speak of an action at a point in *past* time, i.e., at His
resurrection-ascension-enthronement. Hence, the scores of references to Him as "Lord" throughout the New Testament. In fact,
"Christ is Lord" evidently becomes a creedal statement of sorts in
the apostolic era.[32]

Christians Are Now Seated in Rule With Him

In light of the above, Christians now rule and reign with Him
in the world.[33] Ephesians 1:3 declares we are blessed "in heavenly
places." Ephesians 2:6 specifically teaches: "And He hath raised us
up together, and made us sit [aorist tense] together in heavenly
places in Christ Jesus." We are, in the eyes of God, seated with
Christ in heavenly places (which, in essence, is the idea of Rev.
20:4-6), i.e. in regal position.

Interestingly, the epistle to the Ephesians is virtually an anti-
dispensational polemic by the Apostle Paul![34] Notice the teaching
in Ephesians regarding matters antithetical to dispensationalism:
Christ is held as presently in His position as a kingly Lord
(1:19-22) and, as just pointed out, we are presently seated with
Him (1:3; 2:6). Paul applies the application of "the promises of *the*

---

32. Romans 10:9; 1 Corinthians 12:3; Philemon 2:11.

33. For the nature of this rule (spiritual) see Chapter 11 on "The Nature of the
Kingdom."

34. Thus, it is surprising to read House and Ice suggest that Ephesians is
detrimental to Reconstructionism: "Ephesians 2 and 3 is probably the most extensive passage in the New Testament explaining the nature and purpose of the
church age. However, in the volumes of Reconstructionist literature, there are
only a few faint references to this aspect of these crucial passages." House and
Ice, *Dominion Theology*, p. 172.

covenant" (literally) to Gentiles in the Church (2:10-12). He emphasizes the removal of the distinction of the Jew and the Gentile (2:12-19). He refers to the building up of the Church as being the building of the temple (2:20-22).[35] The New Testament phase of the Church is declared to have been taught in the Old Testament, though not with the same fullness and clarity (3:1-6). Christ's kingly enthronement is celebrated by the pouring out of gifts upon His Church/kingdom (4:8-11) with the expectation of the historical maturation of the Church (4:12-14). Paul mentions the kingdom in such a way as indicative of its spiritual, rather than political, nature (5:5).

In 1 Corinthians 3:21-22 Christians are shown their noble status: "For all things are yours; whether Paul, or Apollos, or Cephas, or the world, or life, or death, or things present, or things to come; all are yours." Elsewhere the present kingly status of Christians is evidenced (e.g., Rom. 5:17; Col. 3:3; 2 Tim. 2:11-12).

Objections

Although enough material has been generated to point to the presence of the kingdom since the days of Christ, a brief sampling of some of the verses put forth by House and Ice in opposition to the Reformed or Reconstructionist view would be in order.

One passage they use is 2 Timothy 4:1: "I charge thee therefore before God, and the Lord Jesus Christ, who shall judge the quick and the dead at his appearing and his kingdom." They write: "Paul puts in the future both the 'appearing' of our Lord and 'His kingdom' in his charge to Timothy to preach the word (2 Timothy 4:1)."[36]

There are three live possibilities beyond the dispensational interpretation (which has been shown to be inadequate on other

---

35. Cp. also 1 Peter 2:4-5; 1 Corinthians 3:16-17; 6:19; 2 Corinthians 6:16; Revelation 3:12.

36. House and Ice, *Dominion Theology*, p. 224. In their next paragraph they point to 2 Timothy 4:18 as a proof of a future kingdom. To use that verse thus requires that we give credence to their mere assertion without argumentation that it does not refer to heaven, so we will not deal with that reference.

grounds) as to how to approach this passage. First, it could be that
Paul looks to the coming of the kingdom *with power,* which powerful, judgment-coming was to occur in that generation (cp. Mark
9:1; Luke 21:31).[37] Thus, it would refer to the destruction of the
temple, when Christ manifested His judgment through fulfillment
of His prophetic word (Matt. 24:1-34), bringing wrath upon the
Jews (Matt. 23:29-24:2; 1 Thess. 2:16). That was future from
Paul's vantage point.

Or, second, in that we hold with the great majority of evangelicals the idea of a "now, not yet" kingdom (as House and Ice well
know),[38] and in that we assert the gradualistic[39] expansion and
historical development and ultimate, consummative, and per-
fected glory[40] of that kingdom, it is not difficult to see that this
passage could speak of the introduction of the final, consummative, eternal phase of the kingdom at Christ's Second Advent.[41]

Third, a more accurate translation of the verse suggests
another more reasonable interpretation (which we adopt): "I
solemnly charge you in the presence of God and of Christ Jesus,
who is to judge the living and the dead, and *by* His appearing and
His kingdom."[42] The charge, then, would be with a two-fold emphasis on the basis of the fact that Christ Jesus, who is the Judge,
will judge the living and the dead, *"both* [by] the appearance of
him and [by] the kingdom of him,"[43] that is, by His Second Advent and by His kingdom. As Warfield says: "Each item [appear-
ing and kingdom] is adduced entirely separately; the Apostle is
accumulating the incitement to action, not giving a chronological

---

37. See Chapter 16, "The Preterist Interpretation of the Kingdom."
38. See discussion at opening of the present chapter.
39. See Chapter 13, "The Mission of the Kingdom."
40. See exposition of 1 Corinthians 15 in Chapter 14, "The Victory of the
Kingdom."
41. See exposition of 1 Corinthians 15:20ff. in Chapter 14, "The Victory of the
Kingdom."
42. Emphasis mine. Taken from the New American Standard Bible, a well-
known premillennial-leaning translation.
43. This literal translation is taken from Alfred Marshall, *The Interlinear Greek-
English New Testament* (2nd. ed.; Grand Rapids, MI: Zondervan, 1959), p. 842
(emphasis mine).

list."[44] In this case, we would understand the passage to teach that those Christians who are alive at His Second Advent will be judged, but also those who die even now and enter heaven (the heavenly aspect of the kingdom, 2 Tim. 4:8), as Paul was about to do (2 Tim. 4:6), will be judged. There is no compelling reason to adopt a dispensationalist interpretation.

Certain other passages speaking of the future aspect of the kingdom seem clearly to refer to the eternal, heavenly form of the kingdom. Acts 14:22, cited by House and Ice, is a case in point: "Through many tribulations we must enter the kingdom of God." They comment: "If they were in the kingdom, this statement would make no sense. Since they were not in the kingdom, nor are we, they spoke of it as yet future."[45] This is taken by virtually all non-dispensationalists to refer to our ultimate entry into heaven. Does not Jesus teach that "ye must be born again" to enter the kingdom of God (John 3:3)? Is he not in John 3:3 talking of the realm of salvation, which finds its ultimate goal to be heaven? Besides, John writes that he was in *both* the "tribulation" and "kingdom" (Rev. 1:9). Any tribulation which we encounter in the earthly phase of the kingdom simply prepares us for the heavenly phase by burning away the dross.

Another of the several passages they employ is Matthew 25:31-32. "This passage clearly says that Messiah returns first from heaven and then rules in the kingdom of glory."[46] Had they read a little further they would have learned that the outcome of this "coming" is that all people are assigned at that time (the General Judgment, cp. John 5:28-29) to their final, eternal destiny (Matt. 25:46), not to a temporary, earthly kingdom.

In a remarkably ill-conceived argument House and Ice write: "Shortly before his death, Peter said that believers are 'to make certain about His calling and choosing you' (2 Peter 1:10). The

44. B. B. Warfield, *Biblical and Theological Studies*, ed. by Samuel G. Craig, (Phillipsburg, NJ: Presbyterian and Reformed, [1886] 1952), p. 499.
45. House and Ice, *Dominion Theology*, p. 225. Oddly enough, Pentecost agrees with our interpretation of this verse! See: Pentecost, *Things to Come*, p. 278.
46. *Ibid.*, p. 226.

reason he gave was 'in this way the entrance into the eternal kingdom of our Lord and Savior Jesus Christ will be abundantly supplied to you' (1:11). If he was already in the kingdom when he wrote
this in A.D. 66, why then did he put it in the future?"[47] Here it is
crystal clear that Peter is speaking of the heavenly aspect of the
kingdom, for it is "eternal," not a thousand years in length! After
reviewing their confusion in this regard it almost leads one to ask
of them what Hunt asks of us: "Whatever happened to heaven?"[48]
Where are their verses for heaven?

Neither may we conceive of the kingdom as a future earthly
millennial reign on the basis of the various references to our *inheriting* it. House and Ice write: "That the kingdom is yet future is
also implied in a number of passages which speak of the church
inheriting this kingdom (1 Corinthians 6:9-10; 15:50; Galatians
5:21; Ephesians 5:5; James 2:5)."[49] One of the very verses they
employ specifically says "that flesh and blood cannot inherit the
kingdom of God" (1 Cor. 15:50). The heavenly aspect of the kingdom is in view.

As we have shown, Christ's enthronement is a present reality
that began in the New Testament era subsequent to His ascension. The confident refrain relative to His coronation and enthronement is replete in the New Testament record; we today are
not to be presently awaiting a future kingship of Christ. He is now
on His throne. Indeed, in the New Testament one of the most
quoted or alluded to Old Testament passages is Psalm 110. That
passage records God the Father's word to Christ the Son: "Sit at
my right hand until I make your enemies a footstool for your feet."
In one form or another it appears sixteen times in the New Testament: Matthew 22:44; 26:64; Mark 12:36; 14:62; 16:19; Luke
20:42-43; 22:69; Acts 2:34-35; Romans 8:34; 1 Corinthians 15:25;
Ephesians 1:20; Colossians 3:1; Hebrews 1:3, 13; 8:1; and 10:12.

---

47. *Ibid.*, pp. 226-27. To this passage we could add their references to 1 Corinthians 6:9-10; 15:50; Galatians 5:21; Ephesians 5:5; James 2:5 (pp. 232, 233).
48. Hunt, *Whatever Happened to Heaven?*
49. House and Ice, *Dominion Theology*, pp. 232-33.

The sitting at the "right hand" of God is a semantic equivalent to sitting on God's throne, as is evident in Revelation 3:21: "I also overcame and sat down with My Father on His throne."

Summary

1. The prophesied kingdom of Christ came near in the early ministry of Christ, because the "time was fulfilled" for it to come (Mark 1:14-15).

2. John the Baptist is a marking line separating the fading Old Testament era from the dawning kingdom era (Matt. 11:11-14; Mark 1:14-15).

3. Christ's power over demons was evidence the kingdom had come in His earthly ministry (Matt. 12:28); it was not to await some future, visible coming (Luke 17:20-21).

4. Christ claimed to be king, while on earth (John 12:12-15; 18:36-37) and was enthroned as king following His resurrection and ascension, at Pentecost (Acts 2:30ff.). From then on we hear of his being in a royal position, at the right hand of Almighty God (Rom. 8:34; Eph. 1:20; 1 Peter 3:22).

5. Because of this, first century Christianity proclaimed Him as king (Acts 3:15; 17:7; Rev. 1:5) with regal dignity, authority, and power (Eph. 1:22; Phil. 2:9).

6. Beginning with the first century, people are, at their conversions, translated into the kingdom of Christ (Col. 1:12-13; 4:10; 1 Thess. 2:12).

7. Christians are composed as Christ's kingdom (Rev. 1:6; 9) and are now mystically seated with Him in rulership position (Eph. 1:3; 2:6; 1 Cor. 3:21-22).

8. Christ's kingdom is multi-dimensional, including salvation while on earth (Col. 1:13) and its ultimate fruition in heaven (2 Peter 1:11).

13

THE MISSION OF THE KINGDOM

A Biblical study of the Gospel regarding both its divinely ordained starting point (personal redemption) and ultimate goal (Christian cultural renewal).

In this chapter various issues related to the theoretical mission and practical expectation of the kingdom will be dealt with. Earlier in Chapter 11 the spiritual nature of the kingdom was discussed. That material will form a necessary backdrop for the basic question to be dealt with here and will be especially important to keep in mind for the first two sub-headings below.

The Gospel Focus of the Kingdom

House and Ice often speak of Reconstructionism as entailing a misguided primary focus for the Church.[1] This is due to their radical misunderstanding not only of the nature of the kingdom, but the Reconstructionist view[2] of the essential focus of the gospel and the wide-reaching nature of redemption.[3]

---

1. "The Reconstructionist view of dominion is misdirected. Only the God-Man, Jesus Christ, is destined to rightfully rule over the people of this earth." H. Wayne House and Thomas Ice, *Dominion Theology: Blessing or Curse?* (Portland, OR: Multnomah, 1988), p. 141.

2. Frankly, I would just as soon speak of our views as Reformed as "Reconstructionist." I feel that House and Ice are merely sloganizing in the way they attack "Reconstructionism." Invariably what they end up with is a broadside against historic Reformed theology, even though Tommy Ice claims (incredibly, I believe) that he is Reformed: "I agree that the Reformed faith (of which I am in that family) has historically placed a great emphasis, not on biblical law, since they did not talk about that, but Mosaic law. . . . My view can be found within the historic Reformed faith as can your view" (Personal letter from Tommy Ice to Steven F. Hotze, November 28, 1988, p. 2). What in the world does he mean by "Reformed"?

3. A treatment of their radical misconstrual of Reconstructionism on this point is dealt with in Part III, where their various argumentative shortcomings are highlighted.

It must be understood that Reconstructionists believe that evangelism is the absolute pre-condition to worldwide, postmillennial, theocratic[4] success. House and Ice know this, though they seek to obscure and repress it.[5] But we deeply believe in the "gospel of the kingdom" (Matt. 4:23; 9:35; 24:14; Mark 1:14-15). We insist that cultural influence and change are to be promoted by God's people — who are saved by grace alone (Eph. 2:8-10) — at large in their callings, not by the institutional Church as such. But House and Ice prefer to paint Reconstructionists as those who see evangelism as a superaddition to Christian enterprise in the world: "Evangelism has certainly been added to the Cultural Mandate by the Christian Reconstruction movement, but their real goal is the Cultural Christianization of the world."[6]

How can "Christianization" occur without the priority of evangelism? According to the order in Matthew 28:19-20: Evangelism, leading to baptism, comes first. *Then* follows teaching the *converts* all things Christ taught, with a full assurance of Christ's age-long presence with them to promote more evangelism and more teaching of all things He taught! We deeply believe that "apart from Me you can do nothing" (John 15:5), but that we "can do all things through Christ which strengtheneth me," because "God shall supply all our need according to his riches in glory by Christ Jesus" (Phil. 4:13, 19). Thus, our faith is such that "If ye have faith as a grain of mustard seed, ye shall say unto this mountain, Remove hence to yonder place; and it shall remove; and nothing shall be impossible unto you" (Matt. 17:20b). This leads us to "Work out [our] own salvation [in all of life] with fear and trembling. For it is God which worketh in [us] both to will and to do of his good pleasure" (Phil. 2:12-13). In the final analysis, "with God nothing shall

---

4. The definition of "theocracy" is "God's rule," not rule by Ayatollah Khomeini types. It must be understood as fundamentally different from any "ecclesiocracy," which House and Ice admit Reconstructionists argue, even though House and Ice suggest it must inexorably lead to such. House and Ice, *Dominion Theology*, p. 71, see especially their Chapter 4.

5. They admit that our view is such that "true Christian conversion by the masses is a prerequisite for reconstruction" (House and Ice, *Dominion Theology*, p. 71).

6. *Ibid.*, p. 150.

be impossible" (Luke 1:37). All of this hope has but one foundation: the gospel of the resurrected Christ (Acts 4:12; 1 Cor. 3:11). Hence Paul's testimony regarding his approach: "I determined not to know any thing among you, save Jesus Christ, and him crucified" (1 Cor. 2:2).[7]

An objection that House and Ice bring against our confidence in the success of the Great Commission is that Christians are to be the "called out from" the world (Rev. 7:9; Acts 15:19) and the church is an *ekklesia*, a "called out" body. Hence, "the preaching of the gospel draws out a people from among the peoples or nations of the world — a group of people called the church, a spiritual nation from among the nations. . . . Just as God called Abraham out of Ur of the Chaldeans, so Christ is calling out of the nations a people for his own name — the Body of Christ."[8] "God's intent for this age is to 'take out' from among the nations a people for his name, not to convert the nations and make them into Christian republics."[9]

In light of the following wealth of evidence for a converted world, this objection is wholly without warrant for several reasons: (1) The writers are writing to people in a particular historical context in which they were, in fact, a minority at the very beginning of world-wide progress. A similar argument is answered by Warfield: "It would be manifestly illegitimate to understand these descriptions as necessarily covering the life of the whole dispensation on the earliest verge of which the prophet was standing."[10] The designation does not imply that Christians will *always* be a minority. (2) Actually, the "called out" idea is more of an ethical designation than a prophetic pronouncement. It tells us *from whence* we have come (an ethically fallen world), not *how many* we shall be ("a

---

7. By this he obviously did not mean that he only taught about the gospel details, for he taught them about church divisions (1 Cor. 1-2), church discipline (Chapter 5), marriage (Chapter 7), etc., not to mention all the other things he taught to them and others.

8. House and Ice, *Dominion Theology*, p. 159.

9. *Ibid.*, p. 164.

10. B. B. Warfield, *Biblical and Theological Studies*, ed. by Samuel G. Craig (Phillipsburg, NJ: Presbyterian and Reformed, [1886] 1952), p. 500.

little flock"). If 5/6 of the world's population were to become
Christian in the next century or two, would they not still be "called
out" from an ethically fallen world? (3) In addition, when the
Lord returns, He will return to a wheat field with tares in it — not
to a tare field with wheat in it (Matt. 13:24-30).

The Full-Orbed Character of Redemption

The basic theological problem with House and Ice is that which
Gary DeMar and Peter Leithart have so well captured in the title
of their recent book: "The Reduction of Christianity." They restrict
the focus and effect of redemption: "The purpose of the church[11]
in this present age [is] that of a *witness.*"[12] In the context, that "witness" is rather narrowly defined: "Believers are here to witness to
the coming kingdom, not to inaugurate the kingdom rule."[13] "The
biblical approach is to expose evil with the light (Ephesians 5:13)
and to call men to escape the wrath to come by trusting in Jesus
Christ as their Savior and having their names recorded among those
who will participate in the coming of the future kingdom of God."[14]
They aver that the words of the Great Commission "refer exclusively to Christian evangelism and soteriological salvation,"[15] by
which they mean the salvation of individuals. Of the evangelistic
mandate in Mark 16:15 and Luke 24:46-47, it is claimed: "There is
no language or tone in either of these passages that would support
the notion of Christianizing the world."[16] "Our calling in the present age is primarily evangelism and discipleship."[17]

Let us consider the biblical data.

---

11. Here their use of "church" must mean the church universally considered,
i.e., the mass of believers, rather than the institutional church. This is due to the
next quotation cited.
12. House and Ice, *Dominion Theology*, p. 165.
13. Citing Saucy, *ibid.*
14. *Ibid.*, p. 342.
15. *Ibid.*, p. 151.
16. *Ibid.*, p. 152.
17. *Ibid.*, p. 168.

The Christian Calling

Clearly the initial focus of the Great Commission (Matt. 28:18-20) is evangelism, for the result of our going forth is the baptism of converts.[18] With House and Ice we agree "no one doubts that in the Great Commission the intent of the preaching of the gospel is salvation from sin." The other, supplemental commissionings of Christ recorded in Mark 16:15 and Luke 24:47-49, which are cited by House and Ice, emphasize the salvation of men, as well. But as House and Ice perceptively note with regard to the second "all" in the Great Commission: "the controversy is over the scope of what Christ has commanded."[19]

It is important to understand that the "all" here is used in the distributive[20] sense: It speaks of *every* form of authority as being at His command, whether in heaven or on earth. This is the authority of God Almighty (Matt. 11:25; Amos 1:3-2:3; Oba. 1; Isa. 10:5-34). He has not just the authority of spiritual and moral persuasion among individuals and in the inter-personal realm, to which House and Ice limit it in current practice.[21] He also has authority in the ecclesiastical and familial, as well as in realms such as the societal, political, economical, and so forth. As Revelation 1:5 says of Him *in the days when John wrote*, He *is* "the ruler of the kings of the earth." As Philippians 2:10 and Romans 14:11 teach, He *now* has a Name above *every* name.

---

18. Acts 2:38; 8:12, 36; 9:18; 10:47; 16:15, 33; 18:8.

19. House and Ice, *Dominion Theology*, p. 154. To keep things in perspective, it should be noted that the "Reconstructionist" view of the Great Commission is held by non-Reconstructionists: Harold John Ockenga in his introduction to Carl F. H. Henry's *The Uneasy Conscience of Modern Fundamentalism* (Grand Rapids: Wm. B. Eerdmans, 1947), p. 14: "A Christian world- and life-view embracing world questions, societal needs, personal education ought to rise out of Matt. 28:18-20 as much as evangelism does. Culture depends on such a view, and Fundamentalism is prodigally dissipating the Christian culture accretion of centuries, a serious sin. A sorry answer lies in the abandonment of social fields to the secularist."

20. A. B. Bruce, "Matthew," in W. Robertson Nicoll, *The Expositor's Greek New Testament*, 5 vols. (Grand Rapids, MI: Wm. B. Eerdmans, 1951), vol. 1, p. 339.

21. Regarding the Great Commission: "Those outside the Christian Reconstruction movement say that God's will is individual salvation now and social salvation at the coming of Christ. Thus, the 'all' refers to the directives given to the church to carry out its mission of individual evangelism and teaching in order to build up believers" (House and Ice, *Dominion Theology*, p. 154).

Following upon this claim to universal authority, He delivers
to His few followers the obligation and plan for world conquest:
"Go therefore and make disciples of all the nations, baptizing
them in the name of the Father and the Son and the Holy Spirit,
teaching them to observe all that I commanded you" (Matt. 28:19-
20). The command of the resurrected Christ who possesses "all
authority" is for His followers to bring all nations to conversion
and baptism. This is precisely the expectation of so many of the
Old Testament prophecies, which foresaw all nations flowing to
Mount Zion (e.g., Isa. 2:1-4; Mic. 4:1-4), and which anticipated
"no more shall any man teach his neighbor, 'Know the Lord, for
they shall all know the Lord'" (Jer. 31:34; cp. Isa. 11:9).

In addition, the Commission urges our "teaching them to observe *all* things whatsoever I have commanded you." House and
Ice assert that "worldwide evangelism is the calling of the church
in this age, not Cultural Christianization."[22] (Yet they deny the
success of the worldwide evangelism, despite its being based on
"all authority" and promoted with Christ's age-long presence:
"Scripture indicates that a majority of people will not come to
Christ during the church age.")[23]

In essence, though, they undermine their own view against
cultural Christianization by admitting on the very next page:

> Premillennialists believe that the New Testament does have so-
> cial and cultural ramifications. But they also believe that the em-
> phasis on social and cultural issues reflects the purpose God has
> for this age, namely the individual duties of a Christian before a
> watching world, rather than the redemption and conversion of
> institutions. A look at Gentry's examples [with biblical refer-
> ences — KLG] in the above citation tells how individual believers
> are supposed to behave in relationship to the different spheres of
> life: marriage, charity, employer-employee relationships, citi-
> zenship, and finances. Nowhere in the New Testament does it
> teach the agenda of Christianizing the institutions of the world.[24]

---

22. *Ibid.*, p. 160.
23. *Ibid.*, p. 145, cp. pp. 159, 164, 236, 351.
24. *Ibid.*, p. 155.

Consider how this is damaging to their view. Do not the examples agreeably alluded to by them speak of various "institutions," i.e., marriage, business, government, and so forth? If Christians are to be taught "how individuals are supposed to behave" (presumably on the basis of "all things" Christ taught) in each sphere of life, are they not *ipso facto* being instructed in biblical and Christian culture? And if Christ's commission commands us to "baptize all nations," would not the logical conclusion be that, with His authority (Matt. 28:18), presence (v. 28:20), and command (v. 28:19) we shall get the evangelistic work done? And if so, would it not be the case that when "all nations" have been baptized and the mass of "individuals" in them have been taught how they "are supposed to behave," that the world would, then, have been culturally Christianized? What is "culture" but the sum deposit of the normative labors of men in the aggregate over time?

Should not the "repentance for forgiveness of sins" (Luke 24:47) we are to preach be particular and discrete rather than general and vague? That is, should not repentance be a "change of mind"[25] regarding the *particulars* of our conduct in *all* of life, so that we strive to live differently (i.e., Christianly)? According to Luke 3 should not we then be urged to bring forth particular fruits worthy of repentance (Luke 3:8), i.e. a change of our external behavior by being transformed by God rather than conformed to the world (Rom. 12:1-2), such as caring for the poor (Luke 3:11), being honest governmental officials (Luke 3:12-14), or whatever?

Should not the Christian realize that as a portion of the "all things" of Scripture "the weapons of our warfare are not carnal, but mighty through God to the pulling down of strongholds; Casting down imaginations, and every high thing that exalteth itself against the knowledge of God, and bringing into captivity every thought to the obedience of Christ" (2 Cor. 10:4-5)?[26] And if we cast down "every high thing that exalteth itself against the

---

25. The Greek term *metanoia* means a "change of mind."
26. According to House and Ice, "this is not a passage telling us to develop a Christian worldview." House and Ice, *Dominion Theology*, p. 157.

knowledge of God" and bring "into captivity every thought to the obedience of Christ," will we not be engaging in culture-transforming change? If we are going to "witness" to the people of the world how they are to behave, should we not behave ourselves according to our witness and strive to get *them* to live according to our witness, by the grace of God? Should not we do all things — whether eating or drinking or whatever we do in word or deed — to the glory of God (1 Cor. 10:31; Col 3:17)? Especially since we will give account of every word and deed before Christ (2 Cor. 10:5; Matt. 12:36; Rom. 14:12)? In other words, should not redemption affect *all of life*? May not redemption involve the turning from sin in all of life, even to the point of issuing forth in a distinctive sociopolitical culture, since Israel's "redemption" did such?[27]

In the Great Commission He not only commands them on the basis of universal authority, but He closes with the promise that He will be with them to its completion (Matt. 28:20). There is no inkling of failure for the Church or the perpetual obscurity of the faith here. If we let the Old Testament victory passages[28] speak for themselves, this Great Commission harmonizes perfectly with them.[29] The Victory Motif is enhanced and accelerated by this command of the exalted Christ. This leads us to consider:

---

27. A major distortion of soteriology by dispensationalists blinds them to appropriate Christian duty: a refusal to acknowledge that with personal salvation there must be personal commitment to Christ. We hold that when Christ is accepted as "Savior," He must also be accepted as "Lord." Ryrie is a notorious example of the refusal to acknowledge this (Ryrie, *Balancing the Christian Life* [Chicago, IL: Moody Press, 1969], Chapter 17). I am greatly encouraged though, that John F. MacArthur, an endorser of House and Ice's book, has made a public break with that anemic thinking, even challenging his fellow dispensationalists on the matter — even by favorably citing my own Reconstructionist writing in this regard! (MacArthur, *The Gospel According to Jesus* [Grand Rapids, MI: Zondervan, 1988], pp. 207-8). From what I understand, however, Dallas Seminary professors are preparing to publish rebuttals to it!

28. See Chapter 10 above.

29. For a fine summary exposition of the Great Commission see B. B. Warfield, *The Selected Shorter Writings of Benjamin B. Warfield*, ed. by John E. Meeter, 2 vols. (Nutley, NJ: Presbyterian and Reformed, [1915] 1970), vol. 1, pp. 351-54.

The Breadth of Redemption

All of this discussion regarding the Great Commission comes home to the eschatological argument when we consider the biblical expectations regarding redemption. But first a word study regarding the Greek word *kosmos*, translated "world," will prove helpful.

The nominal form of the word originally meant "order, adornment." The verbal form meant "to put in order, to adorn." The verbal idea of "put in order" is evident in Matthew 12:44 where the demon that is cast out returns to his former "house" and finds it "clean, swept, and *put in order.*" The idea of "adorn" is found frequently.[30] Our modern word "cosmetic" comes from this Greek term. With cosmetics a woman "gets her face in order."

The noun originally had to do with building something from individual parts to form a whole. It came to be applied to relations between men, as in the case of ordering soldiers in armies and governments in matters of state. The Greek idea of beauty and adornment naturally arose from the original conception, in that the Greeks were enamored with that which was "well ordered." Eventually *kosmos* came to speak of the well ordered universe, and was an important term in Greek philosophy.

In the Old Testament there was no Hebrew word for "universe." The coupling of "heavens and earth" served this function. But in the New Testament the word *kosmos* spoke of the sum of all created being, including animate creation. Acts 17:24 speaks of God creating the "world and all that is in it," much as Exodus 20:11 does; it signifies the universe and all that it contains. In that God is not a God of "confusion," but of "order" (1 Cor. 14:33)[31] the universe He created is an orderly creation, as is evident from Genesis 1.

The word "world" as employed in the passages below refers to *the world as the orderly system of men and things.* That is, the world that God created and loves is His creation as it is intended to be: a world in subjection to man who in turn is in subjection to God. Thus, God

---

30. Revelation 21:2; 1 Timothy 2:9; 1 Peter 3:5; Luke 21:5; Matthew 23:29.
31. It should be noted that a different Greek word is here used, *taxis.*

loves His created order of men and things, not for what it has become (sinful and corrupted), but for what He intended. This world order was designed to have man set over it, to the glory of God (Psalm 8; Heb. 2:6-8). This is why at the very beginning of human history man was a cultural creature: Adam was to "cultivate" the world (Gen. 1:26-28),[32] beginning in Eden (Gen. 2:15).

---

32. House and Ice castigate *Reconstructionists* for teaching that the Genesis 1:26-28 Cultural Mandate involves dominion over men, as well as animals (pp. 139-42). This is despite the fact that the full exercise of such dominion necessarily involves men as social creatures working together, whether locally as husbands and wives ("helpmeets," Gen. 2:18) or societally, in governmental arrangements (which God has ordained, Rom. 13:1-4). Interestingly, dispensationalist Henry Morris understands the Cultural Mandate to include governmental arrangements (*The Biblical Basis for Modern Science* [Grand Rapids, MI: Baker Book House, 1984], pp. 41-46). Dispensationalist Herman Hoyt writes: "The issue of dominion is introduced in the opening chapter of the Bible. Immediately after creating man in the image of God the first command given to him concerns the exercise of sovereign control over creation (Gen. 1:26, 28). *This theme unfolds in progressive wonder through the Bible until at last the throne of God is established* on the earth (Rev. 22:1, 3) and the redeemed saints reign with Christ forever (Rev. 22:5)" (Hoyt in *Four Views of the Millennium*, p. 64). Dispensationalist John J. Davis (not to be confused with postmillennialist John Jefferson Davis) writes: "This call [i.e., Gen. 1:26ff.] to rule is a call to *advance civilization* and regulate natural forces" (*Paradise to Prison* [Grand Rapids, MI: Baker Book House, 1975], p. 81). German Dispensationalist Erich Sauer (cited favorably by House and Ice, p. 207) writes of Gen. 1:26-29: "These words plainly declare the vocation of the human race to rule. They also call him to progressive *growth in culture*. Far from being something in conflict with God, *cultural achievements are an essential attribute of the nobility* of man as he possessed it in Paradise. *Inventions and discoveries, the sciences and arts, refinement and ennobling, in short, the advance of the human mind*, are throughout the *will of God*. . . . [T]he call to be ruler signifies a vocation to *advancing civilization* and is a God-given regulation in creation" (Sauer, *The King of Earth* [Grand Rapids, MI: Wm. B. Eerdmans, 1962], pp. 80-81). Anti-Reconstructionist, Presbyterian theologian O. Palmer Robertson agrees regarding Genesis 1:26-28: "This subduing involves the bringing out of all the potential within the creation which might offer glory to the Creator. Such an ordinance, embedded in the creational responsibilities of man, clearly intends to affect his *entire life-pattern*." And after making reference to the Cultural Mandate, he writes: "The explicit repetition of these creation mandates in the context of the covenant of redemption expands the vistas of redemption's horizons. Redeemed man must not internalize his salvation so that he thinks narrowly in terms of a 'soul-saving' deliverance. To the contrary, redemption involves his *total life-style as a social, cultural* creature. Rather than withdrawing narrowly into a restricted form of 'spiritual' existence, redeemed man must move out with a total world-and-life perspective" (Robertson, *The Christ of the Covenants* [Phillipsburg, NJ: Presbyterian and Reformed, 1980], pp. 80, 110). (All emphases above are mine.) See also: Hal Lindsey, *Satan Is Alive and Well on Planet Earth*, (Grand Rapids, MI: Zondervan, 1972), p. 56.

Even early fallen man was driven to cultural exploits (Gen. 4:20-22) well beyond the expectations of humanistic anthropologists and sociologists. Man, then, was created and given a mandate to bring order to all of God's creation. As is evident in their close relation in Genesis 1:26, the dominion drive is a key aspect of the image of God in man. Culture is not an accidental aside of the historical order.

Now it should not go without notice that the New Testament often speaks of the redemption of the "world"—the very system of men and things of which we have been speaking. Although we are prone to speak of Christ as "my personal Savior" (and certainly He is!), we too often overlook the fact He is also declared to be "the Savior of the *world*." There are several passages which speak of the world-wide scope of redemption. These passages are quite instructive in their eschatological data. Let us lay them before you.

Redemption of the World

In John 1:29, John the Baptist sees Jesus and utters these words: "Behold, the Lamb of God who takes away the sin of the world." As such these words are compatible with 1 John 4:14 which informs us of the divine purpose of Christ's incarnation: "The Father has sent the Son to be the Savior of the World." In John 3:16-17 we read that "God so loved the world that He gave His only begotten Son, that whoever believes in Him should not perish, but have eternal life. For God did not send the Son into the world to judge the world; but that the world should be saved through Him" (cp. John 12:47). 1 John 2:2 teaches that "He Himself is the propitiation for our sins; and not for ours only, but also for those of the whole world." In 2 Corinthians 5:19 Paul conceives of Christ's active labor thus: "God was in Christ reconciling the world to Himself."

These passages clearly present Christ in His redemptive labors: He is the Lamb of God; He takes away sin; His purpose in coming was to save; He provides propitiation for the sinner; He is reconciling sinners to Himself. But a point frequently overlooked in these passages is that these verses just as clearly speak of the divinely assured world-wide outcome of His redemption.[33] In 1 John 4:14

---

33. See B. B. Warfield, "Christ the Propitiation for the Sins of the World," in *Selected Shorter Writings*, Vol. 1, Chapter 23.

we discover the divinely covenanted goal of the sending of the Son: He was, in fact, to be the "Savior of the world." Thus, in John 3:17 it is set forth very clearly that "God did not send the Son into the world to judge the world; but that the world should be saved through Him." John 1:29 views Him as in process of actually saving the world: "the Lamb of God who takes away the sin of the world." The verb translated "takes away" is actually a present, active participle: *airon*. Here Jesus is said to be in process of taking away the sin of the world (by His active obedience). Even more strongly put is 1 John 2:2 where it is said that Jesus Christ is "the propitiation for our sins; and not for ours only, but also for those of the whole world." Paul, too, applies the reconciling work of Christ to the world (2 Cor. 5:19).

It undeniably is the case that these verses speak of a redemption that has the world in view. But how are we to understand the nature of this redemption, which has as its scope this "world"? It is vitally important to discern the exact nature of the statements made in regard to Christ's salvific purpose. A close consideration of the passages disallows the notion that what is in view is the *general* tendering of an offer of salvation, or the mere provision of the resources, either of which awaits the response of the individual. The terms employed are too potent to allow such conceptions.

Consider John 1:29. Here it is stated that Christ is presently in process of "taking away" sin. "Taking away" here is the translation of a participle based on the verb *airo*. The idea is to actually "take away, remove, lift up and carry off." In 1 John 3:5 it is stated that Jesus was manifested for the very purpose of bearing away His people's sins. There is no suggestion of a mere possibility or offer; there is no restriction of the force of the statement by use of an "if." In some way Christ was in process of actually bearing away sin. And if the Son Whom the Father sanctified and sent into the world was endeavoring to bear away sin, we may rest assured that sin will be borne away.

In John 3:17 the force is equally potent. The inspired representation of the incarnational motive was that "God did not send the Son into the world to judge the world; but that the world should be saved through Him." In the syntactical construction of this verse we have the conjunction of purpose, *hina*, followed by an aorist, subjunctive verb, *sozo*. Such grammatical structure constitutes a purpose clause. And when used of God's actions it signifies His divine intent (cf. John 1:7; 1 John 5:20; Rev. 20:3), a divine intent that is by the very nature of the case unthwartable (Isa. 46:10; 55:11; Dan. 4:35). As a matter of fact, this very construction occurs in John 3:16, where we read: "He gave His only begotten Son that [*hina*] whoever believes in Him should not perish" [aorist subjunctive]. May we suggest that there are those who truly believe in Him that will perish? Syntactically the certainty of accomplishment of the purpose is expected; historically it is assured by the force of the divine will.

Again there is no mere potentiality suggested in the passage; there is divinely purposive expectation. The expectation is of salvation, of making whole, of healing, not of proffering salvation, hoping for salvation, or mere assisting toward the claiming of salvation.

The 1 John 4:14 passage does not use the purpose clause, but does speak of Christ as being sent by God as the *soter* ("savior") of the world. He is not intended to be a helper toward salvation or to offer Himself as the potential or conditional Savior *if.* . . . Conditional constructions were available to John. He could have used *ean* plus the subjunctive — suggesting the idea of a "more probable future condition" and indicating that some uncertainty is implied; or *ei* and the indicative — suggesting the idea of "simple condition" and expressing a wish. Though these were available to John, he did not employ them in 1 John 4:14.

In 1 John 2:2 the force of the teaching does not depend on syntactical features such as purpose clauses, but upon strong redemptive terminology: "He Himself is the propitiation for our sins; and not for ours only, but also for those of the whole world." The word "propitiation" (*hilasmos*) is one of the more potent redemptive terms available in Scripture. This term is disliked by liberals because of its involvement of the wrath of God against sin (it speaks of appeasing God's wrath by the provision of a covering sacrifice). Thus, here John informs us that Christ is "the propitiation." He is the one Who stands in for us to receive God's wrath, so that it might be turned away from us. One who has Christ acting as His propitiator has Christ standing in his place so that he will never have to receive the wrath and curse of God. Christ's acting as propitiator is not equivalent to His merely offering propitiation.

Reconciliation

In 2 Corinthians 5:19 another significant redemptive term is employed: "reconciliation." Reconciliation has to do with the bringing back of a favorable relationship between God and man. It speaks of actual relief from the consequence of sin (vv. 19, 21). Notice the emphasis on God's action: Verses 18 and 19 say, "All these things were from God, who reconciled us . . . namely, that God was in Christ reconciling the world to Himself." Later in verse 21 it is said that "He made Him that knew no sin to be sin on our behalf." This, as Warfield comments, is a very "high supernaturalism"—God is at work, not man. And God's word is that of reconciliation through the provision of Christ as our sin-bearer.

Thus, in each of the passages passing under our scrutiny, we have reference to the sure provision of full and free salvation. A variety of redemptive terms of significance are employed to underscore the serious nature of the salvation provided. It is impossible to read these passages as teaching a purely potential universalism in the death of Christ—a provision that needs to be made effective in each instance by the actions of fallen sinners.

Consequently, when these verses speak of God's actions in Christ as being in process of "taking away the sin of the world" (John 1:29), as setting forth Christ as "the Savior of the world" (1 John 4:14), as not intended to "condemn the world," but to "save" it (John 3:17), as being "the propitiation for the sins of the world" (1 John 2:2), as "reconciling the world to Himself" (2 Cor. 5:19), the idea must be a protensive concept. That is, Christ's redemptive labors are designed eventually to effect the redemption of the created order of men and things. And that redemptive activity extends out into the future. There is coming a day when the accomplished result of Christ's labors will be evident in a world redeemed by Gospel forces already long operative.

Though these passages do not teach an "each-and-every universalism," as in liberal thought, they do set forth the certain divinely assured prospect of a coming day in which the world *as a system* (a *kosmos*) of men and things, and their relationships, will be redeemed. A day in which the world will operate systematically upon a Christian ethico-redemptive basis. Christ's redemptive labors will have gradually brought in the era of universal worship, peace, and prosperity looked for by the prophets of the Old Testament. As John put it to the first-century Christians who were undergoing various tribulations: Christ is the propitiation not for their sins only, they being few in number (a little flock, Luke 12:32), but for the sins of the world as such. There is coming a day, in other words, in which Christ will have sought and have found that which was lost (Luke 19:10): the world. Hence, the Great Commission command to baptize "all nations" (Matt. 28:19).

The Drawing of All Men

Another class of passages that have an identical import is that which speaks of Christ's labors as having fruition among "all men." Particularly relevant are two passages: John 12:32 and 1 Timothy 2:6. In John 12:32 Jesus is comforting His disciples while in the shadow of the cross: "And I, if I be lifted up from the earth, will draw all men to Myself." In 1 Timothy 2:6 Paul is encouraging Christians to effectual fervent prayer for all men (1 Tim. 2:1) because: Christ "gave himself a ransom for all, the testimony borne at the proper time." We will only briefly deal with these two passages, in that the idea is basically the same as that already presented in the passages that make reference to the world.

The John 12:32 passage, although set in the context of "the shadow of death," as it were, is filled with covenantal hope for the disciples. Though Christ will soon be taken from the disciples and by wicked hands crucified, nevertheless, there is a bright ray of hope as the Gospel Victory Motif penetrates the clouds of despair. And that hope is just this: "And I, if I be lifted up from the earth, will draw all men unto me." Here the Lord does set up a condition for His redemptive labors. The condition set forth in the protasis

is: "If I be lifted up from the earth." The apodosis sets forth the
result: "I will draw all men to Myself." The condition is not founded
upon the action of the creature — a fallen creature, at that. Rather,
it is firmly established upon His own divine plan and action.

It is without a doubt a fact that Jesus was "lifted up from the
earth" (whether this refers to the crucifixion or to the ascension or
to both). Thus, upon His word we may rest assured that He "will
draw all men" to Himself. Upon the completion of the lifting up,
there is the declared future expectation that he will draw (future
tense) all men to Himself. The word for "draw" involves the idea
of resistance; but it is a resistance which is overcome. This statement harmonizes perfectly with the Old Testament creational,
covenantal, and prophetical expectations, as well as with the New
Testament redemptive expectations set forth above.

Paul's statement in 1 Timothy 2:6 is no less clear. He employs
strong redemptive language when he says Christ "gave Himself a
ransom for all." Christ's "ransom" (*antilutron*) is given "in behalf of"
(*huper*) "all" (*panton*). Then he reminds us that this fact will be testi-
fied in due time. That is, the day for its accomplishment will come.
Paul, with John, looks to the eventual outcome of Christ's redemptive labor: "all" the world will one day be ransomed. After all,
that is why "God was in Christ reconciling the world to Himself."

This is why "Reconstructionists say that since it is God's will to
bring both personal and social salvation before Christ returns, it
is necessary to redeem institutions as well as people."[34] House and
Ice's partial citations of technical lexicons cannot overthrow this
conception by reference to Ephesians 5:11: "The Greek word *elegchete* translated 'expose' in Ephesians 5:11 means 'to show someone
his sin and to summon him to repentance.' We are to give the biblical perspective on 'the unfruitful deeds of darkness' so that a person will repent of sin and leave the kingdom of darkness. Paul had
a perfect opportunity to tell the troops to get out and Christianize
the darkness, but he did not."[35] Their partial citation of the *Theo-*

---

34. House and Ice, *Dominion Theology*, p. 154.
35. *Ibid.*, p. 155.

logical Dictionary of the New Testament is interesting, for that work goes on to say of the word in question: "The word does not mean only 'to blame' or 'to reprove,' nor 'to convince' in the sense of proof, nor 'to reveal' or 'expose,' but 'to set right,' namely, 'to point away from sin to repentance.' It implies educative discipline."[36] This is what Reconstructionists are interested in.

Neither is their futile reference to Acts helpful: "Throughout Acts, the proclamation is always the soteriological gospel. Never are the apostles and evangelists involved in the Christianization of the culture"[37] If this were correct, we would be left to wonder why the Christians were considered to be "turning the world upside down" (Acts 17:6). Or why they were calling upon "all men everywhere" to repent (Acts 17:30), so that the converts engaged in burning their once revered magical books (Acts 19:19), leading to the assertion of Luke that "mightily grew the word of God and prevailed" (Acts 19:20). This led further to resistance by the idol industry of the region (Acts 19:24ff.), which feared that "she [Artemis] whom all of Asia and the world worship should even be dethroned from her magnificence" (Acts 19:27, NASB). So rather than Reconstructionism leading to apostasy, as House and Ice believe,[38] the preaching of repentance leads to Reconstruction, i.e., Christians faithfully living for the Master in all of life.

Thus, we have seen, in essence, that we are to "love the Lord thy God with all [our] heart, and with all [our] soul, and with all [our] mind, and with all [our] strength" (Mark 12:30). We are not to be concerned just with the "inner spiritual life,"[39] but also with the totality of life, even engaging our strength (labor) to promoting the will of God. This is why "Reconstructionists believe this calling will be achieved by Christ through his people because of his resur-

---

36. Friedrich Buschel, "*elegcho*," in Gerhard Kittel, ed., *Theological Dictionary of the New Testament*, 10 vols. (Grand Rapids: Wm. B. Eerdmans, 1964), vol. 2, p. 474.

37. House and Ice, *Dominion Theology*, p. 152.

38. *Ibid.*, p. 160.

39. "The church age is a time of development, but not the kind Reconstructionists advocate. It is a time that stresses development of the inner spiritual life" (*ibid.*, p. 167).

rection, his ascension to heaven, and his current mediatorial reign from the throne of heaven."[40]

The reductionist methodology of House and Ice leads them into all manner of confusion. For instance, they state: "True Christianity requires a person to be regenerated by God. . . . Something cannot be Christian without the dynamics of spiritual regeneration."[41] Apparently, by this they mean there are no Christian colleges or Christian bookstores, since a college or a store cannot be literally regenerated! But then on the very next page they write: "For the kingdom to be established, the earth, as well as the individual, must be regenerated."[42] Are the rocks and trees of "the earth" to be "regenerated"? Do they possess "the dynamics of personal regeneration"?

Summary

1. The primary focus of the kingdom of Christ is the Gospel of salvation (Matt. 4:23; 9:35; 24:14).

2. Evangelism is the essential pre-condition to postmillennial, theocratic success. Apart from Christ we can do nothing (John 15:5); in Christ we can do all things (Phil. 4:13, 19; Matt. 17:20).

3. In that He possesses "all authority in heaven and on earth" (Matt. 28:18), Christ's Great Commission expects His people to win converts, who are then baptized into His body, and then instructed in "all things" He taught (Matt. 28:19).

4. Due to the glorious presence of Christ with us, the Great Commission expects the conversion of all nations, as do the prophets (Matt. 28:19; Isa. 2:1-4; Mic. 4:1-4).

5. The Christian witness involves exposing evil (Eph. 5:11) and calling men to repentance from *all* unrighteousness in *every* realm (Luke 24:47; 3:8), so that "every thought" is taken captive to Christ (2 Cor. 10:5).

---

40. *Ibid.*, p. 50.
41. *Ibid.*, p. 350.
42. *Ibid.*, p. 351.

6. Christians are to live and act in every area of life—inner-personal, personal, social, political—with body, soul, mind, and strength (Mark 12:37) to the glory of God (1 Cor. 10:31; Col. 3:17), for they will give an account of every word and deed (Matt. 12:36; 2 Cor. 10:5).

7. God's redemption provided in Christ is designed to bring the world as a system to salvation (John 1:29; 3:17; 1 John 2:2) and redeem mankind (John 12:31; 1 Tim. 2:6).

8. Thus, Christians cannot omit cultural endeavors as they seek the redemption of all of life to God's glory.

14

THE VICTORY OF THE KINGDOM

An exegetical study of key Scripture passages which demonstrate the victorious prospects for the Gospel in history through currently operative means.

The postmillennial system expects the great majority[1] of the people of the world to be converted to Christ at some point in time before the Second Advent of Christ, and that this blessed condition will prevail upon the earth for an extensive period of time, bringing to the world an abundance of righteousness, peace, security, and prosperity, such as has not been known in any previous era of earth history. As House and Ice state it, we are committed to "believing in the eventual earthly triumph of the church"[2] (being careful to understand "church" as the universal church, i.e. Christianity). This is, in essence, the Gospel Victory Motif, which we discover in both Old and New Testament prophecy.[3] In further elucidation of the postmillennial hope, let us turn to consider the following issues.

The Expected Outcome of Gospel Victory

On the basis of our previous discussion of the confidence of the Old Testament expectations of victory[4] and the authoritative commission granted the Church,[5] we clearly have a *biblical* war-

---

1. A possible indicator of the general proportion of the converted to the lost at that time might be indicated in Isaiah 19:18. J. A. Alexander agrees with John Calvin and suggests there will be *"five* professing the true religion to *one* rejecting it" (J. A. Alexander, *The Prophecies of Isaiah*, 2 vols. [Grand Rapids, MI: Zondervan, (1875) 1977], vol. 1, p. 357.

2. H. Wayne House and Thomas Ice, *Dominion Theology: Blessing or Curse?* (Portland, OR: Multnomah, 1988), p. 23.

3. See earlier discussions in Chapters 9-12.

4. See Chapter 10, "The Expectation of the Kingdom."

5. See Chapter 13, "The Mission of the Kingdom."

rant for the expectation of victorious progress of redemption in history. We firmly believe that "the Gospel is the power[6] of God unto salvation."[7]

1 Corinthians 15:20-28

Not only is Christ presently enthroned,[8] but He is enthroned and ruling with a confident view to the subduing of His enemies. A brief exposition of the important 1 Corinthians 15:20-28 passage will prove helpful at this juncture.[9] (We will employ the New International Version as our basic English translation.)

In 1 Corinthians 15:20-22 Paul speaks of the resurrection order: Christ has been resurrected as a first-fruits promise of our resurrection. In verses 23-24 we read more of the order of and events associated with the resurrection: "But each in his own turn:[10] Christ the first fruits, then, when he comes, those who belong to him. Then the end will come." With Paul we are now in the era awaiting the end-time coming of Christ when all believers will be resurrected in glory. *When Christ comes this will be "the end"!*[11] There will be no millennial age on the present earth to follow. But notice the expectation preceding the end:

Verse 24 says, "the end will come, when he hands over the kingdom to God the Father." The end of earth history is brought

---

6. The word for "power" here is *dunamis*.

7. Romans 1:16; cp. 1 Corinthians 1:18, 24; 2:4; 1 Thessalonians 1:5; 2 Timothy 1:8.

8. See Chapter 12, "The Presence of the Kingdom." House and Ice see Christ as only "anointed king" and "given the place of honor at the right hand of God" at His ascension, not enthroned. House and Ice, *Dominion Theology*, p. 235.

9. *If* I were prone to proffer simplistic solutions, I would point to this passage in response to Ice's challenge: "Show me *one* passage that requires a postmillennial interpretation" (*ibid.*, p. 9). For fine 100-year-old (i.e., pre-Reconstructionist) expositions of this passage see B. B. Warfield, *Biblical and Theological Studies*, ed. by Samuel G. Craig (Phillipsburg, NJ: Presbyterian and Reformed, [1886] 1952), pp. 478ff. and David Brown, *Christ's Second Coming: Will It be Premillennial?* (Grand Rapids, MI: Baker Book House, [1876] 1973), pp. 153-66.

10. For a discussion of the Greek word *tagma* ("turn") — often confused by dispensationalists — see Warfield, *Biblical and Theological Studies*, p. 484.

11. The Scripture is clear that the resurrection is a "general resurrection" of both the righteous and unrighteous (Dan. 12:2; John 5:28-29; Acts 24:15), which will occur on the "*last* day" (John 6:39-40, 44, 54; 11:24; 12:48).

about "whenever."[12] Christ "hands over" the kingdom to the Father. In the syntactical construction before us, the "handing over" (NIV) or "delivering up" (KJV) of the kingdom must occur in conjunction with "the end."[13] Here the contingency is of the date: "whenever" it may be that He delivers up the kingdom, *then* the end will come. Associated with the predestined end here is the prophecy that the kingdom of Christ will be delivered up to the Father only "*after* he has destroyed all dominion, authority and power."[14]

Gathering this exegetical data together, the conclusion must be that the end is contingent, but it will come whenever it may be that He delivers up the kingdom. When Christ turns over the kingdom to the Father, the end has come. But this will not occur until "after He has destroyed all dominion, authority and power." Consequently, the end will not occur, Christ will not turn the kingdom over to the Father, until after He has abolished His opposition. Here again is the Gospel Victory Motif in the New Testament in a way co-ordinate with Old Testament covenantal and prophetic expectations.

And notice further: Verse 25 demands that "He must[15] reign until He has put all His enemies under His feet." Here the present infinitive ("reign") indicates the continuance of his reign. We have already seen that He is presently reigning, and has been so since His ascension.[16] Here we learn that He must continue to reign, He must continue to put His enemies under His feet—but until when? The answer is one that is identical to that which has already been concluded. It is expected to occur before the end of

---

12. A better translation of *hotan* is "whenever." We know not "when" this will be (Matt. 24:36).

13. The Greek for "hands over" here is *paradidoi*, which is in the present tense and subjunctive mode. When *hotan* is followed by the present subjunctive it indicates a present contingency that occurs in conjunction with the main clause: here the coming of the end. Arndt-Gingrich, *Lexicon*, p. 592.

14. In the Greek text the *hotan* is here followed by the aorist subjunctive, *katargese*. Such a construction indicates that the action of the subordinate clause precedes the action of the main clause. William F. Arndt and F. Wilbur Gingrich, *A Greek-English Lexicon of the New Testament and Other Early Christian Literature* (Chicago, IL: The University of Chicago Press, 1957), p. 592.

15. Greek: *dei*.

16. See Chapter 12, "The Presence of the Kingdom."

history. Earlier it was awaiting until all rule, authority and power were abolished; here it is said to await occurrence until "He has put all His enemies under His feet." The repetition of the expectation of His sure conquest before the end is significant. Furthermore, the last enemy that will be subdued will be death, which is subdued in conjunction with the Resurrection that occurs at His coming. [17] But the subduing of all other of His enemies occurs before this, before the Resurrection.

In verse 27 it is clear that He has the title to rule, for the Father "has put everything under His feet." This is the Pauline expression (borrowed from Psalm 8:6) that is equivalent to Christ's declaration that "all authority has been given Me." Christ has the promise of victory; He has the right to victory. Psalm 110, especially as expounded by Paul in 1 Corinthians 15, shows He will have the historical, pre-consummation victory as His own before His coming. This verse from Psalm 110 is one of the most frequently referred to Old Testament promises to appear in the New Testament; [18] the expectation is a frequently recurring theme!

Romans 11

In addition, Romans 11 is helpful for the understanding, not only of the worldwide conquest of the Gospel, but of the Jewish hope for salvation. In Romans 11 Paul presents a sustained argument for the future conversion of the Jews. In verses 1-10 he shows very clearly that he has in mind the racial Jew, and not the spiritual Jew (i. e., the Christian): He speaks of tribal distinctions (v. 1) and the rebellion of this nation (vv. 3-10). Later he sets them over in contrast to Gentiles (vv. 11-13, 25). Thus, he is speaking directly to the question: "Has God forever rejected the Jews to certain, irrevocable, and final doom?"

---

17. Contrary to dispensationalist confusion, the resurrection of the lost is not mentioned here only because his primary concern (as in 1 Thess. 4:13) is with Christians and their ethical actions.

18. See Matthew 22:44; 26:64; Mark 12:36; 14:62; Luke 20:42-43; 22:69; Acts 2:34-35; Ephesians 1:20-22; Hebrews 1:13; 10:13; 1 Peter 3:22. There are a number of other allusions to it (e.g., Rom. 8:34 and Col. 3:1), but those listed are fuller and include the idea of expected dominion.

Verse 11 asks: "I say then, they did not stumble so as to fall, did they? May it never be! But by their transgression salvation has come to the Gentiles, to make them jealous." By the fact of the demise of God's special favor to the Jew due to their transgression (i.e., the rejection of the Messiah), they have fallen, encouraging the message of salvation to spread to the Gentiles. In verse 12 we read: "Now if their transgression be riches for the world and their failure be riches for the Gentiles, how much more will their fulfillment be!" Here the expectation is that the number of faithful Jews will be brought back into fullness (*pleroma*) with God.

But there is more. In verse 15 Paul speaks of their rejection as "the reconciliation of the world." In verse 25 he expects massive conversions among the Gentiles: "A partial hardening has happened to Israel until the fullness of the Gentiles has come in." The Gentiles will be converted in full numbers. This "reconciliation of the world" and "the fullness of the Gentiles coming in" seem to be equivalent concepts, betokening worldwide revival.

Interestingly, the worldwide fullness of the Gentiles will provoke the Jews to a jealousy for salvation (vv. 25, 11). This will lead the Jews to mass conversions, as verse 12 indicates. This in turn will lead to further Gentile conversions: "How much more will" the Jews' fullness bring riches to the world of Gentiles (v. 12). This ends with a situation where "all Israel will be saved" (v. 26).

The Gradualistic Principle of Biblical Gospel Victory

The theological truths presented above require the introduction of an important redemptive-historical principle of divine action. Contrary to covenantal postmillennialism, the dispensationalist holds *catastrophism* as the basic *modus operandi* of the kingdom. That is, in their theological system, the kingdom of Christ in all of its attendant glory will invade history in terms of "cataclysmic interventionism"[19] introduced by wars and rumors of wars, as it is imposed on a recalcitrant world (via the Battle of Armageddon).

---

19. House and Ice, *Dominion Theology*, p. 232, cf. pp. 239, 269, 295.

The General Principle as Used in Scripture.

The postmillennialist discerns a contrary operative principle at work: divinely ordained gradualism (in a sense, this involves a macrocosmic version of individual sanctification). This principle expects the gradualistic, developmental, incremental expansion of the kingdom. The postmillennialist sees this as God's common *modus operandi.*[20] Evidences of this principle are apparent throughout biblical revelation. Even the *creation* of the universe proceeded upon a gradualistic principle — an accelerated, anti-evolutionary gradualism, to be sure. Rather than God's creating the word in totality by one instantaneous fiat, He employed a series of successive divine fiats stretched out over a period of six days (Gen. 1). Rather than accomplishing *redemption* immediately in Eden, He promised its coming fruition, a fruition that followed thousands of years after Adam (Gen. 3:15). Rather than giving His total special *revelation* of Himself and His will, He gradualistically revealed His word to men over a period of 1500 years (Heb. 1:1-2). Even in salvation, *sanctification* comes by process, rather than instantaneously (Col. 1:10; 2 Thess. 1:3; 1 Peter 2:2; 2 Peter 3:18). Likewise is it with His redemptive kingdom: it proceeds along gradualistic lines. The kingdom is to come incrementally. Let us survey several relevant passages in this regard.

The Principle as Applied to the Kingdom.

The root concept to a gradualistic development of the kingdom is found in the Old Testament conquest of the Promised Land. There it is specifically stated as to why God operates gradualistically in that situation; in other words, it was not just "a matter of natural course." In Deuteronomy 7:22 the principle is enunciated: "And the Lord your God will clear away these nations before you little by little; you will not be able to put an end to them quickly, lest the wild beasts grow too numerous for you" (cf. Exodus 23:29-30).

---

20. Despite insinuations by House and Ice (p. 336) it has *nothing whatsoever* to do with naturalistic, evolutionary progress, which is a mythical, humanistic construct. See R. J. Rushdoony, *The Mythology of Science* (Nutley, NJ: Craig Press, 1967).

The gradualistic principle was for the good of God's people, allowing them to conquer where they could maintain godly control (a point, when understood in its spiritual implications, is directly relevant to the progress of the kingdom today).

In Daniel 2:35ff. the kingdom of Christ is said to come down to the earth as a stone to smite the Roman kingdom. As we read through the passage we learn that eventually it becomes a great mountain in the earth. In Ezekiel 17:22-24 God promises to establish the kingdom as a small "sprig from the lofty top of the cedar." Then He will nurture it until it becomes "a stately cedar." In Ezekiel 47:1-9 redemption flowing forth from the temple of God is stated to come in stages. The waters of life coming out from under the altar come first "to the ankles" (v. 3), then to the knees (v. 4a), then to the loins (v. 4b), then it "was a river that I could not ford" (v. 5). This is the river of life (v. 9).

In Matthew 13 the kingdom parables speak of its remarkable increase in size (mustard seed) and total penetrative and transformational influence (leaven). Matthew 13:31-33 speaks of its external growth as that of a mustard seed to a great plant and its internal permeation as a little leaven that leavens three pecks of meal. Both parables indicate a small beginning and a magnificent ending.[21] In Mark 4:26-29 the kingdom of God is said to begin as mere seed (v. 26), then it puts forth the blade, then the head, the mature grain (v. 27).

---

21. The incredible contortions the kingdom parables of Matthew 13 and parallels suffer in the hands of dispensationalists are enough to indicate the desperation of that system. Pentecost argues that the mustard seed growth "refers to the perversion of God's purpose" and the "leaven refers to a corruption of the divine agency" (*Things to Come: A Study in Biblical Eschatology* [Grand Rapids, MI: Zondervan/ Academie, (1958) 1964], p. 148). He does so despite their being illustrative of "the kingdom of heaven" that Christ preached and promoted! And despite the kingdom of heaven's being considered something of unparalleled value (Matt. 13:44-46). Just as the symbol of a "lion" does not always represent evil (cp. 1 Peter 5:8 with Rev. 5:5), neither does leaven invariably portray evil in Scripture (see Lev. 7:13; 23:17). Pentecost also points to Matthew 13:3-9 as showing the "course of the [present] age" will experience "a decreasing response to the sowing of the seed, from 'a hundredfold' to 'sixty' to 'thirty' " (p. 146). Despite the fact the parallel in Mark 4:8 has the exact opposite progression, indicating the order of increase was not significant. Besides, who would not be pleased with a thirty-fold increase?

In Romans 13:11-14 and 1 John 2:8 the apostles see the kingdom light as already shining, ready to dispel the darkness. The progress and growth of the kingdom will not be thwarted by Satan, for the "gates of hell will not be able to prevail against it" (Matt. 16:18). Though slow, it will advance in God's good time (cp. 2 Peter 3:8-9).

In light of the Gradualism Principle, it is useless for House and Ice to point to alleged "failures" in the history of the church as evidence that the postmillennial hope, as such, is wrong.[22] Nowhere in the definition of the postmillennial hope is it *necessary* that we *already* have had the requisite growth;[23] theoretically it could well be entirely future from our time! Postmillennialist Warfield could admit to the presence of "evil men waxing worse" without forfeiting his postmillennialism: "Some of these evils [of which Paul speaks] had already broken out in his own times, others were pushing up the ground preparatory to appearing above it themselves. It is historically plain to us, no doubt, that they suitably describe the state of affairs up to at least our day. But we must remember that all the indications are that Paul had the first stages of 'the latter times' in mind, and actually says nothing to imply either that the evil should long predominate over the good, or that the whole period should be marked by such disorders."[24] With that word of caution in mind, we do not agree, however, that there has been no progress in history — *when the long run is viewed.* We do believe there has been progress made from the times the Christians were thrown to the lions to the times of the successful establishment of Dallas Theological Seminary and Multnomah Press.

The postmillennial system has built into it the expectation of long, slow, incremental growth, as House and Ice are aware.[25]

---

22. "How do Reconstructionists account for, even by their own admission, so much false doctrine and so little orthodoxy in Christendom today?" House and Ice, *Dominion Theology*, p. 263, cp. pp. 336-40, 351.

23. There is no postmillennial *sine qua non* demanding that by the year 1989 (or any other year) there must be the fullness of the kingdom.

24. Warfield, *Biblical and Theological Studies*, p. 500.

25. House and Ice, *Dominion Theology*, pp. 232, 240.

House and Ice even speak of America in the year A.D. 40,225 in their straw man scenario of a Reconstructed America.[26] In other words, on that (hypothetical) basis we are now only 1/20 of the way there!

Gradualism and Imminence

It is much more difficult, however, for dispensationalists to justify *their* vigorous assertions of the "any-moment" expectation or the "imminence" of the coming of Christ,[27] when, in fact, almost 2000 years have come and gone. What in the world are we to make of 2000 years of "eagerly awaiting Christ's *any-moment* coming"?[28] Dave Hunt, an endorser of House and Ice, attempts to resolve the problem, with conclusions that totally evacuate the meaning of an "any-moment" Return of Christ:

> Why has it taken so long for our Lord to return? Could it be another 2000 years, or even more, before His promise is fulfilled? . . . [S]ince previous "dispensations" in human history — such as the period from Adam to the Flood, from the Flood to the Promised Land, and the Jewish era prior to the birth of the church at Pentecost — have occupied similar lengths of time, it hardly seems unreasonable that the church should be on earth for 2000 years as well.
>
> That Christ has not yet returned does not change the fact that the early church, in obedience to His clear commands, was waiting and watching for Him to come at any moment.[29]

---

26. *Ibid.*, p. 63.

27. See Pentecost, *Things to Come*, pp. 168, 169, 203; John F. Walvoord, *The Rapture Question* (Grand Rapids, MI: Zondervan, 1957), p. 192. Interestingly, dispensationalist Alan Patrick Boyd has written that the early church fathers "had no concept of imminency or of a pretribulational Rapture of the Church. . . . [Thus] the findings of the thesis regarding imminency would invalidate the [Dispensationalists'] historical claims regarding imminency in the following writings:" Pentecost, *Things to Come*, pp. 168ff.; 203 and Walvoord, *The Rapture Question*, p. 192; Alan Patrick Boyd, "Dispensational Premillennial Analysis of the Eschatology of the Post-Apostolic Fathers (Until the Death of Justin Martyr)," unpublished master's thesis, Dallas Theological Seminary, 1977, p. 90 and footnote 1.

28. House and Ice, *Dominion Theology*, p. 232 (emphasis mine), see also pp. 166 and 231.

29. Dave Hunt, *Whatever Happened to Heaven?* (Eugene, OR: Harvest House, 1988), p. 39.

And in another place, he writes:

> We do well to consider why this continual expectancy of His im-
> minent return, which is unquestionably commanded by Christ,
> should have such a special purifying effect. Oddly enough, it
> seems quite apparent that its value for us, and the importance
> the Bible obviously attaches to it, do not depend upon whether
> the Lord's return is actually imminent or not. It is the eager *ex-
> pectancy* that counts. . . . While there are many indications that
> the Lord's return may very well be imminent for *us*, we now
> know in retrospect that it was *not* imminent for all those genera-
> tions of Christians who came before us.[30]

Hal Lindsey (another endorser of House and Ice), the *Scofield
Reference Bible*, and John F. Walvoord, even argue that the Letters
to the Seven Churches in Revelation 2-3 provide an historical
panorama of Church history to its end — including the Reformation and our own era![31] How could the coming of Christ have
been "imminent" if 2,000 years of history had to transpire? And if
this is what "imminence" means, postmillennialists will gladly
hold to it!

Interestingly, House and Ice themselves make express reference to Luke 19:11-27, which indicates a great length of time will
separate His ascension and His Second Coming. They even recognize and mention that this parable was given because the people "supposed that the kingdom of God was going to appear sud-
denly. In contrast to this popular expectation, Christ spoke of a
nobleman who went on a long journey to a far country."[32]

The Divine Gifts for Gospel Victory

House and Ice assert: "God has not given the church a proper

---

30. *Ibid.*, pp. 58-59.
31. Hal Lindsey, *There's a New World Coming* (Santa Ana, CA: Vision House,
1973), pp. 38ff.; *The Scofield Reference Bible*, ed., C. I. Scofield (New York: Oxford,
1909), pp. 1331-32. See also *The New Scofield Reference Bible*, rev. ed., E. Schuyler
English (New York: Oxford, 1967), p. 1353; and Walvoord, *Revelation*, p. 52. See
also: Pentecost, Ryrie, and Boyer.
32. House and Ice, *Dominion Theology*, p. 228.

dose of grace to Christianize the world."[33] "We should learn from history that every time Christians have tried to establish the kingdom on earth, it has led to disastrous results. We believe the reason for this lack of success is that God has not given the church the necessary tools and graces to establish an earthly kingdom."[34] Elsewhere Ice's testimonial reports his conviction: "I now know that God has not been pleased to give the necessary graces to his church for the kind of victory dominionists decree."[35]

These are incredible statements in that they greatly diminish the richness of the gracious gifts of God to His people. Did Christ not command His disciples to wait in Jerusalem "for power on high" (Luke 24:46-49)? Did He not inform His followers that their faith (which overcomes the world, 1 John 5:3-4) was such that it could remove mountains (Matt. 17:20)? Did not the apostles greatly rejoice in the super-abundant grace of God and unsearchable riches of Christ (Rom. 5:17; Acts 4:33; 1 Pet. 4:10; Eph. 1:7, 18; 2:7; 3:8), declaring that God had blessed us with "all spiritual blessings" (Eph. 1:3) because of Christ's ascension and pouring out of His wondrous gifts upon His people (Eph. 4:8-11)? Was it not by that grace that they felt they could do "all things" through Christ and that God would supply all they had need of "according to his riches in glory by Christ Jesus" (Phil. 4:13, 19)? In short, were they not convinced that "with God nothing shall be impossible" (Luke 1:37)? We have ample gifts and graces to get the job done, in obedience to the Great Commission.[36] Let us just quickly cite a few.

---

33. *Ibid.*, p. 340.

34. *Ibid.*, p. 351. Ironically, dispensationalism sees even a kingdom personally, visibly administered by Christ as ending in disaster! Pentecost, *Things to Come*, pp. 547-53. Also see footnote 13, Chapter 11 above.

35. House and Ice, *Dominion Theology*, p. 7.

36. House and Ice take offense at the notion that the "victory," "dominion," "conquest," and the like will be won by Christians (the body of Christ) acting according to the leading of His Spirit on the basis of His redemptive labors, employing spiritual graces (and not armed aggression!) rather than by Christ's physical return to the earth: "Reconstructionists often say they do not believe that they are to bring in the kingdom. While it is true that they believe the kingdom was established by Christ at his first coming, they clearly believe that some phase of the kingdom is to be mediated by Christ through the agency of the

First, we have the very presence of the Risen Christ with us. The Great Commission specifically promised this (Matt. 28:20). He will never leave nor forsake us (Heb. 13:5). *Second*, since the Ascension of Christ, we have the indwelling of the Holy Spirit (John 7:39; 14:16-18), who will convict the world of sin, righteousness, and judgment (John 16:7-15). In fact, it was "expedient" for us that Christ go away so that we might have His presence in the Person of the Holy Spirit (John 16:7). It is no regression in redemptive history, no diminishing of our resources, no "mere" mystical presence: The Holy Spirit's coming is glorious in every respect. His coming is "power from on high" (Luke 24:49).

Third, it is the Father's delight to save sinners (Eze. 18:23; Luke 15:10; 1 Tim. 2:5). *Fourth*, we have the Gospel, which, as mentioned previously, is the power of God (Rom. 1:16; 1 Cor. 1:18, 24). *Fifth*, we have full access to God in prayer (Heb. 4:16), through Jesus' name (John 14:13-14; 15:16; 16:23, 24, 26; 1 John 3:22; 5:14-15), which even promises greater works than Christ (John 14:12) and opens the full resources of heaven to us (John

---

church during the present age. As a result, Dominionists often use 'take over,' 'bringing in,' or 'establishing' the kingdom language" (*ibid.*, p. 407). It should be noted that this is no "Reconstructionist" *distinctive*, for other postmillennialists do the same: David Brown writes: "That more fidelity on the Church's part would have hastened the predicted consummation, is language which we are fully warranted in using [toward the] long promised *subjugation of the world* to Christ." And "There is a satisfaction unspeakable in anticipating the endless ways in which the Spirit may get himself renown, by what he will yet do in and by the church. . . . [T]he heart delights to think of [these instrumentalities] as destined to effect that *universal submission* to the sceptre of Christ which is to characterise the latter day" (Brown, *Christ's Second Coming*, pp. 323-24, cp. p. 156). Warfield writes: "Christians are His soldiers in this holy war, and *it is through our victory that His victory is known*" (Warfield, *Biblical and Theological Studies*, p. 493). And: "There is the church struggling here below—the 'militant church' we may call it; the *triumphing church* he would rather teach us to call it, for the essence of his presentation is not that there is continual strife here to be endured, but that there is continuous victory here to be won. The picture of this *conquering church* is given us in" Revelation 19 (*Selected Shorter Writings*, ed. by John E. Meeter, 2 vols. [Nutley, NJ: Presbyterian and Reformed, (1915) 1970], vol. 1, p. 348). Still again: "It is the distinction of Christianity that it has come into the world clothed with the mission to *reason* its way to its *dominion*. . . . And it is solely by reasoning that it will put all its enemies under its feet" (Warfield, *Selected Shorter Writings*, vol. 2, pp. 99-100). Emphases mine. See Chapter 12, note 26.

14:13; James 4:15; 1 John 5:14). *Sixth*, in His ministry, Christ witnessed the falling of Satan's kingdom as His followers exercised authority over demoniacs (Luke 17:10). In fact, Satan was cast down (John 12:31) and bound by Christ in order that Christ might "spoil his goods" (Matt. 12:28-29; cp. Rev. 20:2-3). Christ specifically came that He might "destroy" Satan (Heb. 2:14) and his "works" (1 John 3:8), making a show of him and openly triumphing over him (Col. 3:15), having judged him (John 16:11). Consequently, his people might not only resist the devil so that he will flee from them (James 4:7), but even expect to "bruise Satan under" their feet (Rom. 16:20), "because greater is he that is in you, than he that is in the world" (1 John 4:4). Because of all this, the Gospel has the power to "open their eyes, and to turn them from darkness to light, and from the power of Satan unto God" (Acts 26:18).

Now, of course, this does not prove that God intends that the world should be "Christianized" (that has been demonstrated on other grounds). But it should embarrass any diminishing of the potentialities of the gifts and grace of God. Let us hear no more of this talk of "the church age [being] a time in which Satan and his rebellious court refuse to give up their rule."[37] Who cares that Satan "refuses to give up"?!

The Intrinsic Pessimism of Dispensationalism

Due to space considerations we will not deal at length with the following matter. It should be at least briefly broached, however. House and Ice are dismayed at the Reconstructionist characterization of dispensationalism as "pessimistic": "Christian Reconstructionists often misrepresent the premillennial view by saying that our position is inherently a pessimistic one."[38] Nevertheless,

---

37. House and Ice, *Dominion Theology*, p. 235.

38. *Ibid.*, p. 146, cf. discussion on their pages 142-49, 161, 180, 170, 182-88. It must be recognized that it is not just Reconstructionists who so characterize dispensationalism. Even liberal commentators point to the "lethargy" inherent in dispensationalism (e.g., Ted Peters, *Futures: Human and Divine* [Atlanta, GA: John Knox Press, 1978], pp. 28-36). House and Ice state that "the gospel in history is

the characterization is valid.

Although House and Ice call postmillennialists Gary North and R. J. Rushdoony pessimists,[39] a world of difference lies between the two forms of pessimism. In response to their question, "How is their pessimism different from premillennialists,"[40] we answer: North and Rushdoony have a pessimism regarding the deleterious influence of secular humanism when left unchecked; House and Ice have a pessimism regarding the hope of Christian progress in the present age because of the inexorable plan of God. Reconstructionists believe the humanistic danger is real, but will be overcome by the grace of God working presently in His people. The dispensationalists believes in predestined evil times that cannot be overcome by our faithful, Spirit-impulsed labor to the glory of God. Their hope for the success of the gospel requires a *miracle beyond* the current order (the Second Advent); ours requires *providence in* the current order.

The Reconstructionist urges believers to remember that "what a man sows, that shall he reap," but that God nevertheless is at work to establish righteousness in the earth and, thus, "your labor is not in vain in the Lord" (1 Cor. 15:58).[41] The dispensationalist urges believers to accept the view that "the church age will end in apostasy, not revival" because so destined by God.[42] Further, believers today are taught by this view: "This current world is headed toward judgment. After that judgment, Christ will take over control of the world and rule it. But until that happens, the message and activities for believers should be, 'Flee the wrath to come by finding safety in Jesus Christ.' "[43] They dogmatically teach their

---

not doomed to failure. The extent of the success of the gospel during this current age is dependent upon God's sovereign purpose for it. So to argue, in principle, that premillennialists do not believe in the victory of the gospel is to distort the real issue about God's purpose for the gospel" (p. 145).

39. House and Ice, *Dominion Theology*, p. 146.

40. *Ibid.*, p. 148.

41. The backdrop of this statement is Isaiah 65:23, which has as its covenantal context Deuteronomy 28:1-14, promising cause-and-effect blessings to flow to God's people, who are the "new creation" (2 Cor. 5:17; Gal. 6:14).

42. House and Ice, *Dominion Theology*, pp. 390, 378.

43. *Ibid.*, p. 356.

followers: "Christians have no immediate solution to the problems of our day."[44] In fact, they aver that "to attempt to establish a long-term change of institutions before Christ returns will only result in the leaven of humanism permeating orthodox Christianity."[45] They even castigate Reconstructionists (or anyone else, for that matter) for trying: "Tragically, this will contribute to the further unfaithfulness of the church in these last days before the return of Messiah."[46]

The pessimism of House and Ice is flushed out in their answer to Jesus' question in Luke 18:8: "When the Son of man cometh, shall he find faith on the earth?" As pessimists House and Ice write: "This is 'an inferential question to which a negative answer is expected.' So this passage is saying that at the second coming Christ will not find, literally, 'the faith' upon the earth."[47]

There is, however, some doubt as to whether this question is even dealing with the future existence of Christianity.[48] But if it does, why is a negative prospect expected? Could not Christ be seeking to motivate His people, driving them to strive to see that the answer issue forth in an optimistic prospect, as Peter's answer was an optimistic one to another question in John 6:67-68.[49] Could it not be that "the question is asked for the purpose not of

---

44. John F. Walvoord, in Charles Lee Feinberg, *Prophecy and the Seventies* (Chicago, IL: Moody Press, 1971), p. 212. Walvoord continues: "A solution to this unrest and turmoil is provided in the Bible, and there is no other. That solution is that Jesus Christ Himself is coming back to bring peace and rest to the world" (p. 210).

45. House and Ice, *Dominion Theology*, p. 340.

46. *Ibid.*, p. 161.

47. *Ibid.*, p. 229. Ironically, not even House and Ice believe that at either the Secret Rapture Coming or the Second Advent there will be a total absence of the Christian faith.

48. Warfield convincingly suggests that the reference to "the faith" has to do with the faith-trait under question in the parable: perseverance. He doubts the reference even touches on whether or not the Christian faith will be alive then, but rather: "Will Christians still be persevering in the hope of the Lord's return?" See Warfield, "The Importunate Widow and the Alleged Failure of Faith," in *Selected Shorter Writings*, vol. 2, pp. 698-710.

49. For similar ethical promptings, see Warfield, *Biblical and Theological Studies*, pp. 334-50.

speculation but of self-examination. Let each answer for himself."[50]

Reconstructionists believe that dispensationalism is pessimistic in that it asserts the present dispensation of the Holy Spirit lacks any hope of discipling the nations according to Christ's command, authority, and presence. They are pessimists in regard to current prospects for currently available gifts of God and the labors of His people.

Jeremiahs' Hope

Strangely, House and Ice unnecessarily cut their own throat with an illustration of what they would deem an appropriate pessimism: "Jeremiah was a pessimist. God sent him to the people of Israel to tell them that they were under his judgment. They could have repented, but God said through Jeremiah's prophecy that they would not, and therefore they would be destroyed. . . . What would have been the prudent course of action in light of God's plan? It certainly would not have been to start a Reconstructionist movement to return the nation to its roots. That had already been tried by the prophets. The godly response would be to act in accordance with God's message."[51]

What, indeed, would have been "the prudent course of action" in these circumstances? One would think that it would *not* have been a good idea to invest money in a long-term real estate venture in light of the approaching siege and destruction awaiting Jerusalem, but (as a faithful postmillennial Reconstructionist!) that is exactly what Jeremiah did (Jer. 32)! With the *New Bible Commentary* we must agree: Jeremiah 32 was written "a short time before the final collapse of Jerusalem. But, in spite of the encircling gloom, the prophet maintains a steady and impressive optimism. . . ."[52]

---

50. William Hendriksen, *The Gospel of Luke* in *New Testament Commentary* (Grand Rapids, MI: Baker Book House, 1978), p. 818. See also Francis Davidson, ed., *New Bible Commentary* (2nd ed.; Grand Rapids, MI: Wm. B. Eerdmans, 1954) p. 857.

51. House and Ice, *Dominion Theology*, p. 357.

52. F. Cawley, "Jeremiah" in Francis Davidson, ed., *The New Bible Commentary* (2nd. ed.; Grand Rapids, MI: Wm. B. Eerdmans, 1954), p. 627. See also John Gill, *An Exposition of the Books of the Prophets of the Old Testament* (Streamwood, IL: Primitive Baptist Library, [1810] 1976), (at Jer. 32:9) and Matthew Henry, *Matthew Henry's Commentary on the Whole Bible*, 6 vols. (Old Tappan, NJ: Fleming H. Revell, 1976), vol. 4, p. 611.

But also, is it not the case that God's threatenings of judgment can be "repented of" by Him (Exodus 32:14; 2 Sam. 24:16; 1 Kings 21:29; 1 Chron. 21:15; 2 Chron. 12:7; Jer. 26:19; Amos 7:3, 6)? For instance, what of the case with Nineveh, when Jonah preached God's prophecy against them: "Yet forty days, and Nineveh shall be overthrown" (Jonah 3:4)? Yet we read "God saw their works, that they turned from their evil way; and God repented of the evil, that he had said that he would do unto them; and he did it not" (3:10).

House and Ice teach that "the Bible speaks of things progressing from 'bad to worse,' of men 'deceiving and being deceived' (2 Timothy 3:13). We look out at our world and see how bad things really are."[53] Their understanding of this passage is exegetically careless and anti-contextual. Note that: (1) Paul is instructing *Timothy* on this matter. He is speaking of things that *he* will have to face and endure (v. 10, 14). He is not prophesying regarding the long term in history. (2) Verse 1 of 2 Timothy 3 teaches that perilous "times" (Gk: *chairoi*) shall come. This Greek term indicates "seasons." It is the logical error of quantification to read this reference to (some) "seasons" of perilous times as if it said *all* times in the future will be perilous. Postmillennialists are well aware of the "seasons" of perilous times that beset the church under the Roman Empire and at other times. (3) Their piecemeal citation of 2 Timothy 3:13 leaves the impression, further, that "things" shall become worse in history. But the verse actually says: "evil men and seducers shall wax worse and worse." Paul is speaking of individual evil men becoming worse; he is speaking of their progressive personal degeneration—their anti-sanctification, as it were. He says absolutely *nothing* about their numbers increasing! (4) Paul clearly tells Timothy that these evil men (cp. v. 1) "shall proceed no further: for their folly shall be manifest unto all men" (v. 9). He speaks as one expecting victory![54]

---

53. House and Ice, *Dominion Theology,* p. 183

54. See the discussion of 2 Timothy 3 in Gary DeMar, *The Debate over Christian Reconstruction* (Ft. Worth, TX: Dominion Press, 1988), pp. 53-55.

Summary

1. Biblical prophecy expects that there is coming a time when the majority of the world's population will have been converted to Christ by means of the Gospel.

2. Christ is presently ruling and reigning from heaven (1 Cor. 15:25a).

3. He will not return in His Second Advent until "the end" of history (1 Cor. 15:24), when He turns His rule over to the Father (1 Cor. 15:28).

4. At Christ's Second Advent, He will have already conquered His enemies (1 Cor. 15:24)—the last one, death, being conquered at His Return, when we are resurrected (1 Cor. 15:26).

5. The falling away of the Jews allowed for mass conversions among the Gentiles (Rom. 11:12).

6. Eventually the vast majority of Jews and Gentiles alike will be converted, leading to the "reconciliation of the world" (Rom. 11:15).

7. God normally works in history in a gradualistic manner, as evidenced in His gradual unfolding of His plan of redemption and His revelation of Himself in Scripture.

8. The kingdom comes gradualistically, as well, growing and ebbing ever stronger over the long run (Dan. 2:35ff.; Eze. 17:22-24; 47:1-9; Matt. 13:31-33; Mark 4:26-29).

9. The imminence doctrine of Christ's return, which is held by dispensationalism, is meaningless in that it may mean either very soon or thousands of years distant.

10. The imminence doctrine is also unbiblical in that Scripture anticipates a long time delay in Christ's return (Matt. 24:48; 25:5, 19; Luke 19:11-27).

11. Dispensationalism denigrates the gifts that God has given the Church.

12. Christ's gifts to the Church well equip it for its task of winning the world to Christ through its members.

13. The Church has the very presence of Christ (Matt. 28:20) and the Holy Spirit (1 Cor. 3:16).

14. God the Father delights in the salvation of sinners (Eze. 18:23; Luke 15:10).

15. The Gospel is nothing less than "the power of God unto salvation" (Rom. 1:16; 1 Cor. 1:18, 24).

16. Satan's binding was effected in principle in the ministry of Christ (Matt. 12:28-29), thus casting him down from his dominance (John 12:31; Luke 17:10) on the basis of Christ's redemptive labor (Col. 3:15).

17. Christians may resist the devil, causing him to flee (James 4:7); they may even crush him beneath their feet (Rom. 16:20) because "greater is he that is in you, than he that is in the world" (1 John 4:4).

18. Dispensationalism is intrinsically pessimistic in that it denies any hope that the gifts Christ gave the Church might turn back evil; evil is prophetically inevitable. The church age must end in apostasy.

19. Postmillennialism is intrinsically optimistic in the long run. The church age will end in victory.

15

HISTORY OF THEOLOGY ON THE KINGDOM

A response to dispensationalism's faulty historical analysis of the history of eschatology, demonstrating the recency of dispensationalism and the antiquity of nascent postmillennialism.

In House and Ice's Chapter 10 the unwary Christian is left with some fundamental misconceptions regarding the history of eschatological understanding, or the exposition of the kingdom, if you will. This is particularly disappointing in that dispensationalists have in the past been notorious for their errors in this field.

Despite the blatant errors involved in dispensationalist historical analysis, which have been pointed out time and again, House and Ice continue to pass on that data. By and large the faulty data is often traceable to the long discredited claims of George N. H. Peters.[1] Boyd even urges his fellow dispensationalists to "avoid reliance on men like Geo. N. H. Peters . . . , whose historical conclusions regarding premillennialism . . . in the early church have been proven to be largely in error."[2] Noted dispensationalists are prone to resist up-dating their textbooks that remain in print, thereby fostering the misconceptions.[3] In addition to correcting such misconceptions, we will respond to a few of the other errors in their Chapter 10, even beyond these well-known ones.

---

1. For example, see rebuttals of Peters in Alan Patrick Boyd, "A Dispensational Premillennial Analysis of the Eschatology of the Post-Apostolic Fathers (Until the Death of Justin Martyr)," unpublished master's thesis, Dallas Theological Seminary, 1977, p. 92; D. H. Kromminga, *The Millennium in the Church* (Grand Rapids, MI: Eerdmans, 1945).

2. Boyd, "Dispensational Premillennial Analysis," p. 92.

3. E.g., J. Dwight Pentecost, *Things to Come: A Study in Biblical Eschatology* (Grand Rapids, MI: Zondervan/Academie, [1958] 1964), and Charles Ryrie, *Dispensationalism Today* (Chicago, IL: Moody Press, 1965).

233

Confounding Premillennialism and Dispensationalism

It is common practice for most dispensationalists to equate historic premillennialism and dispensationalism. This, of course, is necessary if they desire to defend themselves against what Ryrie calls "the charge of recency."[4] House and Ice employ this remarkable confusion in an attempt to demonstrate the antiquity of their position. Unfortunately, they do so in such a way that the unsuspecting reader has no inkling that this approach has been long discredited by all but certain dispensationalists.[5] Although House and Ice are *dispensationalists* (a *fourth* school of eschatology), they state that there are but "Three Major Views of Eschatology."[6] They later state: "The three schools of eschatology are: amillennialism, premillennialism, and postmillennialism."[7] This approach involves a major misunderstanding of the matter, as can be seen in the following.

First, it is worthy of note that historic premillennialists strongly disavow any systemic commonality with dispensationalism. Premillennialist George E. Ladd vigorously protests the equation of dispensationalism and historic premillennialism.[8] Dispensationalist Herman Hoyt responds to a paper by Ladd, noting: "It is very clear from Ladd's discussion of hermeneutics that he is decidedly opposed to the dispensational system."[9] This explains why the popular book edited by Robert G. Clouse is entitled: *The Meaning*

---

4. Ryrie, *Dispensationalism Today*, pp. 66-78.

5. See Clarence B. Bass, *Backgrounds to Dispensationalism: Its Historical Genesis and Ecclesiastical Implications* (Grand Rapids, MI: Baker Book House, [1960] 1977), pp. 13ff.; Boyd, "Dispensational Premillennial Analysis," *passim*; Gary DeMar, *The Debate over Christian Reconstructionism* (Ft. Worth, TX: Dominion Press, 1988), pp. 107-8.

6. H. Wayne House and Thomas Ice, *Dominion Theology: Blessing or Curse?* (Portland, OR: Multnomah, 1988), p. 193.

7. *Ibid.*, p. 419.

8. George E. Ladd, *The Blessed Hope* (Grand Rapids, MI: Wm. B. Eerdmans, 1956), pp. 31ff. See also: Erickson, *Contemporary Options*.

9. Herman Hoyt, in Robert G. Clouse, ed., *The Meaning of the Millennium: Four Views* (Downer's Grove, IL: Inter-Varsity Press, 1977), p. 42. See Ladd's article, *ibid.*, pp. 19-29.

of the Millennium: Four Views, instead of following House and Ice's practice of speaking of "three views."

Second, some dispensationalists admit the futility of equating dispensationalism and ancient premillennialism. There is an excellent Master's Thesis on this very topic, which was presented to the faculty of Dallas Theological Seminary eleven years before the publication of *Dominion Theology.*[10] In it Alan Patrick Boyd confesses that "he originally undertook the thesis to bolster the [dispensational] system by patristic research, but the evidence of the original sources simply disallowed this. . . . [T]his writer believes that the Church *rapidly* fell from New Testament truth, and this is very evident in the realm of eschatology. Only in modern times has New Testament eschatological truth been recovered."[11] He goes on to admit that "it would seem wise for the modern [i.e., dispensational] system to abandon the claim that it is the historical faith of the Church."[12] He points to the error of such dispensationalist worthies as George N. H. Peters, Lewis Sperry Chafer, Charles C. Ryrie, J. Dwight Pentecost, and John F. Walvoord in assuming a basic similarity between ancient premillennialism and modern dispensationalism.[13] Boyd's conclusion is significant. Of Ryrie's bold statement that "Premillennialism is the historic faith of the Church," he states: "It is the conclusion of this thesis that Dr. Ryrie's statement is historically invalid within the chronological framework of this thesis."[14]

---

10. Those interested may borrow this thesis through the inter-library loan program of their local library. Alan Patrick Boyd, "A Dispensational Premillennial Analysis."

11. Boyd, "Dispensational Premillennial Analysis," p. 91n.

12. *Ibid.,* p. 92.

13. *Ibid.,* p. 2, note 1: George N. H. Peters, *The Theocratic Kingdom of Our Lord Jesus, the Christ,* 3 vols. (New York: Funk and Wagnalls, 1884), vol. 1, pp. 494-97; L. S. Chafer, *Systematic Theology,* 5 vols. (Dallas, TX: Dallas Seminary Press, 1947), vol. 4, pp. 271-74; Charles Ryrie, *The Basis of the Premillennial Faith* (Neptune, NJ: Loizeaux Bros., 1953), pp. 20-23; Pentecost, *Things To Come,* pp. 375-76; John F. Walvoord, *The Millennial Kingdom* (Grand Rapids, MI: Zondervan, 1959), p. 43.

14. *Ibid.,* p. 89.

Though he does not seem to realize the implications, even Ryrie can point to fundamental differences between the two schools of eschatology, as he defines *dispensationalism*: "Perhaps the issue of premillennialism is determinative. Again the answer is negative, for there are those who are premillennial who definitely are not dispensational. The covenant premillennialist holds to the concept of the covenant of grace and the central soteriological purpose of God. He retains the idea of the millennial kingdom, though he finds little support for it in the Old Testament prophecies since he generally assigns them to the Church. The kingdom in his view is *markedly different* from that which is taught by dispensationalists since it loses much of its Jewish character due to the slighting of the Old Testament promises concerning the kingdom."[15] John S. Feinberg, another dispensationalist agrees: "The [dispensational] system does not flow logically from premillennialism. If one holds the dispensationalist's hermeneutic, holds his position on the covenants, and makes the dispensationalist's point about Israel and the church, he will be led to premillennialism of a dispensational sort. But this only illustrates that for a dispensationalist, premillennialism is not *logically* prior to other foundational intellectual commitments."[16]

Dispensationalism's Supposed Antiquity

Third, that it would, indeed, "seem wise" for House and Ice to "abandon the claim" to antiquity is evident in that dispensational distinctives create a radically different *system* from ancient premillennialism. One important dispensational distinctive is that the present church age is "a work separate and distinct from that of Israel in God's plan"[17] and that the Church does not take over the promises to Israel.[18] Yet none of the ancient premillennialists is in agreement with such a notion.

---

15. Ryrie, *Dispensationalism Today*, p. 44 (emphasis mine).

16. John S. Feinberg, ed., *Continuity and Discontinuity: Perspective on the Relationship Between the Old and New Testaments* (Westchester, IL: Crossway Books, 1988), p. 339.

17. House and Ice, *Dominion Theology*, p. 194. Ladd would have vehemently disagreed with such a (re)definition; Ladd, in Clouse, *The Meaning of the Millennium*, pp. 19-29, 94 and Ladd, *Crucial Questions about the Kingdom of God* (Grand Rapids, MI: Eerdmans, 1952), Chapter 5.

18. House and Ice, *Dominion Theology*, pp. 180-82.

For example, one apostolic father proudly pointed to by dispensationalists is Papias (A.D. 60-130).[19] Yet dispensationalist Boyd confesses that "Papias applied much of the Old Testament to the Church,"[20] thus "it seems safe to assume that his chiliasm was of a markedly different character than the modern variety."[21] Of ancient premillennialist Justin Martyr (A.D. 100-165),[22] Boyd writes: "He claims that the Church is the true Israelitic race, thereby blurring the distinction between Israel and the Church."[23] This is a crucial distinctive in that "the doctrine of the Church, is the touchstone of dispensationalism."[24] In addition, Boyd documents from Ryrie, Walvoord, Pentecost, and others various dispensational distinctives that do not appear in early premillennialists. These include: hermeneutic literalism, an imminent rapture followed shortly by the Second Advent, the Jewish character of the Millennium, and the mystery form of the Church.[25]

Fourth, even House and Ice recognize, in their better moments, that there are serious differences between historic premillennialism and dispensationalism: "There is a greater discontinuity between premillennialism, *especially the dispensational version*, and postmillennialism."[26]

In short, as Boyd honestly admits: "Dispensational premillennialism is the product of the post-Reformation progress of dogma."[27] This point is irrefutable. Even Ryrie has admitted that "it is granted by dispensationalists that as a system of theology dispensationalism is recent in origin."[28] Thus, even *if* we were to accept the notion that *"Premillennialism* was first held by the early

---

19. *Ibid.*, pp. 200-1.
20. Boyd, "Dispensational Premillennial Analysis," pp. 60-61.
21. *Ibid.*, p. 62.
22. House and Ice, *Dominion Theology*, pp. 201-2.
23. Boyd, "Dispensational Premillennial Analysis," p. 86. Boyd cites Justin's *Dialogue* 119, 120, 123, 125, 130, 131, 135. See especially 116:3; 11:5.
24. Ryrie, *Dispensationalism Today*, p. 132. Cp. House and Ice, *Dominion Theology*, p. 418.
25. Boyd, "Dispensational Premillennial Analysis," Chapter 1.
26. House and Ice, *Dominion Theology*, p. 46 (emphasis mine).
27. Boyd, "Dispensational Premillennial Analysis," p. 91, n2.
28. Ryrie, *Dispensationalism Today*, p. 67.

church fathers who were closest to the original apostles,"[29] this would have *no* bearing on the debate with *dispensationalists*! Furthermore, House and Ice's confounding of the two views is all the more incredible in light of their statement regarding Reconstructionist David Chilton: Chilton "redefines some of the issues 'broad enough' so that he can hitch the more recent postmillennialism to the wagon of amillennialism and say that this historic orthodox position of the church includes his view."[30] Is not dispensationalism hitched to the wagon of premillennialism by dispensational advocates?

Misrepresentation of the Eschatology of the Ancient Church

Not only do House and Ice illegitimately confound dispensationalism and premillennialism, but they misrepresent the eschatology of historic Christianity: "Premillennialism was the pervasive view of the earliest orthodox fathers"[31] for "the first two and a half centuries" of our era.[32] "The early church was solidly chiliastic until the time of Augustine."[33] This is common dispensational fare, for Pentecost states that "a premillennial belief was the *universal* belief in the church for two hundred and fifty years after the death of Christ."[34] G. N. H. Peters is favorably quoted by Pentecost as saying: "Now let the student reflect: here are *two* centuries . . . in which positively no direct opposition whatever arises against our

---

29. House and Ice, *Dominion Theology*, p. 210 (emphasis mine).

30. *Ibid.*, p. 208. This becomes all the more remarkable in that they state: "It should be pointed out that amillennialists and postmillennialists have more in common with each other" (p. 195).

31. *Ibid.*, p. 202.

32. *Ibid.*, p. 203.

33. *Ibid.*, p. 200. If "solid" and "pervasive" are roughly interchangeable terms in these two quotations, then one quotation claims solid chiliasm until A.D. 250 and the other until Augustine (about A.D. 400)!

34. Pentecost, *Things to Come*, p. 374 (emphasis his). But then he quotes Schaff as saying it was not creedally endorsed by the church, but was "widely current" among distinguished teachers. How he leaps from "widely current" to "universal" we will never know.

doctrine."[35] Such assertions are extremely important to House and Ice[36] and other dispensationalists;[37] unfortunately, they are quite mistaken.

Actually "an inquiry into the extent of ancient chiliasm will serve to show the untenableness of the claim that this doctrine was held with practical unanimity by the Church of the first few centuries."[38] Even dispensationalist Boyd recognizes the futility of such claims: "Indeed, this thesis would conclude that the eschatological beliefs of the period studied [until Justin Martyr, *d.* A.D. 165] would be generally inimical to those of the modern [i.e., dispensational — KLG] system (perhaps, seminal amillennialism, and not nascent dispensational premillennialism ought to be seen in the eschatology of the period)"![39] Boyd even states: "This validates the claim of L. Berkhof . . . 'it is not correct to say, as Premillenarians do, that it (millennialism) was *generally* accepted in the first three centuries. The truth of the matter is that the adherents

---

35. Pentecost, *Things to Come*, p. 375, citing Peters, *Theocratic Kingdom*, vol. 1, pp. 494-96.

36. On page 201 they assert: "The earliest times of the church were in many ways some of the least pagan of all church history, since the church at her birth was almost totally Jewish and often purged by persecution. It is as the church became more Gentile, and consequently more pagan, that the pagan idea of *spiritualization* began to take root, and orthodoxy moved from premillennialism to Augustinian amillennialism." Their combination of Zionistic sympathies and an *a priori* commitment to literalism often blinds them to the fact that the Jews were the ones who rejected the Messiah in preference to Caesar (John 19:15). (Interestingly, one of Pentecost's defenses of the literal hermeneutic is that it was "the prevailing method of interpretation among the Jews at the time of Christ" [Pentecost, *Things to Come*, p. 17]. Undoubtedly, this played no small part in their rejection of Him [John 6:15] and of His disciples' confusion regarding Him [Luke 24:25].) Boyd, who has done extensive original research on the eschatology of the era to Justin Martyr comes to the *exact opposite* conclusion: "It is the present conviction of this writer that there was a rapid departure from New Testament eschatological truth in the early patristic period" (Boyd, "Dispensational Premillennial Analysis," Preface).

37. E.g., Ryrie, regarding premillennialism, asserts that it was "the faith of the early church" and "this was true in the first and purest centuries of the Church" (Ryrie, *Basis of the Premillennial Faith*, p. 33).

38. Kromminga, *The Millennium*, p. 30.

39. Boyd, "Dispensational Premillennial Analysis," pp. 90-91.

of this doctrine were a rather limited number.' "[40]

The difference between Boyd's conclusions and those of House and Ice is that Boyd researches the original writings and analyzes and reports the data; House and Ice merely assert their belief and, for the most part, parade before the reader long-disproved secondary sources.[41] A clear example of this problem of secondary sources is their treatment of Daniel Whitby: "Whitby clearly believed that the early church held to a premillennial eschatology." They even use their secondary source to hold that Whitby held that the first Nicene Council was premillennial.[42] In his "A Treatise on the True Millennium," however, Whitby himself clearly states: "The doctrine of the Millennium was never generally received in the church of Christ."[43] He also writes: "The doctrine of the millennium was not the general doctrine of the primitive church from the times of the apostles to the Nicene council . . . for then it could have made no schism in the church, as Dionysius of Alexandria saith it did."[44]

Ancient Non-Millennialists

Furthermore, it is clear upon reading certain of the ancient champions of premillennialism that they faced opposition from orthodox non-millennialists. For instance, consider Justin Martyr's response to Trypho regarding the hope of "a thousand years in Jerusalem, which will then be built": "I admitted to you formerly, that I and many others are of this opinion, and [believe] that such will take place, as you assuredly are aware; but, on the other hand, I signified to you that *many* who belong to the pure and

---

40. *Ibid.*, p. 92, n1.

41. Extreme dependence on secondary sources is stock-in-trade for dispensationalists. For instance, when Pentecost sets out to refute covenant theology, he opens with a definition of the covenant — a definition provided by dispensationalist Lewis Sperry Chafer (Pentecost, *Things to Come*, pp. 65-66)! When he defines postmillennialism he quotes Walvoord (*ibid.*, p. 386)!

42. House and Ice, *Dominion Theology*, p. 206.

43. Daniel Whitby, "A Treatise on the True Millennium," in Patrick, Lowth, Arnald, Whitby, and Lowman, *Commentary on the Gospels and Epistles of the New Testament*, 4 vols. (Philadelphia, PA: Carey and Hart, 1845), vol. 4, p. 1118.

44. *Ibid.*, pp. 1122-23. He cites Dionysius 5:6; Eusebius, *Eccl. Hist.* 7:24.

pious faith, and are true Christians, think otherwise."[45] Note the reference to "many" who "think otherwise."

Another premillennialist, Irenaeus (*ca.* A.D. 180), observes that "some who are reckoned *among the orthodox*" do not hold to his premillennial views.[46] Eusebius (*ca.* A.D. 325) points to premillennialist Papias (A.D. 60-130) in explaining the spread of premillennialism: "But it was due to him that so many [not "all"!] of the Church Fathers after him adopted a like opinion, urging in their own support the antiquity of the man."[47] The fact that premillennialism was in no way approaching "universal" in extent is evident also in that Dionysius (A.D. 190-264) successfully dealt with "this doctrine" in a certain area where it prevailed and split "entire churches." He wins the day in that Egyptian district and turns the majority away from premillennialism.[48] Later Epiphanius (A.D.

---

45. Justin Martyr, *Dialogue with Trypho the Jew*, 80 (emphasis mine). Pentecost makes two serious blunders in interpreting this passage, because he (1) consults only a secondary source and (2) only partially uses even that source (Pentecost, *Things to Come*, p. 377). He refers to Kromminga's citation of Justin's statement, where Justin warns that there are some who are "blasphemous, atheistical, and foolish" who resist the millennial view. But Kromminga in the very next paragraph shows that "there was dissent from Christian chiliasm on two widely divergent bases" and that Justin clearly allows that many who are *orthodox* dissent — as we have cited in the text to which this footnote is appended (Kromminga, *The Millennium*, p. 45). Kromminga even goes on to note that G. N. H. Peters (*Theocratic Kingdom*, vol. 1, p. 480) has to argue for an emendation of Justin without manuscript evidence and in such a way as to introduce needless repetition into the text in order to get around the obvious significance (Kromminga, *The Millennium*, p. 46)!

46. Irenaeus, *Against Heresies* 5:31:1 (emphasis mine). W. G. T. Shedd comments on this statement: "Irenaeus . . . speaks of opposers of Millenarianism who held the catholic faith, and who agreed with the Gnostics only in being Anti-Millenarians; although he is himself desirous to make it appear that Anti-Millenarianism is of the nature of heresy" (*A History of Christian Doctrine*, 2 vols. (Minneapolis: Klock & Klock, [1889] 1978), vol. 2, p. 394). This is so in that Irenaeus goes on to state: these non-premillenarians "are ignorant of the methods by which they are disciplined beforehand for incorruption, they thus entertain heretical opinions."

47. Eusebius, *Ecclesiastical History* 3:39. Pelikan observes: Eusebius "was certainly speaking for a large body of theological opinion in the East when he called Papias's millenarianism 'bizarre' and 'rather mythological.'" Jaroslav Pelikan, *The Christian Tradition*, 5 vols. (Chicago, IL: University of Chicago Press, 1971), vol. 1, p. 125.

48. Eusebius, *Ecclesiastical History* 7:24; cf. Dionysius 5:6.

315-403) writes: "There is indeed a millennium mentioned by St. John; but the most, and those pious men, look upon those words as true indeed, but to be taken in a spiritual sense."[49]

Still further, we must be aware that *none* of the early Christian creeds encoded a statement establishing or even evidencing premillennialism! Irenaeus and Tertullian were both premillennialists within the period supposedly "solidly" premillennial. Yet in their writings directed against heretics, they record brief statements of the accepted faith of the Church—statements *totally devoid of any premillennialism!*[50] Neither does the Apostles' Creed have any premillennialism evident in it—a fact quite strange if the church were pervasively and solidly premillennial! In fact, Robert G. Clouse, a scholar used by House and Ice, even writes that at "the Council of Ephesus in 431, belief in the millennium was condemned as superstitious."[51]

It is interesting that, as Philip Schaff and others have shown, in ancient Christian literature there are a number of mini-creeds, which express the catholic faith of the era, many well before A.D. 250. Yet *not one* of these—which Schaff records in full—mentions anything premillennial, despite the fact that some of these are recorded by premillennialists (Irenaeus and Tertullian). The following references can be noted in this regard: Ignatius (A.D. 107), Irenaeus (A.D. 180), Tertullian (A.D. 200), Novatian (A.D. 250), Origen (A.D. 230), Gregory Thaumaturgas (A.D. 270); Lucian (A.D. 300), Eusebius (A.D. 325), Cyril of Jerusalem (A.D. 350), Epiphanius (A.D. 374).[52]

---

49. Epiphanius, *Heresies*, 77:26.
50. For documentation, see footnote 52.
51. Clouse, *The Meaning of the Millennium*, p. 9.
52. Philip Schaff, *The Creeds of Christendom*, 3 vols. (New York: Harper and Bros., 1919), vol. 2: "The Greek and Latin Creeds, with Translation", pp. 11ff.: Ignatius, *Trallians* 9; Irenaeus, *Against Heresies* 1:10; 3:4; 4:33; Tertullian, *Virgin* 1; *Praxeus* 2; *Prescription* 13; Novatian, *De Trinitius*; Origen, *Principles* 1, 4-6; Gregory Thaumatergius; Lucian from Athanasius, *Epist. Arini.* 23; Eusebius, *Ecclesiastical History* 2:10, 18; Cyril of Jerusalem, *Katecheseis* 17:3; 18:32; Epiphanius, *Ancoratus* 119, 120.

In a strange distortion of the evidence, House and Ice claim the Council of Nicea as evidence of premillennialism! Apparently, an ancient explanation of the Council—not the Creed itself!— states: "For that reason we look forward to new heavens and a new earth according to the Holy Scriptures: the appearance in the Kingdom of our great God and Savior, who will become visible to us." House and Ice comment: "Notice that although the word *millennium* is not used, the creed is clearly referring to a future, not present, kingdom; a future, not present-age resurrection. This early church statement came over three hundred years after the kingdom is said by postmillennialists to have been instituted. . . . [T]he premillennial view can be clearly and strongly identified."[53] Only a strained reading of the text, however, would suggest "the premillennial view can be clearly and strongly identified." House and Ice are quite familiar with the notion of a "now, not yet" kingdom, with the "not yet" involving the eternal order, which is the "new heavens and new earth" mentioned in their quotation.[54] How they get a millennium out of the statement is beyond us.

This leads us to consider the problem of dispensationalism's:

Misreading the Fathers' Eschatology

Since House and Ice assert a solid two and one-half centuries (at least) for the dominance of premillennialism, one would think that they could document a great number of adherents to premillennialism. Despite their grandiose claims, they actually (and wisely) list only five fathers: Papias (A.D. 60-130); Justin Martyr (A.D. 100-165), Irenaeus (A.D. 130-202), Tertullian (A.D. 160-220), and Hippolytus (A.D. 170-236).[55] In that they accept the reliability of Peters and Pentecost, we may justly surmise, however, that they also misread the eschatology of a number of the church fathers.[56] Otherwise how could we explain their references to premillennial-

---

53. House and Ice, *Dominion Theology*, p. 206.
54. *Ibid.*, pp. 220, 227. For a discussion of the Nicene Creed and premillennialism, see Gary DeMar, *The Debate over Christian Reconstruction* (Ft. Worth, TX: Dominion Press, 1988), pp. 99-101.
55. *Ibid.*, pp. 197, 201-2.
56. Such misreading of the evidence is common among dispensationalists. See Chapter 15.

ism in the early church as "pervasive," "solidly chiliastic," and so forth?[57] Besides those to whom we have already referred, dispensationalists commonly list the following as premillennial: *The Didache* (*ca.* A.D. 100), Clement of Rome (A.D. 30-100), Hermas (first century), Barnabas (first century), Ignatius (*ca.* A.D. 107), Polycarp (*ca.* 69-155), and Melito of Sardis (*d.* A.D. 190).[58]

Such a listing is wholly erroneous, as even dispensationalist Boyd has admitted after careful research. Space fails to allow us to enter into a discussion of the evidence, but the following writers can be consulted most profitably. The three leading, most detailed, and helpful are: Alan Patrick Boyd, D. H. Kromminga, and Ned Stonehouse.[59] Also noteworthy are: W. G. T. Shedd, Louis Berkhof, Philip Schaff, Albertus Pieters, and W. J. Grier.[60] Kromminga carefully examines the sub-apostolic writings, including: Clement of Rome's *1 Clement*, the pseudo-Clementine *2 Clement*, *The Didache*, the Ignatian epistles, Polycarp's *Epistle*, *The Letter of the Church at Smyrna on the Martyrdom of Polycarp*, Barnabas, Hermas, Diognetus, Fragments of Papias, and *Reliques of the Elders*.[61] He convincingly shows that *only Papias among the sub-apostolic fathers is premillennial*. Dispensationalist Boyd agrees: "Clement of Rome, Barnabas, Hermas, Ignatius, Polycarp, and Hegesippus can not be claimed as premillennialists."[62]

---

57. *Ibid.*, pp. 200, 202.

58. Ryrie, *Basis of Premillennial Faith*, pp. 20-22; G. N. H. Peters, *Theocratic Kingdom*, vol. 1, pp. 482ff.; Pentecost, *Things to Come*, pp. 374-77. For discussion of the dates of Hermas and Barnabas, see Gentry, *The Beast of Revelation* (Tyler, TX: Institute for Christian Economics, 1989), Chapter 13.

59. Boyd, "Dispensational Premillennial Analysis," *passim*; Kromminga, *The Millennium*, pp. 29-112; Ned Stonehouse, *The Apocalypse in the Ancient Church* (Goes, Holland: Oosterbaan and LeCointre, 1929), pp. 13ff.

60. Louis Berkhof, *The History of Christian Doctrines* (Grand Rapids, MI: Baker Book House, [1937] 1975), p. 262; Philip Schaff, *History of the Christian Church*, 7 vols. (5th ed.; Grand Rapids, MI: Wm. B. Eerdmans, 1910), vol. 2, p. 615; Albertus Pieters, two articles: "Chiliasm in the Writings of the Apostolic Fathers" (1938; cited by Kromminga, *The Millennium*, p. 41); W.J. Grier, *The Momentous Event* (London: Banner of Truth, 1970 [1945]), pp. 19ff.

61. Kromminga, *The Millennium*, pp. 41-42.

62. Boyd, "Dispensational Premillennial Analysis," p. 92.

Put in the best light, the most that could be said is: "It would seem that very early in the post-apostolic era millenarianism was regarded as a mark neither of orthodoxy nor of heresy, but as one permissible opinion among others within the range of permissible opinions."[63] What has happened to the evidence for "pervasive" premillennialism?

Error Regarding the Origins of Postmillennialism

We have seen heretofore that premillennialism has *never* been without competition from non-premillennial thought in the history of the Church, despite House and Ice's asseverations to the contrary. Now we move on to respond briefly to their analysis of the historic origins of postmillennialism.

Contradictions Regarding Postmillennial Origins

In reading House and Ice it is difficult to determine exactly when they feel postmillennialism originated. There is much confusion in their tracing of its supposed origins, although it is clear they deem it a late arrival on the eschatological scene. They argue that "postmillennialism was the last of the major eschatologies to develop. It was *first* taught within the church in the seventeenth century."[64] Elsewhere they specify that "the founder of postmillennialism . . . [was] Daniel Whitby (1638-1726)."[65] Even more specifically do they assert the time when its "founder" published his founding view: "Daniel Whitby first put forth his view in a popular work entitled *Paraphrase and Commentary on the New Testament* (1703)."[66] Thus, "it did not originate as a system until the early 1700s."[67]

Now consider the mass of temporal contradiction, which is so characteristic of their research. They say that postmillennialism, as

---

63. Jaroslav Pelikan, *The Christian Tradition*, vol. 1, p. 125.
64. House and Ice, *Dominion Theology*, p. 420 (emphasis mine).
65. *Ibid.*, p. 206.
66. *Ibid.*, p. 209.
67. *Ibid.*, p. 209.

an eschatology, "was first taught within the church in the seventeenth century." But then they state that Daniel Whitby was its "founder" and he published his view in 1703. But 1703 is in the *eighteenth* century! Incredibly the endnote appended to the quotation stating that postmillennialism "did not originate as a system until the early 1700s," contradicts the statement it is supposed to support! The book titles and other references cited speak of postmillennialism "from about 1600 on."[68] The several references to the early and mid-1600s belie the assertion of postmillennialism's founding in 1703!

Misunderstanding Whitby's Role in Postmillennialism

House and Ice assert that Whitby was the "founder" of post-millennialism,[69] but the two sources they quote to back this up merely say he "popularized" it (John J. Davis) and gave it "its most influential formulation" (Robert Clouse).[70] As we look into their discussion of Whitby, we discover a rather strange implication being drawn from Whitby's work:

> Daniel Whitby first put forth his view in a popular work entitled *Paraphrase and Commentary on the New Testament* (1703). It was at the end of this work that he first set forth what he calls in his own words "A New Hypothesis"[71] on the millennial reign of Christ. Thus, the system called postmillennialism was born in the early 1700s as a hypothesis. Whitby and his modern followers present their arguments and explanations based upon unproved assumptions — assumptions resulting in a hypothesis rather than something which is the fruit of the study of Scripture or even the voice of the church.[72]

---

68. *Ibid.*, p. 215, n52.
69. *Ibid.*, p. 206.
70. *Ibid.*, p. 209.
71. They do not give documentation for their statement here and we seriously doubt they have even read the article by Whitby. In the edition of Whitby's work that we consulted, the statement "a new hypothesis" was found buried in a sentence toward the end of a paragraph in the body of the work and was not at all capitalized (as if a heading or title) as House and Ice have done.
72. House and Ice, *Dominion Theology*, p. 209.

So this is why postmillennialism is in error? It is based on "unproved assumptions" because Whitby set forth "a new hypothesis"? Absurd. With this statement we become convinced House and Ice have *never* read Whitby.[73] In the first place, even a cursory reading of Whitby's article (which is an appendix to a massive commentary on the Bible!) quickly evidences the fact that he has brought to bear on the matter numerous Scripture passages. His particular argument—though we do not adopt it—is extremely well-put and quite rigorously defended from various Scripture passages.

Secondly, had they read the article they would note that the view he is presenting is not newly created by himself, for he expressly states he picked up on it from "the best commentators."[74] Thirdly, the new hypothesis has to do with *one* aspect of eschatology—Israel's future role and her relation to Revelation chapters 20-21—*and not a whole system of eschatology* (postmillennialism). He compares Romans 11:15 with Revelation 20:4 and various Old Testament references and determines that the bride of Revelation 21 is the Jewish church, "the new birth, reviviscence, resurrection of their dead church and nation."[75] Finally, Whitby's "hypothesis" reference is simply a humble way of suggesting a new understanding of a biblical question, instead of the way in which dispensationalists are criticized for doing.[76] Does not dispensationalist Hunt call the Rapture the "rapture *theory*"?[77] Did not premillennialist Nathaniel West rebut pretribulationism, labeling it the "any-moment theory"?[78]

---

73. We say this without necessarily endorsing anything he believed.

74. Whitby, *A Critical Commentary*, vol. 4, p. 1118.

75. *Ibid.*

76. Ladd has written of dispensationalist Herman Hoyt: "Hoyt's essay reflects the major problem in the discussion of the millennium. Several times he contrasts nondispensational views with his own, which he labels 'the biblical view'. . . . If he is correct, then the other views, including my own, are 'unbiblical' or even heretical. This is the reason that over the years there has been little creative dialogue between dispensationalists and other schools of prophetic interpretation." Ladd in Clouse, ed., *Meaning of the Millennium*, p. 93.

77. Dave Hunt, *Whatever Happened to Heaven?* (Eugene, OR: Harvest House, 1988), Chapter 3.

78. Cited by Richard Reiter in Gleason L. Archer, et. al., *The Rapture: Pre-, Mid-, or Post-Tribulational?* (Grand Rapids, MI: Zondervan, 1984), p. 16.

Returning to our main concern, it should be noted that Whitby was not the founder of postmillennialism—even of its more systematic, modern expression. Rodney Peterson writes in an excellent work in honor of dispensationalist S. Lewis Johnson, Jr.: "This perspective [amillennialism] had undergone changes, particularly since Thomas Brightman (1562-1607), such that some understood those promises to occur literally in a new millennial age opening up in the world prior to Christ's return to judgment, a position now termed postmillennialism."[79] Brightman, who died in 1607, was one of the fathers of Presbyterianism in England. His postmillennial views were set forth in detail in his book *A Revelation of the Revelation*. C. A. Briggs has written of this work: "Few books have been published at so many different places, and in so many different editions, and so widely read."[80] This *book* was a century before Whitby's 1703 *article*.

As their own quotations show, Whitby's work was influential in "popularizing" postmillennialism because it represented postmillennialism's "most influential formulation."[81] They even note that John Calvin (1509-1564) "paved the way for the full flowering of the postmillennial view in English Puritanism."[82] Whitby was simply *not* the "founder" of postmillennialism.

Early Origins of Postmillennialism

It is clear that postmillennialism has undergone great systematization since the time of Calvin. In its simplest form, however, adumbrations of it appear in antiquity. Simply put, postmillennialism is the view that Christ will return to the earth after the Spirit-blessed Gospel has had overwhelming success in bringing Christianity to the "world." Obviously, systematization is developmental, issuing from the diligent labors of many minds over a period of time as they build on the research of those who have

---

79. In "The Debate Throughout Church History" in Feinberg, *Continuity and Discontinuity*, p. 31.

80. Charles A. Briggs, "Thomas Brightman," in Philip Schaff, *A Religious Encyclopedia*, 3 vols. (Chicago, IL: Funk and Wagnalls, 1887), vol. 1, p. 327.

81. House and Ice, *Dominion Theology*, p. 209.

82. *Ibid.*, p. 209, citing John J. Davis.

gone on before. House and Ice should not have any problem with the slow development of systematization, for they write: "The futurist interpretation is the approach used by the earliest church fathers. We do not argue that they had a sophisticated system, but the clear futurist elements were there."[83] We would argue similarly for postmillennialism. After all, did not Ryrie argue regarding dispensationalism's "recency": "Informed dispensationalists . . . recognize that as a system dispensationalism was largely formulated by Darby, but that the outlines of the dispensationalist approach to the Scriptures are found much earlier."[84]

House and Ice question Gary North: "Who are the early church fathers who were postmillennial? There are none."[85] Interestingly, two paragraphs later they cite as a source for their argument the historical work of Robert G. Clouse on millennial views. Clouse apparently would not agree that antiquity provides no evidence of the postmillennial hope, for he clearly states of premillennialism, amillennialism, and postmillennialism: "Although these interpretations have *never* been without adherents in the history of the church, in certain ages a particular outlook has predominated."[86] We will just briefly survey some of the evidence for the existence of the postmillennial hope centuries prior to Whitby.

As a matter of fact, there are indicators in antiquity of a genuine hope for the progress of the Gospel in history. Tertullian (A.D. 160-220) was a Montanist and Montanists were by and large premillennial. Nevertheless, as Kromminga, an amillennialist, has noted, although most Montanists were premillennialists, "others were at least containing also the germs for later fullfledged Postmillennialism."[87] This nascent postmillennialism was resultant

---

83. *Ibid.*, p. 275.
84. Ryrie, *Dispensationalism Today*, p. 66.
85. *Ibid.*, p. 208.
86. Clouse, *The Meaning of the Millennium*, p. 9 (emphasis mine).
87. Kromminga, *The Millennium*, p. 76. Even the premillennialist Tertullian could have something of a postmillennial hope: "We pray, too, for the emperors, for their ministers and for all in authority, for the welfare of the world, for the prevalence of peace, for the delay of the final consummation" (Tertullian, *Apology*

from the hope (rooted in Scripture) that there would be a period of the Holy Spirit's dominance in the affairs of history.[88]

Although much in Origen (A.D. 185-254) is not acceptable, he is a noteworthy church father of considerable influence. As Philip Schaff has noted regarding Origen's views, there was in them a place for a great evidencing of the power of the Gospel: "Such a mighty revolution as the conversion of the heathen emperor was not dreamed of even as a remote possibility, except perhaps by the far-sighted Origen."[89]

In Eusebius (A.D. 260-340) there is a fuller expression of hope that is evident. In Book 10 of his *Ecclesiastical History* he believes he is witnessing the dawning of the fulfillment in his day of Old Testament kingdom prophecies. Of Psalms 108:1-2 and 46:8-9, which he specifically cites, he writes: "Rejoicing in these things which have been clearly fulfilled in our day."[90] Later in Chapters 4 through 7 of Book 10 he cites dozens of other such passages as coming to fulfillment. He writes: "For it was necessary and fitting that as her [the Church's] shepherd and Lord had once tasted death for her, and after his suffering had changed that vile body which he assumed in her behalf into a splendid and glorious body, leading the very flesh which had been delivered from corruption to incorruption, she too should enjoy the dispensations of the Saviour."[91] After quoting several passages from Isaiah he writes: "These are the things which Isaiah foretold; and which were anciently recorded concerning us in sacred books; and it was necessary that we should sometime learn their truthfulness by their fulfillment."[92]

---

39). The prayer for the delay of the end and peace is spoken of as a liturgy of the church. Although there is chiliasm, there are also some adumbrations of cosmic hope in prayer. In his *Scapula* there is a desire for the saving of all men (*Scapula* 3:3-4). See Pelikan, *The Christian Tradition*, vol. 1, p. 130.

88. Kromminga, *The Millennium*, p. 84.

89. Philip Schaff, *History of the Christian Church*, vol. 2, p. 591.

90. Eusebius, *Ecclesiastical History*, 10:1:6.

91. *Ibid.*, 10:4:46.

92. *Ibid.*, 10:4:53, cp. sections 46-52. Citing Isaiah 51:10-11; 54:4; 54:6-8; 51:17-18, 22-23; 52:1-2; 49:18-21.

Athanasius

Athanasius (A.D. 296-372) might properly be called "the patron saint of postmillennialism."[93] He was certain of the victory of Christ for now "the Saviour works so great things among men, and day by day is invisibly persuading so great a multitude from every side, both from them that dwell in Greece and in foreign lands, to come over to His faith, and all to obey His teaching. . . ."[94] "For where Christ is named, and His faith, there all idolatry is deposed and all imposture of evil spirits is exposed, and any spirit is unable to endure even the name, nay even on barely hearing it flies and disappears. But this work is not that of one dead, but of one that lives — and especially of God."[95] In fact regarding idols, Christ "chases them away, and by His power prevents their even appearing, yea, and is being confessed by them all to be the Son of God."[96] He goes on to exult in Christ's continuing victory:

> The Saviour does daily so many works, drawing men to religion, persuading to virtue, teaching of immortality, leading on to a desire for heavenly things, revealing the knowledge of the Father, inspiring strength to meet death, shewing Himself to each one, and displacing the godlessness of idolatry, and the gods and spirits of the unbelievers can do none of these things, but rather shew themselves dead at the presence of Christ, their pomp being reduced to impotence and vanity; whereas by the sign of the Cross all magic is stopped, and all witchcraft brought to nought, all the idols are being deserted and left, and every unruly pleasure is checked, and every one is looking up from earth to heaven. . . . For the Son of God is "living and active," and works day by day, and brings about the salvation of all. But death is daily proved to have lost all his power, and idols and spirits are proved to be dead rather than Christ.[97]

---

93. David Chilton, *The Days of Vengeance* (Ft. Worth, TX: Dominion Press, 1987), p. 5.

94. Athanasius, *Incarnation*, Sec. 30:4.

95. *Ibid.*, Sec. 30:6.

96. *Ibid.*, Sec. 30:7.

97. *Ibid.*, Sec. 31:2-3. This is particularly significant in that idolatry was a world-wide phenomenon (2 Kings 17:29; 1 Chron. 16:26; Psa. 96:5) in which Satan exercised control of men through demonic power (Lev. 17:7; Deut. 32:17; Psalm 106:37; 1 Cor. 10:19-20). Satan's binding (Rev. 20:2-3; Matt. 12:28-29) is increasing "day by day."

Athanasius applies prophecies of the triumph of Christ to the Church age and even rhetorically asks: "But what king that ever was, before he had strength to call father or mother, reigned and gained triumphs over his enemies?"[98] He then writes: "All heathen at any rate from every region, abjuring their hereditary tradition and the impiety of idols, are now placing their hope in Christ, and enrolling themselves under Him."[99] "But if the Gentiles are honouring the same God that gave the law to Moses and made the promise to Abraham, and Whose word the Jews dishonoured, — why are [the Jews] ignorant, or rather why do they choose to ignore, that the Lord foretold by the Scriptures has shone forth upon the world, and appeared to it in bodily form, as the Scripture said. . . . What then has not come to pass, that the Christ must do? What is left unfulfilled, that the Jews should not disbelieve with impunity? For it, I say, which is just what we actually see, — there is no longer king nor prophet nor Jerusalem nor sacrifice nor vision among them, but even the whole earth is filled with the knowledge of God, and the gentiles, leaving their godlessness, are now taking refuge with the God of Abraham, through the Word, even our Lord Jesus Christ, then it must be plain, even to those who are exceedingly obstinate, that the Christ is come, and that He has illumined absolutely all with His light. . . . So one can fairly refute the Jews by these and by other arguments from the Divine Scriptures."[100] "It is right for you to realize, and to take as the sum of what we have already stated, and to marvel at exceedingly; namely, that since the Saviour has come among us, idolatry not only has no longer increased, but what there was is diminishing and gradually coming to an end: and not only does the wisdom of the Greeks no longer advance, but what there is now fading away. . . . And to sum the matter up: behold how the Saviour's doctrine

---

98. Athanasius, *Incarnation*, Sec. 36:1. He cites sections from Num. 24:5-17; Isa. 8:4; Isa. 19:1 (Sec. 33 [context = Secs. 30-31]); Dan. 9:24ff.; Gen. 49:10 (Sec. 40); Isa. 2:4 (Sec. 52:1); 11:9 (Sec. 45:2; *Discourse Against the Arians* 1:59); Psalm 110:1 (*Discourse Against the Arians* 2:15:14, 16); etc.

99. Athanasius, *Incarnation*, Sec. 37:5.

100. *Ibid.*, 40:5, 7.

is everywhere increasing, while all idolatry and everything opposed to the faith of Christ is daily dwindling, and losing power, and falling. . . . For as, when the sun is come, darkness no longer prevails, but if any be still left anywhere it is driven away; so, now that the divine Appearing of the Word of God is come, the darkness of the idols prevails no more, and all parts of the world in every direction are illumined by His teaching."[101] Many other such references could be cited from Athanasius.[102]

Later Pre-Whitby Postmillennialists

Somewhat later in history, but still pre-Whitby, is the case of the medieval Roman Catholic Joachim of Floris (1145-1202). Several non-postmillennial scholars cite him as a postmillennialist,[103] due to his view of a coming outpouring of the Spirit, initiating the Age of the Spirit.[104] As Kromminga puts it: "In fact, modern Postmillenarianism of the orthodox type with its expectation of a glorious final Church Age, brought about through the ordinary operation of the Word and the Spirit, embodies nothing but this Pure Church ideal, dissociated from Joachim's expectation of a future coming of the Holy Spirit."[105] Other postmillennialists well before Whitby include the Franciscans Peter John Olivi (*d. ca.* 1297) and Abertino de Casale (fl. 1305); the Dominicans Ghehardinus de Burgo (fl. 1254), Mechthild of Magdeburg (*d.* 1280), Fra Dolcino (fl. 1330); another Roman Catholic scholar Arnaldus of Villanova (fl. 1298); and the forerunner of John Huss, Jan Miliciz of Kremsier (fl. 1367).[106]

---

101. E.g., *Ibid.*, 55:1-3.
102. E.g., *Ibid.*, 46-48; 50; 52-55.
103. See Kromminga, *The Millennium*, pp. 20; 129ff.; Benz, *Zeitschrift für Kirchengeschichte*, 1931. Schaff, *A Religious Encyclopedia*, vol. 2, p. 1183; and Ryrie, *Basic Theology* (Wheaton, IL: Victor, 1986), p. 443.
104. Joachim of Floris, *Concordia Veteris et Novi Testamenti, Expositio super Apocalypsin*, and *Psalterium Decem Chordarum*.
105. Kromminga, *The Millennium*, p. 132.
106. *Ibid.*, pp. 135-36, 159ff., who cites the following sources: Johann Heinrich Kurtz, Henry Hart Milman, J. A. W. Neander, and Johann Jacob Herzog. See also Möller in *Religious Encyclopedia*, vol. 2, p. 1183; Williston Walker, *A History of the Christian Church* (3rd. ed., New York: Charles Scribner's Sons, 1970) p. 237; Kenneth Scott Latourette, *A History of Christianity*, 2 vols. (rev. ed.; New York: Harper and Row, 1975), vol. 1, p. 435.

Besides, do not House and Ice cite Chilton's admission of certain postmillennial embarrassing advocates, including "the Munster Revolt of 1534"?[107] Is not the Savoy Declaration of 1658 a strong and unambiguous postmillennial document promising that "in the latter days, antichrist being destroyed, the Jews called, and the adversaries of the kingdom of His dear Son broken, the churches of Christ being enlarged and edified through a free and plentiful communication of light and grace, [they] shall enjoy in this world a more quiet, peaceable, and glorious condition than they have enjoyed."[108] After a lengthy and informative discussion of a host of names, amillennialist Kromminga has concluded: "In actual fact there is quite a strain of Postmillennialism in Reformed theology from Cocceius [1603-1669] onward. . . . Reformed theology can therefore in view of these phenomena not well be said to have been uniformly amillenarian, as is rather frequently assumed."[109]

Simply put: Whitby was not the "founder" of postmillennialism. Postmillennialism's distinctive theme of Gospel Victory in history is hoary with age.

Summary

1. Dispensationalists are noted for their misreading church history in regard to the eschatology of the fathers and for their continuing to promote their mistaken views.

2. Dispensationalists are also noted for attempting to equate modern dispensationalism with ancient premillennialism, despite resistance from some dispensationalists and a number of pre-, post-, and amillennial scholars.

3. Dispensationalism and premillennialism are quite diverse systems of eschatology, with dispensationalism being a recent phenomenon.

---

107. House and Ice, *Dominion Theology*, p. 375.
108. Philip Schaff, *The Creeds of Christendom, With a History and Critical Notes*, 3 vols. (6th ed.; New York: Harper and Bros., 1919), vol. 3, p. 723.
109. Kromminga, *The Millennium*, p. 303.

4. Premillennialism was never the "universal belief" of the church, despite dispensational assertions; in fact, it is found in *no* ancient, ecumenical church creed.

5. Early premillennialists like Justin Martyr and Irenaeus recognized a number of orthodox believers were not premillennial.

6. Postmillennialism is not a post-reformation phenomenon.

7. Postmillennial traits are discoverable in some forms of ancient Montanism, even though most Montanists, like Tertullian, were premillennial.

8. Postmillennialism is discoverable in such early church fathers as Eusebius and Athanasius, as well as in medieval writers such as Joachim of Floris (1145-1202), Peter Olivi (*d.* 1297), Jam Miliciz of Kremsier (fl. 1367), and others.

9. Despite frequent dispensational claims, Daniel Whitby was not the founder of postmillennialism in 1703; he was an important systematizer and popularizer of postmillennialism.

10. There is a strong strain of postmillennialism in reformed theology, from John Calvin, through Thomas Brightman (1562-1607), the Savoy Declaration (1658) and Cocceius (1603-1669) as well as in the Westminster Confession of Faith.

16

THE PRETERIST INTERPRETATION
OF THE KINGDOM

An exegetical and historical defense of the application of certain prophecies of Scripture to the destruction of Jerusalem.

In Chapters 12 and 13 of *Dominion Theology*, House and Ice critique the *preterist* approach to prophecy, particularly regarding the Book of Revelation and the Olivet Discourse. The preterist approach to these passages teaches that many of the prophecies of Revelation and much of the Olivet Discourse have already been fulfilled, *although they lay in the future when originally uttered.*[1] Matthew 24:1-34 (and parallels) in the Olivet Discourse was fulfilled in the events surrounding the fall of Jerusalem in A.D. 70. In Revelation, many of the prophecies before Revelation 20 find fulfillment in either the fall of Jerusalem (A.D. 70) or in both Jerusalem's (A.D. 70) *and* Rome's (A.D. 410) falls. This view has been revived recently by some Reconstructionists, and is becoming increasingly popular among others, even among many outside of Reconstructionism. In the first half of Chapter 12, the authors critique David Chilton's *Days of Vengeance*, focusing much of their attention on his brief notes regarding Revelation's date.

Preliminary Observations

Before we engage the main point of the discussion, a few preliminary matters need to be disposed of.

---

1. The emphasized phrase is a vitally important qualification often blurred by House and Ice.

Preterism and Reconstructionism

One frustrating aspect of the debate over Reconstructionism is the tendency of opponents to confuse the issues. The opening statement in their Chapter 12 evidences this problem: "The validity of the Christian Reconstruction agenda is vitally dependent upon the last book in the Bible, the book of Revelation." By this they mean Revelation as interpreted from "the preterist, postmillennial viewpoint."[2] Elsewhere they state that "The *preterist* (Latin for 'past') view is the one advocated by Reconstructionists."[3] This is a logical fallacy, known as hasty generalization.

First, it has only been in recent years of Reconstructionist thought that serious and sustained attention has been focused on the Book of Revelation. Chilton's commentary itself was not published until 1987, with its forerunner, *Paradise Restored*, preceding it by only two years. Earlier, in its "Symposium on the Millennium," *The Journal of Christian Reconstruction* did not even make reference to preterism![4] Second, though in 1970 R. J. Rushdoony published a study entitled *Thy Kingdom Come: Studies in Daniel and Revelation*, it takes an *historicist*, rather than a preterist, approach.[5] Is not Rushdoony a "Reconstructionist"?[6] Third, that which Reconstructionism actually depends upon in eschatology is not preterism (an interpretative *approach* to eschatology), but rather postmillennialism (an eschatological *system*). House and Ice well know this, for they list such as one of the five distinguishing features of Reconstructionism.[7]

---

2. H. Wayne House and Thomas Ice, *Dominion Theology: Blessing or Curse?* (Portland, OR: Multnomah, 1988), p. 249.

3. *Ibid.*, p. 422.

4. Gary North, ed., *The Journal of Christian Reconstruction* (Winter, 1976-1977), *passim.*

5. House and Ice should know this, for they summarize its contents (*Dominion Theology*, p. 436).

6. *Ibid.*, p. 45. They call him "the patriarch of Reconstructionism."

7. *Ibid.*, p. 17. In addition, they specifically note that a 1987 meeting of 100 Reconstructionists "produced a list of ten points of belief 'which all saw as the fundamentals of the Christian Reconstruction Movement.' Point seven insisted on a postmillennial view of the kingdom of God" (p. 301). Preterism was not even mentioned. Preterism is an hermeneutic approach to prophecy; eschatology is a locus of systematics. The two are not interchangeable.

The Matter of Revelation's Date

House and Ice state that "the interpretation of no other book in the canon of the Bible is affected by the date in which it was written as much as the Revelation of Jesus Christ."[8] Unfortunately, their refutation of the early date (pre-A.D. 70), which they attack as Reconstructionist, and their defense of the late date (*ca.* A.D. 96), are embarrassingly flawed.

First, House and Ice speak as if there were a uniform church tradition regarding the date of Revelation: "Chilton questions *the voice* of church tradition concerning the date of Revelation, since it strongly negates his early date viewpoint."[9] The conclusion of the general readership doubtless will be: "Ancient Christianity harmoniously held that Revelation was written later than A.D. 70." Chilton, however, is *not* set against "*the* voice of church tradition." In fact, he specifically mentions "there are other early writers whose statements indicate" that Revelation was written under Nero.[10] And he is correct. We have noted elsewhere that there are a number of significant early date evidences that may be garnered from antiquity.[11]

Clement of Alexandria (despite House and Ice[12] — and others) asserts that all revelation ceased under Nero's reign.[13] The Muratorian Canon (*ca.* 170) has John completing Revelation *before* Paul had written to seven different churches (Paul died in A.D. 67 or 68). Tertullian (A.D. 160-220) places John's banishment in conjunction with Peter's and Paul's martyrdom (A.D. 67/68).[14] Epiphanius (A.D. 315-403) twice states Revelation was written under "Claudius [Nero] Caesar."[15] The Syriac versions of Revela-

---

8. House and Ice, *Dominion Theology*, p. 249.

9. *Ibid.*, p. 251 (emphasis added).

10. Cited in *Ibid.*, p. 253.

11. Kenneth L. Gentry, Jr., *Before Jerusalem Fell: Dating the Book of Revelation* (Tyler, TX: Institute for Christian Economics, 1989).

12. House and Ice, *Dominion Theology*, p. 253.

13. Clement of Alexandria, *Miscellanies* 7:17.

14. Tertullian, *Exclusion of Heretics* 36.

15. Epiphanius, *Heresies* 51:12, 33. Nero's full name is often found on inscriptions: Nero Claudius Caesar.

tion (sixth century) have as a heading to Revelation: "written in Patmos, whither John was sent by Nero Caesar."[16] Arethas (sixth century) applies a number of the prophecies to the fall of Jerusalem in A.D. 70, noting that Eusebius merely "alleges" that Revelation was written under Domitian.[17] Though Andreas (sixth century) holds to a Domitianic date, he notes that "there are not wanting those who apply this passage [Rev. 6] to the siege and destruction of Jerusalem by Titus,"[18] thus evidencing a number of early-date advocates before him. Also we can probably add to the list Papias (A.D. 60-130), who teaches that John the Apostle died before Jerusalem fell, and *The Shepherd of Hermas* (*ca.* A.D. 80?), which evidences influence by Revelation.[19] We seriously suspect that House and Ice have not even read the original references from Clement of Alexandria and Origen, which they put forth as two of their four non-Irenaean "witnesses" supporting the late date.[20] *Neither mentions the name of Domitian!*[21] Apparently for historical evidence, they adopt the common jargon: "It goes without saying"!

There simply is no "voice [singular] of church tradition concerning the date of Revelation." Neither may it be stated, as they do, that Clement of Alexandria (!), Origen (!), Victorinus, and Eusebius "had *no* witnesses to the contrary." Nor should it be said that "if there were some validity to the early date, some trace of this competing tradition should have surfaced. However, it has not!"[22] To quote House and Ice against themselves: Their critique of the early church tradition seems to be "speculative" and a "debater's technique."[23]

---

16. Moses Stuart, *Commentary on the Apocalypse*, 2 vols. (Andover: Allen, Morrill, and Wardwell, 1845), vol. 1, p. 267.

17. Cited by A. R. Fausset, in Robert Jamieson, A. R. Fausset, and David Brown, *A Commentary Critical and Explanatory on the Old and New Testaments* (Hartford, CT: Scranton, n.d.), vol. 2, p. 548.

18. See Stuart, *Apocalypse*, 1:267.

19. See Gentry, *Before Jerusalem Fell*, Chapters 5 and 6.

20. House and Ice, *Dominion Theology*, p. 253.

21. See *Before Jerusalem Fell*, pp. 68ff. and 97ff. See Clement of Alexandria, *Who Is the Rich Man that shall be Saved?* 42; Origen, *Matthew* 16:6.

22. House and Ice, *Dominion Theology*, pp. 253-54 (emphasis mine).

23. *Ibid.*, pp. 252-53.

Irenaeus and the Date of Revelation

Second, as we continue through their argument, it becomes obvious that although they are confident in their employment of *Irenaeus* against early date advocacy, they do not appear to be as prepared to deal with his evidence as is requisite for their task. Note that after citing Irenaeus's passage from *Against Heresies*, they employ a debater's technique by attempting to promote their point as "clear." They write: "How does Chilton deal with such a clear statement?"[24] Unfortunately, Irenaeus's modern translators have commented on the difficulty of translating and interpreting him.[25] In light of such a problem, how could Irenaeus's debated statement be deemed "clear" evidence?

Then after citing a particular *English translation* of Irenaeus (who wrote in Greek), House and Ice comment: "Chilton questions whether [Irenaeus's] 'that was seen' refers to 'the apocalyptic vision' or to John himself. Since the impersonal pronoun 'that' is used we can assume that it refers to John's 'apocalyptic vision.'"[26] This is a serious blunder. The original Greek of *Against Heresies* has no "impersonal pronoun 'that'"![27] The "that" which forms the basis of their argument is an English translator's interpolation!

Irenaeus's famous statement reads (with options listed): "We will not, however, incur the risk of pronouncing positively as to the name of Antichrist; for if it were necessary that his name should be distinctly revealed in this present time, it would have been announced by him who beheld the Revelation. For 'he' [John?] or 'it' [Revelation?] was seen . . . towards the end of Domitian's reign."[28] Actually it is a matter of debate as to what Irenaeus intended by his famous statement: Did he mean to say that John,

---

24. *Ibid.*, p. 251.
25. See Gentry, *Before Jerusalem Fell*, pp. 47-57. The first English translation of Irenaeus's work even notes: "Irenaeus, even in the original Greek, is often a very obscure writer. . . . [U]pon the whole, his style is very involved and prolix" (A. Cleveland Coxe, *The Apostolic Fathers* in Alexander Roberts and James Donaldson, eds., *Ante-Nicene Fathers* (Grand Rapids, MI: Wm. B. Eerdmans, 1985) vol. 1, p. 312.
26. House and Ice, *Dominion Theology*, p. 251.
27. See Gentry, *Before Jerusalem Fell*, pp. 46ff. for the Greek text and comments on it.
28. Irenaeus, *Against Heresies* 5:30:3.

who wrote Revelation was seen (thus John was alive), actively ministering in Domitian's reign? Or did he mean that John wrote Revelation in Domitian's reign?

Revelation and the Neronic Persecution

Third, in contradiction to the argument for early date advocacy's Neronic Persecution backdrop for Revelation, House and Ice suggest that "a stronger case can be made for more severe persecution under Domitian than Chilton admits" and "there is no hard evidence of persecution under Nero in Asia during any part of his reign."[29] But there is *absolutely no* contemporary or near contemporary evidence for or any secular witness to a Domitianic persecution *at all*, whereas Roman historians Tacitus and Suetonius supply us with such for a severe Neronic persecution.[30] Even premillennialist late-date advocate George E. Ladd warns: "The problem with this [Domitian] theory is that there is no evidence that during the last decade of the first century there occurred any open and systematic persecution of the church."[31]

What is worse, their argument involves them in self-contradiction. The passages evidencing "severe persecution,"[32] which are necessary for late-date advocacy, are largely found *after* the Seven Letters in the main text of Revelation, beginning in Revelation 4. Interestingly, House and Ice cite favorably Donald B. Guthrie, who writes: "In certain passages regarding the great harlot (i.e. Rome) there are statements about her being drunk with the blood of the saints (xvii.6, xviii.24, xix.2, cf. also xvi.6, xx.4). . . . The next question which arises is whether this persecution situation fits best into the Domitianic period."[33] The use of such Scripture texts to prove the late-date of Revelation is schizophrenic since House and Ice see *everything* from Revelation 4 and after as being in the distant future![34]

---

29. House and Ice, *Dominion Theology*, p. 255.

30. Nero "inflicted unheard-of punishments on those who . . . were vulgarly called Christians" (Tacitus, *Annals* 15:44). Suetonius praises Nero for the persecution of Christians, but mentions no Domitianic persecution (*Nero* 16).

31. George E. Ladd, *A Commentary on Revelation* (Grand Rapids, MI: Wm. B. Eerdmans, 1972), p. 8.

32. House and Ice, *Dominion Theology*, p. 255.

33. *Ibid.*, pp. 255-56.

34. *Ibid.*, p. 278.

How could it evidence the situation under Domitian in A.D. 95?

Fourth, in a strange misnomer, House and Ice label the evidence drawn from the Seven Letters and from Revelation's allusions to emperor worship as "external evidence"![35] All the "external" arguments they present for a late date in that section have been answered in *Before Jerusalem Fell* and will not be rehearsed here.[36] But we must stand again in wonder at the blatant self-contradiction in their argument! House and Ice dogmatically argue that Revelation is to be interpreted from a futurist viewpoint; that is, they aver that its prophecies in Revelation 4:1-22:5 regard distantly future events.[37] But then they "prove" a late date by pointing to emperor worship in the text of Revelation and apply it to Domitian! The references to emperor worship that are used by late-date advocates are found in Revelation 13 primarily, as their major sources, H. B. Swete and Charles R. Erdman, show.[38] Which is it? Are those references speaking of a Domitianic emperor worship (as used in the late-date argument)? Or are they referring to the centuries-distant Great Tribulation (as used in the futurist approach to Revelation)?

Fifth, there are strong internal indicators of Revelation's pre-A.D. 70 composition. For example, in Revelation 17 an angel undertakes *carefully to explain to John* (Rev. 17:7, 9a) one of the dramatic visions (Rev. 17:3), which otherwise would have been difficult to understand (Rev. 17:6-7). The reason for the difficulty was that the seven heads of the beast are said to have a *double* referent, not a single one: seven mountains *and* seven kings (Rev. 17:10-11). The seven mountains would immediately speak of Rome, the famed seven-hilled city, which was in control of the seven cities of Asia

---

35. *Ibid.*, p. 256. Scholars consider *external* evidence to be that drawn from tradition, not from within the work in question. See Guthrie, *New Testament Introduction*, (3d ed.; Downers Grove, IL: Inter-Varsity Press, 1970), p. 956; W. G. Kümmel, *Introduction to the New Testament* (17th ed.; Nashville, TN: Abingdon, 1973), pp. 466-67. Their error points out a degree of carelessness in their method.

36. See Gentry, *Before Jerusalem Fell*, Chapters 12, 16, 17, and 19.

37. House and Ice, *Dominion Theology*, pp. 260ff., see particularly pp. 261 and 278, where Walvoord and Tenney, respectively, are cited.

38. *Ibid.*, p. 280 (notes 29-30).

Minor and Palestine, *as John wrote.* The seven kings are interpreted *to John* as including a series of five kings who have died. This would be Julius Caesar, Augustus, Tiberius, Caligula, Claudius.[39] These five are followed by the sixth one, who "is" as John writes, i.e., Nero (*d.* A.D. 68). He in turn is followed by the seventh, who, as John writes, "is not yet come; and when he cometh, he must continue a short space." This is Galba, who reigned from June, A.D. 68 to January, A.D. 69, the shortest rule theretofore. Clearly, Nero is alive at the date of writing. In addition, the numerical evaluation of Nero's name is "666" (see Rev. 13:18), Nero persecuted the Christians for 3½ years (Rev. 13:5, from Nov., A.D. 64 until his death in June, A.D. 68), the Jewish Temple is still standing (Rev. 11:1-2), and more.[40]

The Exegetical Basis of Preterism

Foundations of Preterism

In answer to a specific, section-heading question "Why a Preterist Interpretation?," House and Ice point to three unrelated, out-of-context statements by Chilton and North in an attempt to set forth the "reasons" for preterism. These include: *"First,* the canon of Holy Scripture was *entirely* completed before Jerusalem fell"; *"second"* the relevance of the Olivet Discourse and Revelation to the original audience; and *"third"* the interpretive approach involving a "fusion of covenant and symbol."[41]

The very order (which they emphasize), superficiality, and irrelevance of most of their treatment present an intolerably unfair distortion. Actually their second point should properly be first and it should be detailed with more than a passing reference to Revelation 1:1 (to which they never again return). Their first point is poorly put and largely irrelevant. It is not at all necessary for a preteristic approach to certain passages that "the canon of Holy

---

39. For the enumeration, see John's contemporary, Josephus, *Antiquities of the Jews,* 18:2:2, 10; 19:1:11. Also see Roman historians Suetonius (*Lives of the Twelve Caesars*) and Dio Cassius (*Roman History* 5).

40. For a detailed treatment of the evidence see Gentry, *Before Jerusalem Fell.*

41. House and Ice, *Dominion Theology,* p. 53. The emphasis is theirs.

Scripture was *entirely* completed before Jerusalem fell." Jesus spoke the Olivet Discourse 40 years prior to it. And what does it matter if some of the books — excluding Revelation — are dated later? House and Ice drew their documentation from a context in Chilton that deals with the dating of Revelation, not with the general question of preterism.

Their third point either speaks of a distinctive hermeneutic employed by Chilton and Jordan, which is not universally held among Reconstructionists,[42] or is a statement regarding general Reformed hermeneutics, which would be irrelevantly employed *at this juncture*. If it is a reference to Reformed hermeneutics, it should be the Christian's practice that: (1) the clearer statements interpret the less clear (and the following didactic time statements are extremely clear, in contrast to the dramatic imagery in certain of the prophecies)[43] and (2) our hermeneutic should not be *a priori*, but derived from Scripture itself, allowing Scripture to interpret Scripture.[44]

For the intellectually honest and genuinely interested reader, we now set forth a (regrettably!) brief introductory defense of the exegetical basis of preterism.

Regarding the Olivet Discourse: The fulfillment of Matthew 24:4-33 in the destruction of Jerusalem is a most reasonable and even necessary conclusion. House and Ice even admit: "The Olivet discourse did predict the coming destruction of Jerusalem, which is today a past event, but at the same time the bulk of the passage deals with the yet future events of Christ's coming and the end of the age."[45] But that Matthew 24:4-33 *en toto* has been fulfilled is obvious on the two following bases:

---

42. As they well know: They read both Gentry's and Bahnsen's articles disavowing "interpretive maximalism." See House and Ice, *Dominion Theology*, pp. 205, 250.

43. They, however, put the cart before the horse: "Since the phrase 'all these things' governs the timing of 'this generation' (regardless of how it has been used in other contexts), one has to determine what 'all these things' are and when they will be fulfilled. Then we will know whether 'this generation' referred to those in Christ's day or to a future generation" (*ibid.*, p. 286).

44. A flaw of dispensationalism is its *a priori* "literal" hermeneutic.

45. House and Ice, *Dominion Theology*, p. 271.

First, its introductory *context* strongly suggests it. In Matthew 23 Jesus sorely rebukes the "scribes and Pharisees" *of His own day* (Matt. 23:2ff.), urging *them* finally to "fill up then the measure of your fathers" who killed the prophets (23:31-32). He says that they are a "generation" of vipers (23:33) that will persecute and slay His disciples (23:34). He notes that upon *them* will come all the righteous blood shed on the earth (23:35). He then dogmatically asserts: "Verily I say unto you, all these things shall come upon *this generation*" (23:36).

Then we immediately come upon Matthew 23:37-24:2, which provides the essential background occurrence and statements leading to the discourse: Jesus weeps over Jerusalem and declares that its temple will be destroyed stone by stone, despite His disciples' surprise. It is to these things that the disciples ask, "When shall these things be?" As a matter of historical record we know the temple was destroyed stone by stone in August, A.D. 70. Despite House and Ice, how could Christ *not* be dealing with the A.D. 70 event in Matthew 24?[46]

Second, its express temporal indicators demand it. We must not miss the clear references to the contemporary expectation. In Matthew 23:36 He specifically points to a judgment coming *in the days of His original audience*. Then bracketing the relevant portion of the discourse, we have Christ's own time-element designation. In 23:36 he dogmatically asserts *"all* these things shall come upon *this* generation." He closes the relevant portion of the prophecy by repetition of the time frame: Matthew 24:34 says, "Verily I say unto you, *this* generation shall not pass, till all these things be fulfilled." And just forty years later Jerusalem was destroyed! Contextually the "this generation" of Matthew 24:34 *must* speak of the same idea as that of Matthew 23:36.[47]

What things shall be fulfilled in "this generation"? *"All these things."* That is, all these things of which He had just spoken. He employs the near demonstrative for the fulfillment of verses 2-34:

---

46. *Ibid.*, pp. 293-94. Cited below, *q.v.*

47. House and Ice make a most feeble attempt to evacuate the significance of the argument from the phrase "this generation" (*ibid.*, p. 286).

These events will come upon "*this* generation." He uses the far demonstrative in 24:36 to point to the Second Advent: "*that* day." As House and Ice admit: "It is probably true that the disciples thought of the three events (the destruction of the temple, the second coming, and the end of the age) as one event. But as was almost always the case, they were wrong."[48] Thus, Christ divided up the events for them. The coming "tribulation" (24:21; cp. Rev. 1:9) was to come upon "this generation" (Matt. 23:36; 24:34; cp. 1 Thess. 2:16) and was to be foreshadowed by certain signs (Matt. 24:4-8). But the Second Advent was to be at "that" far day and hour, and was not to be preceded by particular signs of its nearness, for no man can know it (24:36).[49]

Regarding Revelation: The past fulfillment of most of the prophecies in Revelation 4-19 is compellingly suggested by the various time indicators contained in its less symbolic, more didactic introduction and conclusion. House and Ice rehearse a good principle regarding Matthew 24, which is equally relevant to Revelation and which they should heed: "The key to understanding the discourse is found in the first sentence."[50]

Although they make one passing reference to the fact of the employment of Revelation 1:1 in preterist literature,[51] they *never* engage the *interpretation* of the verse, or of related verses in Revelation! But Revelation 1:1 opens the prophecies of Revelation and prepares the reader to understand them: "The Revelation of Jesus Christ, which God gave unto him, to shew unto his servants things which must shortly come to pass." And this despite the fact they

---

48. *Ibid.*, p. 271.

49. Despite the clarity of Christ's statement that no man can know the day or the hour, House and Ice write of the Tribulation: "The ruler sets up himself as God in the temple by placing his image in the holy of holies. This will occur three and a half years before the second coming of Christ" (p. 288). Sounds quite datable to us! Other elements that space constraints forbid our exploring include, for example, the preparatory parable of the householder (Matt. 21:33-44), which explained the demise of Israel (21:33-44), which was to happen before the very eyes of the chief priests (21:23, 45) and the especial reference to Judea — the tribulation could be escaped by fleeing Judea (24:16).

50. House and Ice, *Dominion Theology*, pp. 299-300.

51. *Ibid.*, p. 53.

specifically ask of the preterists in a sub-heading: "Why Past and Not Future?"[52] The oversight is intolerable. They deal with various phrases in Revelation 1:1, but *never with the relevant one* — even in their chapter entitled " 'Rightly Dividing' the Book of Revelation"![53] The problem, as before, is that they do what they disdain: They have "erected a [preterist] straw man they love to bash."[54]

Read Revelation 1:1 for yourself! Does not John specifically say the things "must *shortly* come to pass"? And in case you miss it he repeats it, using different, though synonymous, terminology in Revelation 1:3c: "*The time is at hand*" (emphasis mine). And in case the reader skipped the introduction, he repeats these ideas as he closes. Revelation 22:6: "These sayings are faithful and true: and the Lord God of the holy prophets sent his angel to shew unto his servants the things which *must shortly be done*." Revelation 22:10: "And he saith unto me, Seal not the sayings of the prophecy of this book: for the *time is at hand*."

House and Ice are much opposed to the preterist's concern with the original relevance — which is a major hermeneutical difference between their dispensationalism and our Reformed approach. For instance: "Chilton has said that Revelation had to have a contemporary fulfillment in order for it to be relevant to those to whom it was written."[55] Now consider typical dispensational approaches to Revelation and related prophecy. Hal Lindsey (an endorser of *Dominion Theology*), citing C. I. Scofield (the leading popularizer of dispensationalism), writes: Revelation " 'is so written that as the actual time of these events approach, the current events will unlock the meaning of the book.' He pointed out that the Book of Revelation didn't have too much meaning to people a few centuries ago, and that for this reason very few people were willing to study its message."[56]

---

52. *Ibid.*, p. 274.
53. *Ibid.*, See pp. 250, 277, 278.
54. *Ibid.*, p. 266.
55. *Ibid.*, p. 271.
56. Hal Lindsey, *There's A New World Coming* (Santa Ana, CA: Vision House, 1973), p. 21. See also: Robert L. Thomas, *Revelation 8-22* (Chicago: Moody, 1995), p. 185.

Another endorser of House and Ice, Dave Hunt, has written similarly regarding certain prophecies, which are related to Revelation: "For at least 200 years, prophecy students had identified Russia, long before it became a world military power, as the leader of a biblically prophesied confederacy of nations that would attack Israel in the last days."[57] What about the *original* readers 1900 years ago? This is a major difference between their dispensational and our Reformed hermeneutic.

The text-bracketing temporal indicators as pointed to by preterists cannot lightly be dismissed, however. John is writing to seven historical churches (Rev. 1:4, 11; 22:16), which are expecting troublesome times (2-3). He testifies to being with them in "the tribulation" (1:9). And despite Lindsey, Hunt, and other dispensationalists, he expects those very churches to hear and understand (1:3; 22:10) the "revelation"[58] (1:1) and to heed the things in it (1:3; 22:7), because of the nearness of the events (1:1, 3; 22:6, 10).

Original relevance, then, is the lock and the time-texts the key to opening the door of Revelation. And think, What terms *could* John have used to speak of contemporary expectation other than those that are, in fact, found in Revelation 1:1, 3; 22:6, 10 and other places?[59]

Objections to Preterism

In that the charges against preterism are sufficiently answered in print by evangelical authors,[60] our consideration of a few of their objections will be quite brief and merely illustrative of the precariousness of their argument.

---

57. Hunt, *Whatever Happened?*, p. 65.

58. "Revelation" means "uncovering, opening up" — not "obscuring, concealing." See John's intention in Revelation 1:3; 22:7.

59. For more references see Gentry, *Before Jerusalem Fell*, pp. 133-45.

60. See J. Marcellus Kik, *An Eschatology of Victory* (n.p.: Presbyterian and Reformed, 1971), *passim*; Cornelis Vanderwaal, *Search the Scriptures*, (Ontario, Canada: Paideia Press, 1979), vol. 10, pp. 82ff.; Gary DeMar, *The Debate over Christian Reconstruction* (Ft. Worth, TX: Dominion Press, 1988); and Gentry, *Before Jerusalem Fell*, *passim*.

1. The Charge of Arbitrary Exegesis. In response to Jordan's see-ing Matthew 24:2-34 as referring to the fall of Jerusalem, and the following verses as referring to the Second Advent, they ask: "Why, on the basis of the hermeneutics Jordan has used to this point in his interpretation of the Olivet discourse, does he sud-denly make an arbitrary leap to the second coming of Christ?"[61] And, "How can Jordan, after taking the references to 'coming' in verses 1-35 as referring to Christ's coming in judgment in A.D. 70, turn around and say that starting at verse 36 through the end of the chapter, it refers to the second coming. Either he is wrong about the first 35 verses, and they do refer to the second coming, or he should take verse 36 and following as a reference to the A.D. 70 destruction."[62]

They apparently heard Jordan's tapes, for they cite them and they rehearse a portion of his argument.[63] They also have read Kik's book.[64] They even mention the key reason themselves, as found in Chilton's work, calling it the "main reason"![65] Jordan, Kik, and Chilton are careful to give the reason — which we have outlined above (Matthew 24:34) — as justifying a change of sub-ject. Yet they still charge preterists with arbitrariness. *There are tex-tually derived indicators; the change of focus is not in the least "arbitrary."*

Now what of *their* arbitrariness regarding the Olivet Discourse? "Luke shifts from the A.D. 70 destruction of Jerusalem in 21:20-24 to the second coming of Christ in 21:25-28."[66] *Where is their textual cue?* True, they take Luke 21:28 as indicating a "redemption," which they hold as a reference to the Second Coming. But (1) this is based solely on their own *arbitrary assertion* that the term must

---

61. House and Ice, *Dominion Theology*, p. 268.
62. *Ibid.*, p. 298. In Jordan's review of *Dominion Theology*, we read: "They want to know why I (and others) take the 'coming' in Matthew 24:30 in a different sense than in verse 37. Well, partly because two completely different Greek words are used!" James B. Jordan, *Review of Dominion Theology* (Tyler, TX: Biblical Horizons, 1988), p. 14.
63. House and Ice, *Dominion Theology*, p. 297.
64. *Ibid.*, p. 442.
65. *Ibid.*, p. 285. See also: p. 54.
66. *Ibid.*, p. 291.

here indicate the Second Coming, and (2) the term comes four verses *after* the supposed shift: How do they know where to shift gears?

Still further, they note regarding the disciples' questions: "The first question is answered in Luke 21:20-24, since Luke is the one who specializes in the A.D. 70 aspects. Luke records Jesus' warning about the soon-to-come destruction of Jerusalem — the days of vengeance. The second and third questions are answered in Matthew 24."[67] This seems rather arbitrary. Why does Matthew list more questions than he answers? Besides, lay Luke 21:20-24 side by side with Matthew 24:15-21; what is the compelling difference that leads us to conclude Matthew is speaking of the Second Advent and Luke of A.D. 70, events totally different and separated thus far by over 1900 years? They have an interpretive bias as opposed to our contextual time indicator.

2. *The Abomination of Desolation.* House and Ice state boldly: "One major reason Matthew 24 could not have been fulfilled in A.D. 70 is that 'the abomination of desolation' (24:15) was not accomplished in the destruction of Jerusalem."[68] Here we also detect an incredible arbitrariness: They aver that Luke 21:20 and Matthew 24:15 speak of "two separate events" because "In the A.D. 70 destruction of Jerusalem there was no image set up in the holy place, no worship of the image required, and no three-and-a-half year period of time between that event and the second coming of Christ. . . . Finally, no image came to life and beckoned men to worship it."[69] Incredibly, they charge that "Chilton cannot make his interpretation of the abomination of desolation fit the text of Scripture. Instead, he ignores the details of the passage he is supposed to be studying and goes to other unrelated passages importing them into the passage."[70]

---

67. *Ibid.*, pp. 293-94.
68. *Ibid.*, p. 287.
69. *Ibid.*, p. 290. The abomination of desolation phrase is important to House and Ice as a "major reason Matthew 24 could not have been fulfilled in A.D. 70 is that 'the abomination of desolation' (24:15) was not accomplished in the destruction of Jerusalem" (p. 286).
70. House and Ice, *Dominion Theology,* p. 290.

We are left in bewilderment to ask: Where in the "details of the passage" is their come-to-life, speaking image? Where do they discover a three-and-a-half year period? Not from Matthew 24! To insert them here is arbitrary in that there is no contextual warrant. We agree with a statement they make elsewhere: "There should not be a conflict between one's theology and the text, resulting in a fancy reworking of the text to fit the proposed theology."[71] In response to this quotation, we offer a (tongue-in-cheek) warning to the reader of House and Ice: "All therefore whatsoever they bid you observe, that observe and do; but do not ye after their works: for they say, and do not" (Matt. 23:3).

A preterist understanding of the passage sees the fulfillment in the whole complex of events leading to the destruction of the temple, particularly those associated with Titus's final five-month siege of Jerusalem. His encircling of Jerusalem in the spring of A.D. 70 finally culminated in the Temple's desolation and destruction in August, A.D. 70. Matthew was written to a Jewish audience, so he focused on the culminating sacrilegious "abomination of desolation." Luke was written by a Gentile to a Gentile audience, so he focused in on the first stage of the desolation: "When ye shall see Jerusalem compassed with armies, then know that the desolation thereof is nigh."

Jewish historian Josephus speaks of Titus's encircling Jerusalem[72] and finally setting up the pagan Roman ensigns in the Temple: Titus's soldiers "brought their ensigns to the temple, and set them over against its eastern gate; and there did they offer sacrifices to them."[73] Matthew and Luke speak of one historical, desolating episode, beginning with the encompassing of Jerusalem (Luke 21:20) and ending with the abomination (worship) that made desolate (Matt. 24:15). Interestingly, a number of early Church

---

71. *Ibid.*, p. 317.

72. See especially Josephus, *Wars* 12:1-2. "When Titus had therefore encompassed the city with this wall . . . (*Wars* 12:2).

73. *Ibid.*, 6:6:1. These ensigns were "military standards which were objects of cult." Mary E. Smallwood, *The Jews Under Roman Rule* (Leiden: E. J. Brill, 1976), p. 346. See also Josephus, *Wars* 2:9:4; Tertullian, *Apology* 16. Tertullian says: "The camp religion of the Romans is all through a worship of the standards, a setting the standards above all gods."

fathers speak of the fulfillment of Daniel's 70 Weeks, including the "abomination of desolation," in Jerusalem's destruction.[74]

3. *The Alleged Differences Between Luke and Matthew.* House and Ice make an issue of the language of "deliverance" found in Luke 21:28. They see it as reflective of Zechariah 12-14, where Jerusalem is surround by the nations: This passage, they say, "fits very well into the language of Matthew 24 — the nations have surrounded Jerusalem. It does not fit the A.D. 70 destruction of Jerusalem, since that was accomplished by one nation — Rome. . . . It would also be difficult to see how a single nation would fit this passage even if hyperbole were used."[75]

Assuming Zechariah 12-14 to be relevant to Matthew 24, it should be noted that historically it cannot be argued that the Jewish War, which saw the destruction of Jerusalem, was "by one nation." The war was not by one nation, but an empire of nations — the Roman Empire that consisted not only of the nation of Italy, but the lands or nations of Syria, Asia Minor, Palestine, Gaul, Egypt, Britain, and others.[76] Furthermore, Josephus points to numerous auxiliaries from a number of nations which participated.[77]

4. *Coming as Lightning.* House and Ice note that the "coming" of Christ in Matthew 24:27 cannot represent the invasion of Rome under Christ's behest as a judgment coming. The problem is that the "language of the coming of Christ is sudden and interventionist,"[78] *i.e.*, like lightning: "It does not matter how swift an army is, it could never come with that kind of speed."[79] The reason they

---

74. See footnote 101 below and preceding text.

75. House and Ice, *Dominion Theology*, p. 291.

76. Joseph Ward Swain, *The Harper History of Civilization* (New York: Harper and Bros., 1958), vol. 1, p. 198. *Webster's New 20th Century Unabridged* defines an empire thus: "a state uniting many territories and peoples under one ruler" or "the territories, regions, or countries under the jurisdiction and dominion of an emperor." The Roman empire was composed of imperial provinces, senatorial provinces, and client kingdoms.

77. For example, in one place he mentions soldiers and horsemen from Caesarea, from Syria, from the kings Antiochus, Agrippa, and Sohemus, and from Malchus, the king of Arabia (Josephus, *Wars*, 3:4:2; cp. 3:1:3).

78. House and Ice, *Dominion Theology*, p. 295.

79. *Ibid.*

give is simplistic. Rome simply came too slow. But how do they know that the "speed" of lightning is the issue here? What if it is the *specifically mentioned* matter of *direction*: from east to west? In Luke 10:18 the fall of Satan from power was likened to lightning. There the *downward* direction was the point, not how rapidly he accelerated. As a matter of historical fact, the Romans (the New Testament version of God's rod of anger against Israel, cp. Isa. Isa. 10:5) entered Judea from the east.[80]

4. The Search for the Second Coming. "If [Jordan] were to take the whole of the Olivet discourse as already fulfilled, as Chilton does the whole book of Revelation, then he is left with the problem of where does the Bible actually teach the second coming?"[81] We must ask, why would one *have* to find the Second Coming in the Olivet Discourse? But, in fact, preterists find it in the Matthew 24:36-25:46, as House and Ice well know.[82]

5. Is Preterism Intrinsically Erroneous? We were quite surprised to read the following comment, which is set out as a criticism: "The Reconstructionist, preterist approach means that many personalities, events, and places referred to prophetically in the Scriptures have already been fulfilled."[83] So? As a matter of fact, that is true; but as a general statement, how is it harmful? What of the dozens of Bible verses related to Christ's first coming— thirty-one of which they list![84] Regarding the verses *they* choose as references to Christ's first coming, *they are preteristic!*

Both the orthodox Jews today and those in antiquity have felt that Christians are misapplying prophecies to past events: In discussing Daniel 9, Athanasius says: "So the Jews are trifling, and the time in question, which they refer to the future, is actually come. For when did prophet and vision cease from Israel, save when Christ came, the Holy of Holies? For it is a sign, and an important proof,

---

80. Josephus, *Wars* 3:1. See Eduard Lohse, *The New Testament Environment*, trans. by John E. Steely (Nashville, TN: Abingdon, 1976), pp. 48ff.

81. House and Ice, *Dominion Theology*, p. 298. Their statements regarding Chilton and Jordan are erroneous, see Chapter 18.

82. *Ibid.*, p. 297.

83. *Ibid.*, p. 54.

84. *Ibid.*, p. 321.

of the coming of the Word of God, that Jerusalem no longer stands, nor is any prophet raised up nor vision revealed to them."[85]

At this point, we are somewhat surprised at their careless use of Daniel 9:24-27 to prove their literalistic hermeneutic. In Chapter 14 they write: "When we look at prophecies of Christ's first coming, we see that they were fulfilled in a literal manner, rather than figuratively. One good example is the precision of the 483 years predicted until the coming of Messiah in the seventy weeks of Daniel (9:24-27). . . . This kind of precise accuracy requires a literal fulfillment."[86] Yet earlier they state, in full con-

---

85. Athanasius, *Incarnation* 40:1. Origen agreed: "The weeks of years, also, which the prophet Daniel had predicted, extending to the leadership of Christ, have been fulfilled" (Origen, *Principles*, 4:1:5).

86. House and Ice, *Dominion Theology*, p. 321. Dispensationalists attempt a literalistic hermeneutic, but inconsistently. For example, the prophecies regarding David's reign in the millennium are not literally understood; they speak of Christ (J. Dwight Pentecost, *Things to Come: A Study in Biblical Eschatology* [Grand Rapids, MI: Zondervan/Academie, (1958) 1964], p. 498). Elijah's coming in Malachi 4:5-6 need not speak literally of Elijah (Pentecost, *Things to Come*, pp. 311-13; cp. E. S. English, "The Two Witnesses," *Our Hope*, [April, 1941] p. 666.) The sacrifices of Ezekiel 45:15-17 are expressly said to provide reconciliation, but dispensationalists say they are merely memorial (Pentecost, *Things to Come*, p. 525). Scofield says of Isaiah 52:15 that Christ has *literally* sprinkled the nations with His blood (*New Scofield Reference Bible*, p. 758)! Pentecost defends literalism by pointing (in part) to its being the method of Christ's day (Pentecost, *Things to Come*, pp. 17-19). Yet, they were the ones who rejected Christ! Besides, we discover a subtle exposé of "literalism" in John's Gospel. Were not the people often confused due to their literalism, by taking literally the references to the temple (John 2:19-21), the new birth (John 3:3-5), water (John 4:10-14), food (John 4:31-34), eating flesh (John 6:51-58), and so forth? We agree with dispensationalist Feinberg and the rest of the evangelical world in this regard: "Ryrie [and the dispensationalism which he represents] is too simplistic" (John S. Feinberg, *Continuity and Discontinuity* [Westchester, IL: Crossway Books, 1988], p. 73). Their entire system demands a viciously circular reasoning: Ryrie claims the dispensational system is developed from an inductive approach to Scripture and that covenantal theology is deductive (*Dispensationalism Today* [Chicago, IL: Moody Press, 1965], pp. 184, 185, 186, 190). But Reformed theology uses both induction and deduction. Ryrie, however, is self-contradictory on this matter: On page 30 of Ryrie's *Dispensationalism Today* we read of the distinguishable features of a dispensation: "[T]he word *distinguishable* in the definition points out the fact that there are some features which are distinctive to each dispensation and which mark them off from each other as different dispensations. These are contained in the particular revelation distinctive to each dispensation." On the very next page he writes: "The understanding of God's differing economies is essential to a proper interpretation of His revelation within

sistency with their dispensationalist Gap Theory: "The better view is that the seventy weeks of Daniel have yet to be completed."[87] In other words, there is a gap between the 69th and 70th weeks of Daniel, which comprises the time between the Triumphal Entry in A.D. 33[88] and the Secret Rapture in *our* future. Now who can take seriously a claim to "precise accuracy" of fulfillment of Daniel 9 on this basis? Consider the situation: Daniel predicts 70 weeks of years. Though the whole prophetic period in Daniel covers 490 years, the dispensationalist has inserted a 1,966 year gap (thus far!) into those weeks-of-years. Thus, the gap has already covered a period of time almost four times larger than the whole period of 490 years! "Precise accuracy?"

The Historical Basis of Preterism

Nascent Preterism in Antiquity

Statements as fallacious as they are bold are made by House and Ice regarding the destruction of Jerusalem in prophecy. In response to Chilton's comment that "Revelation is primarily a prophecy of the destruction of Jerusalem by the Romans," House and Ice ask:[89] "If this were such a clear 'fact,' then why did *none* of the early church writings reflect Chilton's views in their interpretation of Revelation? If the A.D. 70 destruction of Jerusalem fulfilled so much of biblical prophecy, then why is this *not* reflected in the views of the early church? Why is it that *all* of the early fathers, when referring to Revelation and Matthew 24, see these

---

those various economies." That is, you cannot understand the revelation without the feature, but you cannot find the feature without the revelation!

Interestingly, House and Ice write: "The coming of Christ appears to bring a new order in New Testament teaching, and even various statements and actions of Christ in the Gospel accounts seem to indicate his rejection of a literalistic obedience to the law (John 7:53-8:11; Matthew 12:1-4)" House and Ice, *Dominion Theology*, p. 104.

87. House and Ice, *Dominion Theology*, p. 259.

88. *Ibid.*, p. 321.

89. Though writing under the heading of "Internal Evidence," here they slip into the external evidence.

as future events?"[90] And since they spend a good deal of space on the influence of Daniel 9:24ff. on Matthew 24, surely they would include the handling of Daniel 9 in this statement.[91] After all, they attempt to distinguish Luke 21:20-24 from Matthew 24:15 by "comparison of the description in Matthew and Daniel."[92] They even state: "One major reason Matthew 24 could not have been fulfilled in A.D. 70 is that 'the abomination of desolation' (24:15) was not accomplished in the destruction of Jerusalem."[93] Thus, on their own analysis Daniel 9 should be no more preteristically fulfilled than Matthew 24 and should be no more heard of being interpreted preteristically in early Christianity than it is.

It is here we begin to suspect that they have done *no* first-hand reading in patristics, though they write with confidence as if they were well read. Let us note, however, a few samples that falsify such a claim.

Eusebius (A.D. 260-340) details the woes that befell Jerusalem in A.D. 70, mostly by reference to Josephus (the method of Chilton, which is disdained by House and Ice).[94] He writes that "it is fitting to add to these accounts [i.e., Josephus's] the true prediction of our Saviour in which he foretold these very events."[95]

---

90. *Ibid.*, p. 258 (emphasis mine). Also: "If Chilton and Russell's view is correct, then a majority of the New Testament was not recognized as already fulfilled until recently. It was not until fifteen hundred years later that Chilton's preterist interpretation arose . . . When did the preterist interpretation first arise in the history of the church? The promulgation of this view 'in anything like completeness' was by a Spanish Jesuit of Antwerp, named Alcasar, in the beginning of the seventeenth century (1614)'" (p. 272). On p. 273 they cite Beckwith who says: "[Alcasar's] work is the first to attempt a complete exposition of the entire premillennial part of the book." The qualifying statements "in anything like completeness" and "complete exposition" are interesting. Two pages later they write: "The futurist interpretation is the approach used by the earliest church fathers. We do not argue that they had a sophisticated system, but the clear futurist elements were there" (p. 275). We would argue the same for the "elements" of preterism.

91. House and Ice, *Dominion Theology*, pp. 259, 287-90.

92. *Ibid.*, p. 290.

93. *Ibid.*, p. 287.

94. *Ibid.*, p. 289.

95. Eusebius, *Ecclesiastical History* 3:7:1-2. See also: Jerome in *Post-Nicene Fathers*, 6:61-62.

He then cites Matthew 24:19-21 as his lead-in reference and later refers to Luke 21:20, 23, 24! He even states: "If any one compares the words of our Saviour with the other accounts of the historian [Josephus] concerning the whole war, how can one fail to wonder, and to admit that the foreknowledge and the prophecy of our Saviour were truly divine and marvelously strange."[96]

Another ancient document that makes reference to the destruction of the temple based on Matthew 24:2-34 is the *Clementine Homilies*.[97] There we read: "Prophesying concerning the temple, He said: 'See ye these buildings? Verily I say to you, There shall not be left here one stone upon another which shall not be taken away [Matt. 24:3]; and this generation shall not pass until the destruction begin [Matt. 24:34]. . . . ' And in like manner He spoke in plain words the things that were straightway to happen, which we can now see with our eyes, in order that the accomplishment might be among those to whom the word was spoken."[98]

In Cyprian (A.D. 200-258) we have clear reference to Matthew 24 as referring to Jerusalem's A.D. 70 fall.[99] In the entirety of Treatise 12 he is dealing with testimonies against the Jews, including Christ's prophecies.

Clement of Alexandria (A.D. 150-215) discusses the Seventieth Week of Daniel 9 as a past event: "The half of the week Nero held sway, and in the holy city Jerusalem placed the abomination; and in the half of the week he was taken away, and Otho, and Galba, and Vitellius. And Vespasian rose to the supreme power, and destroyed Jerusalem, and desolated the holy place."[100] As a matter

---

96. *Ibid.*, 3:7:7. This shows that Eusebius deemed Luke 21 and Matthew 24 to be parallel accounts.

97. Though not written by a noted church father, it is an important late second century work that touches on the matter before us. House and Ice boldly state that preterism is found in "none of the early church writings" (p. 258). Yet, here is a work that shows early consideration of the matter, apparently picking up on views current in that day.

98. *Clementine Homilies*, 3:15. See Roberts and Donaldson, *Ante-Nicene Fathers*, vol. 8, p. 241.

99. Cyprian, *Treatises*, 12:1:6, 15. See especially Roberts and Donaldson, *Ante-Nicene Fathers*, vol. 5, pp. 507-11.

100. Clement of Alexandria, *Miscellanies* 1:21.

of fact, *several* of the early fathers held a distinctly preteristic interpretation of Daniel 9![101] By way of further example, Tertullian,
though a premillennialist, does as well: "Vespasion, in the first
year of his empire, subdues the Jews in war; and there are made
lii years, vi months. For he reigned xi years. And thus, in the day
of their storming, the Jews fulfilled the lxx hebdomads predicted in
Daniel."[102] Though House and Ice adopt the Gap Theory of Daniel's weeks, which allows them to project the final week into the
distant future, the more standard evangelical interpretative options regarding Daniel's Seventieth Week can be found in Meredith Kline, Edward J. Young, O. T. Allis, and others.[103]

Andreas of Cappadocia (6th century) wrote: "There are not
wanting those who apply this passage to the siege and destruction
of Jerusalem by Titus."[104] Later he wrote: "These things are referred
by some to those sufferings which were inflicted by the Romans
upon the Jews."[105] Also Arethas specifically interprets various
passages in Revelation in terms of the destruction of Jerusalem.[106]

---

101. For a discussion of early interpretive approaches to Daniel 9, see Louis
E. Knowles, "The Interpretation of the Seventy Weeks of Daniel in the Early
Fathers," *Westminster Theological Journal* (7:2), pp. 137-38. Actual preteristic references include: *The Epistle of Barnabas* 16:6; Clement of Alexandria, *Miscellanies*
1:21; Tertullian, *Against the Jews* 8 (despite being a Montanist premillennialist!);
Origen, *Matthew* 24:15; Julius Africanus, *Chronography* (relevant portions preserved in Eusebius, *Preparation for the Gospel* 10:10 and *Demonstrations of the Gospel*
8); Eusebius, *Demonstrations* 8; Athanasius, *Incarnation* 40:1 (cited above), and
Augustine in his 199th epistle.
102. Tertullian, *An Answer to the Jews* 8. His entire chapter is given over to
demonstrating the fulfillment of Daniel 9, in order to vindicate Christianity
against Judaism.
103. Meredith G. Kline, "The Covenant of the Seventieth Week" in John H.
Skilton, ed. *The Law and the Prophets: Old Testament Studies in Honor of Oswald T.
Allis* (Nutley, NJ: Presbyterian and Reformed, 1974), pp. 452ff.; E. J. Young,
The Prophecy of Daniel (Grand Rapids, MI: Wm. B. Eerdmans, 1949), pp. 191-221;
O. T. Allis, *Prophecy and the Church* (Philadelphia: Presbyterian and Reformed,
1945), pp. 111ff.; R. Bradley Jones, *The Great Tribulation* (Grand Rapids, MI:
Baker Book House, 1980), pp. 43-61; Philip Mauro, *The Seventy Weeks* (Swengel,
PA: Reiner, 1923).
104. Andreas on Revelation 6:12.
105. Andreas on Revelation 7:1.
106. He so interprets Revelation 6 and 7.

Surely it may not be stated, as do House and Ice: "Why is it that *all* of the early fathers, when referring to Revelation and Matthew 24, see these as future events?"[107]

Nero and Revelation

House and Ice write: "If Chilton could show that Nero is the ruler spoken of in Revelation, then he would have a major victory for his view. But he cannot."[108] As has been shown in great detail in *Before Jerusalem Fell*, many lines of evidence converge upon Nero:[109] (1) His place as the sixth among the Roman emperors (Rev. 17:10),[110] (2) his being followed by a seventh, briefly reigning emperor (Galba, Rev. 17:10),[111] (3) his name's numerical value of 666 (Rev. 13:18), (4) his living while the temple still stood (Rev. 11:1-2), (5) the prominence of his persecution in first century Christianity (Rev. 13), and more. There is an old adage: If the shoe fits, wear it. Nero's footprints are all over Revelation.

Systemic Futurism as a Modern Phenomenon

House and Ice write that the preteristic approach represents "a new way to deal with the Olivet discourse and the book of Revelation"[112] that "was not recognized . . . until recently. It was not

107. House and Ice, *Dominion Theology*, p. 258 (emphasis mine). In the final analysis, however, one must wonder how their argument carries weight in light of the 1830 J. N. Darby/Plymouth Brethren roots of dispensationalism (which they admit, p. 422). After all, it is Charles C. Ryrie, the chief proponent of dispensationalism and one of the endorsers of the book by House and Ice, who defends dispensationalism from "the charge of recency" by labeling such a charge a "straw man" and arguing from history as a "fallacy." In addition he writes: "The fact that something was taught in the first century does not make it right (unless taught in the canonical Scriptures), and the fact that something was not taught until the nineteenth century does not make it wrong . . ." (*Dispensationalism Today*, p. 66).

108. House and Ice, *Dominion Theology*, p. 259.

109. See Gentry, *Before Jerusalem Fell*, Chapter 12.

110. The first seven emperors were: Julius, Augustus, Tiberius, Gaius, Claudius, Nero, and Galba. See Josephus, *Antiquities* 18:2:2; 18:6:10; 19:1:11; Suetonius, *Lives of the Twelve Caesars*; Dio Cassius, *Julius* 84.

111. Galba reigned from June, A.D. 68 to January, A.D. 69. Josephus, *Wars* 4:9:2, 9.

112. House and Ice, *Dominion Theology*, p. 264.

until fifteen hundred years later that Chilton's preterist interpretation arose."[113]

In keeping with their usual carelessness, they pose a question, document an answer, and then distort that documentary witness: "When did the preterist interpretation first arise in the history of the church? 'The promulgation of this view "in anything like completeness" was by a Spanish Jesuit of Antwerp, named Alcasar, in the beginning of the seventeenth century (1614).' "[114] Their question was "when did the preterist interpretation *first* arise"? Their citation, though, speaks only of its *systematization*, not its "first" arising! And we have shown its early appearance in a number of the church fathers. On the next page they cite Isbon T. Beckwith as an additional proof for their charge that preterism is traceable to Alcasar. But a part of this quotation reads: Alcasar's "work is the first to attempt a complete exposition of the entire premillennial part of the book."[115]

They seem to be ignorant of the fact that *as a system*, the futurist approach is, too, considered a late development! They state: "So the futurist is taking prophetic literature in a way that is consistent with how believers have always understood it. Futurists are not coming up with a special, new way to deal with the Olivet discourse and the book of Revelation as the preterists have done."[116] But where did futurism arise as a system? "In its present form [the futurist interpretation] may be said to have originated at the end of the sixteenth century with the Jesuit Ribera, who moved . . . to relieve the Papacy from the terrible stigma cast upon it by the Protestant interpretation, and tried to do so by referring their prophecies to the distant future. . . ."[117] O. T. Allis agrees: "The futurist interpretation is traced back to the Jesuit Ribera (A.D. 1580) whose aim was to disprove the claim of the Reformers that

---

113. *Ibid.*, p. 272.
114. *Ibid.*
115. *Ibid.*, p. 273.
116. *Ibid.*, p. 264.
117. H. Grattan Buiness, *The Approaching End of the Age* (London: Hodder and Stoughton, 1879), p. 100.

the Pope was the Antichrist,"[118] as does B. B. Warfield.[119]

Summary

1. Preterism is an interpretive approach to certain prophecies that understands them as having now been fulfilled, although they were future to the time of the one who uttered them. For example, evangelical Christians understand Isaiah 7:14 preteristically: The Messiah has already been born of a virgin.

2. Reconstructionism involves a postmillennial eschatology, and sometimes includes a preteristic interpretation of certain prophecies. Preterism is not essential to Reconstructionism, and it is a mistake to argue that it is.

3. Revelation was written in the mid-A.D. 60s, as the book itself evidences, rather than around A.D. 95, as some early fathers thought.

4. Two basic views of the date of Revelation's writing were held among ancient Christian fathers: a date during Nero's reign and a date at the end of Domitian's reign. There is no unified tradition on the matter.

5. Irenaeus, the leading "evidence" for a late-date view of Revelation, is not at all clear in his statement. He may be legitimately interpreted in two very different ways.

6. There is clear evidence for a Neronic persecution of Christianity, but debatable evidence for a Domitianic persecution.

7. For a futurist to attempt to late-date Revelation by references to emperor worship and Roman persecution involves him in contradiction: His futurism demands a fulfillment in *our* future; his late-date evidence demands major appearances of the prophecies in Domitian's day.

8. The preterist approach to Matthew 24 and Revelation demands that the clear statements interpret the less clear; the futurist approach holds the opposite approach.

---

118. Allis, *Prophecy and the Church*, p. 296, n66.
119. B. B. Warfield, "Revelation," *Selected Shorter Writings*, ed. by John E. Meeter, 2 vols. (Nutley, NJ: Presbyterian and Reformed, 1970), vol. 2, p. 90.

9. The clearly stated time-cues in Matthew 24 and Revelation 1 demand an ancient fulfillment of the prophecies to which they relate. Matthew 24:1-34 was to be fulfilled "in this generation." Revelation's prophecies were to occur "soon" and were "at hand."

10. The destruction of the temple and the disestablishment of Judaism are major redemptive-historical events, which receive little emphasis in the futurist approach to prophecy.

11. As *complete systems* of interpretation both preterism and futurism are "modern": Preterism is traceable to 1614 and futurism to 1580.

12. Many ancient fathers were preterists regarding Daniel's Seventy Weeks, the first portion of Christ's Olivet Discourse, and/or Revelation, including the author of the *Clementine Homilies*, Clement of Alexandria, Cyprian, Athanasius, Eusebius, and Augustine.

Part III
THE SCHOLARLY QUESTION

17

ARGUMENTATION ERRORS

An analysis and exposé of the faulty logic used in "Dominion Theology."

We were most gratified to discover in House and Ice's book several expressions of appreciation and words of commendation to Reconstructionist writers and writings. Among these complimentary expressions we find them speaking highly of the thoroughness and breadth of scholarship evidenced in Rushdoony's *Institutes* and Bahnsen's *Theonomy.*[1] Despite their systemic differences with Reconstructionists, they express appreciation for some of the beneficial "insights Reconstructionists have given the church."[2] These insights are particularly in the development of a Christian worldview, including the areas of educational theory, philosophy, pro-life advocacy, economics, and business.[3] In fact, they note that "Reconstructionists have shown that you can be both intellectual and practical by the way they have written and built their organizations."[4]

In commenting thus they recognize the reality of the challenge of Reconstructionism to modern dispensationalism: Reconstructionists "have issued a challenge, especially to dispensationalism, to clarify our position in terms of their contributions. This challenge should be met in the days ahead as we are driven back to Scripture to see if these things are true."[5]

---

1. H. Wayne House and Thomas Ice, *Dominion Theology: Blessing or Curse?* (Portland, OR: Multnomah, 1988), p. 27.
2. *Ibid.*, p. 359.
3. *Ibid.*, p. 362.
4. *Ibid.*
5. *Ibid.*

Unfortunately, despite these few gracious words of appreciation and notices of accepting the challenge, they have little success in engaging the challenge at a serious level. In fact, but for these few words, the overall character of the book is one of caricature and rhetoric.

We would have preferred our response exclusively to be a debate of the exegetical and theological issues engaged. House and Ice's work, however, goes beyond pure intellectual debate. Consequently, we are moved to add this section in order to point out both the scholarly and ethical failures of House and Ice through radical misrepresentation of Reconstructionists views, as well as the evidence of their general theological failure (as already shown).

This book is partly necessitated by the fact that House has refused to engage Bahnsen in a formal debate in which would be allowed cross-examination on the matters under discussion. And this despite such charges in *Dominion Theology* as: "The problem with many Reconstructionists is that they are long on interpretation and theological presuppositions, and short on specific exegesis and 'crux' passages to support their theology. Reconstructionists are good at telling you what their theology is and even at exhorting you to put it into practice, but they cannot give specific verses to back it up."[6] Perhaps the superficiality of the argument contained in the book explains this hesitancy to debate.

It is evident upon reading *Dominion Theology* that criticism of Reconstructionist thought is more of an art than a science. It seems more interested in plucking the strings of the heart by siding with status quo dispensationalism and engaging in rhetoric than with carefully engaging the mind by carefully coming to grips with the substantive issues. Their book is seriously flawed as a general rebuttal to Reconstructionism. Perhaps the reason is betrayed in Ice's preface. Evidently it was rushed into print in order to be the first in the field: "Well, here it is, and as far as we know, it is the first book-length reply to the Christian Reconstruction movement. Other works are currently in the mill, but some-

---

6. *Ibid.*, p. 307.

one had to be the first to return their volley."[7]

Nevertheless, they have an excellent bibliography of Reconstructionist literature, which is abundantly employed. They are obviously *broadly* read in Reconstructionist literature. For this they are to be commended. Unfortunately they are not *carefully* read — despite their claim to "a serious reading of Reconstructionism."[8] In this section we will gather together a number of examples of the carelessness of their method and presentation. Hopefully, the other works seeking to analyze Reconstructionism, which are mentioned by House and Ice, will avoid these pitfalls.

Contradictory Assertions

One of the most frustrating failures in their presentation is their tendency to internal contradiction.[9] And these are not merely occasional slips; they are constant throughout the work — sometimes even appearing in the same sections! Let us cite a few samples. Some of these will already have been touched upon in the preceding sections. Although we regret this duplication of material, these are being gathered here to illustrate the problem of the argumentative failure, beyond their exegetical, theological, and historical shortcomings.

In an attempt to undermine the historicity of the theonomic ethic, they state on one page: "The Puritans wanted a government that would adhere rigidly to the civil code of the Old Testament, thereby creating a model of the kingdom of God on earth for all the world to see."[10] At another place they write: "While it cannot

---

7. *Ibid.*, p. 9.

8. *Ibid.*, p. 77.

9. For an interesting survey of the writings of the endorsers of *Dominion Theology*, see "A Response to *Dominion Theology*" by Gary DeMar (available from American Vision, P.O. Box 720515, Atlanta, Georgia 30328). He shows how these men have inadvertently employed Reconstructionist ideals, even though they seek to discredit Reconstructionism.

10. House and Ice, *Dominion Theology*, p. 15. It will not relieve the tension for them to assert that "the Puritans themselves left mixed messages regarding the nature of theonomy. They did not always echo an identical theonomic perspective" (*ibid.*, p. 95). Their contradictions are much too bold. Besides their primary point (the matter of historicity) does not require monolithic agreement among

be denied that *some* Puritans were theonomistic, the movement as a whole was never in wholehearted agreement."[11] But on the page immediately preceding this they admit: "It is true the Puritans were *generally* theonomistic in outlook."[12] Now which is it? Were "some Puritans" theonomistic? Or were "the Puritans . . . generally theonomistic"?

In another place they note the Reconstructionist "imitation" of the Puritan experiment in these terms: "It is being imitated today by a small and increasingly influential group of persons who believe that only through the establishment and enforcement of Old Testament civil law can America — and the world — be saved from destruction."[13] Their own "Glossary" defines "Reconstructionism" thus: "Because there is no common ground between biblical and non-Christian thought, the Christian is to use the Bible and the Bible alone to govern his thinking."[14] But later, Reconstructionist postmillennialists are decried as trying to adopt the world's system! "The believer is to be a light shining in the darkness, not a light mixed with darkness. On the other hand, postmillennialism leads to a penetration of institutions, resulting in a spirit of compromise so that the institution may function."[15] Again we must ask: Which is it? Does Reconstructionism seek to establish "the Bible alone" as the basis of civil law in America? Or does it "compromise" by intermingling "with non-Christian thought"? To make matters worse Tommy Ice made the following statement in his debate with Reconstructionists: "Premillennialists have always been involved in the present world. . . . And basically, they have picked up on

---

the Puritans. They even allow disagreement between modern Reconstructionists: "This is not to say that Reconstructionists need to agree on every point. There are always differences between people within any framework" (p. 352). This happens even among premillennialists, as they admit: "The debate over the timing of the Rapture has become the major disagreement within premillennialism" (p. 422).

11. House and Ice, *Dominion Theology*, p. 95 (emphasis mine).
12. *Ibid.*, p. 94 (emphasis mine).
13. *Ibid.*, p. 15.
14. *Ibid.*, p. 418.
15. *Ibid.*, pp. 340-41.

the ethical positions of their contemporaries."[16] How does this not contradict their own concern with compromise?

What are the prospects of Christ's Church in history, especially in these "last days"? House and Ice write that God "is demonstrating that, unlike Adam and Israel, this new people, the church, *will be faithful to him* even though it is their lot to suffer persecution and conflict during the darkness of this present age."[17] This idea appears again: "God answers back in history [to Satan], 'Yes, men made new will serve me and remain loyal even through suffering and deprivation. Look at the church, my bride!'"[18] Yet at other places the Church is said to be destined to *unfaithfulness*: "Tragically, this will contribute to the further *unfaithfulness* of the church in these last days before the return of Messiah."[19] At one point they are led to ask: "If common grace has been increasing, why has sin progressed so far? Why has the church become so diluted in her faith and practice?"[20] And, "Common grace is on the decline, especially God's restraint of evil. This accounts for the rising apostasy and decline of Christianity."[21] Which is it? Will the church prove to Satan that it will be faithful? Or will it apostatize?

The Olivet Discourse is found in Matthew 24 *and* 25, as House and Ice point out.[22] Of this passage they state: "Reconstructionists believe the Olivet discourse was fulfilled in A.D. 70."[23] But then just a few pages later they admit the truth: "Reconstructionist James Jordan says, verses 36 and following [of Matthew 24] refer to the second coming."[24] Which is it? Are their readers to believe Reconstructionists hold the Olivet Discourse was fulfilled in A.D. 70? Or that they hold that only *the first 34 verses* of *one* of the two chapters containing it were fulfilled in A.D. 70, with the re-

---

16. Cited in Gary DeMar, *The Debate over Christian Reconstruction* (Ft. Worth, TX: Dominion Press, 1988), p. 185.
17. House and Ice, *Dominion Theology*, p. 170 (emphasis mine).
18. *Ibid.*, p. 180.
19. *Ibid.*, p. 161 (emphasis mine).
20. *Ibid.*, p. 182.
21. *Ibid.*, p. 183.
22. *Ibid.*, pp. 52, 285.
23. *Ibid.*, p. 285.
24. *Ibid.*, p. 297, cp. p. 268.

mainder awaiting the Second Coming? They give *not one* Reconstructionist who speaks of the Olivet Discourse as being fulfilled in A.D. 70, although they mention several who, with Jordan, see *certain portions* of it fulfilled then.

Of Christ's Second Coming they boldly claim: "Reconstructionists do not have a biblical passage that corresponds with the Acts passage since they have 'preterized' them all away."[25] Yet earlier they had already stated: "Chilton apparently does think that 1 Corinthians 15:51-54 and 1 Thessalonians 4:14-17 are passages teaching the second coming. . . ."[26] And the 1 Thessalonians passage very clearly corresponds to Acts 1!

Focusing on David Chilton's works, they allege in one place (in response to Jim Jordan) "If he were to take the whole of the Olivet discourse as already fulfilled, as Chilton does the whole book of Revelation. . . ."[27] Yet the truth hounds them and they admit in two other places: "Thus, Chilton is saying that *most*, if not all, of the Revelation was historically fulfilled in the time of its writing."[28] And "Chilton says, 'Revelation is *primarily* a prophecy of the destruction of Jerusalem.' "[29] They even quote Chilton's statement that Revelation "does briefly point to events beyond its immediate concerns," i.e. at the consummation.[30]

Other illustrations could be cited, as well. But let us move on.

Distortion Through Imprecision

Vivid illustrations of their argumentative failure also appear in their careless use of words through imprecision. We will cite here only two by way of example, although other entries elsewhere in this portion of our book would fit well here, too.

Regarding the kingdom, they write: "We offer the following as a tentative definition of the kingdom: 'The kingdom is the rule of

---

25. *Ibid.*, p. 278.
26. *Ibid.*, p. 282.
27. *Ibid.*, p. 298.
28. *Ibid.*, p. 261 (emphasis mine).
29. *Ibid.*, p. 426 (emphasis mine).
30. *Ibid.*, p. 52.

God through Christ upon the earth.' "[31] We could say the same thing! The kingdom is the rule of God. It is through Christ. And it is upon the earth! To be more precise they should add something like it will be "while Christ is physically present on the earth in the future" and "it will last 1000 years." This "tentative definition" is not only imprecise but needless, for they quote a very clear and precise definition by Ryrie just a few pages later.[32]

Their imprecise use of the word "church" often leaves false impressions: "Believing in the eventual earthly triumph of the church. . . . "[33] "DOMINION THEOLOGY. The belief that the church is to exercise rule over every area of society, people as well as institutions, before Christ returns."[34] These imprecise statements regarding the Church in Reconstructionism are misleading: Is it the institutional Church to which they refer? or the Universal Church as the composite body of Christ, i.e. the mass of individual Christians? To make matters worse, these statements are made despite even their own occasional careful admissions in this regard, admissions which leave a totally different impression. In another context, after quoting a Bahnsen statement, they accurately note: "The universal church is meant rather than the institutional church."[35] Elsewhere they admit a vigorous denial by Reconstructionists of a wrongful involvement of the institutional Church in political affairs: "Reconstructionists vehemently deny that they are advocating control over society by the institutional church, since the church is only one of many spheres. They claim that critics misrepresent their position to be one of 'ecclesiocracy' (theonomists use this word to speak of government by the visible church) rather than their true position in favor of 'theocracy' (rule

---

31. *Ibid.*, p. 218.
32. *Ibid.*, pp. 221-22: "The period of a thousand years of the visible, earthly reign of the Lord Jesus Christ, who, after His return from heaven, will fulfill during that period the promises contained in the Abrahamic, Davidic, and new covenants to Israel, will bring the whole world to a knowledge of God, and will lift the curse from the whole creation."
33. *Ibid.*, p. 23.
34. *Ibid.*, p. 419.
35. *Ibid.*, p. 32.

by God through universal church members governing the various spheres according to God's law)."[36] Again they write: "Reconstructionists often feel misunderstood by others who characterize them as believing that the church is to bring in the kingdom. . . . [I]n fairness, more recent works have attempted to explain their position more clearly."[37] But their quotations above fail of their own "fairness" doctrine! What is more they quote a *1970* statement by Rushdoony that undermines their implication that it is only *recently* that Reconstructionists have made clear it is not the church that will usher in the kingdom. Rushdoony's statement reads: "Christ ushered in the kingdom of God."[38]

Appeal to Emotion

Reconstructionist thought is easy to mock because Christians today basically think in humanistic terms and categories. Frankly, few modern Christians have attempted to bring every thought captive to Christ (2 Cor. 10:5). This problem is evidenced in Ryrie's concern over the churches packed with "carnal Christians."[39] Such a situation opens up the usefulness of fallacious appeals to emotion in the debate over Reconstructionism. House and Ice are not above such tactics.

Though House and Ice state that the Puritans sought to establish Old Testament law in America[40] and that they were "a leading influence in the founding of America,"[41] they deride Reconstructionism for seeking a similar program. Without offering in the least an appropriate theonomic explanation, they state: "If Reconstructionists succeed, and are consistent with their theory, blasphemy would be a criminal offense, homosexuality a capital crime, and slavery (in some form) reinstituted."[42] This has a purely emo-

---

36. *Ibid.*, p. 71.
37. *Ibid.*, p. 49.
38. *Ibid.*, p. 217.
39. Charles C. Ryrie, *Balancing the Christian Life* (Chicago, IL: Moody Press, 1969), p. 170.
40. House and Ice, *Dominion Theology*, p. 15.
41. *Ibid.*, p. 421.
42. *Ibid.*, p. 27.

tional effect in its undefined imprecision.

No Reconstructionist asserts that "homosexuality" should be a capital crime — only homosexual *conduct* (e.g., sodomy), provable in court. A "Reconstructed government" would not seek out those who might be "homosexually inclined" for punishment! And what is the unsuspecting reader to think of this "slavery in some form"? What *is* the Old Testament concept of slavery (which *God* encoded in His revelation to Moses, a form of indentured servitude upheld in the United States Constitution, Amendment XIII, Section 1)? This is the same sort of argument many use against the doctrine of eternal Hell and the condemnation of "tribes in Africa." Surely God would not do such! But closer examination of the doctrines of Hell and lost tribes makes the matters more understandable. Likewise is it with theonomic political ethics — when properly explained. But then the emotional effect of the argument would be forfeited.

And what could be more fraught with emotion than the following? "Most Reconstructionist descriptions of the ideal church follow conspicuously Reformed and especially Presbyterian formulas in areas of organizational structure and sacraments. The fate of any Christian unwilling to conform to those strictures is not stated. . . ." "A larger question is the fate of many now considered orthodox Christians — dispensationalists, for example." "Many [dispensationalists] would be handed over to the civil authorities as those 'at war' with the law-order. In other words, they would be criminals." "From that moment, the First Amendment provision for religious pluralism would be a thing of the past for dispensationalists, amillennialists, and many other Christians, as well as for all non-Christian religious groups."[43]

Where is there *any* hint in Reconstructionist literature that non-Presbyterian Christians would be punished in a Reconstructed government? Or that dispensationalists and amillennialists would have an unknown "fate" as "criminals"? This is pure emotional rhetoric, for they know such is not the case: "Why do Reconstructionists not advocate taking present action against dispensationalists and other religious groups?"[44]

---

43. *Ibid.*, pp. 72, 77, 79.
44. *Ibid.*, p. 79.

Appealing to the patriotic American, House and Ice tug on the Constitutional heart strings: "A serious reading of Reconstructionism raises monumental doubts about the compatibility of [the Reconstructionist] vision with the guarantees of liberty found in the Constitution, and even with the basic three-part structure of the U.S. Government. The first amendment would appear to face the quickest overhaul."[45] And this is despite the admission that "the Bill of Rights is often applauded by theonomists, such as Gary DeMar."[46] They also imply a Khomeini-like tyranny over the land: "Rushdoony declares that all who oppose the law-order in a theonomic society, including criminals and dissidents, are at war with the law-order and with society. Nothing is more heinous in a theocratic society than to *openly question* the law-order. The legitimate institutions must therefore react with 'destruction' or other appropriate punishment to those with whom they are at war."[47] Sounds horrifying, does it not? To merely "question" the law-order is "heinous" and results in one's "destruction"![48]

In House and Ice's scenario, Christian pastors would have to fear imprisonment if their sermons were not theologically approved in a "Reconstructed America": "Would a public sermon interpreting Galatians 3 to refer to sanctification as well as justification be allowed? Would this not be an open declaration of war on the law-order?"[49] Absurd laws would be forbidden free press analysis: "What about a newspaper editorial questioning the requirement against wearing shirts made with mixed types of thread or in favor of reserve banking? The answers to all such questions are the same: opposing the law-order must be met by criminal sanction. Forget the First Amendment."[50]

---

45. *Ibid.*, p. 77. But see the Marsden quote recorded by Bahnsen on p. 14 and the recognition of Puritan influence on America's early history noted by House and Ice (p. 294 above).

46. *Ibid.*, p. 77.

47. *Ibid.* (emphasis mine).

48. See pp. 304ff. below for a refutation of this implication, under "Careless Use of Sources."

49. House and Ice, *Dominion Theology*, p. 79.

50. *Ibid.*

Sweeping Assertions

As frequent as their internal contradictions is their tendency to sweeping assertions. Though more often than not harmless, still there is evidence of careless thinking and expression — a carelessness that will lead the interested reader astray and falls short of the Christian interest in truth.

Regarding the decline of premillennialism in medieval Christianity, they boldly assert: "With the rise of Augustine's view of amillennialism in the fifth century, premillennialism *totally disappeared* for almost twelve hundred years until the early 1600s. . . . *No one* even thought in terms of premillennialism. . . ."[51] At other places they are more careful: "Premillennialism was first held by the early church fathers who were the closest to the original apostles. As the allegorical interpretation of the Book of Revelation became entrenched during the time of Augustine, the amillennial view arose and gained *almost exclusive* dominance until the Reformation."[52]

In making reference to *some* Reconstructionists (Gary North and David Chilton), they include *all* in the following statement: "Therefore, Reconstructionists stress the primacy of symbolism in prophetic interpretation, rather than a more literal approach."[53] And this sweeping statement is made despite Reconstructionist Bahnsen's own vigorous disavowal of "interpretive maximalism," which they cite, as well as Gentry's, which they evidently read.[54]

And can they prove this broad and totally erroneous generalization: "*Most* dominion theology adherents, when challenged to defend the second coming, do not cite Scripture as the basis for their belief; rather they cite the voice of mother church"?[55] They cite only *one* example (Chilton) — and that one is wholly misread![56]

Blatant historical error is foisted upon the reader through the following sweeping assertions: "If the A.D. 70 destruction of Jeru-

---

51. *Ibid.*, p. 421 (emphasis mine).
52. *Ibid.*, p. 210.
53. *Ibid.*, p. 54.
54. *Ibid.*, pp. 58, 249-50, 309.
55. *Ibid.*, p. 269 (emphasis mine).
56. See analysis below in section entitled, "Careless Use of Sources."

salem fulfilled so much of biblical prophecy, then why is this *not* reflected in the views of the early church? Why is it that *all* of the early fathers, when referring to Revelation and Matthew 24, see these as future events?"[57] "If this were such a clear 'fact,' then why did *none* of the early church writings reflect Chilton's views in their interpretation of Revelation? If the A.D. 70 destruction of Jerusalem fulfilled so much of biblical prophecy, then why is this *not* reflected in the views of the early church? Why is it that *all* of the early fathers, when referring to Revelation and Matthew 24, see these as future events?"[58] But we have pointed out that Andreas of Cappadocia and Arethas specifically speak of interpretations of various passages in Revelation in terms of the destruction of Jerusalem. We noted that Eusebius and the *Clementine Homilies* apply Matthew 24 to the event.[59]

In a sweeping assertion bordering on the ridiculous (if taken literally!) House and Ice state: "Preterists understand the book of Revelation, the Olivet discourse, and *virtually all prophecy* as having been fulfilled in God's judgment upon apostate Jews for their rejection of Jesus as Messiah in the A.D. 70 destruction of Jerusalem."[60] What preterist believes the virgin birth, the Triumphal Entry, the crucifixion, and the many other prophecies cited by House and Ice on pages 321-23 were fulfilled in A.D. 70?

Technical Failure

In a strange misnomer for a theological work, House and Ice label the evidence drawn from the Seven Letters and from Revelation's allusions to emperor worship as "external evidence"![61] New Testament scholars consider *external* evidence to be drawn from tradition, not from within the pages of the work in question.[62]

---

57. House and Ice, *Dominion Theology*, p. 258 (emphasis mine).
58. *Ibid.* (emphasis mine).
59. See Chapter 16.
60. House and Ice, *Dominion Theology*, p. 422.
61. *Ibid.*, p. 256.
62. E.g., Donald Guthrie, *New Testament Introduction* (Downers Grove, IL: Inter-Varsity Press, 1970), p. 956; Kümmel, *Introduction to the New Testament* (17th ed.; Nashville, TN: Abingdon, 1973), pp. 466-67.

Though writing under the heading of "Internal Evidence," they slip into the external evidence, when they make several statements regarding the writings of the church fathers.[63]

As pointed out in an earlier chapter, House and Ice say the first centuries were almost universally premillennial: "Premillennialism was the pervasive view of the earliest orthodox fathers"[64] for "the first two and a half centuries" of our era.[65] Yet, even as Dallas Seminary-trained Alan Patrick Boyd has admitted: "Indeed, this thesis would conclude that the eschatological beliefs of the period studied would be generally inimical to those of the modern system (perhaps, seminal amillennialism, and not nascent dispensational premillennialism ought to be seen in the eschatology of the period)."[66] They simply have not done their homework in this area.

Non Sequitur

House and Ice often involve themselves in *non sequitur* arguments. We will cite three examples. For instance, besides other flaws, their argument from Acts 14:22 ("Through many tribulations we must enter the kingdom of God") is a case in point: "Since they were not in the kingdom, nor are we, they spoke of it as yet future."[67] *If* (for sake of argument) the kingdom was established "in power" in A.D. 70 at the destruction of the Temple, how could it be said that since Paul (who died in A.D. 68) was not in the kingdom when he spoke, therefore neither are we? After all, Jesus said only "some" of His followers and hearers would live to see the power-coming of the kingdom (Mark 9:1). The conclusion simply does not necessarily follow the assertion.

Regarding the legitimacy of the futuristic approach to Revelation, we read: "The outline of the book of Revelation is given for us in 1:19. . . . This means that there are two divisions within the

---

63. House and Ice, *Dominion Theology*, p. 258.
64. *Ibid.*, p. 202.
65. *Ibid.*, p. 203.
66. Alan Patrick Boyd, "Dispensational Premillennial Analysis of the Eschatology of the Post-Apostolic Fathers (Until the Death of Justin Martyr)," (unpublished master's thesis, Dallas Theological Seminary, 1977), pp. 90-91.
67. House and Ice, *Dominion Theology*, pp. 224-25.

book of Revelation: 'one, the things that fall within the actual life-time of the seer, the first century [Revelation 1-3], and second, the things which were future to his period [Revelation 4:1-22:5].' An internal textual verification is clearly seen in Revelation 4:1 when it says, 'I will show you what must take place after these things.' As Tenney concludes, 'On this ground the futurist has a good claim for the validity of his method.' "[68] They add: " 'After' means 'after the present moment; hence, the future.' "[69] But how does this prove the *futurist system*? The thrust of the futurist viewpoint is that the future that John spoke about is future even to *our own present era.* But could not John have been talking of events just a few months or years down the road? Why must his use of future expressions imply a future *2000 years away*? Especially is this problematic for the "futurist" in that John specifically speaks of shortly to occur future events (Rev. 1:1, 3).

Finally, "If Reconstructionist eschatology is wrong, then their whole movement is misdirected about the present and their agenda should be redirected."[70] Why is this necessarily so? Does not God command us to be perfect in our daily living (Matt. 5:48), even though we *cannot* be perfect? Could it not be that God wants us to strive to do what is *right* (implement theonomic ethics), even if it would not be *universally successful* (as per postmillennialism)?

Summary

1. House and Ice admit to a number of positive contributions by Reconstructionists, despite their overall negative assault on Reconstructionism.

2. Though House and Ice have read much Reconstructionist literature, they have not read it carefully. This undermines the task they set out to accomplish.

3. Reconstructionism is easy to assault, because it is so rigorously biblical and our era is so infected with secular humanism — even in Christian thinking.

---

68. *Ibid.*, p. 278.
69. *Ibid.*, p. 283.
70. *Ibid.*, p. 301.

4. *Dominion Theology* evidences a widespread problem in much theological debate: careless mistakes and fallacious logical argument.

5. *Dominion Theology* is filled with contradictory statements that cause the work to be self-destructive.

6. House and Ice are carelessly imprecise in their use of terminology and argument, thus causing misunderstanding through unnecessary distortion.

7. House and Ice frequently engage in a fallacious style of argument when they appeal to emotions, particularly when these appeals are based on misinformation and misguided hypothetical projections.

8. House and Ice make a number of fallacious sweeping assertions in their presentation, which lead to overstatements.

9. House and Ice make certain technical failures in their research and analysis of a number of matters regarding issues both of theological understanding and historical fact.

10. House and Ice fall into *non sequitur* arguments that have a surface appearance of cogency, but when carefully considered fail of their intent.

18

DOCUMENTATION INADEQUACIES

An analysis and exposé of the various documentational inadequacies used in "Dominion Theology."

Although we commend House and Ice on their profuse employment of Reconstructionist literature, beyond this employment there are areas of significant dearth in terms of *original* source documentation. For instance, the significance of Chapter 5 of *Dominion Theology* is diminished by its sparse citation of original sources. This failure is particularly significant in that they are attempting to undermine the Reconstructionist historical arguments. Calvin, Luther, and the Puritans play prominently in the chapter, but the Puritans are never quoted from original sources, Calvin only twice, and Luther just once.

Though previously noted, we remind the reader of a serious charge against Reconstructionists — a charge that lacks one iota of documentary evidence, which House and Ice even admit! In discussing the criminal sanctions of the state in a "Reconstructed America" they write: "Most Reconstructionist descriptions of the ideal church follow conspicuously Reformed and especially Presbyterian formulas in areas of organizational structure and sacraments. The fate of any Christian unwilling to conform to those strictures is not stated. . . ."[1]

Assertion and secondary sources are not sufficient to carry the weight of their arguments. But beyond this they evidence the following problems.

---

1. H. Wayne House and Thomas Ice, *Dominion Theology: Blessing or Curse?* (Portland, OR: Multnomah, 1988), p. 72.

Careless Use of Sources

A major problem with dispensational works is their careless-ness in reading. For example, consider the notoriously erroneous assertions by Pentecost, Ryrie, and Walvoord (three leading dis-pensationalist theologians) that B. B. Warfield was an *amillennialist*, despite his being the leading postmillennialist of this century![2]

A terrifying implication is drawn before the reader through a careless use of Rushdoony. "Rushdoony declares that all who op-pose the law-order in a theonomic society, including criminals and dissidents, are at war with the law-order and with society. Nothing is more heinous in a theocratic society than to openly question the law-order. The legitimate institutions must therefore react with 'destruction' or other appropriate punishment to those with whom they are at war."[3] But it is interesting to check the Rushdoony source. Rushdoony is simply arguing that *all* law sys-tems have to have criminal penalties — as America's does even now — or else laws are suggestions.[4] In addition, Rushdoony spe-cifically says in that context: "The law specifically forbad reprisals against Egyptians or any other foreigner. . . . Israel was required to render justice to all Egyptians in terms of their individual obe-dience or disobedience to the law."[5]

In an attempted *reductio ad absurdum* House and Ice totally mis-use Rushdoony (their favorite target, next to Chilton): "Must men

---

2. See J. Dwight Pentecost, *Things to Come: A Study in Biblical Eschatology* (Grand Rapids, MI: Zondervan/Academie [1958] 1964), p. 387; Walvoord, "The Millennial Issue in Modern Theology," *Bibliotheca Sacra* (January, 1948), p. 430; Ryrie, *Basis of the Premillennial Faith*, p. 30. But that Warfield is clearly postmillen-nial see the Warfield articles in: John E. Meeter, ed., *Selected Shorter Writings of Benjamin B. Warfield* "The Gospel and the Second Coming," vol. 1 (pp. 349ff. [written: 1915]); "Jesus Christ the Propitiation for the Whole World" (pp. 167f. [1921]); "Antichrist" (pp. 356ff.). Also see articles in Warfield, *Biblical and Theological Studies* (Nutley, NJ: Presbyterian and Reformed, 1952): "Are There Few That Be Saved?" (pp. 334ff. [1915]); "The Prophecies of St. Paul" (pp. 463ff. [1886]) and Warfield, *The Saviour of the World* (Cherry Hill, NJ: Mack Publishing, rep. 1972 [n.d.]): "The Lamb of God," "God's Immeasurable Love," and "The Gospel of Paul."
3. House and Ice, *Dominion Theology*, p. 77.
4. Rousas John Rushdoony, *The Institutes of Biblical Law* (Nutley, NJ: Craig Press, 1973), pp. 92-94.
5. *Ibid.*, pp. 92-93.

wear Jewish borders and fringes on their garments, in strict obedience on Deuteronomy 22:11-12? Absolutely yes, says Rushdoony, to preserve unity and holiness."[6] *But Rushdoony says absolutely nothing of the kind!* A check of the very page in Rushdoony's *Institutes*, which they cite, clearly says of the "fringe law":

> It is *not* observed by Christians, because it was, like circumcision, the Sabbath, and other aspects of the Mosaic form of the covenant, superseded by new signs of the covenant as renewed by Christ. The law of the covenant remains; the covenant rites and signs have been changed.[7]

In addition they state regarding Rushdoony's views: "For the same reason, no one should be allowed to wear clothing of mixed material: such an 'unnatural union is to despise the order of God's creation.' "[8] Again, a careful reading of Rushdoony shows that he is merely giving an explanation of the meaning of this law *in its original context, for its original time!*[9] He sees certain principles of holiness undergirding the cultural expressions, but he does *not* argue for a literal, contemporary keeping of these cultural expressions.

Another unnecessary misreading of their sources is evidenced in the following statement and endnote observation: "The first major text to examine is Romans 6:14f. Bahnsen says that this passage is 'the most "sloganized" verse in the dispensationalist's polemic.' "[10] In a footnote they write: "Interestingly neither the Old nor the New Scofield nor the Ryrie Study Bible has a note on this verse."[11] Interesting, indeed! They are speaking of the "Romans 6:14f . . . passage" when they offer their observation. But both the *Scofield Reference Bible* and *The New Scofield Reference Bible* have a footnote *immediately* after Romans 6:14 and at the start of Romans 6:15, which simply repeats verse 14! Why did they bother making this unnecessary and erroneous observation?

A scholarly lapse of monumental proportions has to do with their argument regarding Irenaeus. After citing a particular *English*

---

6. House and Ice, *Dominion Theology*, p. 74.
7. Rushdoony, *Institutes*, p. 25 (emphasis in the original).
8. House and Ice, *Dominion Theology*, p. 74.
9. Rushdoony, *Institutes*, p. 87.
10. House and Ice, *Dominion Theology*, p. 113.
11. *Ibid.*, p. 121.

translation of Irenaeus, they comment: "Chilton questions whether [Irenaeus's] 'that was seen' refers to 'the apocalyptic vision' or to John himself. Since the impersonal pronoun 'that' is used we can assume that it refers to John's 'apocalyptic vision.' "[12] It is obvious that they are not even aware that in the original Greek of *Against Heresies*, there is no "impersonal pronoun 'that' "![13] The "that" which forms the basis of their argument is an English translator's interpolation! A careful, scholarly use of the original of Irenaeus would have preserved them from this embarrassment.

In summarizing the gist of J. M. Kik's *An Eschatology of Victory*, House and Ice state that: "He seeks to establish and defend the second coming as having occurred in A.D. 70 in the destruction of Jerusalem."[14] But Kik does *nothing of the kind!* He clearly states in his work that the Second Coming is a future event, which is dealt with in Matthew 24:36ff.[15]

In a major point in their argument, House and Ice assert that Whitby was the "founder" of postmillennialism,[16] but the two sources they quote to back this up merely say he "popularized" it (John J. Davis) and gave it "its most influential formulation" (Robert Clouse).[17] Apparently they have never read Whitby. Had they read the article they would note that the view he is presenting is not newly created by himself, for he expressly states he picked up on it from "the best commentators."[18] And House and Ice even quote titles of books showing postmillennialism's existence in the mid-1600s. As their own quotations show, Whitby was influential in "popularizing" postmillennialism because it represented postmil-

---

12. *Ibid.*, p. 251.

13. See Kenneth L. Gentry, Jr., *Before Jerusalem Fell: Dating the Book of Revelation* (Tyler, TX: Institute for Christian Economics, 1989), pp. 46ff., for the Greek text.

14. House and Ice, *Dominion Theology*, p. 442.

15. See Kik's chapter entitled: "No Personal Coming During the Siege." Kik writes: "With verse 36 Christ commences a new subject, namely, his second coming," J. Marcellus Kik, *An Eschatology of Victory* (Nutley, NJ: Presbyterian and Reformed, 1971), p. 67.

16. House and Ice, *Dominion Theology*, p. 206.

17. *Ibid.*, p. 209.

18. Daniel Whitby, "A Treatise on the True Millennium," in Patrick, Lowth, Arnald, Whitby, and Lowman, *Commentary on the Gospels and Epistles of the New Testament*, 4 vols. (Philadelphia: Carey and Hart, 1845), vol. 4, p. 1118.

lennialism's "most influential formulation."[19] They even note that John Calvin (1509-1564) "paved the way for the full flowering of the postmillennial view in English Puritanism."[20] Whitby was simply *not* the founder of postmillennialism.

An horrendous misreading of Chilton appears in conjunction with a sweeping assertion mentioned previously: "*Most* dominion theology adherents, when challenged to defend the second coming, do not cite Scripture as the basis for their belief; rather they cite the voice of mother church"?[21] They cite only *one* example — Chilton, whom they quote: "Historic, orthodox Christianity everywhere, with one voice, has always taught that Christ 'shall come again, with glory, to judge both the living and the dead' (Nicene Creed). This is a non-negotiable article of the Christian faith."[22]

To arrive at the mistaken conclusion that "most dominion theology adherents" defend the Second Coming by citing "the voice of mother church" rather than Scripture by use of Chilton's quotation reveals either an incredible incompetence in dealing with sources or malice aforethought. On page 264 of his *Days of Vengeance* (where the statement House and Ice use is found) Chilton is warning that there are some who claim to be consistent preterists and who deny the Second Coming. In a footnote he says: "See, e.g., Max R. King *The Spirit of Prophecy* (n.p. 1971). While King's work has a great deal of value for the discerning student, its ultimate thesis — that there is no future Coming of Christ or Final Judgment — is heretical. Historic, orthodox Christianity everywhere, with one voice has always taught that Christ 'shall come again, with glory, to judge both the living and the dead' (Nicene Creed). This is a non-negotiable article of the Christian faith." He is merely pointing out the historical fact that King is at odds with historic Christianity. Chilton elsewhere points to Scripture for a defense of the Second Coming. In fact, in House and Ice's endnote, which appears at the end of the very statement in question, we read:

---

19. House and Ice, *Dominion Theology*, p. 209.
20. *Ibid.*, p. 209, citing John J. Davis.
21. *Ibid.*, p. 269 (emphasis mine).
22. *Ibid.*

"Chilton apparently does think that 1 Corinthians 15:51-54 and 1 Thessalonians 4:14-17 are passages teaching the second coming (*Paradise Restored*, 147-8)."[23]

Now what if we employed this tactic against House and Ice? They state: "Premillennialism was the pervasive view of the earliest orthodox fathers."[24] What if we quoted this statement and then boldly stated: "*Most* dispensational theology adherents, when challenged to defend the second coming, do not cite Scripture as the basis for their belief; rather they cite the voice of mother church"? Elsewhere they state: "We believe the futurist interpretation is the correct interpretive grid, as the discussion that follows will help show. The futurist interpretation is the approach used by the earliest church fathers."[25] After all, it is interesting that these two sentences are the first point in answering the question of the subheading: "Why a Futurist Interpretation"! Would we be justified in saying: "*Most* futurists, when challenged to defend the futurism, do not cite Scripture as the basis for their belief; rather they cite the voice of mother church"?

Partial Citations

Although space limitations always require one's quoting only a portion of an argument, the problem of partial citations becomes epidemic in House and Ice.

They cite a portion of a Rushdoony argument, which deals with the creation mandate given to Adam in Genesis 1, when they write: "Regarding the original covenant, theonomists assert, 'There is not one word of Scripture to indicate or imply that this mandate was ever revoked. There is every word of Scripture to declare that this mandate must and shall be be [sic] fulfilled.' "[26] In the endnote they scathingly denounce Rushdoony by saying: "He cites no such declarative Scripture to support this claim."[27]

---

23. *Ibid.*, p. 282.
24. *Ibid.*, p. 202.
25. *Ibid.*, p. 275.
26. *Ibid.*, pp. 31-32.
27. *Ibid.*, p. 41.

But it is most interesting that Rushdoony's citation is cut off. The next words, which they did not quote, were "and 'scripture cannot be broken,' according to Jesus (John 10:35)." Rushdoony *did* cite Scripture! Besides that, *they themselves* state that this covenant has never been revoked: "The Cultural Mandate has not been withdrawn since its giving and restatement as the Noahic Covenant in Genesis (1:28-30; 9:1-3)"![28]

Later they attempt to undermine the Reconstructionist mission by defining the Greek word translated "expose" in Ephesians 5:11: "The Greek word *elegchete* translated 'expose' in Ephesians 5:11 means 'to show someone his sin and to summon him to repentance.' We are to give the biblical perspective on 'the unfruitful deeds of darkness' so that a person will repent of sin and leave the kingdom of darkness. Paul had a perfect opportunity to tell the troops to get out and Christianize the darkness, but he did not."[29] Their endnote shows they were quoting from the *Theological Dictionary of the New Testament* for support. But TDNT goes on to say: "The word does not mean only 'to blame' or 'to reprove,' nor 'to convince' in the sense of proof, nor 'to reveal' or 'expose,' but 'to set right,' namely, 'to point away from sin to repentance.' It implies educative discipline."[30] This fuller quotation would have undermined their argument, which limited the word to a summons to repentance.

Summary

1. Dispensationalists have a tendency to set up systems they intend to rebut, by citing from secondary sources.

2. When possible, secondary sources should be avoided in negative critiques because of the risk of unfairness. *Dominion Theology* reduces its effectiveness by use of secondary sources at critical junctures.

---

28. *Ibid.*, p. 159.
29. *Ibid.*, p. 155.
30. Friedrich Buschsel, *"elegcho,"* in *Theological Dictionary of the New Testament*, Gerhard Kittel, ed., Geoffery W. Bromiley, trans., 10 vols. (Grand Rapids: Eerdmans, 1964), vol 2, p. 474.

3. House and Ice frequently evidence an extremely careless use of original sources, which promotes a distorted view of Reconstructionism. This is easy for Reconstructionists to expose, but a dangerous practice in that exposures of such errors will not be read by all who read *Dominion Theology*.

4. All research publication requires a use of partial citations of documents, but partial citations should not distort the intent of the author. House and Ice frequently distort Reconstructionist views by partial citation.

19

ETHICAL LAPSES

An analysis and exposé of the various moral failures in "Dominion Theology."

Many of House and Ice's ethical lapses have to do with misrepresentations of Reconstructionist statements. These appear to be deliberate attempts to set forth a "straw man," though they express a disdain for a "straw man" polemic.[1]

Regarding Reconstructionist concerns, House and Ice compare Reconstructionism to the "failed" Puritan experiment and note of its revival: "It is being imitated today by a small and increasingly influential group of persons who believe that only through the establishment and enforcement of Old Testament civil law can America — and the world — be saved from destruction."[2] This assertion paints Reconstructionists as virtually being Ebionitic, concerned only with the Old Testament law, even to the exclusion of the New Testament. They, however, know that this is not true, for later they state: "The law we are to follow is seen by theonomists as broader than the Mosaic code, and includes consideration of all biblical revelation. . . . Reconstructionists are not hesitant to say that God's instructions cannot be limited to the Mosaic law. Rushdoony states that 'the Biblical concept of law is broader than the legal codes of the Mosaic formulation. It applies to the divine word and instruction in its totality.' "[3] Later they write that Reconstructionists "make all the law of Scripture a generic whole

---

1. H. Wayne House and Thomas Ice, *Dominion Theology: Blessing or Curse?* (Portland, OR: Multnomah, 1988), p. 266.
2. *Ibid.*, p. 15.
3. *Ibid.*, p. 35.

311

they call 'Biblical law.' "[4]

Misrepresentations

They totally misrepresent a Jim Jordan statement in another setting: "Premillennialists plead guilty to the desire to have 'a top-down' kingdom. . . . In fact, fellow Reconstructionist James Jordan . . . favors the top-down approach: 'American (evangelicals) like to believe the myth that society is transformed from the bottom up and not from the top down. This flies squarely in the face both of history and of Scripture.' "[5] But Jordan is shocked at their employment of his quotation: "On p. 237 they quote me out of context to make it appear that I believe in a 'top-down' takeover of society, while North believes in a 'bottom-up' approach. Had they read my remarks in context they would have seen that I was speaking of *influence*, not conquest. People follow leaders. No one disputes this. North was speaking of conquest. There is no contradiction between what he wrote and what I wrote, read in context. See Jordan, *The Sociology of the Church* [1986], pp. 17ff."[6]

Elsewhere we read them stating: "With their belief that ultimate victory is assured (the church will set up a theocratic government, will evangelize the world, and will usher in the earthly reign of Christ). . . ."[7] Both the order and manner of their statement in the quotation are significant: They assert, first, that the "church" (not Christians in society) "will set up a theocratic government"! Then (after setting up a theocratic government?) it "will evangelize the world." This clearly suggests an appalling misplacement of priority for the "Church" by Reconstructionists, and leaves the distinct impression, with other of their statements and innuendos,[8] of a Reconstructionist evangelism by the sword!

And they make these statements despite the fact Reconstruc-

---

4. *Ibid.*, p. 184.
5. *Ibid.*, p. 237.
6. James B. Jordan, "A Review of H. Wayne House and Thomas Ice, *Dominion Theology: Blessing or Curse?: An Analysis of Christian Reconstructionism*" (Tyler, TX: Biblical Horizons, 1988), p. 12.
7. House and Ice, *Dominion Theology*, p. 21-22.
8. For example, *ibid.*, pp. 77-80.

tionists have insisted on the priority of evangelism.[9] Gary North forthrightly states that

> We who call ourselves Christian Reconstructionists proclaim a future worldwide revival and the steady, voluntary submission of people to God's law. We believe that Christians will steadily *be given* responsibilities, but not through revolution or tyranny. Instead, He will give us these responsibilities in history through the voluntary submission of those who have no other hope, and who (until that final rebellion of Revelation 20) will be willing to allow Christians to bear these social, political, military, and economic responsibilities.[10]

They continue on in their repeated misrepresentation: "The Reconstructionist theonomists do not eliminate the state, either, though such a distinction appears superficial. The theonomic ideal is that the institutional church and the state are to be autonomous, coequal spheres within a theocentric context. In practice, however, the clergy would determine that theological context; anything else would risk doctrinal anarchy, or at least instances of conflict and crisis. The primacy of the visible church would be essential in areas of open heresy or false teaching. The reality is that in these and other instances the state becomes merely an extension of both the invisible *and the visible* church."[11]

They wrongfully accuse Bahnsen of carelessly throwing around the term "antinomian": "Bahnsen's relegation to antinomianism of all persons who reject his view is oversimplistic reductionism."[12] They say that this relegation is "the underlying assumption of [Bahnsen's] whole book," but that it especially may be seen in his "second preface, xi-xix, and 251ff."[13] Here again, they woefully misrepresent a Reconstructionist writer. Bahnsen does *not* categorize

---

9. See for example "the patriarch of Reconstructionism" (*ibid.*, p. 45), R. J. Rushdoony, *Institutes of Biblical Law* (Nutley, NJ: The Craig Press, 1973), pp. 113, 122, 147, 163, 308, 413, 449, 627, 780. Rushdoony frequently points to the priority of evangelism.

10. Preface to David Chilton's, *The Great Tribulation* (Ft. Worth, TX: Dominion Press, 1987), p. xiii.

11. House and Ice, *Dominion Theology*, p. 93.

12. *Ibid.*, p. 85.

13. *Ibid.*, p. 41, n4.

"all persons who reject his view" as "antinomians." When Bahnsen speaks of latent antinomians, he identifies such as those who reject various portions of God's Word *without Scriptural warrant.*

By misrepresenting what Chilton actually says, House and Ice wrongly accuse him of mishandling Scripture: "This mishandling of history also influences Chilton's handling of the Bible; he interprets those passages that speak of a future reign of Christ in light of his misunderstanding of history. Chilton says at the beginning of his chapter on Revelation 20 that one must have the proper historical understanding before engaging in exegesis: 'If we wish to gain an understanding of the orthodox position, we must understand that the answer to this precise question cannot be determined *primarily* by the exegesis of particular texts.' Historical understanding is an aid to correct interpretation, but the exegesis of the text is the *most essential* ingredient for gaining a proper understanding of the Bible on any subject."[14]

Anyone reading their summation would think that Chilton's interpretation of Scripture is always through the door of historical analysis, despite exegesis. But Chilton is simply answering an interesting historical question, which he himself clearly and innocently poses in the first sentence on the page containing House and Ice's quoted sentence. His inquiry is: "What is the position of the historic, orthodox Church on the question of the Millennium?"[15] The question he is answering is not: "What is the proper understanding of Revelation 20?" He clearly sets up a historical, not an interpretive question. He does not interpret "those passages that speak of a future reign of Christ in light of his misunderstanding of history."[16] He is at that point dealing only with a matter of history; he is not saying anyone must accept what is the history of the interpretation!

Premillennialism

Another misrepresentation is used to make Chilton look foolish and arrogant: "Chilton more specifically charges that premil-

---

14. *Ibid.*, p. 211.
15. David Chilton, *The Days of Vengeance: An Exposition of the Book of Revelation* (Ft. Worth: Dominion Press, 1987), p. 493.
16. House and Ice, *Dominion Theology*, p. 211.

lennialism 'seems to have been originated by the Ebionite arch-heretic Cerinthus, a "false apostle."' This charge *cannot in any way* be supported; it is a *pure fabrication*. There are *no records from church history* that lead to such a conclusion. Chilton needs to *find a historian outside of his own camp* who will support his claim."[17] Now what is the reader of House and Ice's work to think of Chilton? House and Ice clearly lead the reader to stand aghast at Chilton's reckless charge. They state that the "charge cannot in any way be supported," that it is "pure fabrication" from Chilton, that "there are no records from church history" supportive of it, and that there is no "historian outside of his own camp" who agrees with it. In all humility we must respond that this is nothing less than blatant, intentional falsehood, for in the same paragraph as Chilton's statement quoted by House and Ice, Chilton provides source documentation from church father Eusebius to substantiate his claim! There Chilton writes: "For an account of Cerinthus and his heresies, see . . . Eusebius, *Ecclesiastical History*, iii.xxvii.1-6; iv.xiv.6; vii.xxv.2-3."

Now, whether or not that which "seems" to be the case to Chilton is true, the fact of the matter is *he does have footing in history to ponder the possibility*. In Eusebius (A.D. 260-340), "the father of Church history," we read a statement he has gotten from his predecessor Caius of Rome (fl. A.D. 200-220): "But Cerinthus also, by means of revelations which he pretends were written by a great apostle, brings before us marvelous things which he falsely claims were shown him by angels; and he says that after the resurrection the kingdom of Christ will be set up on earth, and that the flesh dwelling in Jerusalem will again be subject to desires and pleasures. And being an enemy of the Scriptures of God, he asserts, with the purpose of deceiving men, that there is to be a period of a thousand years for marriage festivals."[18] Whether or not Caius and Eusebius were wrong, the point remains: There are at least two

---

17. *Ibid.*, p. 197 (emphasis mine).
18. Eusebius, *Ecclesiastical History* 3:28:1-2. See also: 7:25:3: "Cerinthus . . . founded the sect which was called after him the Cerinthian. . . . For the doctrine which he taught was this: that the kingdom of Christ will be an earthly one. . . ."

ancient historical charges that Cerinthus (*ca.* A.D. 100) originated the doctrine. Chilton did *not* personally fabricate the charge; it can be supported from antiquity. The readers would never suspect that, as they scoffed at Chilton upon reading House and Ice. In addition, despite House and Ice's assertions to the contrary, there are other historians outside of Chilton's Reconstructionist "camp" that suggest the same. W. G. T. Shedd (1820-1894) writes of premillennialism: "It appears first in the system of the Judaistic-Gnostic *Cerinthus.*"[19] Even dispensationalist, Dallas Seminary-trained Patrick Boyd calls Cerinthus "the earliest chiliast"[20] — though he obviously would not grant that Cerinthus created premillennialism. He cites other historians pointing to Cerinthus thus: V. Ermoni and Hans Bietenhard. We could also cite amillennialists W. J. Grier and Louis Berkhof,[21] as well as Schaff's *Religious Encyclopaedia*: "The ultimate root of millenarianism is the popular notion of the Messiah current among the Jews. . . . It is found in Cerinthus (Eusebius, *Eccl. Hist.*, 3:28; 7:25), in the *Testaments of the Twelve Patriarchs* (Jud., *ca.* 25; Benjam., *ca.* 10), and amongst the Ebionites (Jerome, *In Jes.*, 40:1, 66:20)."[22]

Origins of Postmillennialism

Postmillennialists are put down by House and Ice as those who operate theologically in a reckless fashion, rather than seeking to understand Scripture: "Whitby and his modern followers present their arguments and explanations based upon unproved assumptions — assumptions resulting in a hypothesis rather than something which is the fruit of the study of Scripture or even the voice of the church."[23] This reference to "unproved assumptions" is based solely on a reference by Whitby to "a new hypothesis."

19. W. G. T. Shedd, *A History of Christian Doctrine*, 2 vols. (9th ed.; Minneapolis: Klock and Klock, [1889] 1978), vol. 2, pp. 390-91.

20. Alan Patrick Boyd, "Dispensational Premillennial Analysis of the Eschatology of the Post-Apostolic Fathers (Until the Death of Justin Martyr)," unpublished master's thesis, Dallas Theological Seminary, 1977, p. 17.

21. W. J. Grier, *The Momentous Event* (Edinburgh: Banner of Truth, 1970 [1945]), p. 26 and Louis Berkhof, *The History of Christian Doctrines* (Grand Rapids, MI: Baker Book House, [1937] 1975), p. 262.

22. Philip Schaff, *A Religious Encyclopedia: Or Dictionary of Biblical, Historical, Doctrinal, and Practical Theology* (New York: Funk and Wagnalls, 1883), vol. 3, pp. 1514-15.

23. House and Ice, *Dominion Theology*, p. 209.

From Whitby's statement they disclaim all legitimacy of postmillennialism, as if all postmillennialists follow Whitby and his "new hypothesis."

Impugning of Motives

House and Ice are so bent on portraying Reconstructionism in a bad light that they even stoop to a form of psychoanalysis in determining why so many are becoming Reconstructionists: "I believe many are attracted to the dominion position because they have an agenda, such as politics or social reform, for which they believe Reconstructionism provides the vision to lead them to success. . . . *Most* are attracted to dominion theology through the back door, rather than through the front door of biblical study."[24] They make this statement on the basis of bare assertion: they present no statistics, or exit polls from persons entering Reconstructionist bookstores, or anything of the sort.

They do so again regarding Chilton's preterism: "Perhaps the real reason Chilton has chosen the preterist approach, since most postmillennialists have not been preterists, is that it is the most antipremillennialist interpretative option on the market."[25] Here Chilton is portrayed as a malcontent seeking *anything* that is as far away from premillennialism as possible.

Poisoning the Well

In the very Preface of the book, House and Ice begin poisoning the well by suggesting that Reconstructionism is antithetical to biblical Christianity. With a personal testimony Ice speaks of his turning away from Reconstructionism to Scripture: "Once I realized the antithesis of the two positions, I had to side with Scripture and leave behind Reconstructionism."[26]

Almost as early in their book, they introduce what theonomy means to Reconstructionists. As they begin, they immediately

---

24. *Ibid.*, pp. 9-10 (emphasis mine).
25. *Ibid.*, p. 275.
26. *Ibid.*, p. 9.

point to supposed negative factors of Reconstructionism, with such foreboding statements as: "if Reconstructionists succeed," "Bahnsen was forced to resign from Reformed Seminary's faculty," "a respected professor at Westminster Seminary, calls Bahnsen's *Theonomy* 'a delusive and grotesque perversion of the teachings of Scripture.' "[27] Far preferable to this sort of treatment was Carl F. H. Henry's most charitable evaluation of Bahnsen's *Theonomy in Christian Ethics*. Henry wrote: "By a wealth of biblical data Greg L. Bahnsen establishes that God's commands impose universal moral obligation; that God's ethical standards ought universally to inform civil legislation; that civil magistrates are ideally to enforce God's social commands and that Christians are involved in covenantal use of divine law."[28] And though he disagrees with certain theonomic distinctives, there is no reference to its grotesqueness.

Guilt by Association

House and Ice attempt to tie postmillennialism to Daniel Whitby in such a way as to discredit postmillennial eschatology. We cite again a statement rehearsed above: "Whitby and his modern followers present their arguments and explanations based upon unproved assumptions — assumptions resulting in a hypothesis rather than something which is the fruit of the study of Scripture or even the voice of the church."[29] It is one thing to point to Whitby as one who carefully systematized postmillennialism, as some do. It is quite another to aver that postmillennialists follow lock-step Whitby's "unproved assumptions," which are not "the fruit of the study of Scripture."

There is an intense effort to pull Reconstructionism to the ocean floor with the millstone of charismatic extremism: "The reason these two [charismatic and Reconstructionist] movements

---

27. *Ibid.*, pp. 27-28.
28. Carl F. H. Henry, *God, Revelation and Authority*, 6 vols. (Waco, Texas: Word Books, 1983), vol. 6, p. 447.
29. House and Ice, *Dominion Theology*, p. 209.

are coming together is simple. They both believe that if a theology is positive, then it must be right. Charismatics have optimism which is applied to their personal life, while Reconstructionists have stressed social optimism."[30] They make this statement despite the fact they had just quoted on the preceding page a statement by Gary North: "If all a person gains from the Christian Reconstruction movement in general is its optimistic eschatology, then he is skating on thin ice. Optimism is not enough. In fact, optimism alone is highly dangerous."[31]

They also state regarding another charismatic leader: "Paulk, like Reconstructionists, does not believe that Israel and the church are distinct entities within God's single plan: 'I believe that references to Israel in Scripture refer both to natural Israel as well as to the Church. . . .' This is another similarity between Reconstructionists and charismatics."[32] This sounds suspiciously like they are doing what they preach against, for earlier they disavowed a Chilton argument regarding Irenaeus thus: "Chilton's approach is nothing more than a debater's technique. When you do not have strong reasons against something then you try to cast doubt upon the reliability of the source."[33] Nevertheless, the view specifically cited (which Paulk apparently holds, as well) is stock-in-trade confessional, Reformed theology; for instance, John Calvin commented on Galatians 6:16 thus: "In a word, he now calls them the Israel of God whom he formerly named the children of Abra-

---

30. *Ibid.*, p. 377. I would like to note that as a Reconstructionist I have authored two works on the errors of the charismatic movement and was involved in a Presbyterian Church in America decision disavowing a major feature of the movement. See Gentry, *Crucial Issues Regarding Tongues* (Mauldin, SC: GoodBirth Publications, 1982) and *The Charismatic Gift of Prophecy: A Reformed Analysis* (Lakeland, FL: Whitefield Seminary Press, 1986). See also: "Gentry, et al., vs. Calvary Presbytery," *Minutes of the Fourteenth General Assembly of the Presbyterian Church in America*, Philadelphia (June 23-27, 1986), pp. 224, 230-31. In addition, I cannot see how dispensationalists can, on the basis of their system, resist tongues-speaking today, in light of their futuristic approach to Joel 2/Acts 2, which justifies tongues as an indicator of the "last days."

31. House and Ice, *Dominion Theology*, p. 376.

32. *Ibid.*, p. 379.

33. *Ibid.*, p. 252.

ham by faith, and thus includes all believers, whether Gentiles or Jews, who were united in the same Church. On the other hand, the Israel of the flesh can claim only the name and the race. . . ."[34]

Too Broad a Tar Brush

In Appendix A the authors attempt to bring together the heretical charismatic cult known as the "Manifest Sons of God" and Reconstructionism by comparing under fourteen separate headings citations of Reconstructionists with those by adherents to the cult. Yet they confess "Reconstructionists are well within the stream of historic, Christian orthodoxy. They believe in the Trinity, the inerrancy of Scripture, the deity and humanity of Jesus, total depravity, salvation by grace through faith, and godliness in the Christian walk. They are orthodox, Reformed Calvinists in most areas of theology."[35] In point of fact, the issues they point to are quite innocent items held by all sorts of evangelicals — many of them even by dispensationalists! Let us cite *their* major points, with *their* Manifest Sons documentation, and then supply dispensational and/or evangelical quotes in the place where they had Reconstructionist statements. The error of such triviality will become readily evident.

"1. Adam's Lost Dominion.

"MSOG: 'Some believe that when Adam and Eve committed "grand treason" and lost dominion over the earth. . . .' *Reconstructionist:* 'Why doesn't God seem to own [the earth] now? Why are

---

34. John Calvin, *Galatians, Ephesians, Philippians, and Colossians* in David W. Torrance and Thomas F. Torrance, eds., *Calvin's New Testament Commentaries*, 12 vols. (Grand Rapids, MI: Wm. B. Eerdmans, 1965), vol. 11, p. 118. "The New Testament evidently regards the Church as the spiritual counterpart of the Old Testament Jerusalem, and therefore applies to it the same name," L. Berkhof, *Systematic Theology* (Grand Rapids, MI: Wm. B. Eerdmans, 1941), p. 558, cp. pp. 571ff. See also Charles Hodge, *Systematic Theology*, 3 vols. (Grand Rapids, MI: Wm. B. Eerdmans, [1873] 1973), vol. 3, pp. 549-52; J. A. Alexander, *Commentary on the Prophecies of Isaiah*, (Grand Rapids, MI: Zondervan, [1875] 1954), p. 71.

35. House and Ice, *Dominion Theology*, p. 384.

some areas of life seemingly under the exclusive control of Satan, the evil one? Because Adam sold his birthright to Satan.' "[36]

Dispensationalist Hal Lindsey: "When man rebelled, the world was legally handed over to Satan. Adam actually became the Benedict Arnold of the universe. When he obeyed Satan, he turned the title deed of himself, all his dominion, and all his descendants over to Satan."[37]

"2. Dominion over the Earth.

"MSOG: 'God's people are going to start to exercise rule, and they're going to take dominion over the power of Satan.' 'We are rulers of this planet — it's time we take over!' "[38]

Premillennialist George E. Ladd: "Christ is now reigning from heaven as God's vice regent. The reign of Christ has as its goal the subjugation of every hostile power. . . . The New Testament does not make the reign of Christ one that is limited to Israel in the millennium."[39]

B. B. Warfield: "It is the distinction of Christianity that it has come into the world clothed with the mission to *reason* its way to its dominion. . . . And it is solely by reasoning that it has come thus far on its way to its kingship. And it is solely by reasoning that it will put all its enemies under its feet."[40]

"3. Kingdom Now.

"MSOG: 'Scripture teaches that the Kingdom of God is always now.' "[41]

Premillennialist Ladd: "Christ is now reigning from heaven as God's vice regent. . . . The New Testament does not make the reign of Christ one that is limited to Israel in the millennium."[42]

---

36. *Ibid.*, p. 385.
37. Hal Lindsey, *Satan Is Alive and Well on Planet Earth* (Grand Rapids, MI: Zondervan, 1972), p. 62.
38. House and Ice, *Dominion Theology*, p. 385.
39. George E. Ladd, in Clouse, *The Meaning of the Millennium*, p. 29.
40. B. B. Warfield, *Selected Shorter Writings*, ed. by John E. Meeter, 2 vols. (Nutley, NJ: Presbyterian and Reformed, 1973 [article from 1903]), vol. 2, pp. 99-100.
41. House and Ice, *Dominion Theology*, p. 385.
42. Ladd, in Clouse, *The Meaning of the Millennium*, p. 29.

Dispensationalist John S. Feinberg: "One need not deny the kingdom's presence in some sense in this age . . . ."[43]

"4. Bringing in or Establishing the Kingdom.

"MSOG: 'The kingdoms of this world must become the Kingdoms of our God. And we are the ones to do it!. . . . I want to . . . see the Kingdom of God established NOW! We will learn how to literally take over a city.' "[44]

B. B. Warfield: "The whole dispensation in which we are living . . . stretches from the First to the Second Advent, as a period of advancing conquest on the part of Christ. . . . In this case, the prophecy promises the universal Christianization of the world. . . . The period between the two advents is the period of Christ's kingdom, and when He comes again it is not to institute His kingdom, but to lay it down. . . . We can only say that if the reigning of the saints refers to a co-reigning with Christ (cf. II Tim. ii. 12), it must be fulfilled before Christ lays down His kingdom. . . . Christians are His soldiers in this holy war, and it is through our victory that His victory is known."[45]

"5. Israel.

"MSOG: 'There is no more old covenant with Israel, and there never will be.' "[46]

Premillennialist Ladd: "I do not keep Israel and the church distinct throughout God's program. . . ."[47] "What then of the detailed promises in the Old Testament of a restored temple? . . . It is inconceivable that God's redemptive plan will revert to the age of shadows. . . . The salvation of Israel must be through the new covenant made in the blood of Christ already established with the church, not through a rebuilt Jewish temple with a revival of the

---

43. John S. Feinberg, *Continuity and Discontinuity* (Westchester, IL: Crossway Books, 1988), p. 68.

44. House and Ice, *Dominion Theology*, pp. 385-86.

45. B. B. Warfield, *Biblical and Theological Studies* (Philadelphia, PA: Presbyterian and Reformed, [1886] 1952), pp. 485, 486, 487, 490, 493.

46. House and Ice, *Dominion Theology*, p. 386.

47. Ladd, in Clouse, *Meaning of the Millennium*, p. 20.

Mosaic sacrificial system. Hebrews flatly affirms that the whole Mosaic system is obsolete and about to pass away. Therefore the popular Dispensational position that Israel is the 'clock of prophecy' is misguided."[48]

"6. Restoration.

"MSOG: 'We do not live in the time of the great falling away. We are leaving that day and entering a new day, a new age, a new beginning of life and restoration.' "[49]

B. B. Warfield: John "teaches the salvation of the world through a process; it may be — it has proved to be — a long process; but it is a process which shall reach its goal. . . . We are a 'little flock' now: tomorrow we shall be the world. We are but the beginnings: the salvation of the world is the end."[50]

"7. The Rapture.

"MSOG: 'Some are also anti-rapture — rather than go to heaven. God's Army of Overcomers will establish the Kingdom of God on earth.' "[51]

Warfield (see above on #4).

"8. Breakthroughs/New Revelation.

"MSOG: 'The offices of apostle and prophet have the anointing to perceive and proclaim new revelation truth. The apostle and prophet have the ministry to establish and lay the foundation for new truth in the Church. . . . Once an apostle or prophet receives by the spirit a new restorational truth and establishes it as a valid ministry then the teacher teaches it in detail.' "[52]

House and Ice: "By the 1830s J. N. Darby began teaching that the timing of the Rapture would be pretribulational."[53]

---

48. George E. Ladd, *The Last Things* (Grand Rapids, MI: Wm. B. Eerdmans, 1978), p. 25.
49. House and Ice, *Dominion Theology,* p. 386.
50. Warfield, *Selected Shorter Writings* [article from 1921], vol. 1, pp. 176-77.
51. House and Ice, *Dominion Theology,* p. 387.
52. *Ibid.,* pp. 386-87.
53. *Ibid.,* p. 422.

Dave Hunt: "For at least 200 years, prophecy students had identified Russia, long before it became a world military power, as the leader of a biblically prophesied confederacy of nations that would attack Israel in the last days."[54]

A. J. Gordon: "Gordon believed the Bible taught a long period of apostasy separated the First and Second comings — a period concealed from believers in former ages but revealed to believers in modern times by the symbols and chronology of Daniel and Revelation. Therefore, he argued that only the final generation, which knew the long interval was drawing to a close, are [sic] justified on scriptural grounds in believing that Christ *could* come for them at any moment."[55]

"9. The Second Coming.

"MSOG: 'Jesus Christ has now done all He can do, and He waits at the right hand of His Father, until you and I as sons of God, become manifest and make this world His footstool. He is waiting for us to say, "Jesus, we have made the kingdoms of this world the Kingdom of our God, and we are ruling and reigning in Your world." ' "[56]

Warfield (see above at #4).

"Onward Christian Soldiers" (Hymn: 1864): "Onward, Christian soldiers,/ Marching as to war,/ With the cross of Jesus/ Going on before:/ Christ the royal Master/ leads against the foe;/ Forward into battle,/ See, His banners go./ Like a mighty army/ Moves the Church of God. . . . Crowns and thrones may perish,/ Kingdoms rise and wane,/ But the Church of Jesus/ Constant will remain;/ Gates of hell can never/ 'Gainst that Church prevail;/ We have Christ's own promise,/ And that cannot fail."

"10. The Manifest Sons of God.

"MSOG: 'Jesus Christ has now done all He can do, and He waits at the right hand of His Father, until you and I as sons of

---

54. Dave Hunt, *Whatever Happened to Heaven?* (Portland, OR: Harvest House, 1988), p. 65.

55. Cited by Richard R. Reiter in Archer, et al., *The Rapture: Pre-, Mid-, or Post-Tribulational?* (Grand Rapids, MI: Zondervan/Academie, 1984), p. 14.

56. House and Ice, *Dominion Theology*, p. 387.

God, become manifest and make this world His footstool. The true Body of Christ, which is the True Church, will eventually become mature and be manifested as God's great family of Sons.' "[57]

Warfield (see also above #4): "At the end of the day there will stand out in the sight of all a whole world, for the sins of which Christ's blood has made effective expiation, and for which he stands as Advocate before the Father."[58]

"11. The Curse Removed.

"*MSOG:* 'When the church becomes so conformed to His image that those who die do not pass through the grave, but become instead gloriously changed in the twinkling of an eye, it will be that church which will bring the Kingdom of God to pass on the earth. . . . Death will not be conquered by Jesus returning to earth. It will be conquered when the church stands up boldly and says, "We have dominion over the earth!' "[59]

Comment: This comparison does not even have a similarity to Reconstructionist thought: physical death is the *last* enemy and will be conquered only at Christ's Second Coming.

"12. The Church as Spiritual/New Israel.

"*MSOG:* 'The church today is Spiritual Israel.' "[60]

Premillennialist Ladd: "The idea of the Church as spiritual Israel is seen in other passages" and "the New Testament . . . identifies the church as spiritual Israel."[61]

Justin Martyr: It is interesting that House and Ice favorably quote Justin Martyr as an early premillennialist, but he says: "As, therefore, Christ is the Israel and the Jacob, even so we, who have been quarried out from the bowels of Christ, are the true Israelitic race. . . ."[62]

---

57. *Ibid.*, p. 387.
58. Warfield, *Selected Shorter Writings*, vol. 1, p. 177.
59. House and Ice, *Dominion Theology*, p. 388.
60. *Ibid.*
61. Ladd, in Clouse, *Meaning of the Millennium*, pp. 24, 21. See also Ladd, *The Last Things*, p. 23.
62. Justin Martyr, *Dialogue with Trypho* 135.

"13. Unity of the Church.

"MSOG: 'When we reach the place where our total beings are devoted to this truth, and we are all hearing the same voice of God, we will be able to demonstrate to the world that we have transcended our doctrinal differences and are witnesses to the unity of the faith, that will bring about the establishment of the Kingdom of God. This is what God has called us to do.' "63

B. B. Warfield: "The prophecy promises the universal Christianization of the world."64

"14. Covenant Theology.

"MSOG: 'In almost any Christian bookstore, about 99% of the books will say that "God's timeclock is Israel" and that "God's covenant is still with Israel." There is no comprehension that, according to God's Word, the old covenant is dead and gone and the new covenant is with the people who accept Jesus Christ as Lord and Saviour. Whatever has been written concerning the law and prophecies about Israel as a nation is now transferred to spiritual Israel, which is the people of God.' "65

Premillennialist Ladd (also see above #5): "Old Testament concepts are radically reinterpreted and given an unforeseen application. What in the Old Testament applies to literal Israel, in Romans 9:25 applies to the church, which consists not only of Jews but also of Gentiles." "It follows inescapably that the salvation of the Gentile church is the fulfillment of prophecies made to Israel." "It is difficult to see how anyone can deny that the new covenant of Jeremiah 31 is the new covenant made by Christ with his church."66

A Taste of Their Own Medicine

But what if *we* did such a comparison of dispensationalism

---

63. House and Ice, *Dominion Theology*, p. 389.
64. B. B. Warfield, *Biblical and Theological Studies*, (article from 1886), p. 486.
65. House and Ice, *Dominion Theology*, p. 389.
66. Ladd, *Last Things*, pp. 22, 23, 27.

with the Jehovah's Witness cult? It would not be difficult to find, as they did, similarities. Consider the following as purely illustrative of the error of such analysis, while keeping in mind their introductory statement: "We also are not saying that all of the categories dealt with below are wrong, just that the two traditions have parallel beliefs."[67]

The Kingdom Was Preached Only to the Jews:

Jehovah's Witnesses: "To the Jews exclusively he preached, saying: 'Repent, for the kingdom of the heavens has drawn near.' . . . After this announcement of the Kingdom Jesus went to John, showing the primary purpose for which he came to earth, namely, to bear witness to God's kingdom. . . . But there is no record they continued to [preach the kingdom] after his ascension on high. Such announcement would not be appropriate until his return. . . ."[68]

Dispensationalists: "The 'gospel of the kingdom' as announced by John . . . proclaimed the good news that the promised kingdom was 'at hand.' Although the news at the first advent was restricted to Israel, prior to the second advent it will be announced not only to Israel but to the whole world." "All the signs mentioned by Christ in Matthew 24 and Luke 21, which were to precede the setting up of the kingdom, had not been fulfilled, thus preventing a reoffer of the kingdom in Acts."[69]

The Kingdom Is Wholly Future:

Jehovah's Witnesses: "The government which will one day exercise dominion over all the earth [is] God's kingdom by Christ Jesus."[70] "In the capacity of priests and kings of God they reign a thousand years with Christ Jesus. This 'royal priesthood' is spoken of by the apostle Peter as 'a holy nation, a people for special possession,' who inherit the Kingdom."[71]

---

67. House and Ice, *Dominion Theology,* p. 385.
68. *Let God Be True* (Brooklyn, NY: Watchtower and Tract Society, 1946), pp. 37, 140.
69. J. Dwight Pentecost, *Things to Come: A Study in Biblical Eschatology* (Grand Rapids, MI: Zondervan/Academie, [1958] 1964), pp. 472, 469.
70. *Let God Be True*, pp. 250-51.
71. *Ibid.*, pp. 137-38.

Dispensationalists: "Premillennial dominion, on the other hand, will be initiated at Christ's second coming, when he will mediate his rule from the New Jerusalem as the Sovereign over a hierarchical structure. Believers will reign with Christ for one thousand years. . . ."[72] "The kingdom is yet future is also implied in a number of passages which speak of the church inheriting the kingdom."[73]

Jesus Taught the Kingdom Awaited His Second Coming:

Jehovah's Witnesses: "Jesus told his disciples that he was going away as to a far-off country and that he would return with Kingdom power at an unannounced time. . . . Until his foes were to be made his footstool he must sit waiting at God's right hand in heaven."[74]

Dispensationalists: "The parable of the nobleman in Luke 19:11-27 is another example of how Jesus spoke of the future nature of the kingdom. . . . Christ spoke of a nobleman who went on a long journey to a far country. . . . So Christ did not set up the kingdom during his first coming; it awaits his return."[75]

God Does Not Use Christians in Expanding His Kingdom:

Jehovah's Witnesses: The "kingdom of Jehovah will not be set up on this earth by his witnesses. They will perform no overt act in the erecting of such government. . . . So they are commanded at Matthew 24:14 to preach the good news of [the kingdom] among all nations before the end of this world comes. Hence they must be neutral. . . ."[76]

Dispensationalists: "But if Bahnsen is complaining that when people converted from postmillennialism to premillennialism they quit trying to establish the kingdom, he is correct. . . ." "Where does the Bible say that we are to be involved in the social, politi-

---

72. House and Ice, *Dominion Theology*, p. 142.

73. *Ibid.*, p. 232.

74. *New Heavens and a New Earth* (Brooklyn, NY: Watchtower Bible and Tract Society, 1953) p. 188.

75. House and Ice, *Dominion Theology*, pp. 228-29.

76. *Let God Be True*, p. 247.

cal, and economic aspects of society during the church age in the way Reconstructionists affirm?"[77]

The Narrow Christian Mission:

Jehovah's Witnesses: "From the foregoing one thing is clearly seen: It is not the duty of the remnant of the congregation yet on earth . . . to enter into political alliances with the nations of this world. . . . No; the responsibility of the remnant . . . is to praise Jehovah's name and bear witness to his supremacy and glory. How? By ministering the spiritual 'food at the proper time' to those hungering and thirsting for the truth, inviting all to partake of the 'water of life freely.' "[78]

Dispensationalists: "The . . . directives given to the church [are] to carry out its mission of individual evangelism and teaching in order to build up believers to live in faithfulness to our Lord during this dark age."[79] "Premillennialists . . . believe that the emphasis on social and cultural issues reflect the purpose God has for this age, namely the individual duties of a Christian before a watching world, rather than the redemption and conversion of institutions."[80]

Satan's Dominant Rule:

Jehovah's Witnesses: "From [Luke 4:6] it is unreasonable to think anything else than that all world government were the Devil's property. How else could he have offered them to Christ?"[81]

Dispensationalists: Satan "is 'the ruler of this world,' which means he is constantly at work in human government and its political systems."[82] "[K]osmos . . . refer[s] to the organized system under the domination of Satan . . ."[83]

---

77. House and Ice, *Dominion Theology*, pp. 341-42, 150.
78. *Let God Be True*, p. 132.
79. House and Ice, *Dominion Theology*, p. 154.
80. *Ibid.*, p. 155.
81. *Let God Be True*, p. 56.
82. Hal Lindsey, *Satan Is Alive and Well on Planet Earth* (Grand Rapids, MI: Zondervan, 1972), p. 77.
83. Pentecost, *Things to Come*, p. 131.

Our Age Is Evil and Getting Worse:

Jehovah's Witnesses: "God's Word of truth tells us very clearly that we are fast nearing a worldwide change. It shows us that our time is the one Jesus Christ had in mind when he foretold the end of this wicked system. . . . He said that the last days of this wicked system would be marked by such things as world wars, food shortages. . . ."[84]

Dispensationalists: "The threat of atomic war, the growing worldwide spirit of lawlessness, . . . worldwide economic instability — these all join to bring mankind into the vortex of an imminent catastrophe."[85] Walvoord: "The peculiar characteristics of unrest in our day fit precisely into what the prophetic Word says will be the world situation at the time of the end. The nations are rejecting God and things that would effect their salvation, but the Scriptures indicate that ultimately their very turmoil and confusion set the stage. . . ." "This turmoil will end in the greatest of all world wars, preceding the coming of Jesus Christ and His solution to the problems. The conflicts that we see in our world today are symptoms of the day in which we live."[86]

We Are to Be Witnesses:

Jehovah's Witnesses: "Jesus plainly declared that the same commission rested upon the members of the congregation. He said to them: 'You will be witnesses of me.' "[87]

Dispensationalists: "Instead of telling the troops to charge, [Jesus] told them to be witnesses."[88]

The Church as a Called-out Kingdom Bride:

Jehovah's Witnesses: "Jesus told his disciples that he was going

---

84. *The Truth that Leads to Eternal Life* (Brooklyn, NY: Watchtower Bible and Tract Society, 1968), p. 8.

85. Charles H. Stevens, in Charles Lee Feinberg, ed., *Prophecy and the Seventies* (Chicago: Moody Press, 1971), p. 238.

86. John F. Walvoord, in *ibid.*, pp. 207, 211.

87. *Let God Be True*, p. 131.

88. House and Ice, *Dominion Theology*, p. 166.

away as to a far-off country and that he would return with Kingdom power at an unannounced time. All his anointed followers
were to keep watch and preserve themselves with virginlike purity
in expectation of his return to take his faithful congregation to
himself as his bride. Until his foes were to be made his footstool he
must sit waiting at God's right hand in heaven, and during that
waiting period the members of his bride, his congregation, were
to be called out from this world."[89]

Dispensationalists: "My blessed hope, however, continues to be
that Christ will soon rapture his Bride, the church, and that we
will return with him in victory to rule and exercise dominion with
him for a thousand years upon the earth."[90] "Our calling is . . . to
be involved as God's instruments for calling out the Bride of
Christ for the coming, future kingdom."[91]

The Church as a Secret Mystery:

Jehovah's Witnesses: "Scripturally 'church' means a congregation
called out from the world for God's purpose. . . . The doctrine
concerning the church or congregation was for a long time a
sacred secret. It was first revealed to those selected from among
men as members of the congregation. (Mark 4:11)."[92]

Dispensationalists: "[T]he concept given to us in the New Testament that the church is a mystery."[93] The Church "is a mystery
not revealed until New Testament times."[94]

Expectation of Ultimate Apostasy and Babylon:

Jehovah's Witnesses: "Instead of showing godly repentance and
Christian conversion Christendom has shown itself to be wicked."[95]
"This means that Babylon the Great is an empire. What kind of
empire? . . . Could it, then, be a religious empire? . . . Because

---

89. *New Heavens and a New Earth*, p. 188.
90. House and Ice, *Dominion Theology*, p. 10.
91. *Ibid.*, p. 157.
92. *Let God Be True*, p. 125.
93. Pentecost, *Things to Come*, p. 200-1.
94. Ryrie, *Basis of the Premillennial Faith*, p. 130.
95. *New Heavens and a New Earth*, p. 192.

it mixes religion and politics. As regards Christendom, the Bible shows that those who claim to serve God but are unfaithful and enter into relations with the political powers are viewed by God as spiritual prostitutes or adulteresses."[96]

Dispensationalists: "The Scriptures also indicate that a world religion will emerge, symbolically represented by the wicked woman of Revelation 17."[97] "One harmful result is that the Reconstructionists will influence a large segment of the church to set its mind on the things that are on earth and not on things above (Colossians 3:2). This wrong perspective will lead to a wrong merger with the things and systems of this world."[98] "Worldwide evangelism is the calling of the church in this age, not Cultural Christianization. Sadly when the two are combined the result is not the bright and shining city on a hill; rather it is Babylon the great, spoken of in Revelation 18, which God will judge in the future."[99] There is "so much false doctrine and so little orthodoxy in Christendom today."[100]

Christ Must Intervene and Destroy the Present World:

Jehovah's Witnesses: "When Jehovah thus vindicates his universal sovereignty by destroying all his foes in heaven and in earth, then he will be again the great Theocrat or theocratic Ruler over all creatures that live. . . . His theocratic law will be obeyed everywhere. . . . Jehovah God will once and for all time have vindicated his universal sovereignty and his holy name against all false charges, reproaches and challenges of his malicious enemies. . . ."[101] "Then the new world of righteousness will begin, and with it the thousand-year day of judgment."[102]

---

96. *The Truth that Leads to Eternal Life*, p. 133.
97. Walvoord in Feinberg, *Prophecy and the Seventies*, p. 209.
98. House and Ice, *Dominion Theology*, p. 390.
99. *Ibid.*, p. 160.
100. *Ibid.*, p. 263.
101. *Let God Be True*, p. 28.
102. *Ibid.*, p. 287.

Dispensationalists: "A premillennialist believes that Christ's intervening judgment will destroy current society and then Christ will institute millennial conditions."[103] "Scripture has a great deal to say concerning the government of the theocracy, inasmuch as the government administered by the King is the very manifestation of the authority that God seeks to re-establish."[104]

Concern with Armageddon's Approach:

Jehovah's Witnesses: "That thousand years God has assigned to the Lord Jesus, to reign then without disturbance from the devil's organization in either heaven or earth. Such the 1,000 year reign of Jesus Christ, as foretold at Revelation 20:1-6, begins after Satan is bound; in other words, after Armageddon, a war which all evidences indicate will begin inside our generation. — Revelation 16:14-16."[105] "God's name must eventually be sanctified by Jehovah's own stupendous act of vindicating himself at the universal war of Armageddon. The means by which his name will be proved to be holy and deserving to be held sacred is his kingdom by his Messiah, which will shortly fight this war of Armageddon to a successful finish against all enemies."[106]

Dispensationalists: "The 1980's: Countdown to Armageddon."[107] "The premillennialist sees Christ intervening catastrophically in a moment of history, resulting in an establishment of his mediatorial rule."[108] "The 'kings of the earth and of the whole world' are to be gathered together through the activity of the trinity from hell to what is called 'the battle of that great day of God Almighty' (Rev. 16:14). This confluence of the nations of the earth is in a place called Armageddon (Rev. 16:16). There God deals in judgment with the nations." "Thus the Lord destroys every hostile force that would challenge His right to rule as Messiah over the earth."[109]

---

103. House and Ice, *Dominion Theology*, p. 9.
104. Pentecost, *Things to Come*, p. 495.
105. *Let God Be True*, p. 179.
106. *Ibid.*, p. 29.
107. Title of Hal Lindsey's book.
108. House and Ice, *Dominion Theology*, p. 140.
109. Pentecost, *Things to Come*, pp. 340, 358.

Dave Hunt laments: "Within the evangelical church today the numbers are dwindling of those who retain in meaningful form the hope of the imminent return of Christ . . . before the whole world explodes in the Great Tribulation judgment and Armageddon."[110] "Everything seemed to be coming together with astonishing precision too set the stage for Armageddon."[111]

The End Is Now Near:

Jehovah's Witnesses: "God's Word of truth tells us very clearly that we are fast nearing a worldwide change. It shows us that our time is the one Jesus Christ had in mind when he foretold the end of this wicked system. . . . He said that the last days of this wicked system would be marked by such things as world wars, food shortages. . . . How thrilling it is to know that we have the hope of shortly entering a new system where we can forever enjoy life to the full."[112]

Dispensationalists: "We are the generation that will see the end times . . . and the Return of Jesus."[113] "What a way to live! With optimism, with anticipation, with excitement. We should be living like persons who don't expect to be around much longer."[114] "God's promise that He will create a new eternal universe for His children to inhabit, into which sin, sickness, and death can never enter, places the fulfillment of life's purpose beyond both our wildest imagination to conceive and our most heroic efforts to achieve."[115]

We Must Set Our Thoughts on the New World:

Jehovah's Witnesses: "The righteous new world is immediately before us. . . . It will be according to his thoughts and will operate according to his will and ways. It is therefore high time for us to find out what God's true thoughts are and what his ways are. Only

110. Dave Hunt, *Whatever Happened?*, p. 9.
111. *Ibid.*, p. 65.
112. *The Truth that Leads to Eternal Life*, pp. 8, 10.
113. Hal Lindsey, *The 1980's: Countdown to Armageddon* (New York: Bantam Books, 1980), back cover copy.
114. Hal Lindsey, *Late Great Planet Earth*, p. 145.
115. Hunt, *Whatever Happened to Heaven?*, p. 21.

by taking this course shall we be able to begin living for the new world, preparing to live in it."[116]

Dispensationalists: "We will . . . reign over this earth with Him. That hope involves a truly new world order far superior to anything we could establish in these mortal bodies. . . ."[117] "[N]othing is more important in shaping how life on earth is lived and what is accomplished both for time and eternity than a person's attitude toward the life to come." "There's a Whole New Universe Coming!" "We find it difficult to turn away from those things in this world upon which we ought not to set our affection. This would not be the case at all if those things which we are to seek 'above, where Christ sitteth' were understood and had captured our affection."[118]

Christ Will Come Before His Kingdom Begins:

Jehovah's Witnesses: "Christ returns before his thousand-year undisturbed reign to put all enemies under his feet at Armageddon."[119]

Dispensationalists: "PREMILLENNIALISM. The belief that Christ will return at the end of this current age (the church age) before the millennium."[120]

Christ's Earthly Rule:

Jehovah's Witnesses: "Christ returns before his thousand-year undisturbed reign to put all enemies under his feet at Armageddon."[121]

Dispensationalists: "Christians are to pray that Christ will return and bring with him the kingdom. Then God's will in heaven will be brought to earth. But not until Christ rules physically from Jerusalem."[122]

---

116. *Let God Be True*, p. 305.
117. Hunt, *Whatever Happened?*, p. 61.
118. *Ibid.*, pp. 7, 19, 46.
119. *Let God Be True*, p. 206, cp. p. 270.
120. House and Ice, *Dominion Theology*, p. 420.
121. *Let God Be True*, p. 206, cp. p. 270.
122. House and Ice, *Dominion Theology*, p. 160.

The Subjects of the Kingdom:

Jehovah's Witnesses: "Surviving the universal war of Armageddon, they will 'multiply and fill the earth' in righteousness, and their children will become obedient subjects of the King Christ Jesus."[123]

Dispensationalists: "The earthly theocratic kingdom, instituted by the Lord Jesus Christ at His second advent, will include all the saved of Israel and the saved of the Gentiles, who are living at the time His return. Scripture makes it very clear that all sinners will be cut off before the institution of the Kingdom." "The Gentiles that are in the millennium will have experienced conversion prior to admission. . . . They will be subject to the Messiah."[124]

The Glory of the Earthly Kingdom:

Jehovah's Witnesses: "It is beyond the imagination of frail men to conceive the blessings that this glorious kingdom will bestow on all who are privileged to live under its righteous rule."[125]

Dispensationalists: "Much Scripture is devoted to stating the untold blessing and glory poured out upon earth through the beneficence of the Lord Jesus Christ in the kingdom."[126]

Literal Thousand Years:

Jehovah's Witnesses: "The thousand years God has assigned to the Lord Jesus, to reign then without disturbance from the devil's organization in either heaven or earth."[127]

Dispensationalists: "Upon his return, Christ will judge the world, bind Satan, and rule from Jerusalem for a thousand years."[128]

We Will Physically Rule With Him:

Jehovah's Witnesses: "In the capacity of priests and kings of God

---

123. *Let God Be True*, p. 139.
124. Pentecost, *Things to Come*, pp. 505-6, 508.
125. *Let God Be True*, p. 144.
126. Pentecost, *Things to Come*, p. 487.
127. *Let God Be True*, p. 179.
128. House and Ice, *Dominion Theology*, p. 420.

they reign a thousand years with Christ Jesus."¹²⁹

Dispensationalists: "Believers are made 'kings and priests' or, better, 'a kingdom, priests unto God and his Father.' " "They are given the special status of priests of God and of Christ, and are privileged to reign with Him for the thousand years."¹³⁰

Satan Bound:

Jehovah's Witnesses: "Revelation 20:1-3 tells us of the time when the archdeceiver will be completely restrained form his activity. He will be bound and abyssed for a thousand years, to mislead the nations and peoples no more until it is God's time to loose him for a little while. In the meantime deceit, lying, and hypocrisy continue."¹³¹

Dispensationalists: On Revelation 20:2ff.: "In verse 2 the angel is seen laying hold of Satan and binding him for 1,000 years after which, in verse 3, Satan is cast into the abyss and its door is shut. A seal is placed upon Satan himself making it impossible for him to deceive the nations until a thousand years have elapsed, after which, the angel declares, Satan must be loosed for a little while. . . . The mounting evidence for Christianity does not seem to have bound Satan in the twentieth century."¹³²

The Law Was Temporary:

Jehovah's Witnesses: "The Law being theocratic and being given under glorious, awe-inspiring conditions at Mount Horeb, it would seem to be perpetual, everlasting, beyond recall, as eternal as its Giver. So it amazes many when informed that such Law was abolished and brought to an end by Jehovah, and that no creatures on earth, not even the Jews, are any longer under it."¹³³

---

129. *Let God Be True*, pp. 137-38.
130. Walvoord, *Revelation*, pp. 38, 299.
131. *Let God Be True*, pp. 62-63.
132. Walvoord, *Revelation*, pp. 290-91.
133. *Let God Be True*, p. 183.

Dispensationalists: "The idea that the unchangeableness of God requires that the specific details of the Mosaic code be transferred to all times and cultures simply does not follow."[134] "Both the typological and nontypological aspects of the law were of temporary purpose 'until the seed should come' (Gal. 3)."[135]

Abraham Was Not Under a Mosaic-type Law:

Jehovah's Witnesses: On Deut. 5:1-15: "In those words it distinctly says that Israel's forefathers, including most prominently of all Abraham, Isaac and Jacob, and the twelve sons of Jacob, were not under this law covenant."[136]

Dispensationalists: "In reaffirming his promise to bless Abraham and his descendants, God makes clear to Isaac that Abraham had been obedient to a pre-Mosaic revelation of God's law."[137]

The Sabbath Was a Sign for Israel Alone:

Jehovah's Witnesses: "The sabbath was a distinguishing feature of Jehovah's covenant arrangement with Israel alone. . . ."[138]

Dispensationalists: "Then the Sabbath was revealed to Israel . . . and invested with the character of a 'sign' between the Lord and Israel."[139]

Christ Fulfilled the Law, Thus Removing It:

Jehovah's Witnesses: On Matt. 5:17ff.: "Destroying the Law by breaking God's law covenant is far different from fulfilling it and thus moving it out of the way and lifting its obligations from his disciples. . . . So, in order to fulfill the Law and the Prophets, Jesus by Jewish birth 'came to be under law'."[140]

---

134. House and Ice, *Dominion Theology*, p. 87.
135. *Ibid.*, p. 42.
136. *Let God Be True*, p. 173.
137. House and Ice, *Dominion Theology*, p. 87.
138. *Let God Be True*, p. 174.
139. *The New Scofield Reference Bible*, ed. C. I. Scofield (New York: Oxford University Press, 1909), p. 1010 (at Matt. 12:1).
140. *Let God Be True*, p. 175.

Dispensationalists: On Matt. 5:17: "Christ begins with a strong denial that he had come as a rebel, a rejecter of law, though he was often accused of being a lawbreaker (Mark 2:24; Luke 6:2). . . . Rather than being a rejecter of law, Christ had come to fulfill the law."[141]

Christians Are Not Under Law but Grace:

Jehovah's Witnesses: "This fact proves that they are not under the old law covenant with its Ten Commandments, but are under the new covenant, by God's undeserved kindness."[142]

Dispensationalists: "We are not under law but under grace. . . ."[143]

We Cannot Distinguish Ceremonial and Moral Laws:

Jehovah's Witnesses: "The law covenant cannot be taken apart, so that a part of it, the ceremonial part, could be abolished, and the other part of it, the so-called 'moral' part, remain."[144]

Dispensationalists: "The codes of Israel reflect the character of God in ceremonial, moral, and civil expressions; none of these manifestations are ever presented as superior to the others nor severable. These three are inseparable parts of the law of God for Israel."[145]

The Nations Are Not Under Moses' Law:

Jehovah's Witnesses: "Thus the sabbath commandment was a component part of God's covenant with Israel, and it could not be separated from that covenant. The Gentile nations were not and never have been under God's Fourth Commandment of the covenant."[146]

Dispensationalists: "The real question is whether the Mosaic law given to Israel is to be practiced by any other nation not under the covenant. The answer is no!"[147]

---

141. House and Ice, *Dominion Theology*, p. 105.
142. *Let God Be True*, p. 194.
143. Ryrie, *Balancing the Christian Life*, p. 151.
144. *Let God Be True*, p. 188.
145. House and Ice, *Dominion Theology*, p. 89.
146. *Let God Be True*, p. 174.
147. House and Ice, *Dominion Theology*, p. 100.

The New Covenant Brings a New Law:

Jehovah's Witnesses: "The Christians are the ones being led by God's . . . spirit in harmony with his Word. This fact proves that they are not under the old law covenant with its Ten Commandments, but are under the new covenant, by God's undeserved kindness."[148]

Dispensationalists: "Christ has instituted a new covenant with a new law . . . ."[149]

Summary

1. Due to our understanding of the omnipresence and the total judgment of God Christians hold to the ubiquity of Christian ethics: everything we do must be governed by our ethic.

2. Christian analysis and debate must be governed by ethical considerations.

3. *Dominion Theology* frequently suffers from ethical lapses through misrepresentation, impugning of motives, predisposing their readers to a negative view of the subject of their analysis (Reconstructionism), engaging in irrelevant and biasing theses.

4. Similarities of a few points between systems does not mean similarity of systems. Christians must avoid such fallacious reasoning.

5. House and Ice draw select comparisons between a few details of Reconstructionism and certain charismatics in an attempt to undercut the Reconstructionist system.

6. It often is helpful in illustrating fallacious arguments to erect fallacious parallel arguments.

7. There are many similarities between the Jehovahs' Witnesses and dispensationalism.

---

148. *Let God Be True*, pp. 191-94.
149. House and Ice, *Dominion Theology*, p. 101.

CONCLUSION

20

WHERE DO WE GO FROM HERE?

The Reconstruction debate demands deeper and further consideration, and despite the failure of House and Ice it should continue.

The issues engaged in the debate to which this work is directed represent an intramural discussion among evangelical Christians. Though a friendly debate between brothers in Christ, it is at the same time one of great importance. The particular debate as engaged with House and Ice is one between two distinct theological schools: dispensational theology and Reformed theology.

The reader should carefully note that we have stated that it is a debate with dispensational *theology*, not simply dispensational *eschatology*. By that we mean to point out that dispensationalism is a complete theological system in itself — it is not simply an eschatology, one aspect of theology. The Reconstructionism represented by the present writers, Bahnsen and Gentry (and by R. J. Rushdoony, Gary North, Gary DeMar, and many others), is a noble species of Reformed theology. Dispensationalists House and Ice have attempted to set forth the errors of Reconstructionism as if a distinctive and even aberrant theology, whereas in actuality it is confessionally rooted in the historic reformed theology and tradition.

The Call to Careful Argumentation

In that the debate is a lively and significant one today, it requires the diligent and careful consideration of thinking Christians, who should be concerned about the Christian faith in the world today. We confess that we were quite disappointed with House and Ice's work, not only in the scholarly and logical errors

343

riddling their methodology, but in the frequent radical misrepresentations of Reconstructionism in their presentation. If the debate is indeed significant, it demands *thoughtful* consideration.[1] Hopefully our survey of some of these errors will demonstrate the need for more careful evaluations in the future.

The Recognition of Systemic Differences

More importantly, however, the failure of House and Ice to make a case against Reconstructionism was not due simply to a matter of methodological error. Were such the case, their attempt might be written off as a bungled refutation. Actually, we have attempted to show that the very system from which they operate — including its attempted exegetical foundations — is itself fraught with error. We hope that our response to House and Ice will further demonstrate the distortion of theology that has been imported into American evangelicalism by dispensational theology.

The erroneous distinctions inherent in dispensationalism and its tendency to "rightly divide the word of truth" distract too many well-meaning Christians from the unity of God's Word. Consequently, they are deterred from an acceptance of the underlying unity of biblical ethics. The absolutism of Christian theistic ethics — underscored by a "thus saith the Lord" — has tended to be washed out by the relativism promoted by the multiplying of distinctions in Scripture and history by dispensationalism.

House and Ice's "wisdom" approach to Christian ethics exchanges a resounding "thus saith the Lord" with a feeble "thus suggesteth the Lord."[2] Hunt even criticizes Reconstructionist critic Charles Colson for attempting to apply biblical standards to the

---

1. How careful is an argument when a 9 line block of text taken from Bahnsen's *Theonomy in Christian Ethics*, p. 432, is ascribed to R. J. Rushdoony, *Institutes of Biblical Law* — and supposedly covers 42 pages, from 739 to 781 (they say)! See H. Wayne House and Thomas Ice, *Dominion Theology: Blessing or Curse?* (Portland, OR: Multnomah, 1988), pp. 100, 102.

2. House and Ice, *Dominion Theology*, pp. 186-88. See also Dave Hunt: "None of the New Testament epistles is written as though it came from a bishop or pope who had to be obeyed under threat of excommunication" (*Whatever Happened to Heaven?* [Eugene, OR: Harvest House, 1988], p. 125).

prison problem: "When all is said and done, however, even Colson — in spite of an excellent discussion of the issues — is short on real answers. And so he should be if he is to be true to the Word of God in dealing with difficult issues upon which it makes no definitive pronouncements."[3]

It is hoped that our section on ethics will warn Christians of the exegetical, practical, and cultural pitfalls associated with a rejection of God's Law as the standard of righteousness. Although House and Ice attempt to disassociate the Mosaic law from the concept of God's Law, it is clear that Scripture deems the Mosaic code to be God's Law. We humbly urge the reader to consider the biblical and theological presentation given above in defense of theonomic ethics.

Perhaps the most prominent feature of dispensationalism is its inherently pessimistic eschatology. For decades great numbers of evangelical Christians have trained up their children with the view that the world is rapidly approaching its effective end, as far as their labors are concerned. Because of this mindset, generations of Christians have lived with a short-range view of the future. This cannot have been without a serious negative effect on the Christian influence in the world.

The distinctions drawn by dispensationalists, generated by a faulty hermeneutic methodology, have caused many to be blind to the pervasive Gospel Victory Theme of Scripture. They have drawn a radical distinction between the Messianic Kingdom and the Church, which has caused them to look elsewhere for the kingdom and victory — despite Jesus' assertion that the kingdom had come. Due to this, their theology tends toward retreat, awaiting the kingdom's establishment in the future, while chiding Reconstructionists for expecting the conquest of the Gospel in Church history.

The Scripture teaches us that "the earth is the Lord's and the fullness thereof." This is a frequent theme in Scripture.[4] In that

---

3. Dave Hunt, *Whatever Happened to Heaven?*, pp. 85-86.
4. Exodus 9:29; 19:5; Deuteronomy 10:14; 1 Chronicles 19:11; Job 41:11; Psalms 24:1; 50:12; 89:11; 1 Corinthians 10:26, 28.

this earth was created by God for His own glory (Rev. 4:11), it is not surprising to learn that Christ's redemption has a view to reclaiming the world through the gospel, as we have noted above. The expectation of world-wide victory for the gospel is a dominant theme in postmillennialism — a theme wholly at odds with dispensationalism.

The Future of the Debate

We would close by urging the reader and all parties to the debate *carefully* to consider the Reconstructionist position. In addition we would invite the reader to adopt the much needed Reconstructionist option to the dominant dispensationalism of our day. We are convinced of the biblical superiority of Reconstructionism as an approach to the Christian life, not on the basis of pragmatics but exegesis. Consequently, we urge the Christian to repossess the Berean spirit and lay aside his theological biases to properly engage this most important debate.

"They received the word with all readiness of mind, and searched the scriptures daily, whether those things were so" (Acts 17:11b).

APPENDIXES

Appendix A

THEOLOGICAL SCHIZOPHRENIA

by Gary DeMar

Jesus said, "Any kingdom divided against itself is laid waste; and any city or house divided against itself shall not stand" (Matthew 12:25).

The authors of *Dominion Theology: Blessing or Curse?* have something of a problem on their hands. Their own writings and the writings of those who endorse their work discredit their contention that Dominion Theology (Christian Reconstruction) is a "curse." There is a great amount of theological schizophrenia from Charles W. Colson, Norman L. Geisler, John MacArthur, Jr., and Hal Lindsey. Since these men endorse *Dominion Theology*, I thought it would be fitting to evaluate their views in the light of the book they are endorsing. Some of these men seem even to disagree with what they themselves have written, while others disagree with House and Ice and traditional dispensationalism, the supporting theological position used to evaluate Christian Reconstruction. The disagreements are not minor as we will see. Moreover, House and Ice seem to have abandoned the essential distinctives of their system, doctrines that make dispensationalism different from historic premillennialism.[1]

---

1. By Thomas Ice's own admission, dispensationalism is not a static theological system. There is development in the system. The question is, Who speaks for today's new and improved dispensationalism? See Vern S. Poythress, *Understanding Dispensationalists* (Grand Rapids, MI: Zondervan, 1987), pp. 30-38; Craig A. Blaising, "Development of Dispensationalism by Contemporary Dispensationalists," Part 2, *Bibliotheca Sacra*, (July-September 1988), pp. 254-80.

Let us reformulate the verse quoted above: "Any theological position divided against itself is laid waste; and dispensationalism divided against itself shall not stand."

Dispensationalism cannot stand since: (1) There are few able defenses of dispensationalism being published since the metamorphosis of the position. Dispensationalism has gone through such a transformation process that it needs a new scholarly defense. (2) Dispensationalism is being questioned by the more orthodox charismatics.[2] Dr. Joseph Kikasola, professor of international studies and Hebrew at CBN University believes that there has been a " 'diminishing of dispensationalism,' especially among charismatics, who, he says, are coming to see that 'charismatic dispensationalist' is 'a contradiction in terms.' "[3] (3) The date-setting element of dispensationalism is losing its fascination with many of its adherents since the fortieth anniversary of Israel's nationhood (1948-88) has passed without a rapture. Dave Hunt, a proponent of the national regathering of Israel as the time text for future prophetic events, writes: "Needless to say, January 1, 1982, saw the defection of large numbers from the pretrib position. . . . Many who were once excited about the prospects of being caught up to heaven at any moment have become confused and disillusioned by the apparent failure of a generally accepted biblical interpretation they once relied upon."[4] He goes on later to assert: Gary "North's reference to specific dates is an attack upon the most persuasive factor supporting Lindsey's rapture scenario: the rebirth of national Israel. This historic event, which is pivotal to dispensationalism's timing of the rapture, as John F. Walvoord has pointed out, was long anticipated and when it at last occurred seemed to validate that prophetic interpretation."[5] (4) The schizophrenia within dispensationalism and evangelicalism over the application

---

2. Traditionally, pentecostalism has been dispensational.

3. Randy Frame, "The Theonomic Urge," *Christianity Today*, (April 21, 1989), p. 38.

4. Dave Hunt, *Whatever Happened to Heaven?* (Eugene, OR: Harvest House, 1988), p. 68.

5. *Ibid.*, p. 64.

of the Bible to society is a major problem for the position. Some say the Old Testament does apply (e.g., Chuck Colson, and in a modified way, House and Ice). Some say Christian activism is mandated in Scripture (House), while others try to make a case against it (Hunt).[6] It's this type of schizophrenia that I want to address.

The following material does not take the form of a review. Rather, I have centered my attention on the inconsistencies of *Dominion Theology: Blessing or Curse?* and those who endorse the book.

Dominion Theology and the Law

One of the major tenets of dispensationalism is the non-applicability of the Mosaic law to the New Covenant era. Nothing in the Mosaic legislation, say the dispensationalists, is for the church today.[7] Moreover, nothing in the Mosaic legislation is for the non-Israelite secular State. With this in mind, note the following bit of schizophrenia.

> The Christian is to love the law of God. Grace does not free the believer from obedience to the will of God. However, *Christians are not under the expression of the law as it was given to Israel.* Instead, we may use the Mosaic legislation as examples of how we may respond individually and corporately; we may gain wisdom from it. Christians are, however, to obey the will of God as it is expressed in the New Testament — the law of Christ — and the law revealed in the Adamic and Noahic covenants.[8]

---

6. Hunt maintains that a consistent dispensationalist should not be involved in social activism. Wayne House teaches otherwise. See H. Wayne House, *Class Syllabus for Systematic Theology 407*, Unit Four, "Christians and the State," Dallas Theological Seminary, 1987 and "What in the World Is the Church Supposed to Do?" A debate between Dave Hunt and Wayne House on the topic of Christian activism was held on May 20, 1989. Tapes of the debate can be obtained from Answers in Action, P.O. Box 2067, Costa Mesa, California 92628.

7. Charles Caldwell Ryrie, *Dispensationalism Today* (Chicago, IL: Moody Press, 1965), pp. 53-54.

8. H. Wayne House and Tommy Ice, *Dominion Theology: Blessing or Curse?: An Analysis of Christian Reconstructionism* (Portland, OR: Multnomah Press, 1988), pp. 118-19.

Instead of embracing the thesis of the Reconstructionists that laws that make up the Mosaic legislation (properly interpreted and applied through the grid of the New Covenant)[9] are binding in the New Covenant era, House and Ice claim that Christians are to use "wisdom" in determining the application of the law. The authors never show us how this works in actual practice or how this might differ from Christian Reconstruction. One is left with the impression, however, that Reconstructionists do not use wisdom when they attempt to apply the Mosaic legislation in the New Covenant era.

Here's another more fundamental question: What if the Reconstructionist and the neo-dispensationalist[10] come to the same conclusion on the applicability of a Mosaic law for the church age in the area of civil penalties, say, for sodomy? What if a group of neo-dispensationalists are elected to public office and determine, based on wisdom, that the death penalty for a public act of sodomy is the wise thing to implement? Both the Reconstructionist and neo-dispensationalist have come to the same conclusion.

---

9. The following is excerpted from a letter by me addressed to the editor of *Christianity Today* in response to "The Theonomic Urge" (April 21, 1989):

"Generally, the movement's proponents hold that the civil laws of Old Testament, theocratic Israel are normative for all societies in all times." We believe that it is more correct to insist that the whole Bible is normative. This implies that in considering how to apply the Old Testament laws, we must also consider the implications of the death, resurrection, and ascension of Christ, the pouring out of the Spirit, and the breaking down of the wall between Jew and Gentile. There are elements of continuity and discontinuity between the covenants, and we cannot afford to ignore either. And, if we affirm that the Bible is God's inerrant Word, how can we in good conscience ignore its teachings in any area of life?

10. Neo-dispensationalist is a reference to the hybrid view of dispensationalism espoused by House and Ice. This is recognized by a recent reviewer of *Dominion Theology*: "Its appreciation of the Law and its proclamation of salvation by grace in every age move it closer to the Reconstructionists' home camp." Robert Drake, "What Should the Kingdom of God Look Like?," *World* (February 11, 1989), p. 13.

Wayne House

For now, let's take a look at what I would call "dispensational schizophrenia" in Wayne House.

(1)

The Constitution arose from the Puritan idea of *covenant*. The first great document of the colonies had been the Mayflower Compact, and state after state adopted similar documents. It is interesting that the biblical book of Deuteronomy — the covenant book — was the most quoted source in political writings and speeches preceding the writing of the Constitution. There is ample reason to believe that the Framers and ratifiers of the Constitution saw themselves as entering into solemn covenant, an act of lasting and binding importance.

The Constitution reflects a genius in its construction.[11]

Comment: Christian Reconstruction also relies heavily on the covenant concept. In fact, covenant theology is contrasted with dispensationalism in Charles H. Ryrie's *Dispensationalism Today*. Moreover, the book of Deuteronomy is one of the most quoted Old Testament books used to support the relationship between obedience/disobedience and societal blessing/cursing.[12] How then can the Constitution reflect "a genius in its construction," but Christian Reconstruction is a "curse" when it follows a similar covenant model with societal application? If a Reconstructionist proposed that our founding fathers used Deuteronomy as a model for the our nation's constitutional government, House and Ice would have a fit. But when a dispensationalist discovers such a

---

11. Wayne House, ed., "Editor's Introduction," *Restoring the Constitution: 1787-1987* (Dallas, TX: Probe Books, 1987), p. 8.

12. The heavy use of the Book of Deuteronomy was the objection of William E. Diehl in his "A Guided-Market Response" to Gary North's "Free Market Capitalism" article in Robert G. Clouse, ed., *Wealth & Poverty: Four Christian Views of Economics* (Downers Grove, IL: InterVarsity Press, 1984). Diehl writes:

That the author [Gary North] is strong on "biblical law" is apparent. The essay provides us with thirty-nine Old Testament citations, of which twenty-three are from the book of Deuteronomy (p. 66).

presupposition in the drafting of the Constitution, calling it "genius," no one bats an eye. This is theological and historical schizophrenia. But if it is true that the book of Deuteronomy was the most quoted book prior to the drafting of the Constitution, then why cannot our nation return to that former "genius" and once again build on similar presuppositions?

(2)

Exodus 20	*1 Timothy 1*
Commandment 7: You shall not commit adultery	Adulterers and perverts (homosexuals)

One may see from the above chart that Paul [in 1 Timothy 1:8-11] had the Ten Commandments in mind. Homosexual sin is viewed by Paul as a violation of the moral law of God given at Mt. Sinai. But additionally, scholars have recognized for a long time that the Decalogue has its roots in the creation teaching of Genesis. . . .[13]

Comment: House and Fowler see a relationship between the Ten Commandments in the Old Testament and the New Testament. But the Ten Commandments are not specific. They merely *summarize* the law. They do not define adultery or what constitutes a "pervert" or a "homosexual." How does the Christian know when adultery, perversion, or homosexuality has taken place? Where does one find a prohibition against homosexuality in the seventh commandment? What if homosexual marriages are legalized by the State? Would this relationship be valid as long as there were no homosexual adultery? Is the prohibition of bestiality included in the adultery prohibition? The New Testament has very little to say on these matters. The case laws of Exodus, Leviticus, and Deuteronomy, define these crimes in great detail. In fact, Wayne House has written an excellent exposition of Exodus 21:22-25 showing that the unborn child is considered a human being de-

---

13. Richard A. Fowler and H. Wayne House *Civilization in Crisis: A Christian Response to Homosexuality, Euthanasia, and Abortion* (2nd rev. ed; Grand Rapids, MI: Baker Book House, 1988), p. 131.

serving of full protection of the law.[14] This is the only passage in Scripture that clearly shows that the unborn child was protected by law. Finally, why take the prohibitions against these crimes but not the punishments?

Tommy Ice on Law

Tommy Ice states that he "used to be a Christian Reconstructionist." He has remarked on a number of occasions that those who call themselves Christian Reconstructionists are attracted to the position because they have found a theology that supports their cultural and societal activism. Tommy Ice believes that for Reconstructionists, ideology supports theology. But doesn't this assessment cut both ways? Can't the Reconstructionist assert that a dispensationalist like Tommy Ice has chosen a theological system that *releases* him from cultural activism? Why doesn't Tommy Ice come out and say that it is wrong — even heretical — for Christians to be involved in anything beyond evangelism? Why does he still advocate a message of societal application of the law of God if it is useless and unbiblical to do so?[15]

What standard does Tommy Ice ask us to use as a standard for righteousness? What should the Christian activist use? The following quotation is the epitome of schizophrenia. It presupposes a culturally activistic Christian and the application of the Mosaic legislation.

---

14. H. Wayne House, "Miscarriage or Premature Birth: Additional Thoughts on Exodus 21:22-25," *Westminster Theological Journal*, vol. 41, no. 1 (Fall 1978), pp. 108-23.

15. Tommy Ice writes: "Nothing in dispensationalism prohibits a strong involvement in social issues." "Dispensationalism, Date-Setting and Distortion," *Biblical Perspectives*, vol 1, no. 5 (September/October 1988), p. 6. This quotation by Ice seems to contradict other statements made by him that involvement in social issues is not the job of the church during the so-called "church age." In a letter written to Houston physician Dr. Steven F. Hotze, Ice writes: "Please, Steve, show me the New Testament passages which instruct us with the obligation of providing a 'Christian alternative in our culture!' " "A strong involvement in social issues" by Christians assumes a "Christian alternative."

Gary North is critical of premillennialists who use resources such as Rushdoony's *Institutes of Biblical Law* as a "reference work on the Old Testament case laws."[16] There is not much difference in how one approaches the Old Testament case laws, whether as law binding for today or as wisdom. Since both views hold that the law is, in some measure, applicable today, adjustments for our current situation must be made for either law or wisdom. Quite frankly, Rushdoony has some good insights into this area. However, the framework in which one views these Old Testament passages is what makes the real difference. Reconstructionists cannot apply the Mosaic law directly since much of it is tied to the physical land of Israel. Therefore, they make modifications similar to those made by someone treating the law as wisdom.[17]

Comment: Ice makes a remarkable admission here. He tells us that "there is not much difference in how one approaches the Old Testament case laws, whether as binding for today or as wisdom." So what's the problem with Christian Reconstruction, especially theonomy? Both positions get the same results. Both make modifications. Both use wisdom. But is this dispensationalism? I don't think so. For most dispensationalists, law in the Old Testament is "Jewish law."[18]

Charles Colson on the Law

Charles Colson has been critical of Christian Reconstruction for some time. He has expressed his criticisms on the Bill Moyer's *God and Politics* segment on Christian Reconstruction, first aired in December 1987. Colson's latest best-selling book, *Kingdoms in Conflict*, briefly addresses Christian Reconstruction. A comparison of

---

16. Gary North, "Publisher's Preface" in David Chilton, *The Days of Vengeance: An Exposition of the Book of Revelation* (Fort Worth, TX: Dominion Press, 1987), p. xxvi.

17. House and Ice, *Dominion Theology*, p. 187.

18. "To be sure, dispensational premillenarians insist that the Old Testament Law was given only to the Jews and not to Gentiles." Norman L. Geisler, "A Premillennial View of Law and Government," *The Best in Theology*, gen. ed. J. I. Packer (Carol Stream, IL: Christianity Today/Word, 1986), vol. 1, p. 259.

"theonomy" in *Kingdoms in Conflict* with statements about the law in an article published in *Transforming Our World*, with the title "The Kingdom of God and Human Kingdoms," makes one wonder whether Mr. Colson is not aware of Reconstruction distinctives or simply unwilling to study them thoughtfully. Of course, there is always a third alternative. Maybe I don't understand Charles Colson. Consider his schizophrenia.

(1)

Recently I addressed the Texas legislature. . . . I told them that the only answer to the crime problem is to take nonviolent criminals out of our prisons and make them pay back their victims with restitution. This is how we can solve the prison crowding problem.

The amazing thing was that afterwards they came up to me one after another and said things like, "That's a tremendous idea. Why hasn't anyone thought of that?" I had the privilege of saying to them, "Read Exodus 22. It is only what God said to Moses on Mount Sinai thousands of years ago."[19]

Comment: Colson does not take the legislators to natural law or Adamic or Noahic law. Rather, he refers them to the Mosaic legislation, a set of laws that dispensationalists tell us were unique to Israel. These laws are not for the Gentile nations, say Scofield and company. According to dispensationalists, they are *Israel*-specific case laws. Even Ted Koppel seems to agree with Colson and (maybe) Reconstructionists against (maybe) dispensationalists: "What Moses brought down from Mount Sinai were not the Ten *suggestions*."[20] House and Ice and their "wisdom" approach want to

---

19. Charles Colson, "The Kingdom of God and Human Kingdoms," James M. Boice, ed. *Transforming Our World: A Call to Action* (Portland, OR: Multnomah, 1988), pp. 154-55. Consider *all* of Exodus 22 for a moment:

You shall not allow a sorceress to live (v. 18).
Whoever lies with an animal shall surely be put to death (v. 19).
He who sacrifices to any god, other than to the LORD alone, shall be utterly destroyed (v. 20).

Colson's article appears in a book distributed by the publisher of *Dominion Theology.*
20. Delivered at Duke University's Commencement in May of 1987.

make the Old Testament commandments "suggestions" since they are not obligatory. Colson seems to believe that Exodus 22 is more than just suggestive. He tells us that the case laws regarding restitution are "the *only* answer to the crime problem."

(2)

[T]he citizens of the kingdom of God living in the midst of the kingdoms of the world provide a respect for the Law that stands beyond human law. It means the presence of a community of people whose values are established by eternal truths. There is no other place that a culture can find those values.

*   *   *   *   *

"How about the revealed propositional truth of Scripture, because that is the Law that is beyond law?" The Bible provides a basis for absolute truth, for true right and wrong. It is only the citizens of the kingdom in the midst of the kingdoms of man that make that discovery possible. [21]

Comment: What is the Law that stands beyond human law? Colson tells us that "the Bible provides a basis for absolute truth, for true right and wrong." Colson does not point us to natural law since he describes this law as "the revealed propositional truth of Scripture." This is what Reconstructionists have been saying: The Bible is the standard. [22] Colson, like Reconstructionists, believes the whole Bible (with some reservations) as the standard.

(3)

In his *Kingdoms in Conflict*, Colson decries a "utopianism" that he says "is often articulated today in contemporary Christian circles." He tells us that "such preoccupation with the political diverts the church from its primary mission" for the salvation of man's soul. But there is another risk, particularly among "those on the political right where many want to impose Christian values on society by force of law."[23]

---

21. Colson, "The Kingdom of God and Human Kingdoms," p. 151.
22. Greg L. Bahnsen, *By This Standard: The Authority of God's Law for Today* (Tyler, TX: Institute for Christian Economics, 1985).
23. Charles Colson, *Kingdoms in Conflict* (Grand Rapids, MI: Zondervan, 1987), p. 117.

Some, such as those in the theonomist movement, even want to reinstate Old Testament civil codes, ignoring Christ's teaching in the parable of the wheat and the tares in which He warns that we live with the good (the wheat) and evil (the tares), and cannot root out the tares. Only God is able to do that and He will— when the Kingdom comes in its final glory.[24]

Comment: Colson would be hard pressed to find a Reconstructionist who believes in utopia or that the Christian's concern should be for the world rather than the salvation of souls. Can't it be both, with the salvation of man's soul a priority? Colon's very biblical and compassionate ministry, Prison Fellowship, is concerned with the souls of prisoners *and* their life in general. The Bible does say that God "so loved the *world*" (John 3:16). Reconstructionists want to know how the saved should act in the world before "the Kingdom comes in its final glory." This is the message of Paul's epistles to the early churches. The Pauline letters were designed to show these new Christians how to live "in this present evil age" (Galatians 1:4). Aren't values like prohibitions against theft and murder imposed on society? One of Colson's heroes is William Wilberforce. Wilberforce was concerned with slaves as they lived *in this world*. Why not just preach the gospel to them and then tell them to remain in the condition in which the gospel found them? The State, according to the Bible, has the power of the sword to enforce these values (Romans 13:4). But it's *Christian* values that Colson objects to. Or is it? He just told us in his article on "The Kingdom of God and Human Kingdoms" that Exodus 22 is a great example for prison reform. In another place he tells us that we should "apply God's laws." The application of God's law to society does not conflict with the theology of the parable of the wheat and the tares. According to Colson's logic, nothing should be done to restrain evil based on the theology of the parable of the wheat and the tares. The Parable of the Wheat and the Tares has to do with *final* judgment. Taking Colson's view, there could be no temporal punishment, either in family government or civil government.

---

24. *Ibid.*

Norman Geisler and Natural Law

What the reader finds conspicuously absent in *Dominion Theology: Blessing or Curse?* is an evaluation of "natural law." The reason for this may be that House and Ice do not subscribe to a natural law ethic. Why then would they call on Dr. Norman Geisler to endorse their book since he is an advocate of natural law?

(1)

Premillennialists, unlike postmillennialists, do not attempt to set up a distinctly Christian government; they work rather for good government. Premillenarians need not work for Christian civil laws but only for fair ones.[25]

Comment: Postmillennialists have in mind a *biblical* government rather than a *Christian* government since the State is jurisdictionally separate from the church as an institution.[26] What determines "good government" and "fair" civil laws? This is the crux of the matter. Every government claims to act on the basis of the good (Plato) and what's fair (Socialism). Putting someone in the Gulag might be considered "good for the nation." Communism's dictum from each according to his ability and to each according to his need is based on "fairness."

(2)

Building on the natural law ethic of Richard Hooker, an Anglican, who followed Thomas Aquinas, [Isaac] Watts argued that "the design of civil government is to secure the persons, properties, the just liberty and peace of mankind from the invasions and injuries of their neighbours."[27]

---

25. Geisler, "A Premillennial View of Law and Government," p. 258.

26. I've made the distinction between "Christian" and "biblical" to separate gospel proclamation (the means by which people are introduced to Christ = *Christian*), the sacraments and church discipline (the exclusive jurisdiction of the church), and civil government's God-ordained authority to wield the sword to "punish evil doers and promote the good" (the exclusive jurisdiction of the state = *biblical* civil government). The State cannot use the power of the sword to force anyone to become a Christian, take the Lord's Supper, or be baptized. The State is, however, under the jurisdiction of the whole Bible to enforce certain *civil* legislation.

27. Geisler, "A Premillennial View of Law and Government," p. 259.

Comment: How does civil government determine how "to secure the persons, properties, the just liberty and peace of mankind"? Geisler says that natural law is fit for the job. But natural law cannot operate independent of biblical law. Natural law advocates "are like the Irishman who preferred the moon to the sun, because the sun shines in the day-time when there is no need of it, while the moon shines in the night time; so these moralists, shining by the borrowed, reflected light of Christianity, think they have no need of the sun, from whose radiance they get their pale moonlight."[28] Hooker showed the relationship between revelation, reason, and history. Without revelation, reason becomes autonomous. Without revelation, history becomes what man makes it. Without biblical law, natural law degenerates into relativism.

Hal Lindsey and Date Setting

Hal Lindsey has sold more books than all dispensationalists combined. Dallas Seminary dispensationalists have tried to ignore him. He is rarely quoted in dispensational literature. House and Ice don't quote him. Neither is he quoted by Walvoord in *The Rapture Question* (revised and enlarged in 1979) or *The Blessed Hope and the Tribulation* (1976). *The Late Great Planet Earth* came out in 1970.

Hal Lindsey popularized date setting in his *The Late Great Planet Earth*. Yet, Tommy Ice despises date setting. In 1988, in response to the adverse publicity that dispensationalists were getting over Edgar Whisenant's *88 Reasons Why the Rapture Is in 1988*, specifically September 11-13, Tommy Ice wisely signed an anti-date-setting manifesto.[29] Consider Lindsey's date-setting propaganda:

---

28. A. T. Pierson, *The Second Coming of Christ* (Philadelphia, PA: Henry Altemus, 1896), p. 35.

29. David A. Lewis, "Manifesto on Date Setting, *Prophecy Intelligence Digest*, vol. 6, no. 3 (1988), p. 1. Dr. Lewis writes that "new names of Christian leaders are being added daily. If you wish your name to be added, please let us know." You can write Dr. Lewis at David A. Lewis Ministries, 304 E. Manchester, Springfield, Missouri 65810.

(1)

The most important sign in Matthew has to be the restoration of the Jews to the land in the rebirth of Israel. Even the figure of speech "fig tree" has been a historic symbol of national Israel.[30] When the Jewish people, after nearly 2,000 years of exile, under relentless persecution, became a nation again on 14 May 1948 the "fig tree" put forth its first leaves.

Jesus said that this would indicate that He was "at the door," ready to return. Then He said, "Truly I say to you, *this generation* will not pass away until all these things take place" (Matthew 24:34, NASB).

What generation? Obviously, in context, the generation that would see the signs — chief among them the rebirth of Israel. A generation in the Bible is something like forty years. If this is a correct deduction, then within forty years or so of 1948, all these things could take place. Many scholars who have studied Bible prophecy all their lives believe that this is so.[31]

---

30. It may be an *historic* figure, but Lindsey has not shown it to be a *biblical* figure. Contrary to Lindsey, Whisenant, and every other date-setter, "the context of Jesus' words in Matthew 24:32-33 gives no warrant to the idea that Jesus was using the figure of the fig tree as anything more than an illustration on how the Jews were able to tell when summer was near." Dean C. Halverson, "88 Reasons: What Went Wrong?," *Christian Research Journal* (Fall 1988), p. 17. For an evaluation of the meaning of the fig tree illustration, see Gary DeMar, *The Debate over Christian Reconstruction* (Ft. Worth, TX: Dominion Press, 1988), p. 143.

Contemporary date-setters use the "fig tree" as a primary indicator for imminent eschatological events. But "orthodox" dispensationalists do not see it this way. Tommy Ice writes:

> Dispensationalism has always affirmed that the signs of the times, the "prophecy clock," would not resume ticking until after the rapture of the church. Therefore, no one could possibly predict the rapture on the basis of events taking place in the current church age because there are no signs relating to the rapture. The fruit of date-setting and many contemporary errors has *not* been gathered from the root called dispensationalism. Thomas D. Ice, "Dispensationalism, Date-Setting and Distortion," *Biblical Perspectives*, vol. 1, no. 5 (Sept./Oct. 1988), p. 1 (emphasis added).

As much as Ice might want to protest, he has just described modern-day dispensationalism: date-setting with a vengeance. I believe a quick survey of the available literature would reveal that date-setting has "been gathered from the root called dispensationalism."

31. Hal Lindsey, *The Late Great Planet Earth* (Grand Rapids, MI: Zondervan, [1970] 1971), pp. 53-54.

Comment: For Lindsey, the rebirth of Israel in 1948 is the key to Bible prophecy. A generation, says Lindsey, "is something like forty years." By adding forty years to 1948, we get 1988. But Lindsey is a *pre*-tribulationist. He believes that the rapture occurs seven years *before* Jesus returns to set up His millennial kingdom. This means that the rapture should have occurred sometime around 1981 with 1988 being the year of the Second Coming. This is date setting with a vengeance. Of course, Lindsey tries to cover himself by hedging his bets with "*something like* forty years," "*if* this is a correct deduction," "forty years *or so*," and "*could* take place."

Lindsey's prophetic guesses were not considered guesses by his readers. Many took the rebirth of Israel and the forty-year generation scenario as date setting. Gary Wilburn, in his review of the film version of *The Late Great Planet Earth*, seems to agree that the '48-'88 scenario makes up the general thesis of the book: "The world must end within one generation from the birth of the State of Israel. Any opinion of world affairs that does not dovetail with this prophecy is dismissed."[32] Lindsey in his *The 1980's: Countdown to Armageddon*, while still hedging, leads his readers to a pre-1990 climax of history: "Many people will be shocked by what will happen in the very near future. *The decade of the 1980's could very well be the last decade of history as we know it.*"[33] Well, we are about to go into the 1990s. Why should we take Lindsey seriously on anything he says? While Lindsey has not said that we will not see the '90s, his intimations lead many Christians to believe that the end is quite near.

(2)

In an interview published in *Christianity Today* in April 1977, Ward Gasque asked Lindsey, "But what if you're wrong?" Lindsey replied: "Well, there's just a split second's difference between a hero and a bum. I didn't ask to be a hero, but I guess I have become one in the Christian community. So I accept it. But if I'm wrong about this, I guess I'll become a bum."[34]

---

32. Gary Wilburn, "The Doomsday Chic," *Christianity Today*, 22 (January 27, 1978), p. 22.

33. Hal Lindsey, *The 1980's: Countdown to Armageddon* (New York: Bantam Books, 1980), p. 8.

34. W. Ward Gasque, "Future Fact? Future Fiction?," *Christianity Today*, 21 (April 15, 1977), p. 40.

Comment: The thing that bothers me, and it should bother many more Christians, is Lindsey's casual attitude about his false predictions. We're told over and over again by dispensationalists that setting dates is out of accord with "orthodox" dispensational teaching. Why haven't Ice and House written an exposé on Lindsey? Lindsey has misled millions, having sold twenty-five million copies of *The Late Great Planet Earth*. It's obvious that Lindsey does not represent "orthodox" dispensationalism. But Lindsey's brand of date-setting dispensationalism is the prevailing system. If Lindsey had not intimated at dates, and used the regathering of unbelieving ethnic Israel to their land as the basis for his speculations, *The Late Great Planet Earth* would have been a publishing novelty. It was the *predictions* that sold the books. Therefore, many who call themselves dispensationalists are really "Lindseyites." If Tommy Ice says that Edgar C. Whisenant is not a dispensationalist because of his penchant for date-setting, then neither is Hal Lindsey. But if you were to ask a typical unread dispensationalist to describe his belief system, it would sound more like Lindsey than Scofield, Pentecost, Ryrie, House, or Ice. To quote Tommy Ice, "By definition, to date-set is to be non-dispensational because it denies the any-moment rapture feature of dispensationalism."[35] So then, what passes as dispensationalism today, according to Tommy Ice, is not dispensationalism.

(3)

In 1977 Lindsey wrote: "I don't know how long a Biblical generation is. Perhaps somewhere between sixty and eighty years."[36]

Comment: Has Lindsey revised *The Late Great Planet Earth* to reflect his changes in thinking? He's had one hundred editions to do it. In an article entitled "The Eschatology of Hal Lindsey," published in 1975, Dale Moody wrote: "If the 'Great Snatch,' as Lindsey repeatedly calls the Rapture, does take place before the Tribulation and by 1981, I will beg forgiveness from Lindsey for

---

35. Ice, "Dispensationalism, Date-Setting and Distortion," p. 3.
36. Gasque, "Future Fact? Future Fiction?," p. 40.

doubting his infallibility as we meet in the air."[37] Lindsey has had 100 opportunities to revise his earlier attempts at date setting. He has chosen not to revise the date-setting propaganda of *The Late Great Planet Earth.*[38]

John MacArthur, Jr.

John MacArthur is pastor of Grace Community Church, Sun Valley, California. MacArthur's latest book, *The Gospel According to Jesus*, is critical of dispensationalism's tendency to create a dichotomy between Jesus as Savior and Jesus as Lord, as if the Christian can choose one without the other. MacArthur notes that "there is nothing new about 'lordship salvation.' "[39] But there is something new about dispensational premillennialism. George Eldon Ladd, a classic premillennialist, states that "we can find no trace of pretribulationism in the early church: and no modern pretribulationist has successfully proved that this particular doctrine was held by any of the church fathers or students of the Word before the nineteenth century."[40] MacArthur, using the historic argument to support his "lordship salvation" thesis, ignores the same argument in evaluating dispensationalism. But he does come close to shipwrecking the system.

---

37. Dale Moody, "The Eschatology of Hal Lindsey," *Review and Expositor,* 72 (Summer, 1975), p. 278.

38. "Actually, Lindsey no longer holds his Israel-as-fig-tree interpretation. Since 1973 he has taught that the Tribulation would come 'upon the generation which saw *all* the signs begin to appear,' not just Israel's rebirth. He believes 'all the signs' are present today, however, and still believes that the Rapture and Tribulation are near, an opinion at odds with most premillennial teachers, who say Christ may return tomorrow or a thousand years from now." Gary Friesen, "A Return Visit," *Moody Monthly* (May 1988), p. 31. Why hasn't Lindsey revised *Late Great* to reflect his change in thinking? He's had 100 printings to do so (*ibid.*, p. 30).

39. John F. MacArthur, Jr., *The Gospel According to Jesus: What Does Jesus Mean When He Says, 'Follow Me'?* (Grand Rapids, MI: Zondervan, 1988), p. 221. "Lordship salvation" is an unfortunate designation for what are really the doctrines of holiness and sanctification.

40. George Eldon Ladd, *The Blessed Hope* (Grand Rapids, MI: Eerdmans, 1956), p. 31. Quoted in Gary DeMar, *The Debate over Christian Reconstruction* (Ft. Worth, TX: Dominion Press), 1988, p. 106. Also see pages 96 and 97 of *Debate* for dispensational support for this assessment.

There is a tendency, however, for dispensationalists to get carried away with compartmentalizing truth to the point that they can make unbiblical distinctions. An almost obsessive desire to categorize everything neatly has led various dispensationalist interpreters to draw hard lines not only between the church and Israel, but also between salvation and discipleship, the church and the kingdom, Christ's preaching and the apostolic message, faith and repentance, and the age of law and the age of grace.

The age of law/age of grace division in particular has wreaked havoc on dispensationalist theology and contributed to confusion about the doctrine of salvation.[41]

Comment: Drawing a "hard line" between Israel and the church is fundamental to dispensationalism. Once these "hard lines" go, the entire system is in jeopardy of collapsing. MacArthur takes issue with Chafer's beliefs about the radical separation between law and grace. He goes on to maintain that other dispensationalists have taken the separation even further than Chafer. "That the teachings of the Sermon on the Mount 'have no application to the Christian, but only to those who are under the Law, and therefore must apply to another Dispensation than this.'"[42] MacArthur calls this a "lamentable hermeneutic."[43] But this "lamentable hermeneutic" is the natural outgrowth of dispensationalism. MacArthur, Ice, and House break with this legacy. But have they told their readers?

---

41. MacArthur, *Gospel*, p. 25.
42. Clarence Larkin, *Dispensational Truth* (Philadelphia, PA: Larkin, 1918), p. 87. Quoted in MacArthur, *Gospel According to Jesus*, p. 26.
43. *Ibid.*

Appendix B

HAL LINDSEY'S
THE ROAD TO HOLOCAUST

As this book goes to press another critique of Reconstruction-ism has appeared, which should be at least briefly alluded to by way of an addendum: Hal Lindsey's *The Road to Holocaust*. Time will not allow a full incorporation of the arguments into the text of the present work; but then, neither is it necessary.[1] Even a cursory glance over Lindsey's work shows a strong dependence upon and even a plagiaristic regurgitation of House and Ice's book. When David went to meet Goliath he took with him five stones, but he only needed one. It seems that such is the case here. Let us briefly illustrate a few of the problems with Lindsey's work.

Lindsey's Scholarship

Lindsey has never been recognized as a scholar, not even by reputable dispensationalist theologians. This book illustrates anew why this is the case.

Plagiarism

Let me begin with just a brief sample or two of Lindsey's pla-giarism of House and Ice. Without any quotation marks or end-note references, Lindsey virtually lifts a number of statements from House and Ice.

---

1. For a refutation of Lindsey's anti-Semitism charges, see Gary DeMar and Peter Leithart, *The Legacy of Hatred Continues: A Response to Hal Lindsey's "The Road to Holocaust"* (Tyler, TX: Institute for Christian Economics, 1989).

Lindsey:

"But David Chilton uses a typical debater's tactic to cast doubt on the reliability of the source. There is no legitimate reason to doubt the veracity of the source. This is why Chilton resorts to the weak statement, ". . . he [Irenaeus] *may* have meant. . . ."[2]

House and Ice:

"Chilton's approach is nothing more than a debater's technique. When you do not have strong reasons against something then you try to cast doubt upon the reliability of the source. But no reason exists to doubt the veracity of the source. Otherwise, Chilton would have given some specific reasons rather than resorting to the use of the word 'may.' "[3]

Lindsey:

"Chilton concludes his argument by making a totally unfounded, unsupported, and speculative statement: 'Certainly, there are other early writers whose statements indicate that St. John wrote the Revelation much earlier, under Nero's persecution.' But then he doesn't give us even one of these phantom 'other early writers' to support his confident boast."[4]

House and Ice:

"Chilton concludes his critique of the early church tradition by making a totally unfounded, unsupported, and speculative statement: 'Certainly, there are other early writers whose statements indicate that St. John wrote the Revelation much earlier, under Nero's persecution.' But he does not produce those other early writers."[5]

Lindsey:

"If the Apostle John were exiled to Patmos and wrote the Book of Revelation during the reign of Nero (A.D. 54-68),

House and Ice:

" 'It would be strange, if the book really was produced at the end of Nero's reign, that so strong a tradition arose as-

---

2. Hal Lindsey, *The Road to Holocaust* (New York: Bantam Books, 1989), p. 245.
3. House and Ice, *Dominion Theology*, pp. 252-53.
4. Lindsey, *Road to Holocaust*, p. 245.
5. House and Ice, *Dominion Theology*, p. 253.

as Chilton and the Dominionists contend, we would expect to see at least some trace of an early tradition to this effect. But there isn't any."[6]

sociating it with Domitian's.' If there were some validity to the early date, some trace of this competing tradition should have surfaced. However, it has not!"[7]

What is worse, Lindsey's fraudulent "scholarship" goes even further: (1) He cites the original documentation references, which House and Ice gave, as if they were researched by himself, and (2) he picks up on the blatant errors in House and Ice's analysis. For instance, he uses a House and Ice argument for which they employ Henry B. Swete as documentation. Yet he footnotes it from Swete *as if he did the original research himself*![8] Apparently a number of his endnote documentation sources were lifted from House and Ice rather than from the original sources, for he quotes the exact same words they do and in the same argumentative contexts![9] In doing so he even gives an improper form of Hort's name — *just as House and Ice did*: all three of them call him "J. A. Hort" instead of "F. J. A. Hort." A good Englishman would not like being limited to only two first initials!

Elsewhere, he lifts the errors from House and Ice regarding the facts related to North, Rushdoony, Bahnsen, DeMar, and others.[10] On page 240 he makes a strong reference to the impersonal pronoun "that" in Irenaeus' work. But as we have shown, House and Ice blundered in assuming such was in the original Greek, and now Lindsey comes along and picks up their argu-

6. Lindsey, *Road to Holocaust*, p. 247.

7. House and Ice, *Dominion Theology*, p. 254.

8. Lindsey, *Road to Holocaust*, p. 241.

9. E.g., Zahn at Lindsey, *Road to Holocaust*, p. 246 (cp. House and Ice, *Dominion Theology*, p. 254); Schaff at Lindsey, *Road to Holocaust*, p. 242 (cp. House and Ice, *Dominion Theology*, p. 252). There are a number of others, as well. Interestingly, a quotation of page 246 is introduced in the text as being from Ice's work, but the endnote says it's from Guthrie! On page 263 he says that "Jesus illustrated the baptism with fire in Matthew 3:12." But that is a quotation from John the Baptist.

10. See Lindsey, *Road to Holocaust*, pp. 32-34 and compare with our treatment of House and Ice, p. 83, n72.

ment (without indicating to his readers that it was first broached by House and Ice) and reproduces their error!

And he accuses *us* of "sloppy scholarship"?[11] Lindsey's work does not even merit the designation "scholarship"—perhaps that is why he almost never is cited even by legitimate dispensational scholars.[12]

For some reason (apparently to bolster his argument before an unassuming audience) Lindsey considers Thomas Ice to be a "church historian"![13] What are Ice's historian credentials? What published contributions has he made to the study of church history? What Chair of Church History has he held? Nevertheless, we must admit that upon reading Lindsey's work we at least have a greater appreciation for House and Ice's work!

Greek Errors

Lindsey advertises himself in such a way that the unwary reader would assume him to be a competent Greek scholar of sorts: "Mr. Lindsey graduated from Dallas Theological Seminary where he majored in the New Testament and early Greek literature."[14] He notes that he does some "personal translations from the original Greek New Testament."[15] And he makes frequent reference to Greek grammatico-syntactical questions. Unfortunately, he misstates and overstates his case frequently. Not only so, but there is a frustrating inconsistency when he prints out the Greek characters. Sometimes they have an accent (pp. 53, 205, 210, 220); most of the time they do not (pp. 49, 138, 144, 167, 169, 174, 177, 199, 210); sometimes they are wrong (e.g., p. 53). Sometimes he does not list the accents, but the breathing marks (pp. 144, 184,

---

11. Lindsey, *Road to Holocaust*, p. 231. What is strange about this charge is that elsewhere he notes certain Reconstructionists as "unquestionably . . . brilliant" (p. 32) and a "brilliant and keen thinker" (p. 33).

12. As an incidental aside, someone should inform Lindsey that Freud was not the creator of the ink blot test (p. 223). It is properly called the Rorschach Test after its creator, Hermann Rorschach.

13. *Ibid.*, pp. 74, 237.

14. *Ibid.*, p. 296.

15. *Ibid.*, p. 295.

203, 218, 220, 225, 261); sometimes breathing marks are absent (pp. 200, 204, 219, 228, 270, 227); sometimes the breathing marks are wrong (p. 203); sometimes he accidentally substitutes accents for breathing marks (p. 53) and breathing marks for accents (p. 218). He erroneously transliterates the Greek *para* by spelling it *pasa*.[16] If he is going to employ the Greek characters he ought to do so properly and carefully.

Of Luke 18:8 Lindsey writes: "In the original Greek, this question assumes a negative answer. The original text has a definite article before *faith*, which in context means '*this kind of faith.*' "[17] But it does not "assume" a negative answer. The classic Greek grammar Funk-Blass-Debrunner notes that when an interrogative particle is used [as in Luke 18:8, KLG], "*ou* is employed to suggest an affirmative answer, *me* (*meti*) a negative reply. . . ."[18] But neither of these particular particles occur here and so the answer to the question is "ambiguous,"[19] in that the one used here (*ara*) implies only "anxiety or impatience."[20] Lindsey's reference to the definite article before "faith" has absolutely nothing to do with the expected answer, it merely defines that to which the question refers, not whether a negative is expected.

Lindsey parenthetically notes in a translation of Matthew 28:19: "make disciples of [Greek = *out of*]."[21] Elsewhere he notes of this very text that "the genitive construction means 'a part out of a whole.' "[22] Two fundamental problems present themselves here: (1) Such evidence would be a mere interpretive bias on his part. The genitival construction can bear ten or more different mean-

---

16. *Ibid.*, p. 220.

17. *Ibid.*, p. 48.

18. Robert W. Funk, ed., F. Blass and A. Debrunner, *A Greek Grammar of the New Testament and Other Early Christian Literature* (Chicago: University of Chicago Press, 1961), p. 226 (section 440).

19. *Ibid.*

20. William F. Arndt and F. Wilbur Gingrich, *A Greek-English Lexicon of the New Testament and Other Early Christian Literature* (Chicago: University of Chicago Press, 1957), p. 103.

21. Lindsey, *Road to Holocaust*, p. 49.

22. *Ibid.*, p. 277.

ings and implications, which are debatable. For him to merely assert a significance here in Matthew 28 would not make it so. (2) Worse still, there is no genitive anyway! He has simply misread the Greek — twice! The Greek for "the nations" is in the accusative case, not the genitive. His elaborate and confident argument from the Greek is wholly mistaken.

He erroneously claims that the Greek word *oikumene* means the "entire inhabited earth."[23] In fact, he boldly asserts that this "is the only possible meaning of the Greek word *oikumene*."[24] But this is absolutely not true. If it were, then when Augustus Caesar sent out a decree that the *oikumene* (Luke 2:1) should be enrolled, he intended this for China, Africa, the Parthian Empire, North America, etc. The Greek lexicons prohibit any such claim as Lindsey repeatedly insists upon.[25]

Faulty Arguments

Illogical argumentation abounds in *The Road to Holocaust*. For example, Lindsey cites 2 Peter 3:3-6, which specifically speaks of those who deny "the promise of his coming." He introduces this text thus: "Peter predicts that there would be false teachers from within the Church (for who else would understand or care about the time of Christ's coming) who would deny that the Lord Jesus' coming is something *that is imminent* or important."[26] Then after the text he says "the Dominionist teachers certainly *do* deny the imminence of the Lord's coming."[27] But Peter is speaking of those who question the *fact* of the Lord's coming; he says *nothing* of its "imminence." How can denying the dispensationalist imminence view of the coming come under Peter's rebuke? Lindsey's argu-

---

23. Lindsey, *Road to Holocaust*, pp. 218, 220.

24. *Ibid.*, p. 219.

25. For example, Arndt-Gingrich, *A Greek-English Lexicon of the New Testament and Other Early Christian Literature* (Chicago: University of Chicago Press, 1957), p. 564; James Hope Moulton and George Milligan, *The Vocabulary of the Greek Testament Illustrated from the Papyri and Other Non-Literary Sources* (Grand Rapids, MI: Wm. B. Eerdmans, [1930] 1974), p. 443.

26. Lindsey, *Road to Holocaust*, p. 231 (emphasis mine).

27. *Ibid.*, p. 232.

ment is horribly superficial. Besides, Lindsey himself clearly teaches that the Seven Churches of Revelation represent seven eras of Church history right up to our own time![28] Does this not deny an imminent coming before our era?

Elsewhere he warns against "eisegesis" and suggests that such describes "the Dominionist method of interpretation."[29] But he is quite adept at eisegesis! For instance, as we have noted, he reads a Greek word into Irenaeus' text and builds an argumentative rebuttal on the basis of it![30] He reads a "genitive construction" into Matthew 28:19, where there is none.[31] Ironically, in attempting to prove a literalistic hermeneutic, he attempts to rebut Chilton's statement that there will be no personal Antichrist. He does so by citing 1 Thessalonians 2:1-12 — despite the fact the word "Antichrist" does not even appear in the text! It *only* occurs in the epistles of John and there indicates that "Antichrist" is not an individual! How could this use of 1 Thessalonians prove a literal Antichrist when it does not even mention him? Is this not eisegesis?

And what of his dealing with a modern scholar's writing? Somehow a quotation by J. L. Neve is supposed to prove the Apostolic Fathers believed in a future Jewish supremacy in the Millennium, Lindsey quotes three paragraphs from Neve and then writes: "Note carefully the following *crucial facts from this quote.* . . . [T]he early church . . . firmly believed that Israel was yet to be redeemed as a Nation and given her unconditionally promised Messianic Kingdom."[32] I have read and re-read the Neve quotation given in Lindsey's work and it simply does not make *any* mention of the Jews or of their becoming a redeemed nation *at all*! Read it yourself. Is this not eisegesis of a modern text?

After analyzing what Lindsey thinks he is reading from Neve he states: "These six prophetic views caused the early Christians to recognize the Jews as a chosen people with whom God will yet

---

28. Hal Lindsey, *There's A New World Coming*, Chapter 1.
29. Lindsey, *Road to Holocaust*, p. 53.
30. *Ibid.*, p. 240.
31. *Ibid.*, p. 277.
32. *Ibid.*, p. 10 (emphasis mine).

fulfill His promises."[33] But even premillennialist Justin Martyr wrote of Christianity: "even so we, who have been quarried out from the bowels of Christ, are the true Israelitic race."[34] Alan Patrick Boyd, a dispensationalist, has admitted "the majority of the writers/writings in this period completely identify Israel with the Church."[35] We challenge Lindsey to produce the evidence that "the Apostolic Fathers believed that Jesus would return to restore Israel."[36] They may mention His coming to rule from Jerusalem and they may mention that the Jews will be saved, but there is no mention of a restoration of national Israel for a place of pre-eminence.

He continues his date-setting antics that have made him a best-seller on the order of the *National Enquirer*. One of his earlier book was *The 1980's: Countdown to Armageddon* (of course, he has the remainder of 1989 before he can be proven wrong). In *The Road to Holocaust* he claims "this is a unique time in history in which all of the predicted signs that were to precede the Second Coming of Christ are coming into focus within the same generation."[37] Later he writes: "I believe the Rapture cannot be far off."[38] I hope his books can be found 20 or 50 years from now and be used as evidence of the foolishness of date-setting, as Whisenant's *88 Why the Rapture Is in 1988* already is.

Lindsey wrongly states that the Apostolic Fathers "were virtually all literalists."[39] We have shown that this is simply not so.[40] Perhaps this is why Lindsey avoids giving any examples of the literal hermeneutic from the writings of the Apostolic Fathers in his section entitled "The Apostolic Fathers Interpreted Literally." All he does is cite secondary sources that speak of the adherence to *premillennialism* among some of them. But this does not prove they

---

33. *Ibid.*, p. 11.
34. Justin Martyr, *Dialogue with Trypho the Jew* 135. See also at Chapters 119, 120, 123, 125, 130-31.
35. Boyd, "Dispensational Premillennial Analysis," p. 47.
36. Lindsey, *Road to Holocaust*, p. 109.
37. *Ibid.*, pp. 54, 202, 282.
38. *Ibid.*, p. 282.
39. *Ibid.*, p. 59; see also: pp. 74ff.
40. See Chapter 15 above.

employed a literalistic hermeneutic, except in one passage of Scripture (Rev. 20)!

In attempting to prove his literalistic hermeneutic, and particularly the double-reference of prophecy, Lindsey argues: "The most important point of interpretation is that Isaiah predicted events of the First and Second Coming within one sentence without any obvious initial indication that this was the case."[41] Yet later he scoffs at Jordan's dividing Matthew 24 at the transition verses (vv. 34-36) — verses which provide specific interpretive cues! "Jordan gives no adequate reason for slashing the context right in the middle of a consecutive and homogeneous message."[42] How can he rebut Jordan for "slashing the context" of a passage of 51 verses when that is supposed to be "the most important point of interpretation" for prophecy, even in the space of but one verse?

Of Peter's quotation of Joel in Acts 2, Lindsey writes "there is simply no way to be honest with the normal, literal meaning of the passage and say that it was ALL fulfilled on the Day of Pentecost, or in the destruction of Jerusalem in A.D. 70."[43] We agree! But Peter dogmatically introduces the Joel 2 passage thus: "But this is that which was spoken of by the prophet Joel" (Acts 2:16). Lindsey is right: his interpretive approach ("literalism") cannot be honestly accepted, because Peter specifically said what Lindsey's hermeneutic will not allow!

Of the Jewish rejection of Christ, Lindsey states: "Those who looked for the coming of the messiah before His First Coming were perplexed as to just how such different themes of prophecy could both be true of the same person."[44] He noted that John the Baptist is evidence of this problem.[45] But then later he derides "theonomics" as "that very system that blinded Israel to their need for a Suffering Savior who would die for their sins."[46] It would seem

---

41. Lindsey, *Road to Holocaust*, p. 64. See also: p. 214 on Luke 4:16-20.
42. *Ibid.*, p. 230.
43. *Ibid.*, p. 71.
44. *Ibid.*, p. 64.
45. *Ibid.*
46. *Ibid.*, p. 159.

that Lindsey's statements regarding prophecy would more account for their rejection than "theonomics." Especially is this so in light of the evidence in John 6:15, which is suggestive of a premillennial, earthly type kingdom expectation.

Lindsey so equates premillennialism with the dispensational view that he never even mentions "dispensationalism," even when he focuses in on dispensational distinctives![47]

Birds of a Feather

Perhaps one of the most revealing statements by Lindsey is found in his dedication at the front of the book. It is here we may put our finger on many of his unusual views. In House and Ice's work, they try to associate Reconstructionism with the Manifest Sons of God cult. But it is terribly interesting to whom Lindsey gives an adoring dedication of his book: *Col. R. B. Thieme!*[48] The dedication reads: "To my spiritual father, Col. Robert B. Thieme, Jr., whose systematic teaching of God's word and personal encouragement changed the entire direction of my life. If I have any crowns in heaven, it will be because of him. Thanks, Dad."

Now this is most interesting for two reasons: (1) In Thieme's Berachah Church tape ministry a few years back, he publicly dragged Lindsey over the coals and accused him of using Thieme's notes to write *The Late Great Planet Earth*. (2) Evangelical Christians have been rightly alarmed at Col. Thieme's cult-like ministry. An excellent Dallas Seminary doctoral dissertation may be consulted for some of the problems associated with Thieme. The dissertation was written by Joe L. Wall, now president of Colorado Christian College. It is entitled "A Critical Examination of the Teachings by R. B. Thieme, Jr., on the Christian Life."[49] It was published as a

---

47. As on p. 128: "If there is still a future for national Israel, and if the Church is a distinct and separate program of God from them, then the Premil position is justified."

48. He also cites him on pages 130ff.

49. Joe L. Wall, "A Critical Examination of the Teachings by R. B. Thieme, Jr., on the Christian Life" (Dallas Theological Seminary: Th.D. Dissertation: 1978).

book entitled *Bob Thieme's Teachings on Christian Living.*[50] Another exposé of Thiemism is Stuart Custer's *What's Wrong with the Teachings of R. B. Thieme?*[51] Thieme is notorious for creating his own religious terminology and doctrines, and for calling certain persons and groups "S.O.B.'s" and "bastards" from his pulpit while preaching.[52] So this is Lindsey's spiritual influence? Thieme is Lindsey's "spiritual father"?

Horrendous Charges

The worst case of poisoning the well I have ever seen, and the worst case of misconstrual of a movement is found in Lindsey's work. The title itself is "The Road to Holocaust" and the first two chapters suggest that Reconstructionism is anti-Semitic and will lead to killing Jews, *in the tradition of Adolf Hitler.* He even mentions Hitler by name in this connection![53] He specifically puts Reconstructionism in a class with Nazi anti-Semitism: "I believe we are witnessing a growing revival of the same false interpretation of prophecy that in the past led to such tragedy for so many centuries by a movement that calls itself either Reconstructionism, Dominionism and/or Kingdom Now."[54]

As with House and Ice he cannot — he does not even try! — cite *one* sentence from Reconstructionist literature that even remotely appears anti-Semitic. It is most unfortunate that Lindsey's ill-informed work has descended far below House and Ice's in tone and content. Lindsey lays this alleged, but undocumented, anti-Semitism at the door of non-premillennial eschatology for two reasons, neither of which is valid: (1) Non-premillennial eschatology (and even some premillennial eschatology, e.g., George Eldon Ladd) denies Israel a *distinct* future *pre-eminence* over the world in

---

50. Joe L. Wall, *Bob Thieme's Teachings on Christian Living* (Houston, TX: Church Multiplication, Inc., 1978).

51. Stuart Custer, *What's Wrong with the Teachings of R. B. Thieme?* (Greenville, SC: Bob Jones University Press, 1972).

52. See Denny Rydberg, "Sieg Heil Houston" in *The Wittenburg Door* (April, 1977), pp. 22-24.

53. Lindsey, *Road to Holocaust*, pp. 2-3.

54. *Ibid.*, p. 25.

the millennial era.[55] (2) The non-dispensational hermeneutic opens the door to a non-literalistic (he calls it "allegorical") interpretation of various prophecies.[56] "From these attitudes evolved the idea that they [the Jews] were blind impostors under the curse of God, and unrepentant Christ-killers."[57] "It is important to note that the only way the Church could arrive at this view was by interpreting prophecy allegorically. For this error in eschatology (the doctrine of last things or prophecy) to outright anti-Semitism was only a matter of time."[58] But this line of reasoning is an absurd *non sequitur* argument. To simply teach that God has "broken down the middle wall of partition" between the Jew and Greek thereby combining two into one body (Eph. 2) and to say that all the saved are of one tree (Rom. 11) does *not* lead to putting Jews to death in the gas chamber!

He horribly misquotes Rushdoony: "Rushdoony adds, 'So central is the law to God, that the demands of the law are fulfilled as the necessary condition of grace.' In other words, we earn grace by keeping the Law."[59] This is a fundamental and apparently intentional distortion of Rushdoony, for Rushdoony's quotation continues: "and God fulfills the demands of the Law on Jesus Christ."[60] What Rushdoony is really saying is that for us to receive God's grace, Christ had to suffer the broken law for us! Rushdoony is clear on this fundamental truth of salvation: "Man's *justification* is by the *grace* of God in Jesus Christ."[61]

Lindsey mocks Rushdoony and North for their differences one with another and their not being on speaking terms, as if this dis-

---

55. *Ibid.*, pp. 7-8. He tries at great length, but without success, to establish a *national* restoration of Israel by exposition of Romans 9-11 (see Chapters 6-9). Paul is definitely speaking of a future conversion of Israel, but not a political, domineering, national establishment complete with a restoration of animal sacrifices. See John Murray, *The Epistle to the Romans* (Grand Rapids: Eerdmans, 1984) at Romans 11.

56. *Ibid.*, pp. 9ff., 24, 27.

57. *Ibid.*, p. 8.

58. *Ibid.*, p. 9.

59. *Ibid.*, p. 157.

60. R. J. Rushdoony, *The Institutes of Biblical Law*, p. 75.

61. *Ibid.*, p. 4 (emphases are Rushdoony's).

counted their ministries.[62] But how is this worse than the fact Lindsey has been married three times?

Lindsey argues that: "Law and Grace are two completely different systems of approaching God. They are antithetical to each other. We must approach God by one or the other, but we can't mix them. If we try to live by any part of the Law system, we are obligated to keep the whole system."[63] But then later he writes: "In all ages men have had to come to God by faith."[64] Since he agrees with us that even in the Mosaic era, when Israel was definitely obligated to the Law of God, God was approached only on the basis of faith, then how can he put down the Reconstructionist ethic founded on the Law of God as if it presupposes a *different* approach to God? Besides, the Reconstructionist does *not* put the believer under the Law as a means of salvation, despite his distortion of our views![65] Interestingly, he proves we are not under the Law of God but under the requirement of walking in the Spirit by quoting Romans 13:8-10[66] — which cites the Law of God! Under a heading entitled "The Holy Spirit Did Not Come to Help Us Keep the Law" his first quoted Bible verse is Hebrews 10:16: "I will put *my laws* in their hearts, and I will write them on their minds"! Reference here to Romans 8:3-4 is conspicuous by its absence.

Conclusion

These few brief comments should illustrate the tremendous problems with Lindsey's superficial and mean-spirited analysis of Reconstructionism. He is even less successful than House and Ice in his assault. In all honesty it seems that the dispensational critiques of Reconstructionist theology are degenerating to ever new lows. They have gone from bad (House and Ice) to worse (Hunt) to worst (Lindsey).

---

62. Lindsey, *Road to Holocaust*, p. 159.
63. *Ibid.*, p. 161, cp. p. 173.
64. *Ibid.*, p. 266.
65. *Ibid.*, p. 164: "If these men are this far off on their interpretation of something that is a main theme of the New Testament (i.e., Law vs. Grace), is it any wonder they are so far off on something as complex as Biblical prophecy?" See also p. 173.
66. *Ibid.*, p. 162.

I am in receipt of your letter of May 18 which makes reference to the March 3, 1989 advertisement in *Publishers Weekly* for the Reverend Lindsey's THE ROAD TO HOLOCAUST. We regret that this ad caused concern to the principals of Dominion Press and The Institute for Christian Economics, but it's not our policy (or that of other trade publishers) to comply with such a request for a copy of the page proofs. As a reputable publisher which has published many other books by Reverend Lindsey, we are confident that, when the book becomes generally available in the normal course of events and you and your clients do see a copy, it will be found to be free of defamatory content and to merely express the opinions of Reverend Lindsey derived from his exhaustive study of the published literature of Dominion Press and its various affiliates. Meanwhile, please feel free to contact me should you have any further questions.

— Lauren W. Field
Associate General Counsel
Bantam Books, 666 Fifth Ave.
New York, New York

The first to plead his case seems just, until another comes and examines him.

— Proverbs 18:17, NASV

FOR FURTHER READING

A Positive Ethical Alternative: Biblical Law

Bahnsen, Greg L. *By This Standard: The Authority of God's Law Today*. Tyler, TX; Institute for Christian Economics, 1985.

Bahnsen, Greg L. *Theonomy and Christian Ethics*. Phillipsburg, New Jersey: Presbyterian & Reformed, (1977) 1984.

Gentry, Kenneth L. Jr. *God's Law in the Modern World: The Continuing Relevance of Old Testament Law*. Phillipsburg, NJ: Presbyterian and Reformed, 1992.

North, Gary. *Tools of Dominion: The Case Laws of Exodus*. 2 vols. Tyler, TX: Institute for Christian Economics, 1989.

Rushdoony, Rousas John. *The Institutes of Biblical Law*. Phillipsburg, New Jersey: Presbyterian & Reformed, (1973) 1988.

Rushdoony, Rousas John. *Law and Liberty*. Vallecito, CA: Ross House Books, (1971) 1988.

General Works on the Millennium

Bock, Darrell L., ed. *Three Views of the End of History*. Grand Rapids: Zondervan, 1997. Debate between dispensationalism, amillennialism, and postmillennialsim.

Clouse, Robert G., ed. *The Meaning of the Millennium: Four Views*. Downers Grove, IL: InterVarsity Press, 1977. The four major views of the millennium presented by advocates of each view.

Works on Dispensationalism

Allis, Oswald T. *Prophecy and the Church*. Philadelphia, PA: Presbyterian and Reformed, 1945. Classic comprehensive critique of dispensationalism.

Bacchiocchi, Samuele. *Hal Lindsey's Prophetic Jigsaw Puzzle: Five Predictions That Failed!* Berrien Springs, MI: Biblical Perspectives, 1987. Examines Lindsey's failed prophecies, yet argues for an imminent Second Coming.

Bass, Clarence B. *Backgrounds to Dispensationalism: Its Historical Genesis and Ecclesiastical Implications.* Grand Rapids, MI: Baker, 1960. Massively researched history of dispensationalism, with focus on J. N. Darby.

Boersma, T. *Is the Bible a Jigsaw Puzzle: An Evaluation of Hal Lindsey's Writings.* Ontario, Canada: Paideia Press, 1978. An examination of Lindsey's interpretive method, and exegesis of important prophetic passages.

Bray, John L. *Israel in Bible Prophecy.* Lakeland, FL: John L. Bray Ministry, 1983. Amillennial historical and biblical discussion of the Jews in the New Covenant.

Brown, David. *Christ's Second Coming: Will It Be Premillennial?* Grand Rapids, MI: Baker, (1976) 1983. Detailed exegetical study of the Second Coming and the millennium.

Cox, William E. *An Examination of Dispensationalism.* Philadelphia, PA: Presbyterian and Reformed, 1963. Critical look at major tenets of dispensationalism by former dispensationalist.

Cox, William E. *Why I Left Scofieldism.* Phillipsburg, NJ: Presbyterian and Reformed, n.d. Booklet; critical examination of major flaws of dispensationalism.

Crenshaw, Curtis I. and Grover E. Gunn, III. *Dispensationalism Today, Yesterday, and Tomorrow.* Memphis, TN: Footstool Publications, 1985. Two Dallas Seminary graduates take a critical and comprehensive look at dispensationalism.

DeMar, Gary. *The Debate over Christian Reconstruction.* Ft. Worth, TX: Dominion Press, 1988. Response to Dave Hunt and Thomas Ice.

Feinberg, John A. *Continuity and Discontinuity: Perspectives on the Relationship Between the Old and New Testaments.* Westchester, IL:

Crossway, 1988. Theologians of various persuasions discuss relationship of Old and New Covenants; evidence of important modifications in dispensationalism.

Gerstner, John H. *A Primer on Dispensationalism.* Phillipsburg, NJ: Presbyterian and Reformed, 1982. Brief critique of dispensationalism's "division" of the Bible.

Halsell, Grace. *Prophecy and Politics: Militant Evangelists on the Road to Nuclear War.* Westport, CN: Lawrence Hill, 1986. Journalist enters the world of dispensationalist Zionism, and warns of political dangers of dispensationalist prophetic teachings.

Hendriksen, William. *Israel and the Bible.* Grand Rapids, MI: Baker, 1968. Amillennial discussion of the place of the Jews in the New Covenant.

Hendriksen, William. *More Than Conquerors: An Interpretation of the Book of Revelation.* Grand Rapids, MI: Baker, (1940) 1982. Amillennial commentary on Revelation.

Jones, R. Bradley. *The Great Tribulation.* Grand Rapids, MI: Baker, 1980. Amillennial study of major themes in millennial discussions.

Jones, R. Bradley. *What, Where, and When Is the Millennium?* Grand Rapids, MI: Baker, 1975. Amillennial; includes critical discussion of dispensationalism.

Jordan, James B. *The Sociology of the Church.* Tyler, TX: Geneva Ministries, 1986. Chapter entitled, "Christian Zionism and Messianic Judaism," contrasts the dispensational Zionism of Jerry Falwell, et al. with classic early dispensationalism.

Kimball, William R. *What the Bible Says About the Great Tribulation.* Phillipsburg, NJ: Presbyterian and Reformed, 1983. Re-examines the Olivet Discourse and the supposed biblical basis for the notion of a future tribulation.

Kimball, William R. *The Rapture: A Question of Timing.* Grand Rapids, MI: Baker, 1985. Exegetical critique of the pre-trib rapture theory.

McPherson, Dave. *The Incredible Cover-Up.* Medford, OR: Omega Publications, 1975. Revisionist study of the origins of the pretrib rapture doctrine.

Masselink, William. *Why Thousand Years? or Will the Second Coming Be Pre-Millennial?* Fourth edition. Grand Rapids, MI: Eerdmans, 1953. Amillennial critique of chiliasm.

Mauro, Philip. *The Seventy Weeks and the Great Tribulation.* Swengel, PA: Reiner Publishers, n.d. Former dispensationalist re-examines prophecies in Daniel and the Olivet Discourse.

Miladin, George C. *Is This Really the End?: A Reformed Analysis of "The Late Great Planet Earth."* Cherry Hill, NJ: Mack Publishing, 1972. Brief response to Hal Lindsey's prophetic works; concludes with a defense of postmillennial optimism.

Poythress, Vern S. *Understanding Dispensationalists.* Grand Rapids, MI: Zondervan/Academie, 1987. Irenic interaction with dispensationalism, focusing on hermeneutical issues.

Provan, Charles D. *The Church Is Israel Now: The Transfer of Conditional Privilege.* Vallecito, CA: Ross House Books, 1987. Collection of Scripture texts with brief comments.

Rutgers, William H. *Premillennialism in America.* Goes, Holland: Oosterbaan & Le Cointre, 1930. Historical study of premillennialism, from the early Church to Scofieldism, with emphasis on America.

Vanderwaal, C. *Hal Lindsey and Biblical Prophecy.* Ontario, Canada: Paideia Press, 1978. Lively critique of dispensationalism and Hal Lindsey by a Reformed scholar and pastor.

Weber, Timothy P. *Living in the Shadow of the Second Coming: American Premillennialism 1875-1982.* Grand Rapids, MI: Zondervan/Academie, 1983. Touches on American dispensationalism in a larger historical and social context.

Wilson, Dwight. *Armageddon Now!* Grand Rapids, MI: Baker, 1977. Premillennialist studies history of failed prophecy, and warns against newspaper exegesis.

Woodrow, Ralph. *Great Prophecies of the Bible*. Riverside, CA: Ralph Woodrow Evangelistic Association, 1971. Exegetical study of Matthew 24, the Seventy Weeks of Daniel, the doctrine of the Antichrist.

Woodrow, Ralph. *His Truth Is Marching On: Advanced Studies on Prophecy in the Light of History*. Riverside, CA: Ralph Woodrow Evangelistic Association, 1977. Exegetical study of important prophetic passages in Old and New Testaments.

Works Defending Postmillennialism or Preterism

Adams, Jay. *The Time Is At Hand*. Phillipsburg, NJ: Presbyterian and Reformed, 1966. Amillennial, but preterist interpretation of Revelation.

Alexander, J. A. *The Prophecies of Isaiah*, *A Commentary on Matthew* (complete through Chapter 16), *A Commentary on Mark*, and *A Commentary on Acts*. Various Publishers. Nineteenth-century Princeton Old Testament scholar.

Boettner, Loraine. *The Millennium*. Revised edition. Phillipsburg, NJ: Presbyterian and Reformed, (1957) 1984. Classic study of millennial views, and defense of postmillennialism.

Brown, John. *The Discourses and Sayings of Our Lord* and commentaries on Romans, Hebrews, and 1 Peter. Various Publishers. Nineteenth-century Scottish Calvinist.

Campbell, Roderick. *Israel and the New Covenant*. Tyler, TX: Geneva Divinity School Press, (1954) 1983. Neglected study of principles for interpretation of prophecy; examines themes in New Testament biblical theology.

Chilton, David. *The Days of Vengeance: An Exposition of the Book of Revelation*. Ft. Worth, TX: Dominion Press, 1987. Massive postmillennial commentary on Revelation.

Chilton, David. *The Great Tribulation*. Ft. Worth, TX: Dominion Press, 1987. Popular exegetical introduction to postmillennial interpretation.

Chilton, David. *Paradise Restored: A Biblical Theology of Dominion.* Ft. Worth, TX: Dominion Press, 1985. Study of prophetic symbolism, the coming of the Kingdom, and the book of Revelation.

Clark, David S. *The Message from Patmos: A Postmillennial Commentary on the Book of Revelation.* Grand Rapids, MI: Baker, 1989. Brief preterist and postmillennial commentary.

Dabney, Robert L. *Lectures in Systematic Theology.* Grand Rapids, MI: Zondervan, (1878) 1976. Southern Presbyterian theologian of the last century.

Davis, John Jefferson. *Christ's Victorious Kingdom: Postmillennialism Reconsidered.* Grand Rapids, MI: Baker, 1986. Biblical and historical defense of postmillennialism.

DeMar, Gary and Peter Leithart. *The Reduction of Christianity: A Biblical Response to Dave Hunt.* Ft. Worth, TX: Dominion Press, 1988. Critique of Dave Hunt, and historical and biblical defense of postmillennialism.

Edwards, Jonathan. *The Works of Jonathan Edwards.* 2 volumes. Edinburgh: The Banner of Truth Trust, (1834) 1974. Volume 2 includes Edwards' postmillennial "History of Redemption."

Gentry, Kenneth L. Jr. *The Beast of Revelation.* Tyler, TX: Institute for Christian Economics, 1989. Preterist study of the identity of the beast in Revelation.

Gentry, Kenneth L. Jr. *Before Jerusalem Fell: Dating the Book of Revelation.* Tyler, TX: Institute for Christian Economics, 1989. Exhaustively researched study on the dating of Revelation.

Gentry, Kenneth L. Jr. *He Shall Have Dominion: A Postmillennial Eschatology.* 2d. ed.: Tyler, TX: Institute for Christian Economics, 1996. A thorough presentation and defense of theonomic postmillennialism.

Henry, Matthew. *Matthew Henry's Commentary.* 6 volumes. New York: Fleming H. Revell, 1714. Popular commentary on the whole Bible.

Hodge, A. A. *Outlines of Theology.* Enlarged edition. London: The Banner of Truth Trust, (1879) 1972. Nineteenth-century introduction to systematic theology in question-and-answer form.

Hodge, Charles. *Systematic Theology.* 3 volumes. Grand Rapids, MI: Eerdmans, (1871-73) 1986. Old standard Reformed text; volume 3 includes extensive discussion of eschatology.

Kik, J. Marcellus. *An Eschatology of Victory.* Phillipsburg, NJ: Presbyterian and Reformed, 1975. Exegetical studies of Matthew 24 and Revelation 20.

Murray, Iain. *The Puritan Hope: Revival and the Interpretation of Prophecy.* Edinburgh: Banner of Truth, 1971. Historical study of postmillennialism in England and Scotland.

North, Gary, ed. *The Journal of Christian Reconstruction*, Symposium on the Millennium (Winter 1976-77). Historical and theological essays on postmillennialism.

Pate, C. Marvin, ed., *Four Views of the Book of Revelation.* Grand Rapids, Zondervan, 1997. A presentation of the futurist, preterist, idealist, and historicist views of Revelation.

Owen, John. *Works,* ed. William H. Goold. 16 volumes. Edinburgh: The Banner of Truth Trust, 1965. Seventeenth-century preacher and theologian; volume 8 includes several sermons on the Kingdom of God, and volume 9 contains a preterist sermon on 2 Peter 3.

Rushdoony, Rousas John. *God's Plan for Victory: The Meaning of Postmillennialism.* Fairfax, VA: Thoburn Press, 1977. Theological study of the implications of postmillennialism for economics, law, and reconstruction.

Rushdoony, Rousas John. *Thy Kingdom Come: Studies in Daniel and Revelation.* Phillipsburg, NJ: Presbyterian and Reformed, 1970. Exegetical studies in Daniel and Revelation, full of insightful comments on history and society.

Shedd, W. G. T. *Dogmatic Theology.* 3 volumes. Nashville, TN: Thomas Nelson, (1888) 1980. Nineteenth-century Reformed systematics text.

Strong, A. H. *Systematic Theology.* Baptist postmillennialist of late nineteenth and early twentieth centuries.

Sutton, Ray R. "Covenantal Postmillennialism," *Covenant Renewal* (February 1989).

Terry, Milton S. *Biblical Apocalyptics: A Study of the Most Notable Revelations of God and of Christ.* Grand Rapids, MI: Baker, (1898) 1988. Nineteenth-century exegetical studies of prophetic passages in Old and New Testaments; includes a complete commentary on Revelation.

Postmillennialism and the Jews

De Jong, J. A. *As the Waters Cover the Sea: Millennial Expectations in the Rise of Anglo-American Missions 1640-1810.* Kampen: J. H. Kok, 1970. General history of millennial views; throughout mentions the importance of prophecies concerning the Jews.

Fairbairn, Patrick. *The Prophetic Prospects of the Jews, or, Fairbairn vs. Fairbairn.* Grand Rapids, MI: Eerdmans, 1930. Nineteenth-century scholar Fairbairn changed his mind about the conversion of the Jews; this volume reproduces his early arguments for the historic postmillennial position, and his later arguments against it.

Sutton, Ray R. "A Postmillennial Jew (The Covenantal Structure of Romans 11)," *Covenant Renewal* (June 1989). Sutton has a conversation with a postmillennial Messianic Jew!

Sutton, Ray R. "Does Israel Have a Future?" *Covenant Renewal* (December 1988). Examines several different views of Israel's future, and argues for the covenantal view.

Toon, Peter, ed. *Puritans, the Millennium and the Future of Israel: Puritan Eschatology 1600-1660.* Cambridge: James Clarke, 1970. Detailed historical study of millennial views with special attention to the place of Israel in prophecy.

SCRIPTURE INDEX

OLD TESTAMENT

Numbers

14:16-21	153
15:39	43
24:17-19	153, 158
35:33	120

Deuteronomy

4:2	43, 133
4:5-8	38
4:6-9	122, 134
4:26	167
5:1-15	338
5:16	117
6:14-16	167
7:6	169
7:22	218
11:26-28	167
13	li
14:2	169
14:21	35, 100
21:18-21	78
21:19	120
22:8	31, 32
22:11-12	304
24:6	122
24:7	122
24:10-13	122
26:18	169
28:1-14	226
28:15ff.	167
30:15	167
31:19	167
31:21	167
31:26	167
32:4	37, 95
32:17	251

2 Samuel

24:16	229

1 Kings

18	xxi
21:29	229

2 Kings

2	xxi
17:29	251

1 Chronicles

16:26	251
21:15	229

2 Chronicles

12:7	229
26	48

Psalms

1:1-2	37
2	154, 158
2:10-12	135
8	151, 202
8:1	150
8:6	216
18:30	95
19:1	150
19:7	37, 95
19:7-10	48
19:9-12	134
22	154, 158
24:1	140
34:12-13	53
46:8-9	250
66:4	154
68:31-32	154
72	127, 154, 156, 158
82:8	154
86:9	154
89:34	30
96:5	251
98:1-2	250
106	37, 251
106:38	120
110	216
111:7	30
119	127

NEW TESTAMENT

Luke

24:21-27	173
24:25	239
24:25-27	160
24:26-27	32
24:27	75
24:44-49	161
24:46-47	196, 199
24:46-49	223
24:47-49	197, 210
24:49	224

John

1:7	205
1:29	203, 204, 206, 211
2:22	172
3:3	173, 178, 189
3:3-5	275
3:16	359
3:16-17	203-6
3:17	211
3:30	179
3:36	xi
4:10-14	275
4:31-34	275
5:39	75
5:19	184
5:30	184
5:28-29	189
6:15	160, 173, 376
6:51-58	275
6:67-68	227
7:39	163, 173, 224
7:53-8:11	276
8:28	184
10:35	309
11:53	167
12:12-15	182-83, 191
12:15-16	162
12:16	172
12:31	211, 225, 231
12:32	207-8
12:44	106

John

12:47	203
12:49	184
13:34-35	33
14:10	184
14:12	224
14:12-18	23
14:13-14	224, 225
14:15	37
14:16-18	224
14:23-24	42
15:1-7	152
15:5	194, 210
15:7-10	23
15:10	37
15:12-13	33
15:14	37
15:16	224
16:4	172
16:7-11	23
16:7-15	224
16:11	225
16:12-13	172
16:23	224
16:24	224
16:24	224
17:15-18	82-83
17:17	4, 43
18	167
18:30-31	167
18:33-37	161, 183
18:36	35, 173, 178
18:36-37	185, 191
18:37	173
19	167
19:15	239
21:22ff.	172

Acts

1	292
1:6	171-72, 174
1:7	180

NAME INDEX

SUBJECT INDEX

407

WHAT IS THE ICE?

by Gary North, President, ICE

The Institute for Christian Economics is a non-profit, tax-exempt educational organization which is devoted to research and publishing in the field of Christian ethics. The perspective of those associated with the ICE is straightforwardly conservative and pro-free market. The ICE is dedicated to the proposition that biblical ethics requires full personal responsibility, and this responsible human action flourishes most productively within a framework of limited government, political decentralization, and minimum interference with the economy by the civil government.

For well over half a century, the loudest voices favoring Christian social action have been outspokenly pro-government intervention. Anyone needing proof of this statement needs to read Dr. Gregg Singer's comprehensive study, *The Unholy Alliance* (Arlington House Books, 1975), the definitive history of the National Council of Churches. An important policy statement from the National Council's General Board in 1967 called for *comprehensive economic planning*. The ICE was established in order to *challenge* statements like the following:

> Accompanying this growing diversity in the structures of national life has been a growing recognition of the importance of competent planning within and among all resource sectors of the society: education, economic development, land use, social health services, the family system and congregational life. It is not generally recognized that an effective approach to problem solving requires a comprehensive planning process and coordination in the development of all these resource areas.

The *silence* from the conservative denominations in response to such policy proposals has been deafening. Not that conservative church members agree with such nonsense; they don't. But the conservative denominations and associations have remained silent because they have convinced themselves that *any* policy statement of any sort regarding social and economic life is *always* illegitimate. In short, there is no such thing as a correct, valid policy statement that a church or denomination can make. *The results of this opinion have been universally devastating.* The popular press assumes that the radicals who do speak out in the name of Christ are representative of the membership (or at least the press goes along with the illusion). The public is convinced that to speak out on social matters in the name of Christ is to be radical. *Christians are losing by default.*

The ICE is convinced that conservative Christians must devote resources to create alternative proposals. There is an old rule of political life which argues that "You can't beat something with nothing." We agree. It is not enough to adopt a whining negativism whenever someone or some group comes up with another nutty economic program. We need a comprehensive alternative.

Society or State

Society is broader than politics. The State is not a substitute for society. *Society encompasses all social institutions*: church, State, family, economy, kinship groups, voluntary clubs and associations, schools, and non-profit educational organizations (such as ICE). Can we say that there are no standards of righteousness – justice – for these social institutions? Are they lawless? The Bible says no. We do not live in a lawless universe. But this does not mean that the State is the source of all law. On the contrary, God, not the imitation god of the State, is the source.

Christianity is innately decentralist. *From the beginning, orthodox Christians have denied the divinity of the State.* This is why the Caesars of Rome had them persecuted and executed. They denied the operating presupposition of the ancient world, namely, the legitimacy of a divine rule or a divine State.

It is true that modern liberalism has eroded Christian orthodoxy.

There are literally thousands of supposedly evangelical pastors who have been compromised by the liberalism of the universities and seminaries they attended. The popularity, for example, of Prof. Ronald Sider's *Rich Christians in an Age of Hunger*, co-published by Inter-Varsity Press (evangelical Protestant) and the Paulist Press (liberal Roman Catholic), is indicative of the crisis today. It has sold like hotcakes, and it calls for mandatory wealth redistribution by the State on a massive scale. Yet he is a professor at a Baptist seminary.

The ICE rejects the theology of the total State. This is why we countered the book by Sider when we published David Chilton's *Productive Christians in an Age of Guilt-Manipulators* (fifth printing, 1990). Chilton's book shows that the Bible is the foundation of our economic freedom, and that the call for compulsory wealth transfers and higher taxes on the rich is simply *baptized socialism*. Socialism is anti-Christian to the core.

What we find is that laymen in evangelical churches tend to be more conservative theologically and politically than their pastors. But this conservatism is a kind of *instinctive conservatism*. It is *not* self-consciously grounded in the Bible. So the laymen are unprepared to counter the sermons and Sunday School materials that bombard them week after week.

It is ICE's contention that *the only way to turn the tide in this nation is to capture the minds of the evangelical community*, which numbers in the tens of millions. We have to convince the liberal-leaning evangelicals of the biblical nature of the free market system. And we have to convince the conservative evangelicals of the same thing, in order to get them into the social and intellectual battles of our day.

In other words, *retreat is not biblical*, any more than socialism is.

By What Standard?

We have to ask ourselves this question: *"By what standard?"* By what standard do we evaluate the claims of the socialists and interventionists? By what standard do we evaluate the claims of the secular free market economists who reject socialism? By what standard are we to construct intellectual alternatives to the humanism of our day? And by what standard do we criticize the social institutions of our era?

If we say that the standard is "reason," we have a problem: Whose reason? If the economists cannot agree with each other, how do we decide who is correct? Why hasn't reason produced agreement after centuries of debate? We need an alternative.

It is the Bible. The ICE is dedicated to the defense of the Bible's reliability. But don't we face the same problem? Why don't Christians agree about what the Bible says concerning economics?

One of the main reasons why they do not agree is that the question of biblical economics has not been taken seriously. Christian scholars have ignored economic theory for generations. This is why the ICE devotes so much time, money, and effort to studying what the Bible teaches about economic affairs.

There will always be some disagreements, since men are not perfect, and their minds are imperfect. But when men agree about the basic issue of the starting point of the debate, they have a far better opportunity to discuss and learn than if they offer only "reason, rightly understood" as their standard.

Services

The ICE exists in order to serve Christians and other people who are vitally interested in finding moral solutions to the economic crisis of our day. The organization is a *support ministry* to other Christian ministries. It is non-sectarian, non-denominational, and dedicated to the proposition that a moral economy is a truly practical, productive economy.

The ICE produces several newsletters. These are aimed at intelligent laymen, church officers, and pastors. Included in our publication schedule are these newsletters:

Biblical Economics Today (6 times a year)
Christian Reconstruction (6 times a year)
Biblical Chronology (monthly–available only via e-mail)
Dispensationalism in Transition (monthly–available only via e-

mail)

Biblical Economics Today is a four-page report that covers economic theory from a specifically Christian point of view. It also deals with questions of economic policy. *Christian Reconstruction* is more action-oriented, but it also covers various aspects of Christian social theory. *Biblical Chronology* deals with studies in the chronology of the Bible as they relate to the reconstruction of ancient history. *Dispensationalism in Transition* is a critique of the various theological and historical errors in dispensational theology. (Contact the ICE office at P.O. Box 8000, Tyler, TX 75711 for information on how to subscribe to the two e-mail newsletters.)

The purpose of the ICE is to relate biblical ethics to Christian activities in the field of economics. To cite the title of Francis Schaeffer's book, "How should we then live?" How should we apply biblical wisdom in the field of economics to our lives, our culture, our civil government, and our businesses and callings?

If God calls men to responsible decision-making, then He must have *standards of righteousness* that guide men in their decision-making. It is the work of the ICE to discover, illuminate, explain, and suggest applications of these guidelines in the field of economics. We publish the results of our findings in the newsletters.

The ICE sends out the newsletters free of charge. Anyone can sign up for six months to receive them. This gives the reader the opportunity of seeing "what we're up to." At the end of six months, he or she can renew for another six months.

Donors receive a one-year subscription. This reduces the extra trouble associated with sending out renewal notices, and it also means less trouble for the subscriber.

There are also donors who pledge to pay $15 a month. They are members of the ICE's *"Reconstruction Committee."* They help to provide a predictable stream of income which finances the day-to-day operations of the ICE. Then the donations from others can finance special projects, such as the publication of a new book.

The basic service that ICE offers is education. We are presenting ideas and approaches to Christian ethical behavior that few other organizations even suspect are major problem areas. *The Christian world has for too long acted as though we were not responsible citizens on earth*, as well as citizens of heaven. ("For our conversation [citizenship] is in heaven" [Philippians 3:20a].) *We must be godly stewards of all our assets*, which includes our lives, minds, and skills.

Because economics affects every sphere of life, the ICE's reports and surveys are relevant to all areas of life. Because *scarcity affects every area*, the whole world needs to be governed by biblical requirements for *honest stewardship* of the earth's resources. The various publications are wide-ranging, since the effects of the curse of the ground (Genesis 3:17-19) are wide-ranging.

What the ICE offers the readers and supporters is an introduction to a world of responsibility that few Christians have recognized. This limits our audience, since most people think they have too many responsibilities already. But if more people understood the Bible's solutions to economic problems, they would have more capital available to take greater responsibility and prosper from it.

Finances

There ain't no such thing as a free lunch (TANSTAAFL). *Someone has to pay for those six-month renewable free subscriptions.* Existing donors are, in effect, supporting a kind of intellectual missionary organization. Except for the newsletters sent to ministers and teachers, we "clean" the mailing lists each year: less waste.

We cannot expect to raise money by emotional appeals. We have no photographs of starving children, no orphanages in Asia. We generate ideas. *There is always a very limited market for ideas, which is why some of them have to be subsidized by people who understand the power of ideas – a limited group, to be sure.* John Maynard Keynes, the most influential economist of this century (which speaks poorly of this century), spoke the truth in the final paragraph of his *General Theory of Employment, Interest, and Money* (1936):

. . . the ideas of economists and political philosophers, both when they are right and when they are wrong, are more powerful than is commonly understood. Indeed, the world is ruled by little else. Practical men, who believe themselves to be quite exempt from any intellectual influences, are usually the slaves of some defunct economist. Madmen in authority, who hear voices in the air, are distilling their frenzy from some academic scribbler of a few years back. I am sure that the power of vested interests is vastly exaggerated compared with the gradual encroachment of ideas. Not, indeed, immediately, but after a certain interval; for in the field of economic and political philosophy there are not many who are influenced by new theories after they are twenty-five or thirty years of age, so that the ideas which civil servants and politicians and even agitators apply to current events are not likely to be the newest. But, soon or late, it is ideas, not vested interests, which are dangerous for good or evil.

Do you believe this? If so, then the program of long-term education which the ICE has created should be of considerable interest to you. What we need are people with a *vested interest in ideas*, a *commitment to principle* rather than class position.

There will be few short-term, visible successes for the ICE's program. There will be new and interesting books. There will be a constant stream of newsletters. There will educational audio and video tapes. But the world is not likely to beat a path to ICE's door, as long as today's policies of high taxes and statism have not yet produced a catastrophe. We are investing in the future, for the far side of humanism's economic failure. *This is a long-term investment in intellectual capital.* Contact us at: ***ICE, Box 8000, Tyler, TX 75711.***

Paradise Restored
A Biblical Theology of Dominion
by David Chilton

In recent years many Christians have begun to realize a long forgotten truth: God wants us to have dominion over the earth, just as He originally commanded Adam and Eve. By His atonement, Jesus Christ has restored us to Adam's lost position, guaranteeing that God's original plan will be fulfilled. God will be glorified throughout the world: "The earth shall be full of the knowledge of the LORD, as the waters cover the sea." Isaiah 11:9.

In order to demonstrate this truth from Scripture, David Chilton begins at the beginning, in the Garden of Eden. He shows how God established basic patterns in the first few chapters of Genesis – patterns which form the structure of later Biblical revelation. In the course of this book on eschatology, the reader is treated to an exciting, refreshingly Biblical way of reading the Bible.

Building on a solid foundation of New Testament eschatology, the author deals at length with the message of the Book of Revelation – often with surprising results. Throughout the volume, the reader is confronted with the fact that our view of the future is inescapably bound up with our view of Jesus Christ. According to the author, the fact that Jesus is now King of kings and Lord of lords means that His Gospel must be victorious: the Holy Spirit will bring the water of life to the ends of the earth. The Christian message is one of Hope.

342 pp., indexed, bibliography, paperback, $17.95
Dominion Press, P.O. Box 7999, Tyler, Texas 75711

Order all 10 books advertised here (a $144.50 value) for 40% off and pay no shipping! Send a check to I.C.E., P.O. Box 8000, Tyler, TX 75711 for $86.70.

Millennialism and Social Theory
by Gary North

Will Jesus' Great Commission be fulfilled in history? Will God bring judgment against His enemies in history? Is there enough time for the healing power of the gospel to do its work? Two millennial views say no, there isn't enough time: premillennialism and amillennialism ("pessimillennialism"). A third view says yes, there is enough time: post-millennialism. By tying a vision of victory in history to the doctrine that the Bible offers specific answers to social problems, a new movement has begun to capture the minds of a generation of Christian activists. This movement is called Christian Reconstruction.

Millennialism and Social Theory presents a detailed critical account of how and why Protestant evangelicalism has retreated from the battlefields on which the war for modern man is being fought. it shows why Christian leaders have given up hope in the power of the gospel to transform societies as well as individual souls. It shows why Christianity is losing, and will continue to lose, as long as pessimillennialism is dominant. It also shows why this defeat is not inevitable, and why we can expect a great reversal.

393 pp., indexed, hardback, $14.95
Institute for Christian Economics, P.O. Box 8000, Tyler, Texas 75711

The Greatness of the Great Commission
The Christian Enterprise in a Fallen World
by Kenneth L. Gentry

"Save Souls, Not Cultures!" This has been the motto of twentieth-century evangelism. Having encountered heavy resistance to the prophets' message of comprehensive revival and restoration in history, modern evangelical Christianity has abandoned the prophets. Unlike Jonah, who grew weary of life in the belly of a whale, modern evangelicalism has not only grown accustomed to the Church's cultural irrelevance today, it has actually proclaimed this pathetic condition as God's plan for the "Church Age." But is it? Not according to Jesus' instructions to His Church: the discipling (putting under God's discipline) of all nations (Matthew 28:19-20).

Paul makes it clear that the progressive expansion of Jesus' kingdom in history will continue until all things are under His dominion, on earth, before He returns physically to judge the world (I Corinthians 15:25-26). This was David's message, too (Psalm 110:1-2).

The war between God's kingdom (civilization) on earth and Satan's kingdom (civilization) on earth is total, encompassing every aspect of life. The Great Commission calls the Church (in this "Church Age") to make a full-scale attack on modern humanist civilization, but always in terms of a positive message and practical program: a better way of life in every area of life. This is the greatness of the Great Commission. It must not be narrowed to exclude culture from God's special grace.

184 pp., indexed, paperback, $9.95; hardback, $25.00
Institute for Christian Economics, P.O. Box 8000, Tyler, Texas 75711

He Shall Have Dominion
A Postmillennialism Eschatology
by Kenneth L. Gentry

The vast majority of those who call themselves evangelical Christians believe that the Church of Jesus Christ has been predestinated by God to fail in history. "It cannot possibly succeed!" Millions of Christians believe that the Church will be "raptured" soon, removing Christians from the turmoils and responsibilities of this life.

Ken Gentry argues otherwise in *He Shall Have Dominion*. He shows that Christians have many great things to accomplish for Christ before He returns bodily to earth.

Two centuries ago, Protestant Christians believed that they would die before Jesus came back to earth. This affected the way they thought, prayed, worked and saved. They built for the future. They were future-oriented. They were upper class. Today, many Protestants believe that Jesus is coming back soon, so they will not have to die. This belief affects the way they think, pray, work, and save. They are present-oriented. They are lower-class. Ken Gentry refutes this outlook, verse by verse.

He Shall Have Dominion is a positive book: positive about the future of the Church. It teaches that Christians will exercise dominion in history. It therefore teaches responsibility. This is why its message is hated. Today's Christians have been taught that they must flee responsibility, for Jesus' sake. They would rather believe that God has predestined His Church to failure than believe that they are personally responsible for transforming society. This is why the Church is so weak in our day.

584 pp., indexed, bibliography, hardback, $19.95
Institute for Christian Economics, P.O. Box 8000, Tyler, TX 75711

Days of Vengeance
An Exposition of the Book of Revelation
by David Chilton

David Chilton has done it. He has finally done it. He has written a book on Revelation that is sure to spark an eschatological revolution.

With **Paradise Restored**, he embalmed the old corpse of "pessimillennialism." But now, with **The Days of Vengeance**, he has nailed shut the sarcophagus, sealed the crypt, and made off into the night rehearsing profound eulogies.

But, not only does he return the zombies of end times doomsaying to the dust from whence they came, Chilton has resurrected with cogency, clarity, and admirable consistency a genuinely Biblical "optimillennialism."

The Days of Vengeance is an extraordinary exposition of the book of Revelation and will undoubtedly be welcomed as a cool drenching rain upon a dry, thirsty ground. Long parched and impoverished by speculative spectacularization, the evangelical scholastic wilderness can do naught but soak in Chilton's careful and literate commentary.

The Days of Vengeance is phenomenal. It is big (nearly 750 pages big, going where no commentator has dared to go before). It is brash (marshalling mountains of long forgotten evidence to the cause). It is a brazen bravura, a delight, a tour de force.

If you have a "must read list," put this book at the top of that list. If you don't have such a list, start one. And start here, with **The Days of Vengeance.**

754 pp., indexed, bibliography, hardback, $24.95
Dominion Press, P.O. Box 7999, Tyler, Texas 75711

No Other Standard
Theonomy and Its Critics
by Greg L. Bahnsen

In 1959, Rousas J. Rushdoony's first book appeared, *By What Standard?*, a study of the philosophy of Cornelius Van Til. Van Til made it clear that the truth of the Bible must be man's presupposition, the standard of his reasoning, and the final court of appeal in history. He rejected natural law philosophy in any form. Rushdoony believed Van Til, so he wrote *Institutes of Biblical Law* (1973) to demonstrate that the only standard that God provides is biblical law.

That same year, 1973, Van Til's student Greg L. Bahnsen completed his Th.M. degree at Westminster seminary. In 1977, an expanded version of his thesis, *Theonomy in Christian Ethics*, was published. This book was an apologetic for biblical law. So was his subsequent introductory book, *By This Standard* (1985). *Theonomy in Christian Ethics* received only sporadic opposition in print but continual and growing opposition within the faculty at Westminster Seminary. The faculty (past and present) published an attempted refutation of Bahnsen in 1990: *Theonomy: A Reformed Critique*.

No Other Standard is Bahnsen's response not only to the Westminster faculty's book, but also to the two other brief critical books against him, and to the various published articles and typewritten, photocopied responses that have circulated over the years. One by one, Bahnsen takes his critics' arguments apart, showing that they have either misrepresented his position or misrepresented the Bible. Line by line, point by point, he shows that they have not understood his arguments and have also not understood the vulnerability of their own logical and theological positions.

345 pp., indexed, paperback: $9.95; hardback: $25.00
Institute for Christian Economics, P.O. Box 8000, Tyler, Texas 75711

The Beast of Revelation
by Kenneth L. Gentry

One of the greatest mysteries of all time is the identity of the dread Beast of the Book of Revelation. The Bible describes him as the ultimate villain in human history. He is the archetype of evil. He is the very incarnation of wickedness and perversion. It is not at all surprising then that many of the brightest minds throughout history have sought to identify and expose him.

Unfortunately, a great majority of those diligent detectives missed one of the most important clues—if not the most important clue—to solving the mystery. That clue according to Kenneth L. Gentry, Jr., is when and to whom the Apostle John actually wrote the Book of Revelation in the first place.

Following that clue, he is able to blow away the dusts of time that have masked the evil culprit's identity for so very long. Like any good detective, Dr. Gentry lets the evidence speak for itself. And he lets you weigh all the facts to decide for yourself. But be forewarned: He has constructed an iron-clad case. This book is thus likely to revolutionize your interpretation of the mystery of the Beast—and the rest of the Book of Revelation as well.

209 pp., indexed, paperback: $9.95; hardback: $25.00
Institute for Christian Economics, P.O. Box 8000, Tyler, Texas 75711

Order all 10 books advertised here (a $144.50 value) for 40% off and pay no shipping! Send a check to I.C.E., P.O. Box 8000, Tyler, TX 75711 for $86.70.

By This Standard
The Authority of God's Law Today
by Greg L. Bahnsen

For over a century, most conservative Christian social thinkers and theologians have denied all three of these assertions. Some of them have even gone so far as to argue that God's law is inherently tyrannical. They have argued that the church can survive and even prosper under *any* legal order, except one: the rule of God's law. In this assertion, they join forces with secular humanists, occultists, and other assorted ethical rebels.

God's law is Christianity's tool of dominion. This is where any discussion of God's law ultimately arrives: the issue of **dominion**. Ask yourself: Who is to rule on earth, Christ, or Satan? Whose followers have the ethically acceptable tool of dominion, Christ's or Satan's? What is this tool of dominion, the biblically revealed law of God, or the law of self-proclaimed autonomous man? Whose word is sovereign, God's or man's?

Millions of Christians, sadly, have not recognized the continuing authority of God's law or its many applications to modern society. They have thereby reaped the whirlwind: cultural and intellectual impotence. They have surrendered this world to the devil. They have implicitly denied the power of the death and resurrection of Christ. They have served as footstools of the enemies of God. But humanism's free ride is coming to an end. This book serves as an introduction to this woefully neglected topic.

372 pp., indexed, paperback, $4.95
Institute for Christian Economics, P.O. Box 8000, Tyler, Texas 75711

Order all 10 books advertised here (a $144.50 value) for 40% off and pay no shipping! Send a check to I.C.E., P.O. Box 8000, Tyler, TX 75711 for $86.70.

Theonomy: An Informed Response
Edited by Gary North

"You can't beat something with nothing!" This is a fundamental law of politics. It applies equally well to theological debate. A critic who challenges the worldview of a rival needs to present a developed, workable alternative. It does no good to label a rival theological position as deviant, heretical, peculiar, and so forth unless your own position is specific, comprehensive, and practical. The faculty of Westminster Theological Seminary ignored this basic rule of confrontation. In the fall of 1990, their collective effort at long last appeared in print: *Theonomy: A Reformed Critique*.

I.C.E. published this book, *Theonomy: An Informed Response* as a response. The authors challenge the Westminster faculty's assertion that biblical civil law is no longer binding in the New Covenant era, especially its mandated negative civil sanctions against convicted criminals. They ask the faculty: What does the Bible require of civil government if a resurrected Old Covenant law-order is not applicable? What is the Bible-sanctioned alternative? In short, *"If not God's law, then whose?"* Westminster needs to answer.

395 pp., indexed, paperback, $16.95
Institute for Christian Economics, P.O. Box 8000, Tyler, Texas 75711

Order all 10 books advertised here (a $144.50 value) for 40% off and pay no shipping! Send a check to I.C.E., P.O. Box 8000, Tyler, TX 75711 for $86.70.